Managerial Economics and Finance

Managerial Economics and Finance

Edited by Swena Lesley

CLANRYE INTERNATIONAL
www.clanryeinternational.com

Clanrye International,
750 Third Avenue, 9th Floor,
New York, NY 10017, USA

ISBN: 978-1-63240-693-4

Cataloging-in-Publication Data

Managerial economics and finance / edited by Swena Lesley.
p. cm.
Includes bibliographical references and index.
ISBN 978-1-63240-693-4
1. Managerial economics. 2. Finance. 3. Business enterprises--Finance. I. Lesley, Swena.
HD30.22 .M36 2018
330--dc23

For information on all Clanrye International publications visit our website at www.clanryeinternational.com

Clanrye International

Printed in China.

Contents

Preface

Economics is the art of understanding the market by studying the demand, supply, production, distribution and marketing of products and services. Financial studies are the backbone of economics as they assess the present condition of any organization through its profit and loss account. It is the study of investment that helps in determining the current scenario of the market. This book aims to equip students and experts with the advanced topics and upcoming concepts in the area of economics and financial studies. It brings forth some of the most innovative theories and elucidates the unexplored aspects of this field. For someone with an interest and eye for detail, this book covers the most significant topics in the field of economics and finance.

This book is the end result of constructive efforts and intensive research done by experts in this field. The aim of this book is to enlighten the readers with recent information in this area of research. The information provided in this profound book would serve as a valuable reference to students and researchers in this field.

At the end, I would like to thank all the authors for devoting their precious time and providing their valuable contribution to this book. I would also like to express my gratitude to my fellow colleagues who encouraged me throughout the process.

Editor

1

Is there a case for fuel subsidy removal in Malaysia?

Nor Azam Abdul-Razak[a], Russayani Ismail[b], Roslan Abdul-Hakim[c]

[a] Senior Lecturer, School of Economics, Finance & Banking, Universiti Utara Malaysia, Malaysia. E-mail: azam@uum.edu.my
[b] Associate Professor, School of Economics, Finance & Banking, Universiti Utara Malaysia, Malaysia.
[c] Professor, Othman Yeop Abdullah Graduate School of Business, Universiti Utara Malaysia, Malaysia.

HIGHLIGHTS:

1. Fuel subsidy constitutes a huge and growing portion of total subsidy provided in Malaysia.
2. Fuel subsidy reform is costly in terms of the higher prices of non-fuel products.
3. Our analysis suggests that the prices of non-fuel products are expected to rise by 7% if fuel subsidy is removed.
4. Our analysis suggests that subsidy removal primarily affects the following three categories of goods: food and non-alcoholic beverages; housing, water and electricity; and transportation.
5. Our findings seem to constitute a case against fuel subsidy removal unless measures are taken to mitigate its adverse impact.

Article History

Keywords:
Fuel subsidy;
Indirect welfare effect;
Malaysia;
Subsidy removal.

ABSTRACT

This paper examines the indirect welfare effect of removing fuel subsidy on the Malaysian households. The analysis is based on the price-shifting model developed by Coady and Newhouse (2006) and carried out using the data from the Household Expenditure Survey 2004-2005 and the input-output table 2004-2005. The analysis yields the following key results: a) The removal of fuel subsidy is expected to have a relatively huge indirect welfare effect on the society; b) The indirect welfare effect is expected to be uneven across different broad categories of goods (of which the most affected ones are: i) Food and Non-Alcoholic Beverages, ii) Housing, Water and Electricity; and iii) Transportation); and c) The indirect welfare effect is expected to be uniform across different income-based segments of households. Overall, the findings seem to constitute a case against fuel subsidy removal unless the adverse impact on the three categories of goods is mitigated in some way.

1.0 Introduction

Fuel subsidy provision has long been a subject of extensive debate among scholars and policymakers. On the one hand, fuel subsidy benefits the society as a whole since its provision raises the standard of living of households through lower input costs as fuel serves as an input to the production of many goods and services. On the other hand, fuel subsidy benefits primarily the higher-income groups in the society since they are the ones who are more likely to consume a larger quantity of fuel and fuel-related goods and services as fuel subsidy usually takes the form of "blanket subsidies" (Global Subsidies Initiative, 2013a). In one study, El-Said and Leigh (2006) reveal that the poorest 30% of households receive only 13% of all the subsidies while the richest 10% of households receive about one-third of the total subsidy. In another study, Baig et al. (2007) report that the bottom 20% of households receive only 7% of the total subsidy while the top 20% receive 43% of the total subsidy.

In light of these arguments, an analysis of fuel subsidy provision and reform in Malaysia is of special interest since its allocation constitutes a huge and growing portion of the total amount of subsidy provided. During the period

2000-2008, for example, fuel subsidy constituted an annualized average of about 48.3% of the total amount of subsidy provided to the public (Ministry of Finance). During the same period, the world fuel price increased from US$24.54 per barrel to US$72.49 per barrel while the domestic fuel price rose from RM1.13 per liter to RM2.10 per liter (Ministry of Domestic Trade, Cooperatives and Consumerism). Since the soaring world fuel price has not been matched by a proportionate increase in the domestic fuel price, the "additional" price must have been absorbed by the government through a larger amount of fuel subsidy. If Malaysia continues to behave this way, a steady upward trend in the world fuel price is expected to raise the amount of fuel subsidy, which in turn, might contribute to the ballooning budget deficit.

In anticipation of this problem, the government took a drastic step by raising the domestic fuel price from RM1.92 per liter to RM2.70 per liter (i.e. an increase of about 40%) in response to a sudden world fuel price hike from US$61.64 per barrel to US$121.00 per barrel (i.e. an increase of about 96%) in June 2008 (Ministry of Domestic Trade, Cooperatives and Consumerism). In an attempt to curb the deficit further, the government has taken an initiative to phase out subsidies on certain goods and services (including fuel), as stipulated in the Tenth Malaysia Plan (Economic Planning Unit, 2010). In order to carry out the initiative, a special task force named the Performance Management Delivery Unit (PEMANDU) was set up in 2009. Immediately upon its establishment, PEMANDU launched a program called the Subsidy Rationalization Program to provide detailed recommendations on the subsidy rationalization process. Basically, the program recommends that, starting from July 2010, the prices of the subsidized fuel products be raised by RM0.10-RM0.15 per liter every six months during the period 2010-2014 (PEMANDU, 2010).

Although this policy initiative seems warranted, it is important to note that subsidy rationalization policy is a risky proposition since the resulting higher fuel price is expected to raise the prices of other goods and services, thereby eroding the purchasing power of households. At the same time, since fuel itself is a component of the basket of goods consumed by households, the higher fuel price is expected to contribute directly to the erosion of the purchasing power of households too. Hence, there are two channels in which an increase in the price of fuel affects households: direct and indirect. In the literature on the economics of fuel subsidy reform, the adverse welfare impact originating from the direct (indirect) channel is referred to as the direct (indirect) welfare effect in the literature on the economics of fuel subsidy reform. In this paper, our main interest is on examining the indirect welfare effect of fuel subsidy rationalization in Malaysia (a separate paper is devoted to the investigation of the direct welfare effect). In particular, we seek to measure the magnitude of the indirect welfare (since the direction of the effect is already understood).

The remainder of this paper is organized as follows. Section 2 provides an overview of the literature on the economics of fuel subsidy reform. Section 3 describes the methodology used in this paper. Section 4 presents the findings of this paper. Section 5 recapitulates the analysis and discusses the policy implications which emerge from the findings.

2.0 Literature review

There is a huge and burgeoning empirical literature on the economics of fuel subsidy reform [see Global Subsidies Initiative (2010, 2013b) for an extensive review]. In general, this literature can be divided into two main methodological approaches: partial equilibrium and general equilibrium. As the name implies, the partial equilibrium approach investigates the impact of a fuel subsidy reform on one sector of the economy; in contrast, the general equilibrium approach examines such impact on all sectors of the economy. In view of the premise that a fuel subsidy reform is likely going to have a widespread impact on the economy, the fuel literature has been overwhelmingly dominated by the general equilibrium approach, a partial list of which include Araghi and Bakhordari (2012), Clements et al. (2007), Dartanto (2013), and Jiang and Tan (2013), Lin and Jiang (2011), Liu and Li (2011), and Yusuf and Resosudarmo (2008).

In almost all of these studies, a standard tool of analysis called the computable general equilibrium (CGE) model is employed. Basically, the CGE model specifies and simulates the individual demand-and-supply behavior for all goods and services in the economy. If one takes into account the possible interactions among those goods (e.g. one good is a substitute for another good, one good is a complement to another good, or one good is an input for another good), then one can model the equilibrium price and quantity for each one of them more sophisticatedly. In order to capture the substitute, complement and input-output relationships, the parameters of demand and supply functions need to be calibrated. Once these are done, the economy-wide impact of a fuel subsidy reform is determined by simulating the CGE model in two steps; i.e. before and after the reform (Global Subsidies Initiative, 2010).

Despite its attractive feature, the CGE-based analysis is not without problems. For one thing, it requires a large amount of data, some of which may not be available. For another thing, it requires the need to calibrate the parameters of demand and supply functions, which may not be accurate (Global Subsidies Initiative, 2010). In response to these problems, an alternative (yet simpler) approach to studying the economy-wide impact of a fuel subsidy reform, known as the price-shifting model, has been introduced. Basically, the model specifies that each non-fuel good is related to other non-fuel good(s) only through the input-output mechanism implied by the input-output table. Then, the economy-wide impact of a fuel subsidy reform is determined by measuring the extent to which the resulting fuel price rise affects the price of each non-fuel product (Coady and Newhouse, 2006).

Within the framework of the price-shifting model, the literature on the economics of fuel subsidy reform can be effectively narrowed down to a relatively few studies such as Andriamihaja and Vecchi (2008), Arze del Granado et al. (2012), Coady and Newhouse (2006), Coady et al. (2006), and El Said and Leigh (2006). In an empirical study on Madagascar, Andriamihaja and Vecchi (2008) found that the indirect welfare effect of fuel subsidy removal was 1.0%. In an empirical study on Ghana, Coady and Newhouse (2006) found that the indirect welfare effect of fuel subsidy removal was 6.7%. In an empirical study on Gabon, El Said and Leigh (2006) found that the indirect welfare effect of fuel subsidy removal was 4.8%. In addition, Coady et al. (2006) compiled previous empirical studies on a relatively small set of countries (namely, Mali, Sri Lanka, Bolivia, Jordan, and Ghana). They reported that the indirect welfare effects of fuel subsidy removal were 0.8% (Mali), 1.2% (Sri Lanka), 3.3% (Bolivia), and 2.4% (Jordan). Finally, ArzedelGranado et al. (2012) collected previous empirical studies on 20 developing countries in Africa, Latin America, Asia, and Middle East. They reported that the average indirect welfare effect for these countries was 3.3%.

A glance at all of the above empirical findings indicates that the magnitude of indirect welfare effect ranges between as low as 0.8% and as high as 6.7% for those countries. This means that the real income of households is expected to drop by 0.8%–6.7% if fuel subsidy in each of the respective countries is removed. Of course, the question of interest is how much our real income is expected to fall if the Malaysian government decides to remove its fuel subsidy. Since we are interested in the indirect channel of fuel subsidy removal, another question of interest is which non-fuel goods are likely to be affected most by the fuel price rise. Since the income level of households might possibly dictate the composition of the basket of goods that they consume, another question of interest is which income-based segments of households are expected to suffer most from the fuel price rise.

3.0 Data and Methodology

As mentioned earlier, indirect welfare effect refers to the impact of a rise in the fuel price through the indirect channel (i.e. through the increase in the prices of other goods). More precisely, it can be defined as the adverse impact of consuming non-fuel products by households when their prices increase in response to the increase in the price of fuel.[1] Algebraically, indirect welfare effect can be expressed as follows:

$$(1) \quad IWE = \sum_{j=1}^{S} w_j \Delta q_j$$

Where w_j is the budget share of the jth good (or service),[2] Δq_j is the change in the consumer price of the jth good (or service), and S is the number of goods available in the economy.

Assuming that the prices of all non-fuel goods (and services) in the economy are affected by a rise in the fuel price, then

$$(2) \quad \Delta q_j = f_j\left(\Delta p^{oil}\right)$$

where $f_j(\Delta p^{oil})$ indicates that the change in the consumer price of jth non-fuel product is a function of the change in the aggregate producer price of the fuel product, Δp^{oil}. (Note that q is used to denote the consumer price of a good while p the producer price of a good.)

Substituting Eq.(2) into Eq.(1) yields

$$(3) \quad IWE = \sum_{j=1}^{S} w_j f_j\left(\Delta p^{oil}\right)$$

Eq.(3) states that indirect welfare effect is the sum of the product of the budget share of the jth good and the change in the price of the jth good which is induced by a change in the aggregate fuel price brought about by fuel subsidy removal.

[1] By the same token, direct welfare effect can be defined as the adverse impact of directly consuming fuel products (e.g. consuming gasoline for private transportation) when the prices of fuel products increase.

[2] The term "budget share of a good (or service)" refers to the ratio of the expenditures on the good (or service) to the expenditures on all goods and services by households.

To calculate the budget shares of all j's goods (i.e. w_j for j = 1, 2, ..., S), we resort to the Household Expenditure Survey (HES) report for Malaysia during the period 2004–2005. The HES report 2004-2005 contains exhaustive monthly data on expenditures and income for a sample of 4,227 selected households in Malaysia during the period 2004–2005.[3] These data are divided into 12 major categories of goods, ranging from "Food and Non-Alcoholic Beverages" to "Miscellaneous Goods and Services". Dividing the expenditures of all households in the sample on the jth good by their total expenditures (i.e. expenditures on the 12 categories of goods) yields the budget share of the jth good. It should be emphasized that one of the categories, namely, "Housing, Water, Electricity, Gas and Other Fuels", contains expenditures on fuel items. Since our goal is to measure the impact of the fuel price rise on the price of non-fuel goods, the fuel-related expenditures in that category are deliberately excluded, yielding a modified category called "Housing, Water and Electricity".

To calculate the change in the price of the jth good induced by a change in the aggregate fuel price [i.e. $\Delta q_j = f_j(\Delta p^{oil})$], we employ the price-shifting model developed by Coady and Newhouse (2006), which involves a mapping fromthe aggregate producer price of fuel to the consumer price of non-fuel products (i.e. from Δp^{oil} to Δq_i). In brief, the model assumes that the production technology of the economy is fully described by the input-output (I/O) matrix, which depicts the use of sectoral inputs in the production of sectoral outputs.In the case of Malaysia, the I/O table for 2004-2005 contains 120 sectors, ranging from "Paddy" to "Other Private Services". From this I/O table, the mechanism through which a change in the input price (i.e. Δp^{oil}) is passed onto the output price (i.e. Δq_j) is determined (see the Appendix for details). Once the mechanism has been set and applied, we obtain the percentage increases in the consumer prices of 120 goods and services.

Since the budget share data are available for merely 12 goods and services, there is a need to convert (or aggregate) the 1×120 vector of the changes in the consumer prices of goods and into the 1×12 vector of consumer prices. The aggregation process is accomplished by matching the codes for the individual expenditure items in the HES report to the codes for the individual expenditure items in the I/O table using a converter furnished by the Department of Statistics.[4] Once the aggregation is done, indirect welfare effect can be calculated by multiplying the budget share of each of the 12 goods and services by the percentage increase in the corresponding price of each of the 12 goods and services.

It remains to specify the change in the aggregate price of fuel products, Δp^{oil}, which is defined as the weighted sum of the change in the prices of all fuel products:

$$(4)\quad \Delta p^{oil} = \sum_{j=1}^{J} \delta_j \Delta p_j^{oil}$$

Where, Δp_j^{oil} is the change in the price of the jth fuel product and δ_j is its quantity share. (This term should not be confused with the term "budget share" which was defined earlier.)[5]

The introductory section implies that there are three major fuel products consumed by households in Malaysia: RON97, RON95 and diesel. Of the three, RON95 captures 56.3% of the quantity share, diesel 35%, and RON97 8.7% (i.e. $\delta_1 = 0.563$, $\delta_2 = 0.35$, and $\delta_3 = 0.087$).[6] Given their current pre- and post-subsidy prices, the price is expected to increase by 54.1% for RON95, 49.1% for diesel, and 28.7% for RON97 should the government remove the entire subsidy for each fuel product (i.e. $\Delta p_1 = 0.541$, $\Delta p_2 = 0.491$, and $\Delta p_3 = 0.287$).[7] Substituting all of these figures into Eq.(4) yields the value of 0.5014.[8] Hence, the aggregate price of fuel is expected to increase by 50.14% if the subsidy on each of the above fuel products is removed.

4.0 Empirical results

[3] To begin with, the HES report 2004-2005 contains the data on expenditures and income for slightly more than 12,000 households in Malaysia. For technical reason, however, the data for merely one-third of the sample (i.e. 4,227 households) are made available to the authors.

[4] The expenditure items in the HES report are documented using the Consumer Price Index (CPI) code while the expenditure items in the I/O table are documented using the Malaysian Standard Industrial Classification (MSIC) code. What the converter does is essentially match these two different codes.

[5] The term "quantity share of a fuel product" refers to the ratio of the quantity of a particularfuel product to thequantity of all fuel products consumed by households.

[6] The data are extracted from the figures provided by the Ministry of Domestic Trade, Cooperative and Consumerism.

[7] As of December 2010, RON97 was sold at RM2.30/liter while its average market price was RM2.96/liter; hence, the government provided a subsidy of 22.3%. By the same token, RON95 was sold at RM1.90/liter while its average market price was RM2.93/liter; thus, the subsidy was 35.26%. Finally, diesel was sold at RM1.80/liter while its average market price was RM2.68/liter; hence, the subsidy was 32.84%.

[8] $\Delta p^{oil} = \sum_{j=1}^{3} \delta_j \Delta p_j^{oil} = (0.563 \times 0.541) + (0.35 \times 0.491) + (0.087 \times 0.287) = 0.5014.$

Table 1 shows basic statistics for a sample of 4,227 households from the HES report 2004-2005. The average household income is RM2954, the average household expenditure is RM1906, and the average fuel consumption is RM185. This means that, on average, household fuel consumption constitutes about 9.7% of its total expenditure, and 6.3% of its income. When the sample is divided into five groups based on the household income level, we find that the average household income is RM749 for the bottom 20% group and RM7339 for the top 20% group. This means that the income ratio of the richest 20% group to the poorest 20% group is 9.8 to 1. In terms of total household expenditure, we find that the average expenditure is RM679 for the bottom 20% group and RM3850 for the top 20% group. This gives the expenditure ratio of the richest 20% group to the poorest 20% group is 5.7 to 1. In terms of fuel consumption, we find that the average consumption is RM44 for the bottom 20% group and RM305 for the top 20% group. This gives the fuel consumption ratio of the richest 20% group to the poorest 20% group of 7 to 1. This last piece of findings is consistent with that found by Arze del Granado et al.(2007), who note that, for a sample of selected countries, the top 20% group receives about 6 times more in subsidies than the bottom 20% group (see Table 3 in their paper).

The basic statistics indicate that the higher income groups consume more fuel than the lower income groups (see the last column). To the extent that this finding means that the benefits of fuel subsidy accrue more to the higher income groups than the lower income groups, it seems that removing fuel subsidy is justifiable on equity ground. However, it is important to note that since fuel serves as an input to the production of many goods and services, a rise in the price of fuel brought about by its subsidy removal is expected to have a multiplier or spiral effect on the economy. This means that the welfare impact of removing fuel subsidy is far more complicated than a rudimentary analysis might suggest. Using the sample of 4,227 households, we calculate the indirect welfare effect on the 12 categories of goods of the fuel price rise due to subsidy removal. The calculation can be performed in two steps: a) for each category of goods, its price change is multiplied by the household budget share; and b) the product is summed over the 12 categories of goods. Table 2 shows the budget shares, the price changes (called the price effects), and the product of the two (called the expenditure effects) for the 12 categories of goods. Adding the expenditure effects for all of the 12 categories yields the indirect welfare effect, which is 6.97. This value means that the real income of households is expected to fall by about 7% if the prices of non-fuel products rise due to the fuel price rise by 50.14%.

Table 01: Average household income, expenditure and fuel consumption (RM/month)

Income groups (Quintile)	Average Income (RM)	Ratio of Average Income to the poorest quintile (Q5)	Average Expenditure (RM)	Ratio of Average Expenditure to the poorest quintile (Q5)	Average fuel consumption per month (RM)	Ratio of Average fuel Consumption to the poorest quintile (Q5)
Q1 (Richest)	7338.91	9.80	3,849.80	5.67	305.47	7.01
Q2	3148.35	4.20	2,136.82	3.15	200.98	4.61
Q3	2119.15	2.83	1,674.95	2.47	128.96	2.96
Q4	1410.26	1.88	1,182.77	1.74	87.81	2.02
Q5 (Poorest)	749.23	1.00	678.70	1.00	43.56	1.00
Total	2953.57	3.94	1905.85	2.81	185.14	4.25

Compared to the findings of the previous studies (see Section 2), the magnitude of indirect welfare effect in our study is very large (in fact, our figure is the largest). In our case, this huge figure is contributed by three broad categories of goods: "Housing, Water and Electricity"; "Transportation"; and "Food and Non-Alcoholic Beverages". Together, these three categories of goods contribute almost 80% of the indirect welfare effect (see the last column), and this means that the three categories of goods are expected to experience the largest price hike following the fuel subsidy removal.

Table 02: Indirect welfare effect of removing fuel subsidies in Malaysia

Categories of Goods	Budget Shares (%)	Price Effects (%)	Expenditure Effects (%)	Total Impact (%)
	1	2	(1 x 2)/100	
01-Food and Non-Alcoholic Beverages	20.66	7.92	1.64	23.48
02-Alcoholic Beverages and Tobacco	1.92	0.89	0.02	0.24
03-Clothing and Footwear	3.44	3.14	0.11	1.55
04-Housing, Water and Electricity	20.96	9.22	1.93	27.73
05-Furnishing, Household Equipment and Routine	4.59	3.31	0.15	2.18
06-Health	1.41	1.37	0.02	0.28
07-Transport	15.90	11.63	1.85	26.53

08-Communication	5.15	0.46	0.02	0.34
09-Recreation Services and Culture	4.45	8.01	0.36	5.12
10-Education	1.86	1.25	0.02	0.33
11-Restaurants and Hotels	11.33	3.28	0.37	5.33
12-Miscellaneous Goods and Services	8.33	5.76	0.48	6.89
Total	100.0	–	6.97	100.00

The large contribution of the above three categories of goods, in turn, is contributed by a combination of their large budget shares and price effects. In terms of the budget shares, our analysis shows that "Housing, Water and Electricity" ranks the first (21.0%), followed by "Food and Non-Alcoholic Beverages" (20.7%), and "Transportation" (15.9%). Interms of the price effects, our analysis shows that "Transportation" records the highest price rise (11.7%), followed by "Housing, Water and Electricity" (9.2%), and "Food and Non-Alcoholic Beverages" (7.9%). (Note that "Recreation Services and Culture" also records a high price increase, which is 8%.)

These results can be compared to those in the previous studies. In Coady and Newhouse (2006), goods and services (or sectors) are divided into nine categories which differ from our classification. Of these, the major ones are "Agriculture" (44.8%), "Manufacturing" (19.4%), and "Transport" (11.9%) (see Table 11.3 in their paper). In Andriamihaja and Vecchi (2008), goods and services are divided into 30 sectors which also differ from our classification. Of these, the major ones are "Food" (63.4%), "Textile" (7.2%), and "Fats" (6.9%) (see Table 11.3 in their paper). In Arze del Granado et al. (2012), goods and services are divided into three categories only: "Food", "Transport", and "Others". Of these, "Food" captures 39.6% of indirect welfare effect while "Transport" captures a mere 10% of indirect welfare effect (see Table 10 in their paper).

Quite often the types and quantities of goods that households purchase depend on their income levels, thereby possibly altering the composition and magnitude of the household budget shares. Accordingly, the magnitude of indirect welfare effect might vary according to the income levels of households. To accommodate this line of thought, we divide our sample of households into five income groups (or quintiles) and repeat the previous analysis. As shown in Table 3, however, we find that the magnitude of indirect welfare effect is uniform across the five quintiles with the value of 7%. It is interesting to note that this pattern of finding is broadly consistent with that in the previous studies by Coady and Newhouse (2006)(see Table 11.2 in their paper), Andiramihaja and Vecchi (2008)(see Table 11.4 in their paper), and ArzedelGranado et al. (2012)(see Table 2 in their paper).

The source of this uniformity has to do with the fact that the same three categories of goods (as a group) consistently dominate the budget shares of households regardless of their income levels. Across the five quintiles, the budget shares of households range from a) 19.9% to 26.0% for "Housing, Water and Electricity"; b) 15.1% to 32.6% for "Food and Non-Alcoholic Beverages"; and c) 7.9% to 18.5% for "Transportation".

Nonetheless, it is interesting to note that the dominance of the household budget shares by each category of goods does vary by the household income levels. A comparison of the budget shares across quintiles reveals two intriguing patterns: a) the magnitude of the budget shares decreases with income levels for "Housing, Water and Electricity" and "Food and Non-Alcoholic Beverages"; and b) the magnitude of the budget shares increases with income level for "Transportation".

Coupled with the price effects (which are uniform across the quintiles), we will be able to determine the relative contribution of the three categories of goods to indirect welfare effect by the levels of household income. A comparison of the expenditure effects across quintiles reveals three interesting patterns: a) the contribution of "Food and Non-Alcoholic Beverages" to indirect welfare effect decreases with income levels; b) the contribution of "Transportation" to indirect welfare effect increases with income levels; and c) the contribution of "Housing, Water and Electricity" to indirect welfare effect decreases with income levels up to a certain point (and stabilizes beyond this point).

5.0 Conclusion and Policy Implications

In this paper, we study the indirect welfare effect of removing fuel subsidy in Malaysia on households. By indirect welfare effect, we mean the increase in the prices of non-fuel goods and services in the economy brought about by the increase in the price of fuel due to the removal of fuel subsidy. The analysis is based on the price-shifting model developed by Coady and Newhouse (2006) and the Malaysian data from the Input-Output Table 2004-2005 and Household Expenditure Survey report 2004-2005 using a sample of 4,227 households.

We begin the analysis by looking at the income, the total expenditure, and the fuel expenditure for a sample of 4,227 selected households in Malaysia. We find that the higher-income households consume much more fuel than the lower-income households. This preliminary finding indicates that the richer section of the society benefits more from the fuel subsidy than the poor one. Inasmuch this outcome defeats the purpose of the subsidy policy, subsidy removal seems justifiable.

We continue the analysis by studying the indirect welfare effect of removing fuel subsidy on households in general. Given the data on the prices and quantities of petroleum goods, the removal of subsidy is expected to raise the fuel price by approximately 50%. Employing the price-shifting model, our analysis yields three main results. First, the magnitude of indirect welfare effect of fuel subsidy removal in Malaysia is expected to be about 7%. Compared to the findings of the previous studies, indirect welfare effect in Malaysia is very strong.

Table 03: Indirect welfare effect of removing fuel subsidies by income groups in Malaysia

GOODS	01	02	03	04	05	06	07	08	09	10	11	12	TOTAL
First Quintile (Richest/Top20%)													
Budget Shares	15.1	1.59	3.09	19.87	5.41	1.62	18.53	5.88	5.58	2.37	11.07	9.9	100
Price Effects	7.919	0.889	3.135	9.221	3.312	1.367	11.630	0.459	8.013	1.249	3.279	5.761	-
Impact on	1.196	0.014	0.097	1.832	0.179	0.022	2.155	0.027	0.447	0.030	0.363	0.570	6.93
Percent of Total	17.25	0.20	1.40	26.43	2.58	0.32	31.08	0.39	6.45	0.43	5.24	8.23	99.99
Second Quintile													
Budget Shares	20.69	1.77	3.52	20.83	4.49	1.5	15.75	5.29	4.32	1.89	12.08	7.88	100
Price Effects	7.919	0.889	3.135	9.221	3.312	1.367	11.630	0.459	8.013	1.249	3.279	5.761	-
Impact on	1.638	0.016	0.110	1.921	0.149	0.021	1.832	0.024	0.346	0.024	0.396	0.454	6.93
Percent of Total	23.64	0.23	1.59	27.72	2.15	0.30	26.43	0.35	5.00	0.34	5.72	6.55	100.01
Third Quintile													
Budget Shares	23.57	2.36	3.75	20.65	3.93	1.18	15.93	4.84	3.98	1.45	11.14	7.23	100
Price Effects	7.919	0.889	3.135	9.221	3.312	1.367	11.630	0.459	8.013	1.249	3.279	5.761	-
Impact on	1.867	0.021	0.118	1.904	0.130	0.016	1.853	0.022	0.319	0.018	0.365	0.417	7.05
Percent of Total	26.48	0.30	1.67	27.01	1.85	0.23	26.28	0.32	4.52	0.26	5.18	5.91	100.01
Fourth Quintile													
Budget Shares	27.79	2.32	3.87	22.28	3.71	1.1	12.17	4.17	2.93	1.15	11.26	7.26	100
Price Effects	7.919	0.889	3.135	9.221	3.312	1.367	11.630	0.459	8.013	1.249	3.279	5.761	-
Impact on	2.201	0.021	0.121	2.055	0.123	0.015	1.415	0.019	0.235	0.014	0.369	0.418	7.01
Percent of Total	31.41	0.29	1.73	29.32	1.75	0.21	20.20	0.27	3.35	0.20	5.27	5.97	100.00
Fifth Quintile (Poorest/Bottom 20%)													
Budget Shares	32.56	2.46	3.68	25.98	3.39	1.08	7.88	3.06	2.26	1.14	11.05	5.45	100
Price Effects	7.919	0.889	3.135	9.221	3.312	1.367	11.630	0.459	8.013	1.249	3.279	5.761	-
Impact on	2.579	0.022	0.115	2.396	0.112	0.015	0.916	0.014	0.181	0.014	0.362	0.314	7.04
Percent of Total Impact	36.62	0.31	1.64	34.02	1.59	0.21	13.02	0.20	2.57	0.20	5.15	4.46	100.00

This suggests that subsidy removal is expected to severely affect the Malaysian households through increases in the prices of non-fuel goods and services. Second, the indirect welfare effect is dominated by three broad categories of goods: "Food and Non-Alcoholic Beverages", "Housing, Water and Electricity", and "Transportation". Together, they contribute about 80% of indirect welfare effect of subsidy removal. This means that subsidy removal is expected to adversely affect the three categories of goods most. Third, the indirect welfare effect is uniform across households of different income groups. This means that subsidy removal is expected to adversely affect the low-, middle-, and high-income groups equally.

Of the three findings, the first two seem to suggest the same policy direction and the third one a different one. In particular, the third finding implies that the impact of fuel subsidy removal is likely to be neutral across households with diverse income groups. Accordingly, the policy is unlikely to contribute to widening income inequality; hence, there seems to be a case for fuel subsidy removal. Unlike the third finding, the first one suggests that the impact of fuel subsidy removal is likely to be serious, and the second one indicates that the burden of fuel subsidy removal is likely to fall on three broad categories of goods more than others. Taken together, these two sets of finding seem to constitute a case against the fuel subsidy removal unless of course the adverse impact on the three broad categories of goods is mitigated in some way.

In order to come up with appropriate mitigating measures, it is useful to understand the nature of the goods in question, namely "Food and Non-Alcoholic Beverages", "Housing, Water and Electricity", and "Transportation". One common feature of these goods is that all of them are necessity goods. Therefore, the demand for each of them is expected to be highly inelastic. This implies that the decrease in the supply of each good (i.e. the leftward shift in the supply curve) brought about by a fuel price rise is expected to lead to a huge increase in the price of each of them.

For concreteness, consider food. Inasmuch as the inelastic feature of food is fixed and on the demand side of the food market, the burden of change is on the supply side of the food market. Question: What is the nature of the supply side of the food market in Malaysia? According to the supply theory, the non-price determinants of supply are the price of inputs, the number of producers, the level of technology, etc. As far as fuel serves as an input into the production of food, a rise in the fuel price is expected to affect the food price. However, a consideration is that how much fuel accounts for the production of food. Although the answer varies according to the type of food, we suspect that the cost share of fuel is quite negligible. Hence, it is reasonable to conjecture that the relatively large decrease in the food supply is contributed by other supply determinants, of which one likely reason is the number of producers.

If we take fish, for instance, we observe that there are a relatively large number of fishermen in the country. However, the price of fish is relatively high. Casual observations tell us that, despite the presence of a relatively large number of fishermen, the number of wholesalers is relatively few. Hence, they have a substantial market power to increase the fish price in response to the rise in fuel price. One policy option to face the powerful wholesalers is by implementing price regulation. However, its success requires a strict and consistent enforcement by the government since price regulation per se in unlikely to be adequate to deal with this kind of market imperfection. (As of now, "price regulation" on fish takes the form of moral suasion and occasional visits made by authorities to the fish markets to ensure that price tags on fish sold are in place.)

Another policy option to confront the powerful wholesalers is by lessening their market power. One way to do this is by encouraging new entries into the wholesale fish business. Quite often, a new entrant into an otherwise monopolistic (or oligopolistic) industry is likely to face price war by established firms. Again, there is a case for a government's intervention in promoting a healthy competitive environment among the wholesalers. Another way to do this is by introducing cooperatives which act as wholesalers for distributing fishes to retailers. Unlike private new entrants, cooperatives are less likely going to face price war because they are owned by many fishermen. However, managing cooperatives might pose a challenge for their survival. Once again, there is a case for the government's intervention in maintaining the cooperatives. In either case, the additional number of producers (i.e. wholesalers in this case) might undermine the market power of individual wholesalers.

Although our discussion was confined to food products, it can be easily generalized to housing and transportation goods. In the case of housing, we also observe that the producers have substantial market power. In order to fight this kind of market imperfection, the government might be called for to implement price regulation. (Lessening market power through new entries or cooperatives may be inappropriate in this case due to the need to raise huge capital.) In this case too, a strict and consistent enforcement by the government is required. In the case of transportation, it is very clear that the producers have substantial market power since the domestic car industry is dominated by our national car producers. In this case, however, the powerful producers are owned by the government. Accordingly, the government has a better control over the car prices in the event of fuel subsidy removal. In a nutshell, active government interventions are needed in the markets characterized by the presence of market power on the part of sellers should the government choose to pursue its subsidy removal policy.

References

Andriamihaja, N. and Vecchi, G. 2008. Evaluation of the welfare impact of higher energy prices in Madagascar, in: Go, D. and Page, J. (Eds.), Africa at a turning point? Growth, Aid and External Shocks.Washington: World Bank.
Araghi, M. and Bakhordari, S.2012. An evaluation of the welfare effects of reducing energy subsides in Iran. Energy Policy. 47(8): 398-404. http://dx.doi.org/10.1016/j.enpol.2012.05.007
ArzedelGranado, J. Coady, D. and Gillingham, R. 2012. The unequal benefits of fuel subsidies: A review of evidence for developing countries. World Development. 40(11): 2234-2248. http://dx.doi.org/10.1016/j.worlddev.2012.05.005
Baig, T., Mati, A., Cady, D. and Ntamatungiro, J., 2007. Domestic petroleum product prices and subsidies: Recent developments and reform strategies. Washington D.C.: International Monetary Fund.
Clements, B. Gupta, J. and Jung, S. 2007. Real and distributive effects of petroleum price liberalization: The case of Indonesia. Developing Economies. 45(2): 220-237. http://dx.doi.org/10.1111/j.1746-1049.2007.00040.x
Coady, D., El-Said, M., Gillingham, R., Kpodar, K., Medas, P., and Newhouse D. 2006. The magnitude and distribution of fuel subsidies: Evidence from Bolivia, Ghana, Jordan, Mali and Sri Lanka. IMF Working Paper. 06(247), Washington D.C: International Monetary Fund.
Coady, D. and Newhouse, D. 2006. Ghana: Evaluating the fiscal and social costs of increases in domestic fuel prices, in: Coudouel, A., Dani, A. andPaternostro, S. (Eds.), Poverty and Social Analysis of Reforms: Lessons and Examples from Implementation. Washington: World Bank.
Dartanto, T. 2013. Reducing fuel subsidies and the implication on fiscal balance and poverty in Indonesia: A simulation analysis.Energy Policy. 58(July): 117-134. http://dx.doi.org/10.1016/j.enpol.2013.02.040
Economic Planning Unit, 2010. Tenth Malaysia Plan 2011-2015, Malaysia: Economic Planning Unit
El Said, M. and Leigh, D. 2006. Fuel price subsidies in Gabon: Fiscal cost and distributional impact. IMF Working Paper, 06(243). Washington D.C: International Monetary Fund.
Global Subsidies Initiative, 2010. The effects of fossil-fuel subsidy reform: A review of modeling and empirical studies. Geneva: International Institute for Sustainable Development.
Global Subsidies Initiative, 2013a.A citizen's guide to energy subsidies in Malaysia.
Global Subsidies Initiative, 2013b.A guidebook to fossil-fuel subsidy reform for policy-makers in Southeast Asia.
Jiang, Z. and Tan, J. 2013. How the removal of energy subsidy affects general price in China: A study based on input-output model. Energy Policy. 60(12): 599-606. http://dx.doi.org/10.1016/j.enpol.2013.08.059
Lin, B. and Jiang, Z. 2011. Estimates of energy subsidies in China and impact of energy subsidy reform.Energy Economics. 33(2): 273-283. http://dx.doi.org/10.1016/j.eneco.2010.07.005
Liu, W. and Li, H. 2011.Improving energy consumption structure: A comprehensive assessment of fossil energy subsidies reform in China.Energy Policy. 39(7): 4134-4143. http://dx.doi.org/10.1016/j.enpol.2011.04.013
Ministry of Domestic Trade, Cooperation and Consumerism.Petroleum Information 2010. Malaysia. Retrieved fromhttp://www.kpdnkk.gov.my/web/guest/index
Ministry of Finance.Economic Report 2010/2011 and others. Malaysia. Retrieved fromhttp://www.treasury.gov.my/index.php?option=com_content&view=category&id=73&Itemid=174&lang=en
PEMANDU, 2010. Opening presentation: Subsidy rationalization lab open day. Kuala Lumpur: Performance Management and Delivery Unit. Retrieved fromhttp://www.slideshare.net/Adamloh/subsidy-rationalization-lab-by-day
Yusuf, A. and Resosudarmo, B. 2008.Mitigating the distributional impact of fuel pricing reform: the Indonesian experience.ASEAN Economic Bulletin. 25(1): 32-47. http://dx.doi.org/10.1355/AE25-1D

Appendix: 01

The price-shifting model assumes that the production technology of the economy can be completely described by the input-output (I-O) matrix, which depicts the use of sectoral inputs in the production of sectoral outputs. In the case of Malaysia, the I-O table for 2004-2005 contains 120 sectors, ranging from paddy to other private services. Hence, the I-O coefficient matrix associated with the I-O table is of dimension 120×120. This I-O coefficient matrix is denoted by A as follows:

$$\text{(A1)}\quad \mathbf{A} = \begin{bmatrix} a_{11} & a_{12} & \cdots & a_{1S} \\ a_{21} & a_{22} & \cdots & a_{2S} \\ \cdots & \cdots & \cdots & \cdots \\ a_{S1} & a_{S2} & \cdots & a_{SS} \end{bmatrix}$$

where a_{ij} (i, j = 1, 2, ..., S) is the cost of the ith input per unitary value of the jth output (units of output are defined in such a way that they have a user price of unity) or, more precisely, a change in the cost of producing one unit of jth output due to a unit change in the price of ith input.

In order to determine the mechanism through which changes in input prices are passed onto output prices, it is assumed that all of the existing sectors (i.e. S = 120) can be grouped into three broad sectors: traded, cost-push, and controlled. As the name implies, the traded sectors are sectors which compete with internationally traded goods; therefore, higher input costs cannot be fully passed onto output prices. In brief, the cost-push sectors are non-traded sectors (such as most government services, construction, public utilities, trade and transportation, and retail and wholesale trade); hence, higher input costs are pushed fully onto output prices. Finally, the controlled sectors are sectors where output prices are controlled by the government; thus, higher input costs cannot be fully passed onto output prices.

Given the above three broad sectors, the pricing scheme for each of them (in terms of how changes in input prices are passed onto output prices) can be expressed as follows:

(A2) $\mathbf{q}^{cp} = \mathbf{p}^{cp} + \mathbf{t}^{cp}$ [cost-push]

(A3) $\mathbf{q}^{ts} = \mathbf{p}^{w} + \mathbf{t}^{ts}$ [traded]

(A4) $\mathbf{q}^{cs} = \mathbf{p}^{*}$ [controlled]

where **q** is the 1×S vector of consumer prices, **p** is the 1×S vector of producer prices (net of sales taxes and/or tariffs), $\mathbf{q}^{cp}$ is the price paid by consumers in the cost-push sectors, $\mathbf{p}^{cp}$ is the price set by producers in the cost-push sectors, $\mathbf{t}^{cp}$ is the sales or excise taxes imposed by the government in the cost-push sectors, $\mathbf{q}^{ts}$ is the price paid by consumers in the traded sectors, $\mathbf{p}^{w}$ is the world prices, $\mathbf{t}^{ts}$ is the trade taxes, $\mathbf{q}^{cs}$ is the price paid by consumers in the controlled sectors, and $\mathbf{p}^{*}$ is the price controls set by the government.

Given these pricing schemes, it can be easily shown that price changes in each of these sectors are given by

(A5) $\Delta\mathbf{q}^{cp} = \Delta\mathbf{p}^{cp} + \Delta\mathbf{t}^{cp}$ [cost-push]

(A6) $\Delta\mathbf{q}^{ts} = \Delta\mathbf{p}^{w} + \Delta\mathbf{t}^{ts}$ [traded]

(A7) $\Delta\mathbf{q}^{cs} = \Delta\mathbf{p}^{*}$ [controlled]

Of all the right-hand side variables, four of them (i.e. $\Delta\mathbf{p}^{w}$, $\Delta\mathbf{p}^{*}$,$\Delta\mathbf{t}^{cp}$, and $\Delta\mathbf{t}^{ts}$) are exogenous while $\Delta\mathbf{p}^{cp}$ is endogenous. The endogeneity of this final variable is due to the fact that the producer prices of goods depend on all factor prices of intermediate goods:

(A8) $\Delta\mathbf{p}^{cp} = \Delta\mathbf{p}^{cp}(\mathbf{q}) \Rightarrow \Delta\mathbf{q}^{cp} = \Delta\mathbf{p}^{cp}(\mathbf{q}) + \Delta\mathbf{t}^{cp}$

where**q** is a vector of intermediate goods included in the I-O table. (Andriamihaja and Vecchi (2008) claim that $\Delta\mathbf{p}^{cp}$ is a function of a price vector of intermediate goods not included in the I-O table as well. Since the data for this price vector are not available, they are disregarded upfront.)

It is important to note that, although **q** is a vector of consumer prices, it is also a vector of input prices for certain sectors. Then, how do changes in **q** pass on to final prices? To get around this problem, Coady and Newhouse (2006) assume that each of the composite commodities is made up of a certain proportion of cost-push, traded and controlled sectors. To fix ideas, let α, β and γ denote the proportion of cost-push, traded and controlled sector, respectively. Then each of them is a positive fraction and they add up to unity:

(A9) $0 \le \alpha_j, \beta_j, \gamma_j \le 1;\ \ \alpha_j + \beta_j + \gamma_j = 1 \qquad (j = 1, 2, ..., 120)$

To illustrate, consider the 28th sector in our I-O table (i.e. the soft drink sector). In order to produce soft drink, suppose its producers buy 30% of inputs from the producers of the cost-push sector, 30% of inputs from the producers of the traded sector, and 40% of inputs from the producers of the controlled sector. Then, $\alpha_{28} = \beta_{28} = 0.30$ and $\gamma_{28} = 0.40$. This means that the change in the price of the soft drink commodity can be expressed as a linear combination of the three broad sectors. In general, the change in the price of the jth commodity can be expressed as a linear combination of the three broad sectors:

$$\text{(A10)}\quad \Delta p_j^{cp}(\mathbf{q}) = \sum_{i=1}^{S} \alpha_i a_{ij} \Delta q_j^{cp} + \sum_{i=1}^{S} \beta_i a_{ij} \Delta q_j^{ts} + \sum_{i=1}^{S} \gamma_i a_{ij} \Delta q_j^{cs} \quad (for\ j = 1, 2, \ldots, S)$$

If we stack over all commodities (i.e. j = 1, 2, ..., S), we obtain

$$\text{(A11)}\quad \Delta\mathbf{p}^{cp} = \Delta\mathbf{q}^{cp}\boldsymbol{\alpha}\mathbf{A} + \Delta\mathbf{q}^{ts}\boldsymbol{\beta}\mathbf{A} + \Delta\mathbf{q}^{cs}\boldsymbol{\gamma}\mathbf{A}$$

where $\Delta\mathbf{p}^{cp}$, $\Delta\mathbf{q}^{cp}$, $\Delta\mathbf{q}^{ts}$, and $\Delta\mathbf{q}^{cs}$ each is a 1×S vector; $\boldsymbol{\alpha}$, $\boldsymbol{\beta}$, and $\boldsymbol{\gamma}$ each is an S×S diagonal matrix; and A is an S×S matrix.

If we substitute Eqs.(A5), (A6), and (A7) into Eq.(A11), we obtain

$$\text{(A12)}\quad \Delta\mathbf{p}^{cp} = \Delta\mathbf{p}^{cp}\boldsymbol{\alpha}\mathbf{A} + \Delta\mathbf{t}^{cp}\boldsymbol{\alpha}\mathbf{A} + \Delta\mathbf{p}^{w}\boldsymbol{\beta}\mathbf{A} + \Delta\mathbf{t}^{ts}\boldsymbol{\beta}\mathbf{A} + \Delta\mathbf{p}^{*}\boldsymbol{\gamma}\mathbf{A}$$

If we collect terms, we obtain

$$\text{(A13)}\quad \Delta\mathbf{p}^{cp} = \Delta\mathbf{t}^{cp}\boldsymbol{\alpha}\mathbf{AV} + \Delta\mathbf{p}^{w}\boldsymbol{\beta}\mathbf{AV} + \Delta\mathbf{t}^{ts}\boldsymbol{\beta}\mathbf{AV} + \Delta\mathbf{p}^{*}\boldsymbol{\gamma}\mathbf{AV},$$

where $\mathbf{V} = (\mathbf{I} - \boldsymbol{\alpha}\mathbf{A})^{-1}$ is an S×S matrix.

Eq.(A13) gives the vector of producer price changes in the cost-push sector. Nevertheless, we are interested in the vector of consumer price changes:

$$\text{(A14)}\quad \Delta\mathbf{q} = \Delta\mathbf{q}^{cp}\boldsymbol{\alpha} + \Delta\mathbf{q}^{ts}\boldsymbol{\beta} + \Delta\mathbf{q}^{cs}\boldsymbol{\gamma}$$

In order to make this transition, we follow Andriamihaja and Vecchi (2008) by making the following assumptions. First, the only exogenous price changes are changes in the controlled sector; thus, $\Delta\mathbf{p}^{w} = \Delta\mathbf{t}^{ts} = \Delta\mathbf{t}^{cp} = \Delta\mathbf{q}^{ts} = 0$. Second, all petroleum products are within the controlled sector whereas all other products are within the cost-push sector; hence, $\beta_j = 0$ and $\alpha_j + \gamma_j = 1$.

Given these assumptions, Eq.(A13) reduces to

$$\text{(A15)}\quad \Delta\mathbf{q}^{cp} \equiv \Delta\mathbf{p}^{cp} = \Delta\mathbf{p}^{*}\boldsymbol{\gamma}\mathbf{AV}$$

If we substitute Eq.(A15) into Eq.(A14), and noting that $\Delta\mathbf{q}^{ts} = 0$ and $\Delta\mathbf{q}^{cs} = \Delta\mathbf{p}^{*}$, we obtain

$$\text{(A16)}\quad \Delta\mathbf{q} = \Delta\mathbf{p}^{*}\boldsymbol{\gamma}\mathbf{AV}\boldsymbol{\alpha} + \Delta\mathbf{p}^{*}\boldsymbol{\gamma} = \Delta\mathbf{p}^{*}(\boldsymbol{\gamma}\mathbf{AV}\boldsymbol{\alpha} + \boldsymbol{\gamma})$$

Eq.(A16) gives the vector of consumer price changes ($\Delta\mathbf{q}$) due to changes in the prices of petroleum products ($\Delta\mathbf{p}^{*}$). (Recall that $\Delta\mathbf{q}$ and $\Delta\mathbf{p}^{*}$ each is a 1×S vector; **A** and **V** each is an S×S matrix; and $\boldsymbol{\alpha}$ and $\boldsymbol{\gamma}$ each is a 1×S diagonal matrix.) Inasmuch as the data for **A** are readily available and the data for $\Delta\mathbf{p}^{*}$ were obtained earlier (i.e. $\Delta\mathbf{p}^{*}$ = [50.14%, 50.14%, ..., 50.14%]), it remains to obtain the data for $\boldsymbol{\alpha}$, $\boldsymbol{\gamma}$ and **V**.

Since α_j and γ_j denote the proportion of inputs needed to produce one unit of output in the sth sector from the cost-push and controlled (or petroleum) sectors, respectively, and $\alpha_j + \gamma_j = 1$, then we need to identify the petroleum sectors in the I-O table. An examination of the table reveals that there are three petroleum sectors: crude oil and natural gas; petroleum refinery; and electricity and gas. For each of the 120 available sectors, γ_j is derived by dividing the sum of the input coefficients in these petroleum sectors by the sum of the input coefficients in all sectors, and α_j is derived residually; i.e. $\alpha_j = 1 - \gamma_j$. Once α_j and γ_j are obtained for the 120 sectors, we construct the matrix for $\boldsymbol{\alpha}$ and $\boldsymbol{\gamma}$:

$$\text{(A17)}\quad \boldsymbol{\alpha} = \begin{bmatrix} \alpha_1 & 0 & \ldots & 0 \\ 0 & \alpha_2 & \ldots & 0 \\ \ldots & \ldots & \ldots & \ldots \\ 0 & 0 & \ldots & \alpha_{120} \end{bmatrix}, \quad \boldsymbol{\gamma} = \begin{bmatrix} \gamma_1 & 0 & \ldots & 0 \\ 0 & \gamma_2 & \ldots & 0 \\ \ldots & \ldots & \ldots & \ldots \\ 0 & 0 & \ldots & \gamma_{120} \end{bmatrix}$$

From the formula $\mathbf{V} = (\mathbf{I} - \alpha\mathbf{A})^{-1}$, we have

$$\text{(A18)}\quad \mathbf{V} = \left(\begin{bmatrix} 1 & 0 & \dots & 0 \\ 0 & 1 & \dots & 0 \\ \dots & \dots & \dots & \dots \\ 0 & 0 & \dots & 1 \end{bmatrix} - \begin{bmatrix} \alpha_1 & 0 & \dots & 0 \\ 0 & \alpha_2 & \dots & 0 \\ \dots & \dots & \dots & \dots \\ 0 & 0 & \dots & \alpha_{120} \end{bmatrix} \begin{bmatrix} a_{11} & a_{12} & \dots & a_{1,120} \\ a_{21} & a_{22} & \dots & a_{2,120} \\ \dots & \dots & \dots & \dots \\ a_{S1} & a_{S2} & \dots & a_{120,120} \end{bmatrix} \right)^{-1}$$

$$= \left(\begin{bmatrix} 1 & 0 & \dots & 0 \\ 0 & 1 & \dots & 0 \\ \dots & \dots & \dots & \dots \\ 0 & 0 & \dots & 1 \end{bmatrix} - \begin{bmatrix} \alpha_1 a_{11} & \alpha_1 a_{12} & \dots & \alpha_1 a_{1,120} \\ \alpha_2 a_{21} & \alpha_2 a_{22} & \dots & \alpha_2 a_{2,120} \\ \dots & \dots & \dots & \dots \\ \alpha_{120} a_{S1} & \alpha_{120} a_{S2} & \dots & \alpha_{120} a_{120,120} \end{bmatrix} \right)^{-1}$$

$$= \begin{bmatrix} 1-\alpha_1 a_{11} & -\alpha_1 a_{12} & \dots & -\alpha_1 a_{1,120} \\ -\alpha_2 a_{21} & 1-\alpha_2 a_{22} & \dots & -\alpha_2 a_{2,120} \\ \dots & \dots & \dots & \dots \\ -\alpha_{120} a_{S1} & -\alpha_{120} a_{S2} & \dots & 1-\alpha_{120} a_{120,120} \end{bmatrix}^{-1}$$

Once all of these data are obtained, $\Delta\mathbf{q}$, which is a 1×120 vector of the consumer prices of goods and services, can be calculated based on Eq.(A16).

2

Financial crises and volatility spillovers among emerging European equity markets

Ugur Ergun [a*], Zehra Mahmutović [a]

[a] Management Department, Faculty of Economics, International Burch University, BIH
[*] Corresponding author's email: uergun@ibu.edu.ba

HIGHLIGHTS:

1. We study the effect of current financial crisis on equity market returns of Balkan transition economies.
2. The study employed generalized autoregressive conditional heteroscedasticity model for daily data spanning from 2006 to 2012.
3. Result suggests that volatility transmission take place from Bosnian and Croatian stock markets to Serbian stock market

Article History

Keywords:
Balkan transition economies;
GARCH (1.1);
Equity markets;
Volatility spillover.

ABSTRACT

Financial crisis not only have statistically but also economically significant impact on global equity market returns. This study analyzes whether current financial crisis affect the equity market returns of Balkan transition economies and what is the extent of such impact by employing Generalized Autoregressive Conditional Heteroscedasticity model is employed on daily data spans from 2006 to 2012 for three transition economies which are Bosnia-Herzegovina, Croatia and Serbia. Empirical result indicates that volatility of Serbian stock price is influenced by the volatility of Bosnian and Croatian stock prices. There is one way volatility transmission from Bosnian and Croatian stock markets to Serbian stock market. High degree of volatility is observed in the stock markets during latest financial crises.

1.0 Introduction

The global economic crisis brings drop in economic activity, illiquidity of real sector, the financing problems of current income, growth and development of companies, depressed consumer spending and aggregate demand, and an enormous increase in the unemployment rate. There is almost no economic sector which was not affected by the emerging market crisis. In today's global world crisis are easily transferred from one market to another. The intensity of its transmission depends on the economic strength of countries in which it originally emerged. Since the U.S. is still economically strongest country in the world, its impact on the world's economy is largest, and the crisis that emerged in U.S. in 1929. ("Great depression."), quickly spread to European and Asian markets as well. As time progresses, the right size and dimension of this crisis became visible, and this U.S. crisis actually demonstrated how interconnected markets, in fact, are. So that the market crisis is not only retained as a local event, rather it takes the global state. A financial crisis can thus be defined as an ongoing issue which brings there cession into many countries, and causes a downward flow into major stock indexes. In 1997, Asian financial crisis emerged. As a major shock, it had a strong influence on investors in emerging markets. Not only were there significant losses on investments, but also many investors had come to believe that rapid and relatively steady economic growth in the region was the norm and foresaw only mild market setbacks. The Asian crisis was followed by the Russian crisis in 1998, and several others. In the period of 2008-2012 global financial crisis known as "Great recession," has took place and is considered by many economists to be the worst financial crisis since the "Great depression" in U.S. The financial crisis has caused the emerging and developing economies to replace advanced economies to lead global economic growth. The mentioned crisis taught us that the confidence of financial market, ones it is shattered, it cannot be easily recovered. The latest analysis of the global financial and economic crisis, are including the possibility that the crisis has touched the bottom, and the worst is behind us, but do not exclude the fact that the full recovery of the world economy could take many years.

The economy of Bosnia and Herzegovina was in structural crisis before the economic crisis, due to its lack of planned development, incompetent government structures, and political interference in economic decision making. The global crisis has just "pulled back the veils" hiding our domestic crisis while opening a large number of other problems, as in other countries in transition. Despite being one of the world's fastest growing countries, Turkey is now facing a number of economic challenges, as a result, of the global economic downturn. The rest of this paper is focusing on the emerging market crisis which started in 2008 and is still present, and how this crisis affects the equity markets of developing countries such Bosnia and Herzegovina, and Turkey are.

The contribution of this study is twofold. At first we conduct an analysis covering old Yugoslavian transition economies focusing on the Croatia, Serbia and Bosnia-Herzegovina; later we employ the GARCH (1.1) to examine volatility spillover and transmission among stock markets of those three countries. At last we analyze the volatility structure of the selected countries 'stock markets before and after the latest world financial crises.

The remainder of this study is structured as follows: Section 2 presents a literature review. Section 3 presents the data and methodology employed in the empirical analysis. Section 4 gives the empirical result, whereas the section 5 concludes.

2.0 Literature review

The global economy and deregulated financial system are once again in crisis, and equity market is experiencing the lowest level in the past 70 years. "Rating agencies might add instability to financial markets in emerging economies, is the conclusion drawn from recent research about emerging market instability" (Kaminsky & Schmukler, 2002). Although with the globalization effect, in which stock markets are expected to show uniform responses to shocks, the degree of stock market reactions to such shocks differs from one region to another, depending on the level of integration with the international economy (Nikkinen et al., 2008).

While financial crises are not a new phenomenon the current financial crisis differs from many of the previously studied crises in that it is both severe and global. It is well-documented that international capital markets react, in terms of returns and volatility, quickly and simultaneously to major events such as the crash of 1987 and the Asian crises in 1997. However, the timing and magnitude of changes in stock returns and volatility differ across markets around the world (Roll, 1988). The central message from the findings conducted by Samarakoon (2011) is that emerging markets have large normal sensitivities to U.S. shocks, and large declines in stock prices in these markets reflected these dependencies rather than contagion. The findings underline the importance of emerging markets as drivers to global asset price developments in recent years (Sáez, Fratzscher, & Thimann, 2009).

The results of IMF study conducted in 2008 and covering 30 countries indicate that emerging market equity prices are influenced by changes in global financial conditions, such as liquidity, credit and market risks, as well as growth and exchange rate expectations. Therefore, global factors constitute a significant channel for spillovers when the international economic environment changes. A number of past financial studies deal with financial market linkages and shock contagion effects between mature and emerging equity markets (e.g. Ratanapakorn and Sharma, 2002; Bessler and Yang, 2003; Chaudhuri and Wu, 2003; Wong and Vlaar, 2003; Syriopoulos, 2004). Summarizing the earlier empirical findings, it can be postulated that the medium to long-term dynamic behavior of the Balkan equity markets can potentially be affected by co-movements and volatility in leading mature, developed equity markets. Nevertheless, the Balkan equity markets have been neglected, and empirical research remains thin on this region (Samitas et al., 2007). Some past studies indicate that emerging stock market behavior increasingly depends on mature stock market volatility swings (e.g. Phylaktis and Ravazzolo, 2002; Swanson, 2003; Yang et al., 2006; Syriopoulos, 2007). There is general agreement that the recent global financial crisis raised the costs and constraints in the financial sector in providing working capital, pre-shipment export finance, export credit insurance and insurance of letters of credit for international trade (Uygur; 2010). The global recovery remains fragile and uneven-sluggish in advanced countries, much stronger in emerging and developing countries. The recent crisis has come to Turkey rather late, but it hit hard swiftly (Ercan, Taymaz & Yeldan; 2010). Bosnia and Herzegovina has been facing the difficult challenge of dealing with the legacies of the crisis and its past unsustainable policies while not hurting the recovery. The most widely applied models in situations where volatility of returns is central issue are ARCH (Engle, 1982) and a generalization of Engels's model known as GARCH introduced by Bollerslev (1986).

3.0 Data and methodology

3.01 Data

To investigate the issue and to analyze the relationship among equity returns and emerging financial crisis this study uses daily equity returns of SASE (Bosnia and Herzegovina), Serbia (BELEX) and Croatia (CROBEX) for the period of 2005 -2012. This data has been applied to estimate the volatility transmission among the selected Balkan countries 'equity returns and the impact of financial crises on the volatility of selected equity returns.

3.02 Generalized autoregressive conditional heteroscedasticity (GARCH)

With the aim of contributing to the development of macroeconomics rational expectations, Professor Robert F. Engle in 1982 in an article has introduced and defined the term ARCH model. The term ARCH stands for autoregressive (depending on its past), conditional, and heteroscedasticity (non-constant variance). By "conditional", it is meant that likelihood is computed based on an estimated set of priming values for the squared innovations (ε_t^2) and the variances (σ_t^2). This means that ARCH model allows the current conditional variance to a function of the past squared error terms. Because of his contribution Engle was considered as the pioneer of the financial econometrics.

The first application of ARCH was in a study of inflation rates (Engle, 1982), and thereafter a variety of parametric and nonparametric specifications of autoregressive conditional heteroscedasticity have been proposed. ARCH models seek to estimate the time-dependent volatility as a function of observed prior volatility. The original ARCH model modeled the variance of disturbances as a linear function of lagged values and provides a framework of analysis and development of time series models of volatility. The ARCH model allows the variance of the error to vary over time, in contrast to the standard time series regression models where the variance is assumed to be constant.

The ARCH model can be written as:

$$y_t = \mu_t + \sigma_t \varepsilon_t$$

$$\mu_t = \mu$$

$$\sigma_t^2 = \alpha_0 + \sum_{i=1}^{q} \alpha_i \alpha_{t-i}^2$$

$$\alpha_t = \sigma_t \varepsilon_t$$

where ε_t is a sequence of independent and identically distributed random variables with mean zero and variance 1; $\alpha_0 > 0$, $\alpha_i \geq 0$, for $i > 0$.

From the structure of the ARCH model, it can be concluded that if there is a large shock in previous periods, in other words if there is a large variance in previous periods, it makes the present period's variance higher. It means that large shocks tend to follow by another large shock. This property of ARCH stands for the volatility clustering in financial time series. As the ARCH models are used to model the volatility, they are also used to understand whether and to what extent the volatility is transmitted across markets. The basic ARCH model has been extended in several ways; in 1986, Bollerslev generalized the autoregressive conditional heteroscedasticity model, and this GARCH is the most influential and widely-used extension of ARCH.

Measuring the relationship between variables at various points in time, rather than using a single correlation coefficient over the entire sample period, provides information on the evolution of the relationship over time. The methodology applied in this paper is GARCH (1.1) modeling, which is widely applied method for analyzing data at different.

The (1.1) in GARCH (1.1) model in Eq. (3.2) refers to the presence of a first-order GARCH term and a first-order ARCH term

$$y_t = \beta x_t + \delta \sigma_t^2 + \varepsilon_t \ldots\ldots\ldots\ldots\ldots\ldots (3.2)$$

$$\varepsilon_{t-1}^2 = \omega + \alpha_i \varepsilon_{t-1}^2 + \beta_1 \sigma_{t-1}^2 \ldots\ldots\ldots\ldots\ldots\ldots (3.2)$$

$$\sigma_{t-1}^2$$

News about volatility from the previous period, measured as the lag of the squared residual from the mean equation (ARCH term) last periods forecast variance (GARCH term)

4.0 Empirical results

In order to evaluate volatility spillovers among three Balkan transition countries stock market return we form three variance equation model as follows;

$$y_t = \beta x_t + \delta\sigma_t^2 + \varepsilon_t$$

$$\sigma_t^2(\text{BELEX}) = \omega_1 + \alpha_1\varepsilon_{t-1}^2 + \beta_1\sigma_{t-1}^2 + \beta_2\text{CROBEX} + \beta_3\text{SASE}\text{............Model 01.........(3.3)}$$

$$\sigma_t^2(\text{SASE}) = \omega_2 + \alpha_2\varepsilon_{t-1}^2 + \beta_4\sigma_{t-1}^2 + \beta_5\text{CROBEX} + \beta_6\text{BELEX}\text{..........Model 02.......(3.4)}$$

$$\sigma_t^2(\text{CROBEX}) = \omega_3 + \alpha_3\varepsilon_{t-1}^2 + \beta_7\sigma_{t-1}^2 + \beta_8\text{SASE} + \beta_9\text{BELEX}\text{...........Model 03.......(35)}$$

Table shows the variance equation estimation results for three models. In all three models, stock market's volatility is being influenced by their past volatility. Significant ARCH coefficient in the variance equation implies that previous day's stock market return information about volatility is an important factor in defining today's market return volatility. It means that all three-stock market´s return volatility is influenced by its own shocks which are ARCH and GARCH factors.

Furthermore, the result from the first model shows that Serbian stock market (BELEX) volatility is being influenced by Bosnian and Croatian stock market returns. In the second and third model outside shocks are not significant. Bosnian stock market and Croatian stock market is not being influenced by the outside shock from two neighbor countries.

Table GARCH (1.1) Estimation Result

Variables	Model 01	Model 02	Model 03
C	4.50E-07	0.00000257	0.00000339
	(0.0003)*	(0.0000)*	(0.0015)*
ARCH	0.01837	0.132604	0.107567
	(0.0000)*	(0.0000)*	(0.0000)*
GARCH	0.707029	0.857954	0.884762
	(0.0000)*	(0.0000)*	(0.0000)*
CROATIA	0.0000791	0.0000557	
	(0.0204)*	(0.5095)	
BIH	-0.000158		0.0000761
	(0.0338)*		(0.4683)
SERBIA		-0.0000201	0.000125
		(0.7751)	(0.2563)

Note: Estimated coefficient with p-values in the brackets. * indicates significantly at the 5% significance level.

In the second model, Croatian and Serbian stock market return is not significant meaning that volatility in CROBEX and BELEX does not transmit to SASE. In the third model also BELEX and SASE is not significant meaning that there is no volatility transmission from those markets to Croatian stock market. We can conclude that unlike Croatian and Bosnian stock markets, Serbian stock market volatility is influenced by the Croatian and Bosnian stock market volatility.

Figure 01: Volatility of BELEX

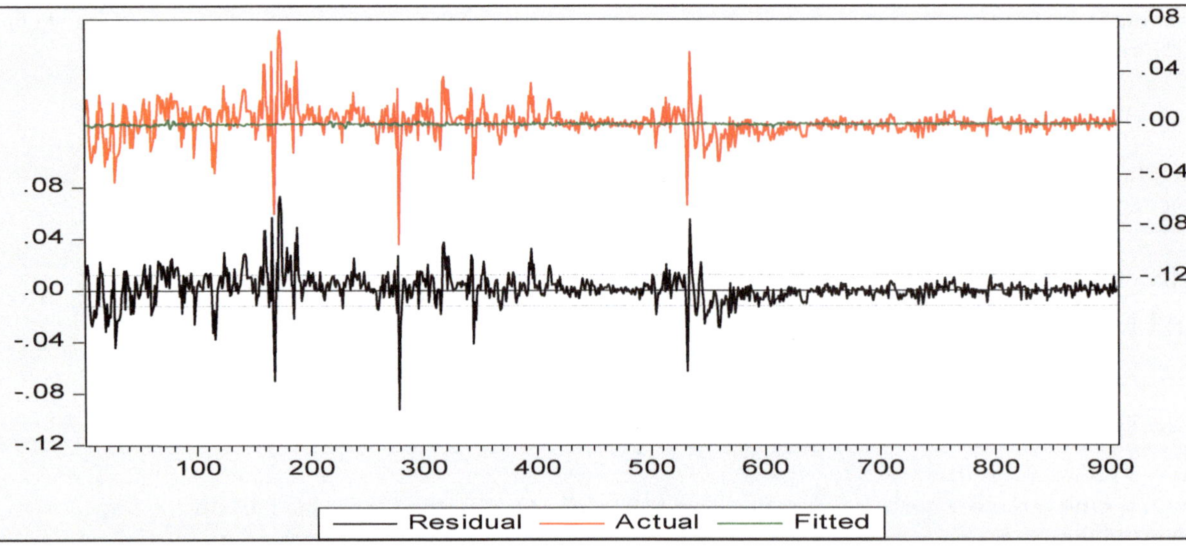

Figure 02: Volatility of COBEX

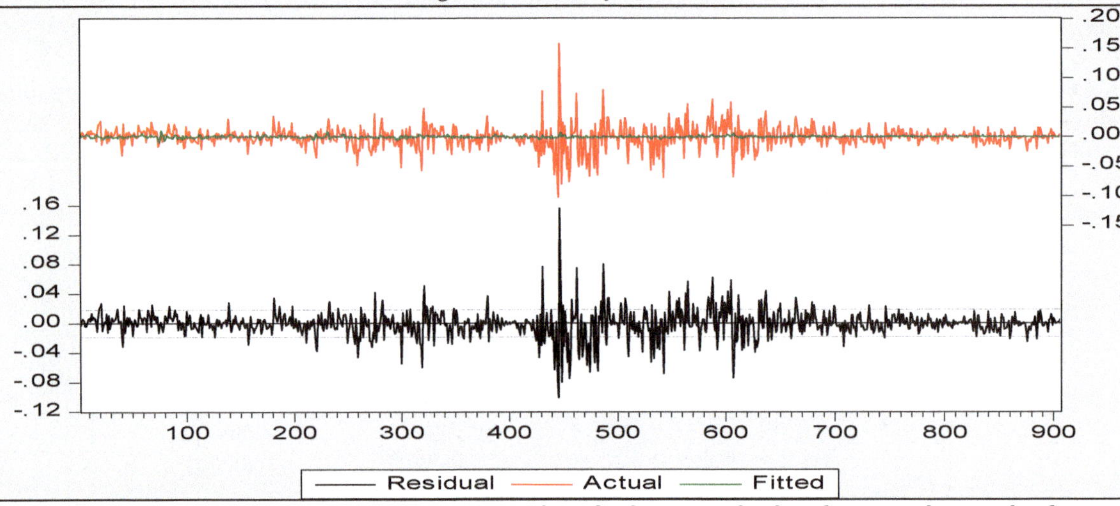

Among the three stock markets in transition, CROBEX has the lowest volatility features during the financial crises free period and moderate volatility in the latest financial crises as shown in Fig.2. After crises, all three stock markets enjoy low and stable volatility.

Figure 03: Volatility of SASE

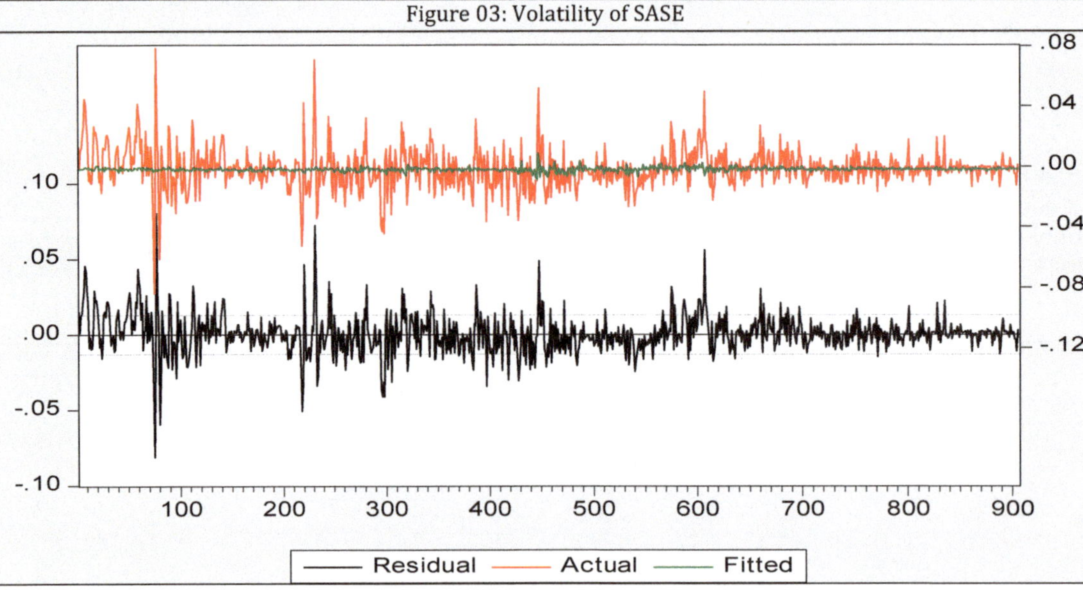

The last large financial crisis began in 2007, reached the bottom in 2008, and is still present. After applying the ARCH modeling to the equity returns data collected for the period of 2007-2010 in several markets of interest for the article, it can be stated that although due to the globalization effect, in which it is expected that stock markets show uniform responses to financial crashes, the degree of stock market volatility differs from one region to another, depending on the level of integration with the international economy. Observing stock markets of the neighbor countries of Bosnia and Herzegovina, Croatia and Serbia, we can see uneven developments and different responses to the emerging financial crisis.

5.0 Conclusion

This study explores the volatility spillover among the three stock markets of Balkan countries in transition which are Croatia, Bosnia and Herzegovina and Serbia. Given that the globalization has integrated financial markets, the hypothesis is that the emerging financial crisis has affected all stock markets worldwide to some degree, although shock sensitivity is significantly more obvious in emerging countries. Result from the GARCH (1.1) model implies that only Serbian stock market volatility is being influenced by the Bosnia and Herzegovina and Croatia.

Lack of external volatility transmission to Bosnian and Croatian stock markets form the other two former Yugoslavian countries are observed. Additionally all three-stock market's volatility is being influenced by its own shocks and information channels. Bosnian and Croatian stock markets have higher volatility features compared to Serbian stock market. All three stock markets show stable low volatility after latest financial crises. Our results have implications for international portfolio investors which are looking for diversified markets.

References

Bessler, D. A., and Yang, J. 2003. The structure of interdependence in international stockmarkets. Journal of International Money and Finance, 22:261-287

Bollerslev, T. 1986. Generalized autoregressive conditional heteroskedasticity. Journal of Econometrics, 31(03):307–327.

Chaudhuri, K., and Wu, Y. 2003. Random walk versus breaking trend in stockprices: evidence from emerging markets. Journal of Banking & Finance 27(4):575–592.

Engle, R. F. 1982. Autoregressive conditional heteroskedasticity with estimates of the variance of U.K. inflation. Econometrica 50(4):987-1007.

Ercan, H., Taymaz, E., &Yeldan, E., 2010. Crisis and Turkey: Impact analysis of crisis response measures. International Labor Organization, 9-15.

Kaminsky, G., & Schmukler, S. L. 2002. Emerging markets instability: Do sovereign ratings affect country risk and stock returns. World Bank Economic Review 16(2):171-195.

Nikkinen, J., Omran, M. M., Sahlström, P., &Äijö, J. 2008. Stock Returns and Volatility Following the September 11 Attacks: Evidence from 53 Equity Markets. Int. Review of Financial Analysis 17:27-46.

Phylaktis, K., and Ravazzolo, F. 2002. Measuring financial and economic integration with equity prices in emerging markets. Journal of International Money and Finance 21(6):879-903.

Ratanapakorn, O., & Sharma, S.C., 2002. Interrelationships among regional stock indices. Review of Financial Economics 11(2):91-108.

Roll, R., 1988. The international crash of October 1987.Financial Analysts' Journal 44(5):19-35.

Saez, L. C., Fratzscher, M., &Thimann, C. 2009. The transmission of emerging market shocks to global equity markets. Journal of Empirical Finance, 16:2-17.

Samarakoon, L. P., 2011. Stock market interdependencies, contagion, and the US financial crisis: The case of emerging and frontiermarkets. International Financial Markets, Institutions and Money 21(5):724-742.

Samitas, A., Kenourgios, D., &Paltalidis, N. 2007.Integration and behavioral patterns in emerging Balkan stock markets.Working paper, EFMA Annual Conference, 5-20.

Swanson, P.E., 2003. The interrelatedness of global equity markets, money markets, and foreign exchange markets. International Review of Financial Analysis 12(2):135-155.

Syriopoulos, T., 2004. International portfolio diversification to central European stock markets. Applied Financial Economics, Taylor and Francis Journals 14(17):1253-1268.

Syriopoulos, T., 2007. Dynamic linkages between emerging European and developed stock markets: Has the EMU any impact? International Review of Financial Analysis 16(1):41-60.

Uygur, E., 2010. The global crisis and the Turkish economy. Third World Network, 131:15-17.

Wong, A. S. K., and Vlaar, P. J. G., 2003.Modelling time-varying correlations of financial markets. WO Research Memorandum, no. 739: 16.

Yang, J., Hsiao, C., Li, Q., and Wang, Z., 2006. The emerging market crises and stock market linkages: further evidence. Journal of Applied Econometrics 21(6):727-744.

3

Data envelopment analysis with missing data: An application to life insurance industry in Taiwan

Yueh-Chiang Lee [a*], Yao-Hung Yang [b*]

[a] Department of Business Administration, Vanung University, Taiwan
[b] Department of Business Administration, Chung Yuan Christian University, Taiwan
[*] Corresponding author's e-mail: yaohungyang@yahoo.com.tw

HIGHLIGHTS:

1. The study uses the financial statement data of Taiwanese insurance industry from 2008 to 2012.
2. The Financial Holding Company's (FHC) cross-selling generate synergy which benefits life insurance.
3. FHC insurance's operational efficiency is better than non-FHC.
4. The use of fuzzy DEA solves the uncertainty of missing data.

Article History

Keywords:
Financial holding company;
Fuzzy data envelopment analysis model;
Life insurance;
Operational efficiency.

ABSTRACT

A fuzzy Data Envelopment Analysis model is adopted in this paper to assess the operational efficiency of life insurance companies in Taiwan. The study was conducted from 2008 to 2012 and the data were taken from Taiwan Economic Journal and related financial statements provided by the Taiwan Insurance Institute. The results indicate that the operational efficiency of insurance companies affiliated to financial holding companies appears to be better than that of insurance companies not affiliated with financial holding companies, signifying that the synergy generated after a financial holding company is formed and the cross-selling between its subsidiary groups are highly beneficial to the management of a life insurance company affiliated to such a financial holding company. The chief contribution of this paper is that, in the past, the data envelopment analysis models applied often could not calculate due to missing input and output data. The study adopts the fuzzy linear mathematics to solve the uncertainty.

1.0 Introduction

Unable to cope with business losses over the years, MetLife Taiwan started to dismiss its conventional business sections at the end of 2006 and also began to consider selling the company. In October 2009, it made the decision to pull out of the Taiwan market. ChinaTrust Financial Holdings purchased all its shares with US$180 million in March 2011. Share transfer was completed in November the same year and MetLife Taiwan became a member of ChinaTrust Financial Holdings. Meanwhile, Dutch-run ING Aetna Life Insurance also withdrew from the life insurance market in Taiwan and sold the business to Fubon Life Insurance, a local enterprise. In early 2009, Prudential Life Insurance Taiwan transferred all the liabilities and assets of insurance policies sold by salespeople to China Life Insurance (Taiwan) and shifted its focus on insurance through telephone marketing and banks. Dutch-based Aegon sold its TransGlobe Life Insurance Taiwan to Chung Wei Yi Co., Ltd., a financial holding company, in the same year. In 2011, Run Chen Investment Holdings signed a contract with US-based AIG and purchased 97.57% of the shares of Nan Shan Life Insurance with US$2.16 billion.

The abovementioned life insurance company mergers aroused the concern of the public about the operational efficiency of foreign life insurance companies and the reason why they pulled out from the Taiwan market one after another. Coincidentally, a significant change also occurred to the financial environment in Taiwan around the same time. The Financial Institutions Merger Act was passed in 2000, allowing banks, securities firms and insurance companies to make cross-industry mergers. In 2001, the Financial Holding Company (FHC) Act was passed and enforced in November the same year. It greatly reduced the restrictions on cross-industry operations between financial institutions, making it possible for banks, securities firms and insurance companies, subsidiaries of financial holding companies, to reduce operating costs and maximize the benefits of consolidated management through cross selling, exchange and use of information, and equipment sharing. This change in the management environment made it even more difficult for insurance companies that were not affiliated with financial holding companies. For this reason, insurance companies had to reexamine and evaluate their operational efficiency to understand their own advantages and disadvantages and distribute their resources effectively.

Data envelopment analysis (DEA) has been extensively applied in a large number of studies on operational efficiency in the financial industry (Yang, 2006; Luhnen, 2009; Lu, Wang & Lee, 2011; Hu, Yu & Lin, 2012). To overcome the lack of management information in one-stage DEA, Seiford and Zhu (1999) first applied two-stage DEA to analyze the profitability and market power of the top 55 banks in the US. The numbers of input and output items were fixed. However, when there were missing input or output data, assessment became impossible. There are 30 life insurance companies in Taiwan and most of them have not yet gone public; hence, collection of complete input and output data is not easy. However, this has led to the idea of using the fuzzy DEA applied by Kao and Liu (2000, 2004) to explore the management performance of life insurance companies in Taiwan. Is it true that life insurance companies affiliated with financial holding companies are able to upgrade their operational efficiency through cross selling between the banks, life insurance companies and securities firms under the same financial holding company or the diversity of business operations or the massiveness of organization can lead to decrease in operational efficiency? Is there difference in operational efficiency between life insurance companies affiliated with financial holding companies and those not affiliated with financial holding companies? The empirical results of this study should be able to shed light on how life insurance businesses in the country can make effective adjustments to their resource distribution and management strategies in order to improve their operational efficiency and competitiveness. In the meantime, it is also hoped that these results can serve as referential management performance indexes for the general public, investment organizations, and supervising agencies.

2.0 Literature review

After decades of development, the life insurance industry in Taiwan has achieved maturity. Progress has been accomplished in various areas, such as the supervision system, product development, and consumer awareness, etc. After the Financial Holding Company Act was passed in 2001 and Taiwan became a member of the WTO in 2002, Taiwan officially entered the bancassurance era. The management of life insurance businesses transformed from relying on salespeople to integrating banks, insurance brokers/agents, and direct marketing, carried out in diverse approaches. Facing fierce competition in the life insurance market, each life insurance company had to adopt the most advantageous management style or strategy, reinforce its management constitution, and expand its operation scale effectively to boost operational efficiency. In addition, the synergic effects generated after financial holding companies were formed made it all the more difficult for insurance companies not affiliated with financial holding companies to compete in the market. To break the deadlock, these life insurance companies started to develop niche products gradually and market them through different channels to fight life insurance companies affiliated with financial holding companies. Therefore, it is necessary for each company to measure its operational efficiency to understand its advantages and disadvantages and make effective distribution of the various resources of the company.

Berger, Hunter Timme (1993) suggested use of DEA to deal with the problem of excessive output or input encountered by decision making units (DMUs), maintain units invariance, and keep the weight unaffected by subjective factors. It was a remarkable overall index for measuring the efficiency of financial institutions. Fukuyama (1997) applied DEA to assess the difference in management performance between mutual insurance companies and regular life insurance companies in Japan and also studied the productivity changes happening between 1988 and 1993. The empirical results showed that there was no significant difference in management performance between the two types of companies. The technical inefficiency of mutual insurance companies was mainly pure technical inefficiency, whereas the technical inefficiency of regular insurance companies was a result of scale inefficiency. Meanwhile, Donni and Fecher (1997) used the Malmquist index (MI) and DEA to study the insurance industry of 15 OECD member states between 1983 and 1991. The results indicated that the growth of productivity in each country was mainly attributed to technological advancements. They further observed certain characteristics of the insurance market in each country and discovered that reinsurance rate and market share seemed able to facilitate efficiency upgrades in these OECD member states. Cummins, Tennyson and Weiss (1999) employed DEA to examine the US life insurance industry from 1988 to 1995 and concluded that companies having engaged in acquisitions outperformed those not having engaged in acquisitions, financially feeble companies were the mostly likely to become acquisition targets, and mergers had a positive effect on the efficiency of life insurance businesses. Diacon (2001) used a DEA BCC model to measure the operational efficiency of British insurance businesses as well as evaluate 431 insurance companies in 6 European countries. The study revealed that the level of efficiency was related to the U-shaped scale of insurance companies. In other words, insurance companies of smaller or larger scales had better operational efficiency. The higher the percentage of the total premiums over the years, the better the operational efficiency would be. In comparison, French and German insurance companies had better technical efficiency than insurance companies in the UK and other countries.

Barros, Nektarios and Assaf (2010) discovered in their study that consolidation to expand operation scales was the driving force for improvement of operational efficiency adopted by Greek life insurance businesses. Moreover, the empirical results also confirmed that, compared to other life insurance companies, life insurance companies of larger scales, listed life insurance companies, and life insurance companies that had gone through consolidation had higher operational efficiency.

Lu, et al. (2011) performed a study on 25 life insurance companies in Taiwan between 2003 and 2006 and applied metafrontier data envelopment analysis to estimate technical efficiency and the metatechnology ratio (MTR). The empirical results showed that old local insurance companies were the most efficient. Besides having the best technical efficiency, they also adopted production technologies closest to metatechnology standards. In addition, the metatechnology ratio values of old local insurance companies and foreign insurance companies were significantly higher than those of new local insurance companies. Hu, et al. (2012) applied two-stage DEA to analyze the efficiency 29 life insurance companies in Taiwan between 2005 and 2009 and adjusted the negative values of input and output items according to the approach employed by Lovell and Pastor (1995). The empirical results revealed that, except for 2009, the overall efficiency of the insurance companies appeared to be rising slightly. They also indicated that insurance companies affiliated with financial holding companies and foreign life insurance companies had higher efficiency values. According to the above literature, a hypothesis is induced as follows.

H: Life insurance companies are affiliated with financial holding companies have better operating efficiency than life insurance companies are not affiliated with financial holding companies in Taiwan.

3.0 Research design

In DEA literature, it is generally assumed that the input and output items are fixed numbers. However, it is not impossible that some input or output data are inaccurate or missing. Kao and Liu (2000, 2004), Inuiguchi and Tanino (2000), and Hsieh and Hsu (2009) therefore adopted fuzzy linear mathematics to cope with such uncertain factors during production process. Besides assessing data with fuzzy features, fuzzy DEA can also be used to construct the upper and lower limits of efficiency value while also obtain valuable information between the intervals contained in these limits. The samples in this study are life insurance companies in Taiwan. As many of them have not yet gone public, collection of data has not been easy and the problem of missing data exists. Therefore, in this paper, fuzzy DEA is employed to analyze the operational efficiency of life insurance companies. This chapter will first describe the sample data sources and variable definitions and then explain the fuzzy DEA and fuzzy sorting.

3.01 Data sources and variable definitions

Some of the sample life insurance companies have not yet gone public; therefore, besides the data from Taiwan Economic Journal, related financial statements provided by the Life Insurance Association of ROC have also been referred to. After taking out companies less than 5 years old and the ones on which there is not enough information, the samples are as follows: 6 life insurance companies that are affiliated to financial holding companies, namely Fubon Life Insurance (FB), Cathay Life Insurance (CA), Shin Kong Life Insurance (SK), First-Aviva Life Insurance (FI), Bank Taiwan Life Insurance (TB), and BNP Paribas TCB Life (CO); and 17 life insurance companies that are not affiliated to financial holding companies, namely China Life (CL), Nan Shan Life (NL), Kuo Hua Life (KL), PCA Life (PCL), Global Life (GL), Hontai Life (HL), Chaoyang Life (CYL), Singfor Life (SL), Farglory Life (FL), Taiwan Life (TL), TransGlobe Life (TGL), Allianz Life (AL), Mercuries Life Insurance (MLI), New York Life (NYL), Prudential Life (PL), CIGNA Life (CL), and Manu Life (ML).

Life insurance companies are deemed in this paper as intermediate organizations to provide financial services. In other words, they are intermediates that transfer financial resources, not producers. Therefore, the intermediate approach is adopted to define the input and output items (Isik & Hassan, 2002; Bonin, Hasan & Wachtel, 2005). In selection of input variables, due to the fact that the business of a life insurance company mainly relies on the field staff to sell policies and the size of field staff is therefore always a few times larger than the size of office staff, this means that field staff is very important to the management performance of a life insurance company. Therefore, the total of the field staff and the office staff is regarded the number of employees of a life insurance company. Other than the number of employees, the input variables also include the fixed assets and operating expenses (Cummins *et al.*, 1999; Lu et al., 2011). As for output variables, besides the premiums collected that are a source of revenue for a life insurance company, the company also has to use its assets to make proper investments. Therefore, investment income is another source of revenue for a life insurance company (Cummins *et al.*, 1999; Lu, et al., 2011; Hu, et al., 2012) See Table 1 for the setting of input and output variables.

Table 01: Definitions of input and output items

Variable	Description	Unit
Employees	Total number of employees on the payroll in the fiscal year	Person
Fixed Assets	Tangible assets having been used at least one year for business purposes, not for sale	Thousand NT
Operating expenses	The expenses for marketing, management, R&D, etc. during the period in concern	Thousand NT
Insurance Premium	The premiums collected for sold policies	Thousand NT
Investment Income	The income from the insurance company's long- and short-term investments	Thousand NT

Since the relative efficiency calculated with DEA is based on the input and output items of each decision-making unit, a certain relationship between the numbers of input and output items and the number of decision-making units has to be maintained; the number of units to be evaluated must be at least two times that of the input items and the output items (Bowlin, 1987; Golany & Roll, 1989). In this study, there are 3 input items, 2 output items, and 23 units to be evaluated. The arrangement complies with the rule.

3.02 Fuzzy data envelopment analysis

In this study, the fuzzy DEA developed by Kao and Liu (2000) to analyze fuzzy interval data is adopted. The input and output variables are defined as a triangular fuzzy number. Using a BCC input-oriented model for the hypothesis and applying α−Cut and the extension principle, the fuzzy DEA model is simplified into a conventional DEA model containing parameters of α level. At specific α levels, the model can be used to obtain the upper and lower limits of efficiency.

Input variables are defined as $\left[(X_{ij})_\alpha^L,(X_{ij})_\alpha^U\right]$, output variables $\left[(Y_{ik})_\alpha^L,(Y_{ik})_\alpha^U\right]$, and efficiency values $\left[(\theta_r)_\alpha^L,(\theta_r)_\alpha^U\right]$ respectively being the upper and lower limit intervals of $\alpha-Cut$ of $\widetilde{X}_{ij}$, $\widetilde{Y}_{ij}$ and $\widetilde{\theta}_{ij}$; $\left[(\theta_r)_\alpha^L\right]$ and $\left[(\theta_r)_\alpha^U\right]$ can be calculated with the following formula:

$$(\theta_r)_\alpha^L = \max\left(\sum_{k=1}^{t} u_k (Y_{rk})_\alpha^L - u_0\right) \Big/ \sum_{j=1}^{s} v_j (X_{rj})_\alpha^U$$

$$s.t. \left(\sum_{k=1}^{t} u_k (Y_{rk})_\alpha^L - u_0\right) \Big/ \sum_{j=1}^{s} v_j (X_{rj})_\alpha^U \le 1$$

$$\left(\sum_{k=1}^{t} u_k (Y_{ik})_\alpha^U - u_0\right) \Big/ \sum_{j=1}^{s} v_j (X_{ij})_\alpha^L \le 1,\ i = 1,2,\ldots,n, i \ne r \qquad (1)$$

$$k = 1,2,\ldots,t,\ j = 1,2,\ldots,s$$

$u_k, v_j \ge \varepsilon > 0, u_0$ There is no positive or negative limit.

$$(\theta_r)_\alpha^U = \max\left(\sum_{k=1}^{t} u_k (Y_{rk})_\alpha^U - u_0\right) \Big/ \sum_{j=1}^{s} v_j (X_{rj})_\alpha^L$$

$$s.t. \left(\sum_{k=1}^{t} u_k (Y_{rk})_\alpha^U - u_0\right) \Big/ \sum_{j=1}^{s} v_j (X_{rj})_\alpha^L \le 1$$

$$(\sum_{k=1}^{t} u_k (Y_{ik})_\alpha^L - u_0) \Big/ \sum_{j=1}^{s} v_j (X_{rj})_\alpha^U \leq 1, i = 1,2,\ldots,n, i \neq r \qquad (2)$$
$$k = 1,2,\ldots,t, j = 1,2,\ldots,s$$

$u_k, v_j \geq \varepsilon > 0, u_0$ There is no positive or negative limit.

$(\theta_r)_\alpha^L$ = the lower limit of efficiency value of target decision-making unit r at α level;

$(\theta_r)_\alpha^U$ = the upper limit of efficiency value of target decision-making unit r at α level;

$(X_{rj})_\alpha^L$ = the lower limit of the quantity of no. j input item of target decision-making unit r at α level;

$(X_{rj})_\alpha^U$ = the upper limit of the quantity of no. j input item of target decision-making unit r at α level

$(Y_{rk})_\alpha^L$ = the lower limit of the quantity of no. k output item of target decision-making unit r at α level;

$(Y_{rk})_\alpha^U$ = the upper limit of the quantity of no. k output item of target decision-making unit r at α level;

$(X_{ij})_\alpha^L$ = the lower limit of the quantity of no. j input item of no. i decision-making unit at α level;

$(X_{ij})_\alpha^U$ = the upper limit of the quantity of no. j input item of no. i decision-making item at α level;

$(Y_{ik})_\alpha^L$ = the lower limit of the quantity of no. k output item of no. i decision-making unit at α level;

$(Y_{ik})_\alpha^U$ = the upper limit of the quantity of no. k output item of no. i decision-making unit below α level;

u_k = the weight of no. k output item; v_j = the weight of no. j input item

$\varepsilon = 10^{-4}$ or 10^{-6} as normally set

u_0 the intercept term

3.03 Fuzzy number comparison index

Unlike the crisp values obtained with conventional DEA models, the efficiency values obtained with the fuzzy DEA model are fuzzy numbers; therefore, it is difficult to conduct sorting on the units evaluated. In this study, the area estimation approach proposed by Chen and Klein (1997) is adopted to sort the fuzzy numbers. At α level, there is the decision-making unit i (i = 1, 2, ..., n) and the upper and lower limits of efficiency value θ_r are respectively $(\theta_r)_\alpha^L$ and $(\theta_r)_\alpha^U$. By definition, h(X) = 1 stands for the maximum height (α = 1) and $\alpha_b = b/w$, b = 0.1, 0.2, ..., w; in other words, $\alpha_0 = 0.0$, $\alpha_1 = 0.1$, ..., $\alpha_{10} = 1$; therefore the comparison index (CI) is:

$$CI_i = \frac{\sum_{b=0}^{w} ((\theta_i)_{\alpha_b}^U - c)}{\left[\sum_{b=0}^{w} ((\theta_i)_{\alpha_b}^U - c) - \sum_{b=0}^{w} ((\theta_i)_{\alpha_b}^L - d) \right]} \qquad (3)$$

$(\theta_i)_{\alpha_b}^L$ = the lower limit of efficiency value of decision-making unit I;

$(\theta_i)_{\alpha_b}^U$ = the upper limit of efficiency value of decision-making unit I;

$c = \min\{(\theta_i)_{\alpha_b}^L\}$ $d = \max\{(\theta_i)_{\alpha_b}^U\}$. The sorting principle is that the larger the CI_i value, the higher the ranking.

4.0 Empirical results

This study was conducted on life insurance companies, 23 in total, in Taiwan between 2008 and 2012. Take the data for 2012 data as an example. The investment income figure for CIGNA Life is missing, as shown in Table 2.

Table 02: Life insurance company input and output variables

DMUs	Input			Output	
	Employees (person)	Fixed Asset (Thousand NT)	Operating expenses (Thousand NT)	Insurance premiums (Thousand NT)	Investment income
TB	5,648	893,222	840,423	56,697,442	10,208,200

TL	4,498	9,836,433	2,624,008	67,610,451	15,343,225
PCL	718	73,043	2,174,019	21,339,630	6,139,689
CA	30,889	20,508,928	16,134,194	471,820,605	119,271,028
CL	5,181	4,854,110	3,341,642	115,577,332	26,472,589
NL	18,092	12,177,214	14,500,158	352,729,473	82,904,992
KL	2,700	400,551	1,492,220	36,771,296	10,896,254
SK	11,356	14,192,745	12,851,151	162,367,489	68,007,294
FB	17,739	7,395,030	13,157,079	401,449,260	68,097,646
GL	614	113,524	479,299	8,516,802	1,180,712
MLI	6,773	4,226,604	3,876,625	103,890,522	15,315,113
CYL	249	155,506	304,794	8,495,689	490,649
SL	686	17,053	760,784	8,693,829	1,790,980
FL	1,763	8,726,315	1,620,986	36,498,273	13,424,564
HL	485	302,639	625,861	22,618,716	5,187,520
AL	1,316	113,180	1,215,181	4,679,402	659,860
FI	188	4,851	364,400	2,474,901	368,779
PL	1,152	1,365,586	1,712,333	11,474,736	1,661,718
TGL	926	178,686	1,796,514	25,191,738	8,825,842
NYL	640	33,067	1,047,296	11,006,193	1,787,727
CL	938	168,366	2,314,288	7,346,983	*
ML	1,376	50,964	921,294	6,892,806	736,459
CO	255	20,748	925,367	3,037,692	171,220

* missing data

In this paper, according to the input and output items, the minimum, maximum and median are selected to be the most pessimistic value, most optimistic value and most likely value to construct a triangular membership function and form the lower limit, upper limit and vertex. Then the data in Table 2 are converted into $\alpha -$ Cut and presented as interval data. The 2012 data, for instance, are as shown in Table A.1.

Next, the calculation approach defined by Kao and Liu (2000) is applied. α is divided into 10 intervals; in other words, $\alpha = 0.0, 0.1, 0.2, \ldots, 1.0$, forming 11 α values. The different upper and lower limit interval values of $\alpha -$ Cut are calculated. Using the 2012 data as an example, the upper and lower limits of efficiency value calculated with the DEA-Solver software are as shown in Table A.2.

After obtaining the upper and lower limits of efficiency value of life insurance companies in Taiwan between 2008 and 2012, the area estimation approach proposed by Chen and Klein (1997) is applied to calculate and establish the fuzzy number comparison index for each year. Then, the indexes are added up and the performance rankings of the life insurance companies are determined in accordance with the total index; the larger the index, the higher the ranking, as shown in Table 3.

Table 03: Life insurance company performance rankings 2008-2012

DMU	2008	2009	2010	2011	2012	Sum	Rank
TB	1.000	1.000	1.000	1.000	1.000	5.000	1
CA	1.000	1.000	1.000	1.000	1.000	5.000	1
FB	1.000	1.000	1.000	1.000	1.000	5.000	1
CYL	1.000	1.000	1.000	1.000	1.000	5.000	1
FI	1.000	1.000	1.000	1.000	1.000	5.000	1
SL	0.774	1.000	1.000	1.000	1.000	4.774	6
HL	0.744	1.000	1.000	1.000	1.000	4.744	6
CL	1.000	0.699	1.000	1.000	1.000	4.699	8
FL	1.000	1.000	1.000	0.896	0.781	4.677	9
CO	0.937	1.000	1.000	1.000	0.682	4.620	10
NYL	0.632	1.000	1.000	1.000	0.978	4.610	11
PCL	0.490	1.000	1.000	1.000	1.000	4.490	12
GL	0.690	0.984	0.998	0.862	0.849	4.383	13
KL	0.833	0.736	0.822	0.974	1.000	4.364	14
TGL	0.841	0.793	1.000	0.674	1.000	4.308	15
NL	0.907	0.901	0.675	0.799	0.985	4.267	16
SK	0.798	0.797	1.000	0.822	0.783	4.199	17
ML	1.000	0.884	0.525	0.674	0.490	3.573	18
MLI	0.798	0.883	0.525	0.478	0.677	3.361	19
CL	1.000	1.000	0.057	0.017	0.610	2.683	20
TL	0.455	0.755	0.457	0.330	0.607	2.603	21
PL	0.723	0.878	0.044	0.041	0.004	1.690	22
AL	0.067	0.020	0.117	0.105	0.088	0.396	23

Table 3 indicates that the operational efficiency of TB, CA, FB, CYL and FI was the best in the five years from 2008 to 2012. Their efficiency value achieved 1 each year, apparently better than the remaining life insurance companies. According to the classification of Norman and Stocker (1991), these five companies are robustly efficient units and are able to remain efficient unless critical changes occur in the future. Their scales of return should be constant; hence, there is no need to increase output or decrease input. They only need to maintain the current production scale. Among these five companies, TB, CA, FB and FI are subsidiaries of financial holding companies. Obviously, the synergy generated after a financial holding company is formed and the cross selling between the subsidiary groups can give an affiliated life insurance company a lot of help.

Besides in 2008, the operational efficiency value of SL and HL achieved 1 each year between 2009 and 2012, indicating increasingly improved operational efficiency. They also need not increase output or reduce input unless critical changes happen to the market in the future. The efficiency value of CL, except in 2009, was 1 in every one of the other years, signifying that the company is efficient and able to adjust its output and input to maintain its operational efficiency in the best condition. The efficiency value of FL, on the other hand, may have achieved 1 from 2008 to 2010, but it has become not so satisfactory in more recent years and needs to adjust its input items appropriately to improve the efficiency value. CO and NYL, however, appeared inefficient in 2008 and 2012 but exhibited decent operational efficiency from 2009 to 2011. It is suggested that they review the input items in 2008 and 2009 and make necessary adjustments. The efficiency value of PCL for 2008 was particularly low but the company immediately adjusted the input items and the operational efficiency value achieved 1 in each of the following years.

The efficiency value of the remaining life insurance companies rarely achieved 1 during the time of study, indicating poor operational efficiency as well as the inability of the managers to adjust the input items in time. The efficiency value of MLI, TL, PL and AL during the time of study was below 0.9 each year, making them distinctly inefficient units. It will be difficult for them to become efficient in a short time. They need to improve the input-output ratio and adjust their production scale simultaneously to become efficient.

5.0 Conclusion and policy implication

Liu et al. (2011) applied metafrontier data envelopment analysis to study life insurance companies in Taiwan. The empirical results showed that the metatechnology ratio of old local insurance companies and foreign insurance companies was significantly higher than that of new insurance companies. Hu et. al. (2012) adjusted the negative values of input or output items and the empirical DEA results indicated that the efficiency value of insurance companies affiliated with financial holding companies and foreign life insurance companies was better. In this paper, it is also proven that the operational efficiency of insurance companies TB, CA, FB and FI, all affiliated to financial holding companies, was indeed superior to that of insurance companies not affiliated to financial holding companies. This is consistent with the empirical results of Hu et al. (2012). Obviously, these four life insurance companies are able to boost their operational efficiency as a result of cross selling through the banks, life insurance companies and securities firms under the same financial holding company. However, the operational efficiency of CO and SK, also affiliated to financial holding companies, is not so decent, probably a result from the diversity of business operations or immensity of organization. Meanwhile, the five life insurance companies proven to be with the best efficiency in this paper are all local companies. This is not consistent with the empirical results of Lu et al. (2011) and Hu et al. (2012). Besides that different DEA models have been used, the difference in time of study and the dissimilarity in input and output items could have led to inconsistent results.

This paper shows that insurance companies that are not affiliated to financial holding companies generally are not efficient. Among them, CYL is the only one with efficiency value achieving 1 every year for five consecutive years. The other insurance companies all need to adjust their input items appropriately to boost efficiency. As life insurance businesses have transformed from relying on salespeople to diversified marketing through banks and securities firms, competition in the life insurance market has intensified and the room for insurance companies not affiliated to financial holding companies has been suppressed, making their further growth increasingly difficult. In the future, they have to adopt the most advantageous management styles and management strategies to differentiate from insurance companies that are affiliated to financial holding companies.

In the past, the DEA models applied were often unable to compute due to missing input and output data. In this paper, fuzzy linear mathematics is employed to solve this uncertainty (Kao & Liu , 2000; Hsieh & Hsu, 2009). In the future, when data collection is difficult or there are missing data, researchers are suggested to adopt fuzzy DEA to analyze operational efficiency.

Reference

Barros CP., Nektarios M. Assaf A., 2010. Efficiency in the Greek insurance industry. European Journal of Operational Research, 205(2): 431-436. http://dx.doi.org/10.1016/j.ejor.2010.01.011
Berger AN., Hunter W C., Timme S G., 1993. The efficiency of financial institutions: A review and preview of research past, present and future. Journal of Banking & Finance, 17(2-3): 221-249. http://dx.doi.org/10.1016/0378-4266(93)90030-H
Bonin JP., Hasan, I., Wachtel P., 2005. Bank performance, efficiency and ownership in transition countries. Journal of Banking and Finance, 29: 31-51. http://dx.doi.org/10.1016/j.jbankfin.2004.06.015
Bowlin W., 1987. Evaluating the efficiency of US Air Force real-property maintenance activities. Journal of the perational Research Society, 38(2): 127-135. http://dx.doi.org/10.2307/2582148
Chen CB., Klein, CM., 1997. A simple approach to ranking a group of aggregated fuzzy utilities. IEEE Transactions on Systems, Man Cybernet. Part B: Cybernet, 27(1): 26-35. http://dx.doi.org/10.1109/3477.552183
Cummins JD., Tennyson S., Weiss MA., 1999. Consolidation and efficiency in the US life insurance industry. Journal of Banking and Finance, 23(2-4): 325-357. http://dx.doi.org/10.1016/S0378-4266(98)00089-2
Diacon SR., 2001. The efficiency of UK general insurance companies. Working Paper, Centre for Risk & Insurance Studies, University of Nottingham.
Donni O., Fecher F., 1997. Efficiency and productivity of the insurance industry in the OECD countries. The Geneva Papers on Risk and Insurance-Issues and Practice, 22(84): 523-535.
Fukuyama H., 1997. Investigating productive efficiency and productivity changes of Japanese life insurance companies. Pacific-Basin Finance Journal, 5 (4): 481-509. http://dx.doi.org/10.1016/S0927-538X(97)00016-4
Golany B., Roll Y., 1989. An application procedure for DEA. OMEGA, 17(3): 237-250. http://dx.doi.org/10.1016/0305-0483(89)90029-7
Hsieh LF., Hsu SM., 2009. A new fuzzy DEA ranking model with an application for bank branch performance evaluation. Journal of Management & Systems, 16(3): 469-486.
Hu JL., Yu S., Lin FL., 2012. Efficiency analysis of life insurance companies in Taiwan: A two-stage data envelopment analysis. Insurance Issues and Practices, 11(1): 21-42.
Inuiguchi M., Tanino T., 2000. Data envelopment analysis with fuzzy input-output data. In Y. Y. Haimes and R. E. Steuer (Eds.), Research and Practice in Multiple Criteria Decision Making, Springer-Verlag, Berlin, 296-307. http://dx.doi.org/10.1007/978-3-642-57311-8_25
Isik I., Hassan MK., 2002. Technical, scale and allocative efficiencies of Turkish banking industry. Journal of Banking and Finance, 26(4): 719-766. http://dx.doi.org/10.1016/S0378-4266(01)00167-4
Kao C., Liu S T., 2000. Data envelopment analysis with missing data: An application to university libraries in Taiwan. Journal of the Operational Research Society, 51: 897-905. http://dx.doi.org/10.2307/254045
Kao C., Liu ST., 2004. Predicting bank performance with financial forecasts: A case of Taiwan commercial banks. Journal of Banking and Finance, 28(10): 2353-2368. http://dx.doi.org/10.1016/j.jbankfin.2003.09.008
Lovell CAK., Pastor JT., 1995. Units invariant and translation invariant DEA models. Operations Research Letters, 18(3): 147-151. http://dx.doi.org/10.1016/0167-6377(95)00044-5
Lu YH., Wang CH., Lee CH., 2011. The differences in technology efficiency of Taiwan's life insurance companies – The application of the Metafrontier DEA model. Journal of Economics and Management, 7(1): 73-100.
Luhnen M., 2009. Determinants of efficiency and productivity in German property-liability insurance: evidence for 1995–2006. The Geneva Papers on Risk and Insurance, 34(3): 483-505. http://dx.doi.org/10.1057/gpp.2009.10
Norman M., Stocker B., 1991. Data envelopment analysis: The assessment of performance? John Wiley and Sons.
Seiford LM., Zhu J., 1999. Profitability and marketability of the top 55 U.S. commercial banks. Management Science, 45(9): 1270-1288. http://dx.doi.org/10.1287/mnsc.45.9.1270
Yang Z., 2006. A two-stage DEA model to evaluate the overall performance of Canadian life and health insurance companies. Mathematical and Computer Modeling, 43(7-8): 910-919. http://dx.doi.org/10.1016/j.mcm.2005.12.011

Appendix tables:

Table a.1: Life insurance company input and output intervals in 2012

DMUs	Employees	Fixed Asset	Operating expenses	Insurance premium	Investment Income
TB	[5648 , 5648]	[893222 , 893222]	[840423 , 840423]	[56697442 , 56697442]	[10208200 , 10208200]
TL	[4498 , 4498]	[9836433 , 9836433]	[2624008 , 2624008]	[67610451 , 67610451]	[15343225 , 15343225]
PCL	[718 , 718]	[73043 , 73043]	[2174019 , 2174019]	[21339630 , 21339630]	[6139689 , 6139689]
CA	[30889 , 30889]	[20508928 , 20508928]	[16134194 , 16134194]	[471820605 , 471820605]	[119271028 , 119271028]
CL	[5181 , 5181]	[4854110 , 4854110]	[3341642 , 3341642]	[115577332 , 115577332]	[26472589 , 26472589]
NL	[18092 , 18092]	[12177214 , 12177214]	[14500158 , 14500158]	[352729473 , 352729473]	[82904992 , 82904992]
KL	[2700 , 2700]	[400551 , 400551]	[1492220 , 1492220]	[36771296 , 36771296]	[10896254, 10896254]
SK	[11356 , 11356]	[14192745 , 14192745]	[12851151 , 12851151]	[162367489 , 162367489]	[68007294 , 68007294]
FB	[17739 , 17739]	[7395030 , 7395030]	[13157079 , 13157079]	[401449260 , 401449260]	[68097646 , 68097646]
GL	[614 , 614]	[113524 , 113524]	[479299 , 479299]	[8516802 , 8516802]	[1180712 , 1180712]
MLI	[6773 , 6773]	[4226604 , 4226604]	[3876625 , 3876625]	[103890522 , 103890522]	[15315113 , 15315113]
CYL	[249 , 249]	[155506 , 155506]	[304794 , 304794]	[8495689, 8495689]	[490649 , 490649]
SL	[686 , 686]	[17053 , 17053]	[760784 , 760784]	[8693829 , 8693829]	[1790980 , 1790980]
FL	[1763 , 1763]	[8726315 , 8726315]	[1620986 , 1620986]	[36498273 , 36498273]	[13424564, 13424564]
HL	[485 , 485]	[302639 , 302639]	[625861 , 625861]	[22618716 , 22618716]	[5187520, 5187520]
AL	[1316 , 1316]	[113180 , 113180]	[1215181 , 1215181]	[4679402 , 4679402]	[659860 , 659860]
FI	[188 , 188]	[4851 , 4851]	[364400 , 364400]	[2474901 , 2474901]	[368779 , 368779]
PL	[1152 , 1152]	[1365586 , 1365586]	[1712333 , 1712333]	[11474736 , 11474736]	[1661718 , 1661718]
TGL	[926 , 926]	[178686 , 178686]	[1796514 , 1796514]	[25191738 , 25191738]	[8825842 , 8825842]
NYL	[640 , 640]	[33067 , 33067]	[1047296 , 1047296]	[11006193 , 11006193]	[1787727, 1787727]
CL	[938 , 938]	[168366 , 168366]	[2314288 , 2314288]	[7346983 , 7346983]	$(171220 + 7311546\alpha$, $119271028 - 111788262\alpha)$
ML	[1376 , 1376]	[50964 , 50964]	[921294 , 921294]	[6892806 , 6892806]	[736459 , 736459]
CO	[255 , 255]	[20748 , 20748]	[925367 , 925367]	[3037692 , 3037692]	[171220 , 171220]
maximum	30,889	20,508,928	16,134,194	471,820,605	119,271,028
minimum	188	4,851	304,794	2,474,901	171,220
median	1,316	302,639	1,620,986	22,618,716	7,482,766

Table A.2: Life insurance company upper and lower limits of efficiency in input and output in 2012

DMU	α= 0		α= 0.1		α= 0.2		α= 0.3		α= 0.4		α= 0.5		α= 0.6		α= 0.7		α= 0.8		α= 0.9		α= 1		score
	L	U	L	U	L	U	L	U	L	U	L	U	L	U	L	U	L	U	L	U	L	U	
TB	1.000	1.000	1.000	1.000	1.000	1.000	1.000	1.000	1.000	1.000	1.000	1.000	1.000	1.000	1.000	1.000	1.000	1.000	1.000	1.000	1.000	1.000	1.000
TL	0.705	0.712	0.705	0.712	0.705	0.712	0.706	0.712	0.706	0.712	0.706	0.712	0.707	0.712	0.707	0.712	0.709	0.712	0.712	0.712	0.712	0.712	0.607
PCL	1.000	1.000	1.000	1.000	1.000	1.000	1.000	1.000	1.000	1.000	1.000	1.000	1.000	1.000	1.000	1.000	1.000	1.000	1.000	1.000	1.000	1.000	1.000
CA	1.000	1.000	1.000	1.000	1.000	1.000	1.000	1.000	1.000	1.000	1.000	1.000	1.000	1.000	1.000	1.000	1.000	1.000	1.000	1.000	1.000	1.000	1.000
CL	1.000	1.000	1.000	1.000	1.000	1.000	1.000	1.000	1.000	1.000	1.000	1.000	1.000	1.000	1.000	1.000	1.000	1.000	1.000	1.000	1.000	1.000	1.000
NL	0.945	1.000	0.961	1.000	0.978	1.000	0.996	1.000	1.000	1.000	1.000	1.000	1.000	1.000	1.000	1.000	1.000	1.000	1.000	1.000	1.000	1.000	1.000
KL	1.000	1.000	1.000	1.000	1.000	1.000	1.000	1.000	1.000	1.000	1.000	1.000	1.000	1.000	1.000	1.000	1.000	1.000	1.000	1.000	1.000	1.000	0.985
SK	0.638	1.000	0.641	1.000	0.646	1.000	0.651	1.000	0.659	1.000	0.703	1.000	0.808	1.000	0.992	1.000	1.000	1.000	1.000	1.000	1.000	1.000	1.000
FB	1.000	1.000	1.000	1.000	1.000	1.000	1.000	1.000	1.000	1.000	1.000	1.000	1.000	1.000	1.000	1.000	1.000	1.000	1.000	1.000	1.000	1.000	0.783
GL	0.889	0.889	0.889	0.889	0.889	0.889	0.889	0.889	0.889	0.889	0.889	0.889	0.889	0.889	0.889	0.889	0.889	0.889	0.889	0.889	0.889	0.889	1.000
MLI	0.761	0.761	0.761	0.761	0.761	0.761	0.761	0.761	0.761	0.761	0.761	0.761	0.761	0.761	0.761	0.761	0.761	0.761	0.761	0.761	0.761	0.761	0.849
CYL	1.000	1.000	1.000	1.000	1.000	1.000	1.000	1.000	1.000	1.000	1.000	1.000	1.000	1.000	1.000	1.000	1.000	1.000	1.000	1.000	1.000	1.000	0.677
SL	1.000	1.000	1.000	1.000	1.000	1.000	1.000	1.000	1.000	1.000	1.000	1.000	1.000	1.000	1.000	1.000	1.000	1.000	1.000	1.000	1.000	1.000	1.000
FL	0.698	1.000	0.703	1.000	0.708	1.000	0.715	1.000	0.726	1.000	0.742	1.000	0.764	1.000	0.799	1.000	0.862	1.000	1.000	1.000	1.000	1.000	0.781
HL	1.000	1.000	1.000	1.000	1.000	1.000	1.000	1.000	1.000	1.000	1.000	1.000	1.000	1.000	1.000	1.000	1.000	1.000	1.000	1.000	1.000	1.000	1.000
AL	0.325	0.325	0.325	0.325	0.325	0.325	0.325	0.325	0.325	0.325	0.325	0.325	0.325	0.325	0.325	0.325	0.325	0.325	0.325	0.325	0.325	0.325	0.088
FI	1.000	1.000	1.000	1.000	1.000	1.000	1.000	1.000	1.000	1.000	1.000	1.000	1.000	1.000	1.000	1.000	1.000	1.000	1.000	1.000	1.000	1.000	1.000
PL	0.260	0.263	0.260	0.263	0.261	0.263	0.261	0.263	0.261	0.263	0.261	0.263	0.261	0.263	0.262	0.263	0.263	0.263	0.263	0.263	0.263	0.263	0.004
TGL	1.000	1.000	1.000	1.000	1.000	1.000	1.000	1.000	1.000	1.000	1.000	1.000	1.000	1.000	1.000	1.000	1.000	1.000	1.000	1.000	1.000	1.000	1.000
NYL	0.984	0.984	0.984	0.984	0.984	0.984	0.984	0.984	0.984	0.984	0.984	0.984	0.984	0.984	0.984	0.984	0.984	0.984	0.984	0.984	0.984	0.984	0.978
CL	0.309	1.000	0.309	1.000	0.309	1.000	0.374	1.000	0.443	1.000	0.513	1.000	0.583	1.000	0.653	1.000	0.723	1.000	0.793	1.000	0.864	0.864	0.610
ML	0.623	0.623	0.623	0.623	0.623	0.623	0.623	0.623	0.623	0.623	0.623	0.623	0.623	0.623	0.623	0.623	0.623	0.623	0.623	0.623	0.623	0.623	0.490
CO	0.765	0.765	0.765	0.765	0.765	0.765	0.765	0.765	0.765	0.765	0.765	0.765	0.765	0.765	0.765	0.765	0.765	0.765	0.765	0.765	0.765	0.765	0.682

4

Can inflation targeting mitigate monetary policy time-inconsistency?

Gabriel Caldas Montes [a*]

[a] Department of Economics, Fluminense Federal University Rio de Janeiro, Brazil.
*Corresponding author email: gabrielmontesuff@yahoo.com.br

HIGHLIGHTS:

1. The paper evaluates whether inflation targeting is able to mitigate the time-inconsistency problem
2. The paper provides evidence based on cointegration tests for Brazil
3. The findings suggest that the central bank needs to manage the regime better than it has done so far
4. It is recommended that commitment technologies must be improved in emerging countries

Article History

Keywords:
Cointegration;
Monetary policy;
Inflation targeting time-inconsistency.

ABSTRACT

Although the adoption of inflation targeting can, on average, bring benefits to developing countries, however, adopting this scheme is not necessarily sufficient to mitigate the time-inconsistency problem of monetary policy. The present paper makes use of two theoretical models in order to analyze for the Brazilian case whether it is possible for the monetary authority to conduct time-inconsistent monetary policies even under inflation targeting. The results obtained for Brazil allow one to conjecture that the traditional argument that the adoption of inflation targeting can avoid the time-inconsistency problem is not necessarily true.

1.0 Introduction

Despite there are several theoretical arguments for the time-inconsistency problem, empirical evidence is scarce on this subject. Even today, as highlighted by Taylor (2012), one of the most important subjects for analysis in modern macroeconomics is the time-inconsistency problem in monetary policy. However, great difficulties exist in terms of evaluating episodes of time-inconsistency, creating a gap with regard to empirical evidence. There are studies, based on Ireland (1999), that have sought to answer whether the time-inconsistency problem has occurred in some countries – these studies consider a bi-variate time series model for CPI inflation and unemployment (Ruge-Murcia, 2003; Akay and Nargelecekenler, 2007; Pierdzioch and Stadtmann, 2011; Montes, de Mendonça and Bastos, 2014) or a tri-variate time series model for CPI inflation, unemployment and U.S. unemployment (Doyle and Falk, 2008). However, in practice, it is still not possible to ensure if time-inconsistency is/was really a problem.

An important reference with regard to empirical analysis about time-inconsistency problem is the work of Ireland (1999). In order to perform an applied analysis for the U.S. economy, Ireland (1999) modified Barro and Gordon's model by assuming that the natural rate of unemployment is an autoregressive process which holds a unit root and by introducing control errors for inflation. After presenting the theoretical model, Ireland (1999) makes cointegration tests between inflation and unemployment in order to identify the time-inconsistency problem of monetary policy in the United States.

Despite the unemployment-inflation trade-off represents an important subject in several researches involving the time-inconsistency problem of monetary policy; in the economy, there exist other trade-offs. Researches in macroeconomics also highlight the output-inflation trade-off, and compare the determinants of these trade-offs and the implications for the economy (de Mendonça, 2009). The present paper uses two different approaches to identify the time inconsistency problem - Ireland (1999) and Gupta and Uwilingiye (2010) - and based on these approaches makes an analysis for the Brazilian case, in order to identify if the time-inconsistency problem of monetary policy is verified under inflation targeting. In this sense, the theoretical model of Ireland (1999) is presented and subsequently modified, as did Gupta and Uwilingiye (2010), to turn possible the analysis for the output-inflation trade-off. The empirical study developed for Brazil seeks to answer, for the period from 1999.6 to 2014.1, whether monetary policy is time-inconsistent and therefore whether inflation targeting represents a sufficient commitment technology to mitigate the time-inconsistent problem. In this sense, the following questions arise: Does the time-inconsistency model of monetary policy apply to Brazil even under inflation targeting? The motivation for this analysis simply emanates from the need to evaluate the performance of the Brazilian monetary authority during the inflation targeting period.

This paper is organized as follows: Section 2 presents a review of the literature based on researches that follow Ireland's (1999) model. Section 3 presents Ireland's (1999) time-inconsistency model of monetary policy and Gupta and Uwilingiye's (2010) model. Section 4 develops an empirical analysis for Brazil. Section 5 presents a discussion section, and section 6 offers the concluding remarks.

2.0 Literature review

The seminal papers by Kydland and Prescott (1977) and Barro and Gordon (1983) gave rise to a large theoretical literature that examines the normative and positive implications of the time-inconsistency problem of monetary policy. Although the basic Kydland and Prescott (1977) and Barro and Gordon (1983) frameworks represent well known and influential models in macroeconomics, there has been relatively little empirical testing of that framework, i.e., the empirical analysis of this type of models has been more limited. Furthermore, policy insiders have questioned the relevance of these models, arguing that the time-inconsistency story is a poor representation of policymakers' behavior (Blinder, 1997). Blinder (1997) argues that "*academic economists have been barking loudly up the wrong tree and could learn a great deal from listening to practitioners*". Is it true? Economists remain skeptical about the subject (Taylor, 2012) and have sought answers through empirical work.

Ireland (1999) examines whether the time-inconsistency problem in Barro and Gordon (1983) can explain the behavior of the U.S. inflation rate. Ireland (1999) derives the restrictions imposed by Barro and Gordon's theory of time-consistent monetary policy on a bivariate time series model for inflation and unemployment and tests those restrictions using quarterly U.S. data from 1960 through 1997. Ireland (1999) tests the cointegration constraint shown in the model to see whether the time-inconsistency problem can explain the long-run behavior of inflation and unemployment. The results show that a simple time-inconsistency model of monetary policy, modified to allow for a time-varying NAIRU, can explain long-run trends in U.S. inflation, i.e., that the data are consistent with the implications of the theory for the long-run behavior of the two variables, indicating that the theory can explain the initial rise and subsequent fall of inflation for the period analyzed.

The work of Ruge-Murcia (2003) tests the predictions of the Barro–Gordon model using U.S. data on inflation and unemployment. To that end, it constructs a general game-theoretical model with asymmetric preferences that nests the Barro–Gordon model and a version of Cukierman's (2000) model as special cases. The model is estimated using quarterly U.S. data on inflation and unemployment. In order to assess the robustness of the results and to allow their comparison with those reported by Ireland (1999), two sample periods are considered (1960:1 to 1999:4 and 1970:1 to 1999:4). Likelihood Ratio tests indicate that the restriction imposed by the Barro–Gordon model is rejected by the data but the one imposed by Cukierman's model is not. These results are robust to the forecasting model for unemployment and to the sample period employed. Hence, the behavior of U.S. inflation appears to be better explained by a model where the central banker has asymmetric unemployment preferences around the expected natural rate, than by the standard text book Barro–Gordon model with quadratic preferences and an unemployment target below the natural rate.

Özlale and Özcan (2005) analyze the time-inconsistency problem for monetary policy in Turkey, but their data set consists of monthly observations in a sample period from 1980.1 to 2001.12, between inflation rate and output series. They show that the time inconsistency problem can explain the long-run behavior of inflation and output in the Turkish economy. The results also reveal that the Turkish monetary policymakers have put more emphasis on output stability than price stability in the period analyzed.

The paper of Akay and Nargelecekenler (2007) analyzes the time-inconsistency problem between inflation and unemployment rate series for Turkey. In order to investigate the long-run effects of the time-inconsistency problem, unit root and co-integration tests are applied. The data (taken from the Central Bank of the Republic of Turkey's database) were annually evaluated between 1955 and 2006. The paper used co-integrating tests for analyzing the relationship between unemployment rate and inflation rate series. The findings indicate that both inflation and unemployment series are not cointegrated. In this sense, the results do not support the Barro-Gordon model's implications for the long-run behavior of inflation and unemployment. Furthermore, the results suggest that the time-inconsistency problem for Turkey can be valid in the short-run, but sufficient proof cannot be found to support the Barro-Gordon model's implications for the long-run. This result does not match Özlale and Özcan (2005).

The paper of Doyle and Falk (2008) asks whether time-inconsistency models of monetary policy can explain inflation trends across OECD economies. The authors investigate two important variants of the hypothesis: i) that time-inconsistency was an important component of central bank behavior in earlier decades, but has become less significant in recent years, and ii) that time-inconsistency problems drive U.S. inflation, which affects inflation rates in other countries as a result of central bankers' attempts to manage nominal exchange rate movements vis-à-vis the U.S. dollar. They find that the first hypothesis fits the data no better than the baseline model. Moreover, they also find some support for the international spillovers version of the model, but the behavior of non-U.S. central bankers with respect to domestic unemployment rates, as viewed through the lens of a time-inconsistency account of monetary policy, remains puzzling. Hence, the behavior of non-U.S. central bankers with respect to domestic unemployment rates is not well described by the time-inconsistency mechanism. According to Doyle and Falk (2008), the failure of the time-inconsistency model to fit the data may be due to a failure of the assumption that the model parameters were unchanged over the estimation period. In this sense, in order to allow for this possibility, the authors extend the baseline model to incorporate time varying model parameters, and show that shifts in these parameters imply structural breaks in the cointegrating relationship. Hence, they investigate whether allowing for structural breaks significantly improves the empirical performance of the model using the Gregory-Hansen test for cointegration in the presence of a possible structural break in the cointegrating relationship. The results imply that allowing for time varying model parameters in this way does not overturn the conclusion that the time-inconsistency framework does not fit the data for most OECD countries.

The work of Gupta and Uwilingiye (2010) derives the econometric restrictions imposed by the Barro and Gordon model of dynamic time-inconsistency on a bivariate time series model of consumer price index (CPI) inflation and gross domestic product (GDP), and tests these restrictions based on quarterly data for South Africa. Unlike Ireland (1999), due to the lack of quarterly data on unemployment for South Africa, they model the supply side using a traditional Lucas-type supply curve rather than an expectational Phillips curve. Specifically, Barro and Gordon's (1983) model is modified by allowing the natural rate of output to follow an autoregressive process that contains a unit root and by incorporating control errors for the rate of inflation. While the first extension allows for the real GDP to be nonstationary, the second modification ensures transitory deviations between the actual real GDP and the natural rate of output. The results show that the data are consistent with the long-run implications of the theory of time-consistent monetary policy. Moreover, when the model is used to forecast one-step-ahead inflation over the period of January 2001-February 2008, i.e., the period covering the starting point of the inflation targeting regime until date, they, on average, obtain lower rates of inflation.

The paper of Pierdzioch and Stadtmann (2011) applied Ireland's (1999) time-inconsistency model to study whether the European Central Bank (ECB) has had a time-inconsistency problem. The data cover the sample period from January 1999 to December 2009. However, because the credibility of the ECB may have changed since it resumed responsibility for monetary policy in European Monetary Union (EMU), the authors analyzed subsample periods and used rolling tests for cointegration between the inflation rate and the unemployment rate. Based on the assumption that the inflation rate and the unemployment rate are nonstationary, the authors used the approach developed by Johansen (1991) to analyze whether the inflation rate and the unemployment rate are cointegrated and analyzed the sign of the estimated coefficient of the cointegration vector. The test results provide no strong evidence of cointegration between the inflation rate and the unemployment rate. Furthermore, the estimated coefficient of the cointegration vector has a negative sign, i.e., the sign of the estimated cointegration coefficient is not in line with a sign restriction imposed by the time-inconsistency model. According to Pierdzioch and Stadtmann (2011), violation of the sign restriction implies that, even if one assumes cointegration between the inflation rate and the unemployment rate, it is unlikely that a potential time-inconsistency problem, at least insofar as it is described by Ireland (1999), was the main driving force of cointegration.

Due to the fact that cointegration is a long-run concept, and because Pierdzioch and Stadtmann (2011) were obliged to study a relatively short sample period, it is quite relevant to ask whether it is reasonable to expect that tests for cointegration can detect economically interesting cointegration patterns in the data that can be interpreted in terms of a time-inconsistency problem. In order to answer this question, Pierdzioch and Stadtmann (2011) collected data for the pre-EMU period (1993.1–1998.12) for three member countries of EMU: France, Germany, and the Netherlands. The authors found evidence of cointegration between the inflation rate and the unemployment rate for France, but they did not find evidence of cointegration in the cases of Germany and the Netherlands. Besides, the authors found that the sign of the coefficient of cointegration estimated for France is in line with Ireland's (1999) time-inconsistency model.

The paper of Montes, de Mendonça and Bastos (2014) makes an empirical analysis concerning time-inconsistency problem (TIP) based on a sample of 12 countries for the period from 1993 to 2011 and it sheds light on four important issues: (1) Has the change in the mindset of monetary policy management from the 1990s eliminated TIP? (2) Is TIP a sickness only for developing countries? (3) Is inflation targeting associated with TIP? (4) Has the TIP increased around the world due to the subprime crisis? The findings indicate that the large majority of countries in the sample have policies that are consistent with long-term goals. Furthermore it is possible to conjecture that the traditional argument that developing countries have weak institutions and thus present a fertile ground for TIP or that the adoption of IT can avoid TIP is not necessarily true.

In this sense, further analysis in relation to an important developing country that operates with inflation targeting (as is the case of Brazil) is required.

3.0 The theoretical models

This section presents Ireland's (1999) model and Gupta and Uwilingiye's (2010) model. The main difference between the models is that the paper of Gupta and Uwilingiye (2010) models the supply side using a traditional Lucas-type supply curve while the work of Ireland (1999) models the supply side using an expectational Phillips curve.

3.01 The model considering the unemployment-inflation trade-off

The inflation rate, π_t, and the unemployment rate, u_t, are linked via an expectations-augmented Phillips curve:

$$u_t = \bar{u}_t - \alpha(\pi_t - \pi_t^e), \quad \alpha > 0, \tag{1}$$

Where, $\bar{u}_t$ is the natural rate of unemployment and π_t^e is the expected inflation rate. In Ireland's (1999) model, a difference-stationary data-generating process describes the dynamics of $\bar{u}_t$:

$$\bar{u}_t = \bar{u}_{t-1} + \lambda(\bar{u}_{t-1} - \bar{u}_{t-2}) + \varepsilon_t, \qquad -1 < \lambda < 1, \tag{2}$$

Where, ε_t is a serially uncorrelated mean-zero shock. The central bank does not observe ε_t when deciding on the planned inflation rate, π_t^P. The actual inflation rate, π_t, differs from the planned inflation rate, π_t^P, by a serially uncorrelated mean-zero control error, η_t, such that $\pi_t = \pi_t^P + \eta_t$. Rational expectations imply $\pi_t^e = \pi_t^P$.

The loss function of the central bank is given by $L = \frac{1}{2}(u_t - k\bar{u}_t)^2 + \frac{b}{2}\pi_t^2$, where $b > 0$, and $0 < k < 1$ gives rise to the usual inflation bias. The central bank chooses π_t^P to minimize the expected value of the loss function. Under commitment, the central bank chooses $\pi_t^P = 0$, and under discretion

$$\pi_t^P = \alpha\frac{1-k}{b}E_{t-1}\bar{u}_t, \tag{3}$$

Where, E denotes the expectation operator. The planned inflation rate depends on the expected unemployment rate, and it is equal to the expected inflation rate ($\pi_t^e = \pi_t^P$). Equations (1) and (3), in conjunction with $\pi_t = \pi_t^P + \eta_t$, yield $u_t = \bar{u}_t - \alpha\eta_t$. Upon using this result together with equation (2), one obtains

$$u_t = \bar{u}_{t-1} + \lambda(\bar{u}_{t-1} - \bar{u}_{t-2}) + \varepsilon_t - \alpha\eta_t, \tag{4}$$

Because equation (2) implies $E_{t-1}\bar{u}_t = \bar{u}_{t-1} + \lambda(\bar{u}_{t-1} - \bar{u}_{t-2})$, and because of $\pi_t^P = \pi_t - \eta_t$, it follows that

$$\pi_t = \alpha\frac{1-k}{b}\bar{u}_{t-1} + \lambda\alpha\frac{1-k}{b}(\bar{u}_{t-1} - \bar{u}_{t-2}) + \eta_t, \tag{5}$$

Taken together, equations (4) and (5) imply that, in the case of discretionary policy, π_t and u_t should be co-integrated:

$$\pi_t - \alpha\frac{1-k}{b}u_t = -\alpha\frac{1-k}{b}\varepsilon_t + (1+\alpha^2\frac{1-k}{b})\eta_t. \quad (6)$$

Equation (6) yields the sign restriction that, because $-\alpha\frac{1-k}{b} < 0$, the coefficient of cointegration in the cointegration vector, $\pi_t = \alpha\frac{1-k}{b}u_t$, should have a positive sign.

3.02 The model considering the output-inflation trade-off

The economy is characterized by the Lucas Supply curve (equation 7):

$$y_t = \bar{y}_t + \beta(\pi_t - \pi_t^e), \quad (7)$$

where, π_t is the actual inflation rate, π_t^e is the expected inflation rate, y is the actual output, $\bar{y}$ is the output at its flexible-price level (natural level) and $\beta > 0$.

The output at its flexible-price level, in turn, fluctuates over time in response to a real shock ξ_t according to the autoregressive process:

$$\bar{y}_t - \bar{y}_{t-1} = \psi(\bar{y}_{t-1} - \bar{y}_{t-2}) + \xi_t, \quad (8)$$

where, $1 > \psi >$ -1 and ξ is serially uncorrelated and normally distributed with mean zero and standard deviation σ_ξ.

The loss function of the central bank is given by:

$$L = (\tfrac{1}{2})(y_t - y^*)^2 + (\tfrac{c}{2})(\pi_t)^2 \quad (9)$$

where, y^* is the *socially optimum* level of *output* and c >0 denotes the relative weight that the policymaker puts on the price stability. Due to imperfections, it is assumed that $y^* > \bar{y}$. Thus, the policymaker has an incentive to push the output above its flexible price level.

Due to $y^* > \bar{y}$, thus, it is possible to consider that $y^* = \theta\bar{y}$, where, θ >1. Hence,

$$L = (\tfrac{1}{2})(y_t - \theta\bar{y}_t)^2 + (\tfrac{c}{2})(\pi_t)^2, \quad (9')$$

Similar to Ireland (1999), it is assumed that the monetary authority cannot commit to a policy rule. Instead, at the beginning of each period t = 0,1,2,..., after private agents have formed their expectation π_t^e, but before the realization of the real shock ξ_t, the policymaker chooses a planned rate of inflation π_t^p. Actual inflation for the period is then determined as the sum of π_t^p and a control error v_t so that

$$\pi_t = \pi_t^p + v_t, \quad (10)$$

where, v_t is serially uncorrelated and normally distributed with mean zero, standard deviation σ_v, and covariance $\sigma_{\xi v}$ with ξ_t.

Substituting (7) and (10) into (9'), the loss function to be minimized is:

$$E_{t-1}\left\{(\tfrac{1}{2})\left[(1-\theta)\bar{y}_t + \beta(\pi_t^p + v_t - \pi_t^e)\right]^2 + (\tfrac{c}{2})(\pi_t^p + v_t)^2\right\}, \quad (11)$$

where E_{t-1} denotes the expectation at the beginning of period t or, equivalently, the end of period t-1. Solving for (π_t^p), the first-order condition is:

$$\beta E_{t-1}\left[(1-\theta)\bar{y}_t + \beta(\pi_t^p + v_t - \pi_t^e)\right] = -cE_{t-1}(\pi_t^p + v_t), \quad (12)$$

Private agents know the structure of the economy and understand the policymaker's time-consistency problem. Thus, in equilibrium, they correctly anticipate the policymaker's actions, so that $\pi_t^e = \pi_t^p$. Using this condition, along with the fact that $E_{t-1}\upsilon_t = 0$, equation (12) simplifies to

$$\pi_t^e = \pi_t^p = -\beta\left[\frac{1-\theta}{c}\right]E_{t-1}\bar{y}_t, \qquad (13)$$

It is possible to observe that when the policymaker acts with discretion, the resulting inflation will be nonzero. The inflationary bias resulting from the policymaker's inability to commit depends positively on $E_{t-1}\bar{y}$. Thus, the equilibrium inflation rate moves together with the output at its flexible-price level.

Equations (7), (10) and (13) imply that:

$$y_t = \bar{y}_t + \beta\upsilon_t, \qquad (14)$$

Which shows how the control error for inflation (υ_t) allows the output to fluctuate, in equilibrium, around the output at its flexible-price level. Combining equation (14) with (8) yields

$$y_t = \bar{y}_{t-1} + \psi\Delta\bar{y}_{t-1} + \xi_t + \beta\upsilon_t, \qquad (15)$$

Where ($\Delta\bar{y}_{t-1} = \bar{y}_{t-1} - \bar{y}_{t-2}$) denotes the change in the output at its flexible-price level during period t-1. Substituting (13) into (10) and combining with equation (8), and considering that $E_{t-1}\bar{y} = \bar{y}_t$, and ξ_t is a white noise, gives

$$\pi_t = -\beta\left[\frac{1-\theta}{c}\right]\bar{y}_{t-1} - \beta\left[\frac{1-\theta}{c}\right]\psi\Delta\bar{y}_{t-1} + \upsilon_t, \qquad (16)$$

It is important to note that, separately, equations (15) and (16) indicate that both inflation and output are non-stationary, inheriting unit roots from the underlying process for the equilibrium output. Together, however, they imply that

$$\pi_t + \beta\left[\frac{1-\theta}{c}\right]y_t = \beta\left[\frac{1-\theta}{c}\right]\xi_t + \left\{1 + \beta^2\left[\frac{1-\theta}{c}\right]\right\}\upsilon_t, \qquad (17)$$

which shows that a linear combination of inflation and output is stationary.

Equation (17), therefore, summarizes the constraint imposed on the long-run behavior of inflation and output; according to the model, these variables should be non-stationary but cointegrated. Equation (17) yields the sign restriction, $\beta[(1-\theta)/c] < 0$, that the coefficient of cointegration in the cointegration vector should have. Thus, it is possible to test whether these conditions are met, and as a consequence, affirm whether the time-inconsistency model describes well the behavior of inflation and output for the period.

4.0 Empirical analysis

Brazil adopted an inflation targeting framework in June 1999. This framework included all the features of a full-fledged inflation targeting regime, including: 1) the announcement of multi-year inflation targets; 2) assigning the National Monetary Council the responsibility for setting the inflation targets and tolerance ranges based on a proposal by the Minister of Finance; 3) giving to the Central Bank of Brazil (CBB) full responsibility to implement the policies needed to attain the inflation targets; 4) establishing procedures to increase the central bank's accountability (specifically, if the target range is breached, the central bank president would have to issue an open letter to the Minister of Finance explaining the causes of the deviation, the measures that will be taken to eliminate it, and the time it will take to get inflation back inside the tolerance range) and, 5) taking actions to improve the transparency of monetary policy.

The independence of Brazil's central bank and the commitment to price stability, however, were not clear cut. Both were based on a presidential decree and confidence in a reliable central bank president, but not on a more formal commitment based on legislation. Despite the initial success, the weakness of some aspects of the institutional framework for fiscal and monetary policy did come back to haunt the inflation targeting regime in Brazil. In the run-up to the presidential election in October 2002, the market had concerns that the front-runner, Luiz Inácio "Lula" da Silva, would weaken fiscal and monetary institutions. Lula had made statements that seemed to indicate that once in office he would encourage fiscal policy to be highly expansionary and would not take steps to prevent a possible default on Brazil's foreign debt. He also indicated that he would not reappoint the highly respected president of the central bank, Arminio Fraga. Moreover, Lula's commitment to the independence of the central bank, price stability and the inflation targeting regime was far from clear. Not surprisingly, the lack of market confidence in Lula, who was then elected President led to a sharp depreciation of the Brazilian Real and a sharp upward spike to inflation to

12.5%, which substantially overshot the inflation target of 3.5% for 2002 (Table 1). The impact of the Brazilian election on the inflation targeting regime illustrate that weak fiscal and monetary institutions are likely to create severe problems for an inflation targeting regime.

Since the premise of the time-inconsistency model is the inability of the monetary authority to commit to an announced goal, the analysis focuses on the period after the adoption of inflation targeting in Brazil (from 1999.6 to 2014.1). Moreover, following Montes, de Mendonça and Bastos (2014), the analysis considers two sub-samples, one corresponding to the period before the subprime crisis (from 1999.6 to 2008.10) and another corresponding to the period that also considers the crisis (from 1999.6 to 2014.1). The idea of separating the period in before and after the financial crisis is to identify a possible change in the behavior of the monetary authority.

Table 01: Inflation, inflation target and tolerance limits

Period	Observed Inflation	Inferior Limit	Superior Limit	Inflation Target
1999	8.9	6.0	10.0	8.0
2000	6.0	4.0	8.0	6.0
2001	7.7	2.0	6.0	4.0
2002	12.5	1.5	5.5	3.5
2003	9.3	1.5	6.5	4.0 / 8.5*
2004	7.6	3.0	8.0	5.5
2005	5.7	2.0	7.0	4.5
2006	3.1	2.5	6.5	4.5
2007	4.5	2.5	6.5	4.5
2008	5.9	2.5	6.5	4.5
2009	4.3	2.5	6.5	4.5
2010	5.9	2.5	6.5	4.5
2011	6.5	2.5	6.5	4.5
2012	5.8	2.5	6.5	4.5
2013	5.9	2.5	6.5	4.5

Source: Central Bank of Brazil. * denotes adjusted inflation target.

Based on the empirical literature (e.g., Ireland (1999) and Pierdzioch and Stadtmann (2011)), after analyzing the results of the cointegration tests and the signs of the estimated coefficients of the cointegration vectors, the following results are possible taking into account the time-inconsistency problem in the Ireland sense:

- *Inflation and unemployment/output are not cointegrated*: this outcome does not support the Kydland and Prescott (1977) and Barro and Gordon (1983) framework's implications for the long-term behavior of inflation and unemployment/output, and does not match with Ireland's (1999) model.
- *Inflation and unemployment/output are cointegrated and the estimated coefficient of the cointegration vector is negative*: this outcome indicates that much of the comovement of the inflation rate with the unemployment/output appears to be business-cycle related. It follows that it is unlikely that a potential time-inconsistency problem of the monetary authority was the main driving force of cointegration between the inflation rate and unemployment/output.
- *Inflation and unemployment are cointegrated and the estimated coefficient of the cointegration vector is positive*: this outcome indicates the monetary authority's inability to commit to a monetary policy that reduces its temptation to exploit the trade-offs present in the Phillips curve and in the Lucas Supply curve. In other words, when the cointegration vector presents a positive coefficient it means that this estimated coefficient is in line with the predictions of the models, and thus the time-inconsistency problem of the monetary authority is the main driving force of cointegration between the inflation rate and the unemployment rate.

4.01 Econometric methodology

In the seminal article of Ireland (1999), the time-inconsistency problem is studied by testing the existence of cointegration between inflation and unemployment rate series. In the present paper, cointegration tests are made considering inflation[1] and unemployment[2] series as well as inflation and output[3] series. In the present paper the standard Engle and Granger (1987) residual-based and Johansen (1991) approaches are compared with Gregory

[1] Inflation is measured by National Consumer Price Index – IPCA – in 12 months – %. The data code for the inflation rate is 13522 (Central Bank of Brazil). Due to the fact that Brazil presents very high inflation in the period, this study follows Montes, de Mendonça and Bastos (2014) and considers inflation "D" for this country, as suggested by Cukierman, Webb, and Neyapti. (1992), instead of percentage change in price level ($D=\pi/(1+\pi)$, where π is the inflation rate).

[2] Unemployment rate is based on the metropolitan region of São Paulo (SEADE-SP Foundation). Available through IPEADATA.

[3] The output is GDP accumulated in the last 12 months - evaluated by the IGP-DI in the month (R$ million) – R$ (million). The data code for the output is 4190 (Central Bank of Brazil).

and Hansen[4] (1996) sequential breaking test procedure. Besides the coefficient obtained from Johansen cointegration test, the coefficient of cointegration in the cointegration vector is estimated using three different methods: Fully-modified OLS (FMOLS), Dynamic OLS (DOLS) and Canonical cointegrating regression (CCR).

A necessary condition for testing for a long-run relationship between two variables is that these variables are I(1), i.e., stationary in first differences. Therefore, the classical unit root test, namely, the Augmented Dickey-Fuller (ADF) test was used. Table 2 below presents the results for the ADF test considering both periods.

Table 02: Augmented Dickey-Fuller (ADF) test

period: 1999.06 to 2013.01				period: 1999.06 to 2008.10			
Variable	Lag	ADF test statistic	Summary	Variable	Lag	ADF test statistic	Summary
u	1	-2.469	I(1)	u	1	-1.233	I(1)
d(u)	0	-10.912		d(u)	0	-8.762	
y	1	-1.770	I(1)	y	1	-1.067	I(1)
d(y)	0	-5.109		d(y)	0	-4.663	
infl	1	-3.497	I(1)	infl	1	-2.949	I(1)
d(inf)	0	-5.403		d(inf)	0	-4.429	

Lag length based on Schwarz information criteria; ADF: constant and linear trend; critical value ADF: 1% = -4.01 (both periods)

Once it is established that the series representing measures of inflation, unemployment and output are I(1), it is possible to proceed to test for a long-run relationship between the series. If such a relationship exists and the signs of the coefficients are positive, it is possible that the time-inconsistency problem is occurring. Before undertaking cointegration tests, it was necessary to specify the relevant order of lags of the vector autoregression (VAR) model. Table 3 presents the results for each case.

Table 03: Order of lags of the vector autoregression (VAR) model

Period	unemployment-inflation	output-inflation
1999.06 to 2013.01	2	2
1999.06 to 2008.10	2	2

Lag order selected by the Schwarz information criterion

The results of the cointegration tests are presented in Table 4. The upper part of Table 4 considers the subprime crisis period. The lower part of Table 4 shows the results for the period before the subprime crisis.

Table 04 (a): Cointegration tests and signs of coefficients

inflation-unemployment				period: 1999.6 to 2013.01		
cointegration test	z	τ		λ_{max}	λ_{trace}	coint. coef.
Engle-Granger	-29.543**	-3.873**	Johansen	18.651**	20.569**	0.559
Gregory-Hansen	ADF* (t-stat)			Method	coint. coef.	
Cointegration with Regime Shift	-5.007**		Cointegrat. Regression	FMOLS	1.183	
				DOLS	1.207	
				CCR	1.182	

Regarding the results for the relation between inflation and unemployment, the findings suggest (for both periods) that inflation and unemployment are cointegrated; besides, positive coefficients were found. In this sense, considering the monetary authority's possibility to exploit the unemployment-inflation trade-off, it seems that, even under inflation targeting, the findings support the Barro-Gordon model's implications for the long-run, and thus the time-inconsistency problem of monetary policy cannot be neglected.

Table 04(b): Cointegration tests and signs of coefficients

inflation-output	period: 1999.6 to 2013.01

[4] The Gregory-Hansen (1996) test is developed within the framework of the Engle-Granger (1987) residual-based cointegration analysis and can be viewed as a multivariate extension of the endogenous break univariate tests of Zivot and Andrews (1992). The null hypothesis of no-cointegration is tested against the alternative of cointegration with a break in the cointegrating relationship. Three models to take account of different types of structural changes in the cointegrating relationships are considered: 1) the "C" level shift model; 2) the "C/T" level shift with trend model; 3) the "C/S" regime shift model which allows the cointegrating vector parameters to shift. The Gregory-Hansen test statistic is the smallest values of ADF across all possible break points. The approximate critical values for the break cointegration tests in presence of structural break, obtained through simulation methods, are reported in Gregory and Hansen (1996, Table 1).

cointegration test	z	τ		λ_{max}	λ_{trace}	coint. coef.
Engle-Granger	-24.305**	-3.479**	Johansen	11.965**	13.74**	-0.000002
Gregory-Hansen	ADF* (t-stat)			Method	coint. coef.	
Cointegration with Regime Shift	-4.524**	Cointegrat. Regression		FMOLS	-0.000009	
				DOLS	-0.000007	
				CCR	-0.000009	

Table 04(c): Cointegration tests and signs of coefficients

inflation-unemployment				period: 1999.6 to 2008.10		
cointegration test	z	τ		λ_{max}	λ_{trace}	coint. coef.
Engle-Granger	-42.588**	-4.127**	Johansen	16.260**	17.46**	-0.879
Gregory-Hansen	ADF* (t-stat)			Method	coint. coef.	
Cointegration with Regime Shift	-4.312**	Cointegrat. Regression		FMOLS	2.058	
				DOLS	2.161	
				CCR	2.056	

Table 04(d): Cointegration tests and signs of coefficients

inflation-output				period: 1999.6 to 2008.10		
cointegration test	z	τ		λ_{max}	λ_{trace}	coint. coef.
Engle-Granger	-17.898**	-2.999**	Johansen	8.980**	12.97**	0.0000006
Gregory-Hansen	ADF* (t-stat)			Method	coint. coef.	
Cointegration with Regime Shift	-3.901**	Cointegrat. Regression		FMOLS	0.0000001	
				DOLS	-0.0000001	
				CCR	-0.0000002	

Engle-Granger and Johansen cointegration tests based on the null hypothesis of no cointegration. (***) denotes rejection of the null hypothesis at the 0.01 level, and (**) denotes rejection of the null hypothesis at the 0.05 level.
Gregory-Hansen Test: the asymptotic critical values are obtained from Gregory and Hansen (1996, Table 1, $m = 1$). The null hypothesis of no cointegration with structural breaks is tested against the alternative of cointegration by Gregory and Hansen approach.

Regarding the findings for the relation between inflation and output, the results do not support the model's implications for the long-run and thus monetary policy is not inconsistent when considered the output-inflation trade-off. For the period 1999.06 to 2013.01, the estimated coefficient of the cointegration vector is negative. In this sense, it is unlikely that a potential time-inconsistency problem of the monetary authority was the main driving force of cointegration between the inflation rate and the output. In turn, for the period 1999.06 to 2008.10, inflation and output are not cointegrated. In general, for both periods, there is no strong evidence of time-inconsistency problem of the monetary policy when considered the relation between the inflation rate and the output.

5.0 Result discussion, policy implication and recommendation

Since the early 1990s, inflation targeting has been adopted by several central banks as a strategy for the implementation of monetary policy. This regime has as its main feature the official announcement of ranges for inflation fluctuations and the explicit recognition that the main objective of monetary policy is to assure a low and stable inflation rate. Inflation targeting works as a guide for inflation expectations and it is associated with an increase in central bank transparency, which, in turn, increases accountability in the implementation of monetary policy and thus improves the central banks' credibility.

An important step in controlling inflation is to guide inflationary expectations, thus one main task of a central bank is to build credibility through the commitment to price stability. According to de Mendonça and de Guimarães e Souza (2012), the effectiveness of this framework for inflation control fuels a controversial debate between policymakers and academics. As a consequence, two key questions are raised: (i) How successful is inflation targeting in reducing and stabilizing the inflation rate? (ii) Are effects caused by inflation targeting sufficiently homogeneous when both developing and industrialized countries are taken into consideration?

Gonçalves and Salles (2008) reproduced Ball and Sheridan's (2005) analysis using data for 36 developing economies, 13 of which have implemented the inflation targeting framework. Their findings suggest that the choice of the inflation targeting regime proved beneficial for emerging economies. In particular, they found that the greater fall in inflation experienced by emerging market targeters can, to some extent, be attributed to the regime itself and not only to mean reversion. Moreover, the often heard claim that inflation targeting regimes hinder economic growth is clearly not sustained by the empirical evidence. In sum, the data so far suggests that the adoption of inflation targeting by emerging economies did contribute towards the attainment of superior outcomes in terms of economic performance.

Considering a sample of 180 countries for the period from 1990 to 2007, de Mendonça and de Guimarães e Souza (2012) analyzed whether the adoption of inflation targeting can reduce inflation and inflation volatility. The sample of 180 countries was split into two sets of countries (advanced and developing). The findings suggest that the adoption of inflation targeting represents a good strategy for developing economies and, in addition to reducing inflation volatility, can drive inflation down to internationally acceptable levels. The empirical literature suggests that inflation targeting may bring benefits to developing countries. Nevertheless, another key question is raised: does inflation targeting represent a framework capable of mitigating the time-inconsistency problem of monetary policy in an important developing country?

Based on the findings of the empirical literature on inflation targeting and on the findings of the present paper, it is suggested that although the adoption of inflation targeting can, on average, bring benefits to developing countries, not necessarily adopting this scheme is sufficient to mitigate the time-inconsistency problem of monetary policy. Then, what kind of strategies should be followed in order to reduce the inflationary bias and mitigate the time-inconsistency problem of the monetary policy? Following Walsh (1995), incentive contracts can be designed to bind the actions of the central bank. Besides, central bank independence can be improved: a lower turnover rate of central bank governors and longer terms of office may improve the reputation of the policymakers. Last but not least, transparency about both objectives and operations of central banks as well as accountability, which is a key element of the inflation targeting regimes, should be increased in order to remove the uncertainties during the policymaking process.

6.0 Conclusion

The results allow one to conjecture that the traditional argument that the adoption of inflation targeting can avoid the time-inconsistency problem is not necessarily true. It is important to note that the findings are different from those presented by Montes, Bastos and de Mendonça (2014) for the specific case of Brazil. Particularly, developing countries present a fertile ground for the occurrence of the time-inconsistency problem due to the history of weak institutions and lack of commitment on the part of policymakers. Inflation targeting seems to not have improved the time-consistency of monetary policy expected out of such a regime. The results, thus, point to the fact that the CBB needs to manage monetary policy under inflation targeting better than it has done so far. In this regard, as Gupta and Uwilingiye (2010) concluded for the South African Reserve Bank, a lower inflation target and possibly also a narrower target band could be of immense help in improving the central bank's credibility and causing inflation expectations to converge to a focal point, and hence, bring down the rate of inflation. Moreover, commitment technologies must be taken seriously if the regime still has the intention to serve as a guide for the formation of expectations and safeguard the stability achieved with the Real Plan.

Recent data on the behavior of inflation and inflation expectations in Brazil point to the loss of reputation of the monetary authority and the weakening of credibility. Based on the findings, the paper provides interesting policy implications: 1) the inflation targeting framework currently operating in Brazil is not enough to mitigate discretionary actions of the monetary authority and therefore is not able to eliminate the time-inconsistency problem; 2) since the management of expectations is a key task for the monetary authority under inflation targeting, the commitment to a low and stable inflation target cannot be abandoned, otherwise once the public knows that policymakers have the incentive to pursue expansionary policies, they will not expect a low and stable inflation; 3)the framework of inflation targeting in Brazil should be redefined in order to increase the commitment of the monetary authority with its main long-term goal; 4) incentive contracts can be designed to bind the actions of the central bank, central bank independence can be improved and, a lower inflation target and a narrower target band could be adopted.

References

Akay, H. K., Nargelecekenler, M., 2007. Is there the time-inconsistency problem in Turkey? Journal of Economic Studies, 34(5): 389-400.

Ball, L., Sheridan, N., 2005. Does inflation targeting matter? In: Bernanke, B.S., Woodford, M. (Eds.), The Inflation-Targeting Debate. University of Chicago Press.

Barro, R. J., Gordon, D. B., 1983. Rules, discretion and reputation in a model of monetary policy. Journal of Monetary Economics, 12(1): 101-121.

Blinder, A., 1997. What central bankers could learn from academics – and vice versa. Journal of Economic

Perspectives, 11(2): 3–19.
Cukierman, A., Webb, S., Neyapti, B., 1992. Measuring the independence of central banks and its effects on policy outcomes. World Bank Economic Review, 6(3): 353-398.
Cukierman, A., 2000. The Inflation Bias Result Revisited. Tel-Aviv University, April, Mimeo.
de Mendonça, H. F., 2009. Output-inflation and unemployment-inflation trade-offs under inflation targeting: Evidence from Brazil. Journal of Economic Studies, 36(1): 66-82.
de Mendonça, H. F., de Guimarães e Souza, G. J., 2012. Is inflation targeting a good remedy to control inflation? Journal of Development Economics, 98(2): 178-191.
Doyle, M., Falk, B., 2008. Testing Commitment Models of Monetary Policy: Evidence from OECD Economies. Journal of Money, Credit and Banking, 40(2-3): 409-425.
Engle, R. F., Granger, C. W. J., 1987. Co-integration and Error Correction: Representation, Estimation, and Testing. Econometrica, 55(2): 251–276.
Gonçalves, C. E. S., Sales, J. M., 2008. Inflation targeting in emerging economies: What do the data say? Journal of Development Economics, 85(1-2): 312–318.
Gregory, A., Hansen, B., 1996. Residual-based Tests for Cointegration in Models with Regime Shifts. Journal of Econometrics, 70(1): 99-126.
Gupta, R., Uwilingiye, J., 2010. Dynamic time inconsistency and the South African Reserve Bank. South African Journal of Economics, 78(1): 76-88.
Ireland, P. N., 1999. Does the time-consistency problem explain the behavior of inflation in the United Sates? Journal of Monetary Economics, 44(2): 279-291.
Johansen, S., 1991. Estimation and hypothesis testing of cointegration vectors in gaussian vector autoregressive models. Econometrica, 59(6): 1551–1580.
Kydland, F., Prescott, E., 1977. Rules rather than discretion: the inconsistency of optimal plans. Journal of Political Economy, 85(3): 473-491.
Montes, G. C., de Mendonça, H. F., Bastos, J. C. A., 2014. Time inconsistency problem: less common than we think. Journal of Economic Studies, 41(5).
Özlale, Ü., Özcan, K. M., 2005. Does time inconsistency problem apply for Turkish monetary policy? METU Studies in Development, 32(2): 467-88.
Pierdzioch, C., Stadtmann, G., 2011. Does the ECB have a time-inconsistency problem? A note. Scottish Journal of Political Economy, 58(2): 189-199.
Ruge-Murcia, F., 2003. Does the Barro-Gordon model explain the behavior of U.S. inflation? A reexamination of the empirical evidence. Journal of monetary economics, 50(6): 1375-1390.
Taylor, J. B., 2012. Monetary policy rules work and discretion doesn't: A tale of two eras. Journal of Money, Credit and Banking, 44(6): 1017-1032.
Walsh, C., 1995. Optimal Contracts for Central Bankers. The American Economic Review, 85(1): 150-167.
Zivot, E., Andrews, D. W. K., 1992. Further evidence on the Great Crash, the oil-price shock and the unit hypothesis. Journal of Business and Economic Statistics, 10(3): 251–270.

5

How to finance investment in Bangladesh: Finding long-run factors in a bounds test method✧

Biru Paksha Paul[a*]

[a] Department of Economics, State University of New York at Cortland, NY 13045, USA.
* Corresponding author email: biru.paul@cortland.edu

HIGHLIGHTS:

1. Bangladesh's growth has remained almost stagnant, because its investment rate has remained stagnant as well.
2. The country has to reduce lending rates and undertake credit expansion policies to enhance investment.
3. Growing demand for Bangladeshi exports has helped increase capital formation in the country.
4. Further liberalization in trade and finance is needed to accelerate investment growth in Bangladesh.

Article History

Keywords:
ARDL Bounds test method;
Bangladeshi economy;
Capital formation;
Investment determinants.

ABSTRACT

Investment in Bangladesh has been at almost one-fourth of the country's output since the early 2000s. Consequently, Bangladesh's growth has also remained stagnant at around 6 percent since then. The question of how to increase investment in Bangladesh has been of crucial discussion of late. This study examines the long run determinants of investment in Bangladesh by applying the bounds test over 1976-2010. There should not be any policy dilemma about the effect of lending rates, which must be reduced to boost investment and domestic credit should be expanded. Further liberalization in trade and finance is recommended since economic openness and financial deepening show a positive impact on capital formation. The policy prescriptions for Bangladesh are not different from those for other nations that embarked on liberalization to augment investment for accelerating growth.

1.0 Introduction

Bangladesh is an emerging market economy in South Asia. Its growth is one of the fastest not only in the region, but also in the world. The country grew at the rate of 5 percent over the last quarter century since 1986 (WDI 2012). Over the last decade, Bangladesh's growth reached close to 6 percent, suggesting an impressive rate of growth, which in turn has created an increasing demand for investment in the country. The investment-Gross Domestic Product (GDP) ratio, which is often defined as the investment rate, has remained in the doldrums in Bangladesh at around 24-26 percent for a decade or so. The capital-output ratio, which gives the amount of capital needed to produce one unit of output, in the region turns out to be around 4. Consequently, this investment rate of 26 percent is capable of generating output growth of 6 percent or slightly above.

✧ The author is thankful to Bangladesh Bank governor Dr. Atiur Rahman for his valuable advice. The support of the Research Division of Bangladesh Bank and Rama Rani Sutradhar in particular is greatly acknowledged. The author has been benefited from the comments of the participants at the international conference on Bangladesh held on February 22-24, 2013 at University of California-Berkeley.

There are no other magical tools to earn and secure sustainable growth of 7 percent or above without lifting the investment-GDP ratio above the current level. In the recent years, Pakistan hardly managed a growth rate below 4 percent with its investment rate at around 13-14 percent. In contrast, India registered 8 percent growth mainly because of its high investment ratio at around 34-36 percent. So the same is true for China. Given this perspective, there are sufficient concerns around national and international corners as to how Bangladesh can increase investment to accelerate its economic growth.

This scenario has raised a number of questions such as: 1) what are the factors that affect Bangladesh's investment significantly in the long run? 2) What policy measures are important to nurture these influential factors? 3) Did liberalization contribute to accelerated capital formation in Bangladesh? The existing literature on the long run determinants of Bangladesh's investment is conspicuously absent. This study fills that gap by addressing the questions.

This work collects a dataset of 13 variables, which are supposed to influence investment in a developing economy, over the period from 1976 to 2010. The issues on the sample size and the selection of variables have been discussed subsequently in detail. The term, capital formation, is used in this paper to mean a change in annual capital stock, which means investment as well. Accordingly, these two terms have been used interchangeably in this paper. Finally, this work examines the determinants of investment in Bangladesh in an Autoregressive Distributed Lag (ARDL) bounds test approach, a modern econometric method to test long-run relationships among selected variables.

In this part, the results of the study can be briefly previewed as follow: this study finds that the lending rate adversely affects investment in Bangladesh in the long-run. Short-run effects of the lending rate on investment are insignificant. Both domestic credit and financial deepening have both long-run and short-run positive impact on capital formation in the country. Both trade and economic openness influence capital formation of the country in a positive fashion. A further investigation reveals that only exports are the significant factor that makes the trade and openness variables significant. The level relationship between foreign aid and investment is significant but negative.

Other variables such as savings, imports, Foreign Direct Investment (FDI), remittances, and market capitalization do not maintain any of the long-run relationships with investment in Bangladesh in a significant way. It appears that the policies on liberalization, export promotion, deregulation, and financial deepening have been beneficial to foster capital formation in an emerging economy like Bangladesh. These findings have policy implications not only for Bangladesh, but also for other developing nations that endeavor to boost capital formation to sustain and often accelerate economic growth in their economies.

This paper comprises six sections. The next section presents a brief literature review. Section 3 discusses data and methodology aspects. Section 4 presents estimations and results. The implications of the results are delivered in Section 5. Section 6 concludes.

2.0 Literature review

The causal effect on how investment or capital formation can contribute to economic growth has been addressed in Krugman (1994), Parida and Sahoo (2007), Das and Paul (2011) and Sahoo and Dash (2012). As a specific work on the South Asian region, Paul (2013) shows that the economic growth-differential between Bangladesh and India is mainly explainable by the investment-growth differential between them. Hence, it becomes necessary to understand both the short-run and long-run contributing factors to investment to promote output growth.

There are not many time-series studies on Bangladesh's investment. The main reason behind this deficiency is the absence of an adequate number of observations. While there is no explicit statement in econometrics on how many observations are needed to get reliable results with annual time-series data, the usual practice is to collect at least 30 observations to make econometric estimates acceptable and robust. As discussed in the introduction, the most annual time series on Bangladesh's macro variables did not become either available or free of massive outliers until the mid or late 1970s. As a result, exercises on Bangladesh's annual time series began to emerge remarkably since the mid-2000s to ensure around 30 observations in the sample. Despite this deficiency, we notice a number of papers on investment or capital formation in mainly South Asian economies and particularly in Bangladesh as discussed below.

Investment determinants can be country specific as argued in Naqvi and Tsoukis (2003). They examined growth and investment performances of six Asian nations: Bangladesh, India, Indonesia, Malaysia, Pakistan, and Thailand. While public and private investments are likely to feed each other, there exist no single relationship between these variables that hold consistently across these countries. Bhattacharyay and De (2005) argue that the open regionalism and integration between China and India can foster investment and growth. They propose to include other neighboring countries such as Bangladesh, Bhutan, Myanmar, and Nepal for promoting capital formation and growth through regional integration.

Dollar et al. (2005) run a study with various micro aspects of the investment climate in China, India, Pakistan, and Bangladesh. They find that the investment is low where the cost of different bottlenecks is high. They show that for many of these costs, the obstacles are lower in China than in Pakistan, India, and Bangladesh. Factor returns are also higher where the investment climate is better. Siriwardana and Yang (2007) argue that thefree trade is beneficial for investment augmentation. They show that the Indian investment in Bangladesh can enhance new supply and export capacities under free trade arrangements.

Wadud (2009) runs a study with India, Pakistan, and Bangladesh over 1976-2008. He finds that the financial development affects economic growth positively in these countries. In essence, financial deepening contributes to investment expansion to increase output. De et al. (2012) find that greater trade integration between Bangladesh and India can promote investment and productivity in both countries. Sahoo and Dash (2012) work with four South Asian countries: India, Pakistan, Bangladesh, and Sri Lanka over 1980-2005. They find a long run equilibrium relationship between output and infrastructure along with capital formation.

Correa and Rao (2004) assert that the neoclassical proposition of the influence of interest rates on investment has little support in the Indian experience. Cole (2009) shows that the credit markets with nationalized banks experienced faster credit growth during a period of financial repression in India, suggesting that lower interest rates do not necessarily increase investment. He argues that India's bank nationalization in 1980 led to lower interest rates and lower-quality intermediation, and may have slowed employment gains in trade and services. Qayyum (2002) finds significant responsiveness of investment to changes in interest rates in Pakistan over a decade before 2002. He shows that a high rate of interest on bank lending negatively affects the demand for bank credit by the business sector, which reduces investment and in turn leads to low aggregate demand and lower output.

Using quarterly dataset for the period of 1976Q4 to 2005Q2, Ahmed and Islam (2004) investigate whether interest-rate liberalization pursued under the Financial Sector Reform Programs (FSRPs) of the early 1990s has been able to create a competitive environment in the financial market of Bangladesh. Their results, however, suggest that investment spending at the aggregate level be non-responsive to interest rates. As they also find, investment spending at the disaggregate level is still not responsive to interest rates except for the private sector investment category, which is only moderately responsive from the lender's point of view in the short run. This study, nevertheless, covers a longer timespan to examine the determinants of investment in Bangladesh.

Kamal (2011) investigates the effect of real interest on investment in Bangladesh for the period from 1976 to 2006. He finds evidence of weak but negative sensitivity of investment to the interest rate in Bangladesh both in the short run and long run. The findings of this work, which contradict some of the previous results, warrant further investigation by extending the sample beyond 2006. Although Kamal uses the ARDL method as is used here, he mainly focuses on the interest-investment nexus only. The approach in this paper includes all possible factors of investment in a more comprehensive way with an extended sample size.

The mixed results on the interest rate-investment relationship have been subject to further investigation when the Budget of Bangladesh's Finance Ministry for the fiscal year 2012-2013 argues that the investment-interest rate correlation is not much significant. This policy document claims that the Bangladesh economy is now in the takeoff stage, and there are ample opportunities for earning high returns on investments. Hence, as the Budget claims, high interest rates are not likely to impede investment in the country (Budget 2012:10).

The studies show that there could be a number of factors to influence investment in South Asia and particularly in Bangladesh. Thus, the influencing factors of investment being different across countries warrant further inquiry for Bangladesh.

3.0 Materials and methods

Data from the World Development Indicators (WDI 2012) of the World Bank were collected. The time series on investment is termed as capital formation in the WDI. The dataset begins in 1976 and ends in 2012. Although Bangladesh became independent in 1971, most economic series exhibit serious volatility and numerous outliers in the initial years of independence since the country had been recovering from a war-ravaged situation. Some variables are not available until 1976. As a result, most time-series studies on Bangladesh begin in 1976 or even after that (see Ahmed and Uddin 2009, Mamun and Nath 2005, Paul 2011, 2012).

There lies another reason for why time-series studies on Bangladesh begin sometime in the post-1975 period. The first regime in the post-independence period took a rigorous path of massive nationalization, centralized control, and socialist planning. This regime ended in 1975, and the country slowly began to proceed towards the market economy and liberalization in a piecemeal approach since 1976. Ahmed and Sattar (2004) assert that Bangladesh's first phase of liberalization began in 1976 after the regime change in 1975. The interactions between economic variables are expected to show more plausible results in a relatively liberalized environment. That also explains why this exercise begins in 1976. The starting point of 1976 leaves us to work on each series with 35 annual observations, a number viewed as a sound sample size for time-serie's estimations.

Since the main objective of this paper is to find the long-run factors behind capital formation, a number of macro variables are collected that are, based on theory and practice, expected to influence investment in Bangladesh. The typical goods market theory dictates including income or Gross Domestic Product (GDP) and interest rates in the first place. The expansion of domestic credit is viewed as a dominant candidate to affect capital formation in emerging economies like Bangladesh. In Keynesian theory, saving may not necessarily be a significant determinant of investment. The Solow model recommends including saving to determine the change in capital stock (Solow 1956). Foreign aid or Official Development Assistances (ODA) and remittances are two major inflows that are expected to contribute to capital formation in Bangladesh.

Based on the recent experience of growth in the country in the wake of liberalization and financial deregulation, the inclusion of variables like trade, foreign direct investments (FDI), and market capitalization becomes imperative. The measure of openness has various versions (Harrison 1996). The most basic measure of openness is the simple trade share, which is exports plus imports divided by GDP (Yanikkaya 2003). The total trade volume is also viewed as a measure of economic openness (see Liu et al. 1997, Sinha and Sinha 2002, Din at el. 2003). The level of financial development in the country is usually measured by the share of domestic credit in the country's GDP (see Adeniyi et al. 2012).

Given this perspective, this study includes 11 variables that are expected to influence investment in Bangladesh such as: 1) GDP 2) the lending rate 3) domestic credit 4) domestic saving 5) remittances 6) foreign aid 7) the total trade volume 8) the trade-GDP ratio or the measure of economic openness 9) the share of domestic credit in GDP, which can be called as the credit-GDP ratio or financial deepening 10) FDI and 11) market capitalization. The variable of trade volume has also been decomposed into exports and imports, making total number of variables be 13. All the basic variables except for the lending rate are first converted into 2000 constant U.S. dollars. The logarithmic values of all the variables are taken afterward. Due to some negative figures, which refuse log conversion, in the series of net FDI until 1985, the series begins in 1986. The series of market capitalization is not available in the WDI until 1988.

The studies that sequentially developed the ARDL bounds test approach include Pesaran and Pesaran (1997), Pesaran and Shin (1999), and Pesaran et al. (2001). There are numerous advantages in the ARDL method, which makes it more useful than others. With a small sample size, as is the case with mine, this method is more efficient than other techniques. In contrast, the Johansen cointegration technique, which is due to Johansen and Juselius (1990), requires larger samples for the results to be valid (Ghatak and Siddiki 2001). The simplicity of this ARDL bounds test method is appealing. As opposed to other multivariate cointegration techniques, it allows the cointegrating relationship to be estimated by the OLS method once the lag order of the model is identified.

As Pesaran et al. (2001) assert, this asymptotic theory provides a simple univariate framework for testing the existence of a single level relationship between a variable and its regressors when it is not known with certainty whether the regressors are purely integrated of order one, *I(0)*, purely *I(1)*, or mutually cointegrated. In contrast, the Johansen test can work only with nonstationary *I(1)* series. Moreover, it is unnecessary that the order of integration of the underlying regressors be ascertained prior to testing the existence of a level relationship. Therefore, unlike typical applications of cointegration analysis, this method is not subject to this particular kind of pretesting problem.

Thus, a long-run relationship can be established with this technique irrespective of the time series properties of the variables in the model. Even when some of the model regressors are endogenous, the bounds testing approach generally provides unbiased long-run estimates and valid *t*-statistics (Narayan 2005, Odhiambo 2008). Moreover this approach provides a method of simultaneously assessing the short-run and the long-run effects of one variable on the other. At the same time, the ARDL has an appealing separation of short-and long-run effects (Bentzen and Ergsted 2001). The long-run relationship can be estimated in the following forms:

$$cap_t = \alpha_{i1} + \beta_i x_t + \theta_i trend + \varepsilon_{it}$$

Where, *cap* denotes capital formation, *x* stands for the 13 variables that are likely to affect capital formation as mentioned in the introduction. Hence, α_i (i = 1...13) stands for intercept terms, β_i (i = 1...13) signifies coefficients on respective variables, θ_i (i = 1...13) stands for the trend terms, and finally ε_{it}(i = 1...13) denotes error terms. To implement the bounds testing procedure, the following conditional ARDL-error correction models (ECMs) are presented, which correspond to the previous equation:

$$\Delta cap_t = c_i + \pi_1 cap_{t-1} + \pi_{2i} x_{it-1} + \pi_{3i} trend_{t-1} + \sum_{i=1}^{p} \theta_i \Delta cap_{t-i} + \sum_{i=1}^{p} \phi_i \Delta x_{t-i} + \sum_{i=1}^{p} \delta_i \Delta trend_{t-i} + u_{it}$$

Where, Δ denotes the first difference operator. c_i (i = 1...13) shows constants, π_i (i = 1...13) signifies coefficients on the lagged levels, θ_i, ϕ_i, and δ_i (i = 1...*p*) denote coefficients on the first differences of the lagged variables and trend, and finally u_i (i = 1...13) stands for error terms. *p* signifies the maximum lag length, which is decided by the user. The researcher usually depends on literature and convention to determine the maximum lag length. The selection criteria such as Schwarz Bayesian Criterion (SBC) and Akaike Information Criterion (AIC) are mainly used to determine the order of the ARDL model. Given the sample size, the SBC is used to determine the lag length of the ARDL, because the SBC chooses the most parsimonious model (see Enders 2010:120, Lutkepohl 1985).

Following Pesaran et al. (2001), *F* and *W* (Wald) statistics are employed to 'bounds test' for the existence of a long-run relationship where the null hypothesis states that the coefficients on the lagged levels are zero: $H_0: \pi_1 = \pi_2, \pi_1 = \pi_3, \ldots\ldots \pi_1 = \pi_{13} = 0$. Pesaran et al. (2001) provide lower and upper bound critical values where the lower bound critical values assume all variables are *I(0)* while the upper bound critical values assume all variables are *I(1)*. If the calculated *F* or *W* statistic exceeds the upper bound, the null hypothesis of no cointegration can be rejected. If they fall below the lower bound, the null hypothesis of no long-term relationship cannot be rejected. However, if they fall within their respective bounds, inference would be inconclusive. Now estimating long-run coefficients and the ECM along with the short-run parameters becomes necessary. The sign of the error correction (EC) coefficient must be negative and significant to ensure convergence of the dynamics to the long-run equilibrium.

4.0 Results and discussion

As discussed before, testing the variables for unit roots in the ARDL estimation is unnecessary, because this estimation can accommodate any variables, which are I(1), I(0), or mutually cointegrated. However, one limitation of the ARDL method is that it cannot be estimated with I(2) series. Although the series this study has undertaken are most likely to be I(1) or I(0), testing them to ensure that none of them are I(2) is required. The Augmented Dickey-Fuller (ADF) test is widely used in this regard (Dickey and Fuller 1979, 1981).

Phillips and Perron (1988) proposed a modification of the Dickey-Fuller (DF) test and have developed a comprehensive theory of unit roots. The Phillips-Perron (PP) test has introduced a t-statistic on the unit-root coefficient in a DF regression, corrected for autocorrelation and heteroskedasticity. Formally, the power of a test is equal to the probability of rejecting a false null hypothesis.

TABLE 1

Phillips-Perron unit root tests with investment and its related series in Bangladesh: 1976-2010

Variables	In levels		In first difference		Integration
	Model A	Model B	Model A	Model B	
Capital formation	-2.23 (0.20)	-4.62 (0.00)	-4.39 (0.00)	-3.81 (0.03)	I(1)/I(0)
Gross domestic product	7.15 (1.00)	0.87 (1.00)	-4.36 (0.00)	-5.91 (0.00)	I(1)
Lending rate	-0.45 (0.89)	-2.42 (0.36)	-5.37 (0.00)	-5.31 (0.00)	I(1)
Domestic credit	0.67 (0.99)	-1.26 (0.88)	-5.79 (0.00)	-6.15 (0.00)	I(1)
Domestic savings	-0.43 (0.89)	-3.36 (0.07)	-8.03 (0.00)	-16.05 (0.00)	I(1)
Trade	0.47 (0.98)	-3.09 (0.12)	-7.64 (0.00)	-7.42 (0.00)	I(1)
Exports	0.19 (0.97)	-2.03 (0.56)	-7.66 (0.00)	-7.94 (0.00)	I(1)
Imports	0.18 (0.97)	-3.94 (0.02)	-9.07 (0.00)	-9.50 (0.00)	I(1)/I(0)
Foreign aid	-1.88 (0.34)	-3.99 (0.02)	-9.16 (0.00)	-8.88 (0.00)	I(1)/I(0)
Foreign direct investment	-0.53 (0.87)	-2.05 (0.55)	-5.15 (0.00)	-5.18 (0.00)	I(1)
Remittances	-3.03 (0.04)	-5.27 (0.00)	-8.46 (0.00)	-8.00 (0.00)	I(0)
Market capitalization	-0.36 (0.90)	-2.22 (0.46)	-4.36 (0.00)	-4.39 (0.01)	I(1)
Economic openness	-0.06 (0.95)	-2.37 (0.39)	-6.97 (0.00)	-7.04 (0.00)	I(1)
Financial deepening	-0.21 (0.93)	-1.84 (0.66)	-6.16 (0.00)	-6.36 (0.00)	I(1)

Note: Model A includes intercept, and Model B includes both intercept and trend. The null hypothesis states that the variable has a unit root. *p*-values are shown in the parentheses under each adjusted *t*-statistic. The critical values and details of the test are presented in Phillips and Perron (1988). I(1)/I(0) indicates that the series's integration order depends on the model chosen. Source: WDI 2012.

Monte Carlo simulations show that the power of the various DF tests can be very low (Enders 2010:234). Maddala and Kim (1998:107) comment that the DF test does not have serious size distortions, but it is less powerful than the PP test. Choi and Chung (1995) assert that for low frequency data, as is the case with this study, the PP test appears to be more powerful than the ADF test. Accordingly, the PP methodology is adopted to test unit roots in the variables.

Table 1 presents the results of the Phillips-Perron unit root tests with the 14 series including capital formation. The results in Table 1 show that 10 out of 14 series are I(1). The rest are either I(0) or I(1) depending on model selection, but none of them are I(2), suggesting their eligibility to be examined in the ARDL bounds test method. The approach provides us with 95 percent critical bounds for the F and W (Wald) statistics. Table 2, however, shows only F-statistics since W-statistics provide the similar results needed to consider the long-run relationships. The critical value bounds are computed by stochastic simulations using 20,000 replications (Pesaran and Pesaran 2009).

TABLE 2

ARDL cointegration tests with capital formation in the LHS: 1976-2010

Forcing variables	F-Statistic	Forcing variables	F-Statistic
Gross domestic product	6.60	Foreign aid	**11.67**
Lending rate	**24.55**	Foreign direct investment	4.18
Domestic credit	**8.64**	Remittances	5.87
Domestic savings	2.81	Market capitalization	4.69
Trade	**12.24**	Economic openness	**21.64**
Exports	**21.12**	Financial deepening	**8.86**
Imports	5.73		

Note: The null hypothesis for the *F*-test denotes that the coefficients on lagged levels are equal to zero. The critical value bounds are computed by stochastic simulations using 20,000 replications (see Pesaran and Pesaran 2009). The 95 percent values for the lower and upper bounds are **7.38** and **8.24**, respectively. Statistics are bold when significant at the 5 percent level. Δ denotes the first order difference operator. Source: WDI 2012.

As Table 2 reports, out of the 13 variables that are likely to affect investment, only 7 variables have been found to have significantly influenced Bangladesh's capital formation over the last 35 years. They are: 1) lending rate 2) domestic credit 3) trade 4) exports 5) foreign aid 6) economic openness and 7) the level of financial development or simply financial deepening. The variables that did not deliver significant effect on investment include: 1) GDP 2) domestic savings 3) imports 4) FDI 5) remittances and finally 6) market capitalization.

Based on the findings of Table 2, all the 7 influential variables are plotted in Figure 1. In Panel A of Figure 1, domestic credit, trade, exports, and foreign aid are plotted along with capital formation. Except for the series of foreign aid, all other series are moving in a positive direction with capital formation, suggesting that the long-run coefficients on these forcing variables will be positive when investment will be regressed on them.

Panel B in Figure 1 plots 3 influential factors of investment. The lending rate is in percent. Other measures are expressed as a percentage of GDP. The figure convinces that both economic openness and financial deepening have been beneficial to capital formation in Bangladesh. The movement between the lending rate and capital formation is divergent over time, suggesting a long-run negative relationship. These relationships are acuter since 1992 when a new form of liberalization had commenced.

Table 3 that presents ARDL estimations of the long-run coefficients and the Error Correction Model (ECM) vindicates the observations of Figure 01. All the results are robust and consistent in that both long-run and short-run estimate bear the same positive sign. In Table 3, the relationship between the lending rate and investment is strongly negative (-0.55) and the coefficient is significant at the 1 percent level.

This finding being theoretically accurate supports Kamal (2011) but contradicts many such as Ahmed and Islam (2004), Correa and Rao (2004), Cole (2009), and Budget (2012). Figure 1: B shows a divergent pattern between the lending rate and investment since the early 1990s. It implies that a lower or slightly falling cost of fund has encouraged the growth of business ventures since the beginning of the new era of liberalization that depressed interest rates down.

FIGURE 1
Influencial factors to capital formation in Bangladesh: 1976-2010

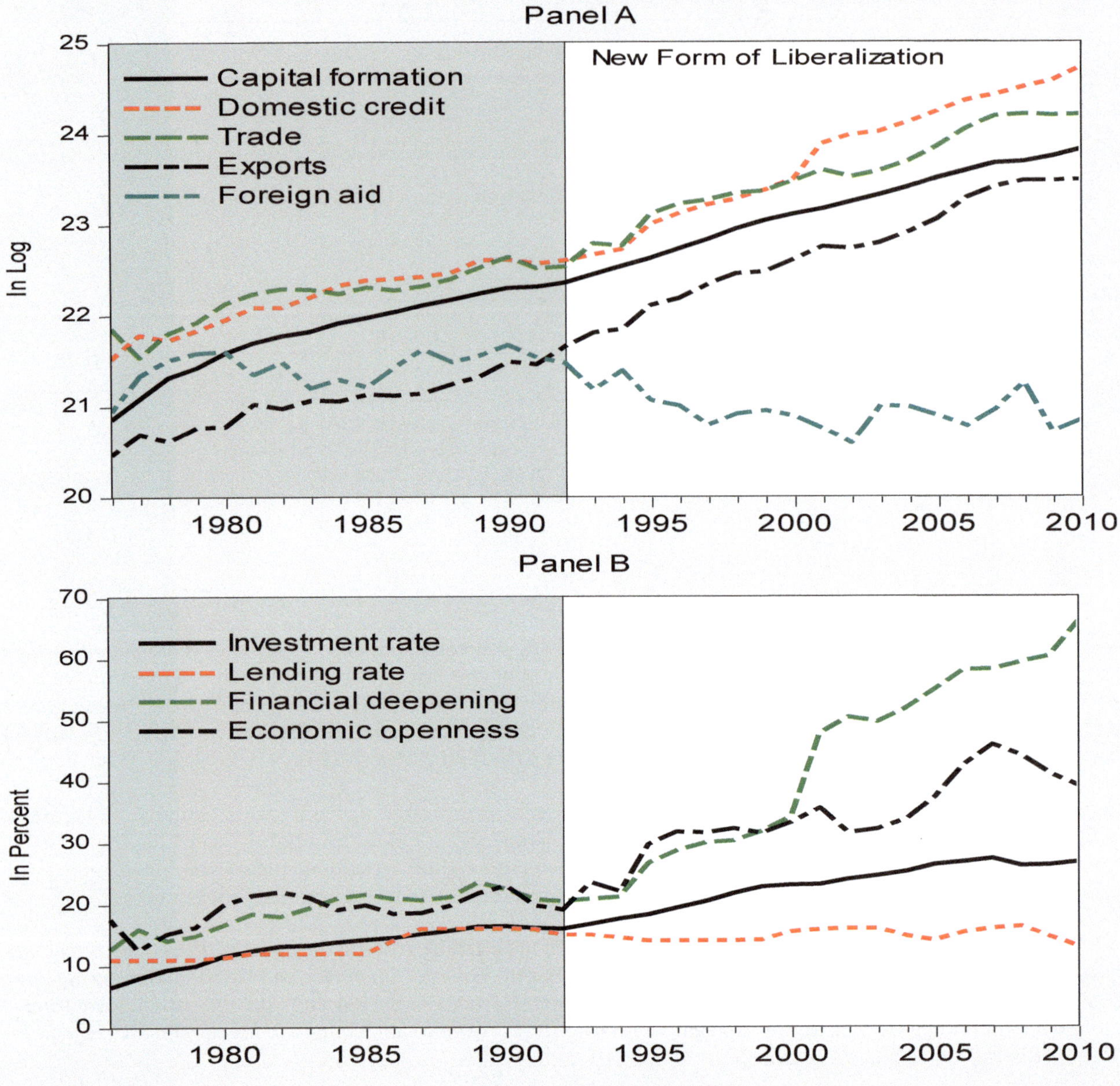

Source: WDI 2012

All other coefficients on the RHS forcing variables in Table 3, except for the one on foreign aid, are not only positive but also strongly significant at the 1 percent level. Domestic credit expansion has both short-run and long-run positive impact on capital formation. The long-run positive effect of trade on investment is mainly coming from exports; it vindicates the trade and investment relationships as found in Siriwanrdana and Yang (2007) and De et al. (2012). Growing exports always necessitate more investments to comply with the growing demand for goods by foreigners. The garments industry is a glaring testimony to this case.

Both economic openness and financial deepening have both long-run and short-run positive and significant effects on capital formation, supporting the findings in Bhattacharyay and De (2005) and Wadud (2009). Economic openness creates more incentives for businesses and necessitates an ever-growing demand for investment. In addition, financial deregulation creates more credit opportunities which in turn promote further capital formation in the economy. That is why we notice a simultaneous upward trend in economic openness, financial deepening, and the investment-output ratio since the early 1990s when liberalization rendered a new impetus to investment in Bangladesh.

TABLE 3

Long run coefficients and error correction estimates of ARDL models on capital formation in Bangladesh: 1976-2010

	RHS variable = Forcing variable						
Long-run estimations with capital formation (t):	Lending rate	Domestic credit	Trade	Exports	Foreign aid	Economic openness	Financial deepening
RHS variable (t)	-0.55*** (0.161)	0.20*** (0.067)	0.32*** (0.079)	0.35*** (0.112)	-0.25*** (0.091)	0.37*** (0.132)	0.25*** (0.073)
Constant	22.68*** (0.435)	17.01*** (1.416)	14.30*** (1.682)	14.22*** (2.222)	26.61*** (2.003)	20.42*** (0.304)	20.61*** (0.182)
Trend	0.08*** (0.001)	0.06*** (0.006)	0.05*** (0.006)	0.04*** (0.011)	0.07*** (0.003)	0.06*** (0.005)	0.06*** (0.004)
ECM estimations with Δcapital formation (t):							
Δcapital formation (t-1)		0.27** (0.12)			0.27** (0.114)		0.28** (0.113)
ΔRHS variable (t)	0.04 (0.081)	0.07** (0.03)	0.14*** (0.032)	0.13*** (0.034)	-0.03 (0.023)	0.11*** (0.028)	0.10*** (0.037)
ΔTrend	0.03*** (0.006)	0.02*** (0.005)	0.02*** (0.005)	0.014** (0.006)	0.02*** (0.005)	0.02*** (0.006)	0.03*** (0.006)
ECM(t-1)	-0.37*** (0.070)	-0.37*** (0.083)	-0.43*** (0.068)	-0.36*** (0.069)	-0.30*** (0.069)	-0.31*** (0.069)	-0.40*** (0.085)
Estimation model	ARDL (1,1)	ARDL (2,0)	ARDL (1,0)	ARDL (1,0)	ARDL (2,1)	ARDL (1,0)	ARDL (2,0)
Adjusted R^2	0.64	0.64	0.63	0.59	0.65	0.60	0.65
Diagnostic tests:							
A: Serial Correlation: $\chi2(1)$	1.01 [0.31]	0.11 [0.75]	3.16 [0.08]	0.89 [0.35]	1.26 [0.26]	0.41 [0.52]	0.23 [0.63]
B: Functional Form: $\chi2(1)$	0.63 [0.43]	1.31 [0.25]	0.42 [0.52]	0.64 [0.43]	4.38 [0.04]	0.17 [0.68]	0.32 [0.57]
C: Normality: $\chi2(2)$	2.08 [0.35]	2.56 [0.28]	1.31 [0.52]	1.44 [0.49]	1.32 [0.52]	2.30 [0.32]	1.27 [0.53]
D: Heteroskedasticity: $\chi2(1)$	1.75 [0.19]	0.65 [0.42]	0.23 [0.63]	0.28 [0.60]	2.71 [0.10]	0.19 [0.66]	0.78 [0.38]

Note: RHS means right hand side, and ECM error correction model. Δ denotes the first order difference operator. *, **, and *** indicate that the coefficients are significant at the 10 %, 5%, and 1% levels, respectively. The SBC selects the order of the ARDL models. In diagnostic tests, the nulls are: (A) no serial correlation, (B) no functional-form misspecification, (C) no non-normal errors, and (D) no heteroskedasticity. The LM version of diagnostic statistics show their respective *p*-values in brackets under each statistic (see Pesaran and Pesaran 1997, Ch. 18 for details). Source: WDI 2012.

The long-run coefficient on foreign aid is negative, implying that investment rises if aid goes down. A note of caution should be made in this regard. Historically, the amount of foreign aid has been gradually evaporating over time. Bangladesh has been making a great deal of progress in self-financed investment and growth. The series of foreign aid and capital formation have shown a divergent pattern. Hence, this negative relationship between foreign aid and capital formation is more of a pattern rather than causality. We also notice that all the estimations, except for the one with foreign aid, in Table 3 are free of the misspecification in the function form. In addition, there is a trace of heteroskedasticity at the 10 percent level in the equation with foreign aid, implying that the estimates under foreign aid are likely to be non-robust. Consequently, the equation can be ignored in considering the investment determinants in this discussion.

All other estimations are free of serial correlation, heteroskedasticity, and non-normal errors, as shown under the diagnostic tests in Table 3. Adjusted R-squared values for all estimations are quite respectable, ranging from 59 to 65 percent. The SBC selected all the parsimonious models, which are stable in the long run, because the ECM values are all negative and significant, as required for stability. They range from -0.40 to 0.31, suggesting that if the long-run relation is ever shocked, the robust values of the ECM will bring the system back in equilibrium in around three years or less.

5.0 Policy implications

The finding on the significant long-run effect of the interest rate on investment is important in that some previous studies provided confounding results in this regard. It also dispels the confusion in the national budget document that argues that high interest rates are not likely to impede investment in Bangladesh (Budget 2012:10). The central bank of the country should promote policy to reduce interest rates across the board. Commercial banks in Bangladesh argue that they cannot reduce the lending rate because of high deposit rates, on which they have to maintain a spread or difference to earn their income for administration and profit. The central bank cannot turn this point down. Rather, the central bank should try to reduce the whole interest rate spectrum so that the operations of the commercial banks become feasible.

Because high lending rates is not simply the presence of high deposit rates or a considerable amount of spread. The reason also lies in institutional factors such as bureaucracy, corruption, and excessive regulations, as argued in Dollar et al. (2005). Only the central bank cannot solve these issues unless the government becomes sincere enough to address them. Financial deregulation and prudent government policy that arguably can reduce the lending rate would be beneficial for the country to finance investment and to spur faster growth.

Since domestic credit expansion has a positive impact on capital formation, the central bank can nurture credit promotion policies to enhance the growth performance of the country. Although trade is beneficial for capital formation, the export sector needs preferential treatment to earn foreign capital and promote growth. There should not be any policy dilemma about economic openness, which lies at the root of investment augmentation and growth acceleration particularly since the early 1990s, as also shown in Siriwardana and Yang (2007) and De etal. (2012).

Apart from these interpretations, the government must ensure macro stability, which again depends on political stability, to create a vigorous investment climate. East Asian economies harvested the benefits of public policy and political stability in boosting investment (see WB 1993). Political instability has always affected investment adversely in Bangladesh. There is no exception to this rule in any developing nations. Since most investment decisions take medium-to-long-term scenarios into account, entrepreneurs are reluctant to risk their new ventures when political uncertainty clouds the future. Accordingly, we have always observed some slowdown in investment during the periods of regime change, but there is no authentic time series on political instability. The construction of this series in an objective way may allow us to include a variable in the estimations of investment in the future.

6.0 Conclusion

While we observe a plethora of research on the investment-output nexus, studies on the determinants of capital formation are evidently scarce. This scarcity becomes even acute when newly emerging countries are considered. In Bangladesh, an emerging nation of South Asia, a comprehensive study on the short-run and long-run determinants of investment is conspicuously absent. This work fills that gap. Working over a relatively liberalized regime of Bangladesh from 1976 to 2010, this exercise engages an ARDL bounds test method. It finds that the lending rate has a long-run negative effect on capital formation in the country, but short-run effects are insignificant.

While domestic savings have no significant impact on investment, domestic credit has. The policies of liberalization and financial deregulation appear to have had a positive impact on capital formation in Bangladesh. Economic openness and financial deepening have shown positive and significant effect on capital formation in the country. Trade or, more specifically, export promotion has contributed to the capital building as expected. These findings have policy implications for other developing nations which aspire to accomplishing rapid capital formation for faster economic growth.

This work raises some additional questions such as: 1) what are the significant underlying channels of financial deepening and economic openness that promote capital formation in Bangladesh? 2) Why is the short-term relationship between lending rates and capital formation insignificant in Bangladesh? 3) Why cannot domestic saving play a significant role in capital formation in Bangladesh? 4) How to assess the impact of political uncertainty on capital formation in Bangladesh? These questions require further study and hence are left for future investigation.

References

Adeniyi, O., Omisakin, O., Egwaikhide, F.O., Oyinlola, A., 2012. Foreign direct investment, economic growth and financial sector development in small open developing economies. Economic Analysis and Policy, 42(1):105-128.

Ahmed, S., Islam, Md. E., 2004.Interest rate responsiveness of investment spending in Bangladesh. Bangladesh Development Studies, 30(1-2):67-109.

Ahmed, S., Sattar, Z., 2004.Trade liberalization, growth and poverty reduction: The case of Bangladesh.South Asia Discussion Paper No.IDP-190, World Bank, Washington.

Ahmed, H.A., Uddin, M.G.S., 2009. Export, imports, remittance and growth in Bangladesh: An empirical analysis. Trade and Development Review, 2(2):79-92.

Bhattacharyay, B., De, P., 2005. Promotion of trade and investments between China and India: The case of Southwest China and East and Northeast India, CESifo working paper no. 1508. http://www.cesifo.de/DocCIDL/cesifo1_wp1508.pdf

Bentzen I., Engsted T., 2001. A revival of the autoregressive distributed lag model in estimating energy demand relationships. Energy 26:45-55.

Budget, 2012. 2012-2013 Budget Speech by AMA Muhith, Finance Minister, Ministry of Finance, Government of Bangladesh, 1-149. http://mof.gov.bd/en/budget/12_13/budget_speech/speech_en.pdf

Choi, I., Chung, B., 1995. Sampling frequency and the power of tests for a unit root: A simulation study. Economics Letters, 49:131-36.

Cole, S., 2009. Financial development, bank ownership, and growth: Or, does quantity imply quality? Review of Economics and Statistics. 91(1):33-51.

Correa, R., Rao, D.T., 2004. Saving, lending and interest rates: A critique of financial liberalization in India. International Review of Applied Economics, 18(3):289-99.

Das, A., Paul, B. P., 2011. Openness and growth in emerging Asian economies: Evidence from GMM estimations of a dynamic panel. Economics Bulletin, 31(3):2219-28.

De, P., Raihan, S., Kathuria, S., 2012. Unblocking Bangladesh-India trade: Emerging potential and the way forward. World Bank Policy Research WP 6155. World Bank, Washington.

Dickey, D, Fuller, W.A., 1979. Distribution of the estimates for autoregressive time series with a unit root.Journal of the American Statistical Association, 74:427-431.

Dickey, D., Fuller, W.A., 1981. Likelihood ratio statistics for autoregressive time series with a unit root.Econometrica, 49:1057-72.

Din, M., Ghani, E., Siddique, O., 2003. Openness and economic growth in Pakistan. Pakistan Development Review, 42(4):795-807.

Dollar, D., Hallward-Driemeier, M., Mengistae, T., 2005.Investment climate and firm performance in developing economies. Economic Development and Cultural Change. 54(1):1-31.

Enders, W., 2010.Applied econometric time series, 3e, John Wiley and Sons, New Jersey.

Ghatak, S., Siddiki, J., 2001.The use of ARDL approach in estimating virtual exchange rates in India. Journal of Applied Statistics, 28:573-583.

Harrison, A., 1996. Openness and growth: A time-series, cross-country analysis for developing countries. Journal of Development Economics, 48:419-47.

Johansen, S., Juselius, K., 1990.Maximum likelihood estimation and inference on cointegration with application to the demand for money. Oxford Bulletin of Economics and Statistics, 52:169-209.

Kamal, M., 2011.Interest rate and investment in Bangladesh: An empirical analysis. Bank Parikrama, 36(2-4):1-10.

Krugman, P., 1994. The myth of Asia's miracle. Foreign Affairs, Nov-Dec, 73(6):62-78.

Liu, X., Song, H., Romilly, P., 1997.An empirical investigation of the causal relationship between openness and economic growth in China. Applied Economics, 29:1679-86.

Lutkepohl, H., 1985. Comparison of criteria for estimating the orders of a vector autoregressive process. Journal of Time Series Analysis, 6:35-52.

Maddala, G. S, Kim, I. M., 1998.Unit Roots, cointegration, and structural change, Cambridge University Press.

Mamun, K.A.A., Nath, H.K., 2005. Export-led growth in Bangladesh: A time series analysis. Applied Economics Letters, 12:361-364.

Naqvi, N.H., Tsoukis, C., 2003. Does public investment crowd out private investment? Evidence on investment and growth in Asia, 1971-2000. European Research Studies, 6(1-2):65-79.

Narayan, P.K., 2005. The saving and investment nexus for China: evidence from cointegration Tests. Applied Economics, 37(17):1979-1990.

Odhiambo, N.M., 2008. Energy consumption and economic growth nexus in Tanzania: An ARDL bounds testing approach. Energy Policy 37(2):617-622.

Parida, P. C., Sahoo, P., 2007. Export-Led growth in South Asia: A panel cointegration analysis. International Economic Journal, 21(2):155-75.

Paul, B.P., 2011. Revisiting export-led growth for Bangladesh: A synthesis of cointegration and innovation accounting. International Journal of Economics and Finance, 3(6):3-15.

Paul, B.P., 2012. Inflation–growth nexus: some bivariate EGARCH evidence for Bangladesh. Macroeconomics and Finance in Emerging Market Economies, 6(1):1-11.

Paul, B.P., 2013. Can Bangladesh grow faster than India? Journal of Bangladesh Studies, 15(1):15-27.

Pesaran M.H., Pesaran B., 1997.Working with Microfit 4.0: Interactive econometric analysis, Oxford University Press.

Pesaran B., Pesaran M.H., 2009.Time series econometrics using Microfit 5.0, Oxford University Press.

Pesaran MH, Shin Y., 1999. An autoregressive distributed lag modeling approach to cointegration analysis.in Econometrics and Economic Theory in the 20th Century: The Ragnar Frisch Centennial Symposium, Strom S (ed.). Cambridge University Press, 371-413.

Pesaran, M.H., Shin Y., Smith R.J., 2001.Bounds testing approaches to the analysis of level relationships. Journal of Applied Econometrics, 16:289-326.

Phillips, P. C., Perron, P., 1988. Testing for a unit root in time series regression. Biometrika, 75(2):335-46.

Qayyum, A., 2002. Demand for bank lending by the private business sector in Pakistan. Pakistan Development Review, 41(2):149-59.

Sahoo, P., Dash, R.K., 2012. Economic growth in South Asia: Role of infrastructure. Journal of International Trade and Economic Development, 21(2):217-52.

Sinha, D., Sinha, T., 2002.Openness, investment, and economic growth in Asia. Indian Economic Journal, 49(4):90-95.

Siriwardana, M., Yang, J., 2007. Effects of proposed free trade agreement between India and Bangladesh. South Asia Economic Journal, 8(1):21-38.

Solow, R.M., 1956. A Contribution to the theory of economic growth. Quarterly Journal of Economics, 70:65-94.

Wadud, M. A., 2009. Financial development and economic growth: A cointegration and error-correction modeling approach for South Asian countries. Economics Bulletin, 29(3):1670-77.

WB, 1993. The East Asian miracle: Economic growth and public policy, A World Bank Policy Research Report, Oxford University Press.

WDI, 2012. World development indicators, World Bank, Washington, http://data.worldbank.org/data-catalog/world-development-indicators

Yanikkaya, H., 2003. Trade, openness and economic growth: A cross-country empirical investigation. Journal of Development Economics, 72:57-89.

6

Capital market, financial deepening and Nigeria's economic growth: empirical evidence

Raymond Osi Alenoghena [a*]

[a] Department of Economics, Faculty of Social Sciences, University of Lagos, Nigeria
* Corresponding author's e-mail: raymondalen@hotmail.com

HIGHLIGHTS:

1. The study investigates the impact of capital market and financially deepening to economic growth in Nigeria.
2. The window of analysis is from 1981-2012.
3. The results from error correction model suggest that financial deepening has significant effect on the economic growth of Nigeria.
4. The result supports policy of government and other stakeholders to improve the liquidity of the financial market to enhance overall economic efficiency of Nigeria.

Article History

Keywords:
Capital market;
Financial deepening;
Economic growth.

ABSTRACT

This study investigates the contributions of capital market and financially deepening to economic growth in Nigeria over the period of 1981 to 2012. The analysis involves examining the stochastic characteristics of each time series variable by testing their stationarity using Augmented Dickey-Fuller (ADF) test and estimates the error correction mechanism model. The study revealed that Stock Market Capitalization, Narrow Money Diversification (involving credit to the private sector) and Interest Rate significantly impacted the promotion of economic growth of the country during the period of study. Though, other measures of liquidity represented by Financial Development (FID) and Monetization Ratio (MTR) were not significant in explaining the trend in economic growth, they exhibited very strong coefficients in the process. The study recommends that Government and other stakeholders in the economy should take measures further to improve the liquidity of the financial market to enhance overall economic efficiency in the country. In addition to proper monetary policy management, the study further recommends that concrete steps be taken to improve the activities of the Nigerian stock market.

1.0 Introduction

The objective of economic development constitutes a primal position in the task of Governance around the world. The financial sector plays a crucial role in the process of economic growth of any nation. The depth of the country's financial sector has been found to relate with the speed of economic progress. Analysts have observed that well-functioning capital markets increase economic efficiency, investment and growth. Capital market development is an important component of the financial sector development and supplements the role of the banking system in terms economic development. Long term capital is deemed crucial for economic development as evidenced by the positive relationship between long-term capital and economic growth (Demirguc and Levine, 1996). It is the responsibility of the capital market to attract funds for long-term capital for the economy at the right price. Specifically, capital markets assist in price discovery, liquidity provision, reduction in transactions costs, and risk transfer. They reduce information cost through generation and dissemination of information on firms leading to efficient markets in which prices incorporate all available information (Yartey and Adjasi, 2007; Garcia and Liu, 1999). Overall, stock markets provide market liquidity that enables implementation of long-term projects with long-term payoffs thereby promoting a country's economic growth. Moreover, efficient capital markets not only avail resources to investors, they also facilitate inflow of foreign financial resources into the domestic economy.

Financial deepening is like one of those strategies whose implementation can quicken the pace of development. However, the effect of this strategy needs to be determined and examined from time to time especially for developing economies. Financial deepening focuses more on the process of financial intermediation. Financial markets undertake this vital role of the intermediation process, by channeling funds from surplus units (savers) to deficit units (investors). When a country's process of financial intermediation is efficient and without repression, the outcome is usually a well-developed and functioning financial sector with the capacity to support economic growth. But where the contrary is the case, the result is an economy beset with "financial shallowness" which is a common problem infecting the growth of development economies (Goldsmith, 1969; Ghani, 1992). Developing Countries possess financial assets and instruments that are narrow, and this is condition is usually akin to shallow financial depth. This condition partly explains why countries in with shallow financial depth experience low or negative per capita income. Opinionating, Nnanna and Dogo (1998) said that financial deepening often refers to a state of an atomized financial system, meaning a financial system that is largely free from financial repression. Oloyede (1998) remarked. Thus, financial deepening is the outcome of accepting appropriate real finance policy such as relating real rate of return to real stock of finance. Where then do we place the Nigerian financial system on the barometer of financial repression and subsequently financial deepening?

It is instructive to note that the vibrant and unprecedented economic growth of the emerging markets of the sub-Saharan Africa (average 6.5%), which became more glaring from early 2001, was however called to question in 2008, no thanks to the global economic and financial meltdown. With the near collapse of Nigerian stock market between 2008 and 2009, Nigeria like other sub-Saharan Africa counterparts, had a taste of the contagion of global economic and financial crises. Between 2008 and 2009, the Nigeria stock exchange lost almost 63% of its market capitalization and 67.2% of her all share indexes. The cumulative loss till date (Nov 2012), stands in the neighbourhood N6 trillion. In fact, the performance of Nigerian stock market from 2008 till date has made nonsense of most known fundamental and technical analysis for equity investment. For instance in 2007, the market capitalization skyrocketed from N2900bn in 2005 to N13294.50bn in 2007. While new issues rose from N552.78bn to N2400bn. This phenomenal growth notwithstanding, the market capitalization represents only 28 percent of the GDP, compared with 167.1 per cent for South Africa, 50.7 percent for Zimbabwe and 130 percent for Malaysia. This indicates that the potentials for growth in the Nigerian market are still very enormous. (Ukeje, Kama, Eluemunor, 2007).

Many Nigerian's for numerous reasons are unbanked and lack access to formal financial services. The result of a survey conducted by Elfin Access in Nigeria in 2012 revealed that 34.9 million adults representing 39.7% of the adults in the Country did utilize the services of formal financial institutions (Efina, 2012). Only 28.6 million adults in Nigeria access and utilize formal financial services and this represents 32.5% of the adult population. In addition, the survey by Efina (2012) also revealed that 23.0 million adults save at home. This means that a huge bulk of the country's currency circulates outside the formal financial sector. This poses real problems to the economy in terms of controlling liquidity and financial deepening process.

Given this background the key objectives of this research study are: (i) to examine the contribution of the Nigerian Capital market to the country's economic growth, (ii) to establish the impact of financial deepening on the Nigeria's economic growth, and (iii) to understand the combined impact of capital market and financial deepening on the Nigerian economic growth process. Therefore, the following hypothesis have been formulated for the study: (i) developments in the capital market have not made an impact on the country's economic growth process; (ii) financial deepening has not made significant impact on the Nigerian growth process (iii) developments in the capital market and financial deepening have jointly not significantly impacted on the Nigerian economic growth process.

The existing literature in this field of study so far has not separated the contributions of financial deepening variables and capital market variables in the analysis of contributions to the country's economic growth. This approach is expected to guide us in a better analysis of the Nigeria's financial markets and, therefore, position us to make improve recommendations on how to improve their contributions to the country's growth process.

The paper is divided into five sections; the first section gives a general introduction to the phenomenon of globalization and serves as background of the paper stating its problem and its objectives, hypotheses and justification. Section 2 looks into the review of existing related literature on the topic while section 3 presents the Analytical Framework. Section 4 discusses the presentation of results. Section 5 is the conclusions and policy recommendations

2.0 Review of literature

The earliest establishment of the link between finance and growth in literature could be traced to the work of Schumpeter (1911) in which he contends that entrepreneurs require credit in order to finance the adoption of new production techniques with banks as key agents to facilitate financial intermediating activities. In this way, it is expected that a well-functioning banking system will provide intermediation services to productive entrepreneurial activities which will spur technological, innovative, and productive activities that increase real sector growth. Gurley and Shaw (1955), Goldsmith (1969) and Hicks (1969) have also argued along this line, positing that development of the financial system is crucial in stimulating economic growth and under-developed financial systems retard economic growth hence policies aimed at expanding the financial system should be formulated in order to foster growth. McKinnon (1973) and Shaw (1973) have also emphasized on the role of financial intermediaries and financial markets in the growth process. The McKinnon model assumes that the investment in a typical developing economy is mostly self-financed hence given its lumpy nature, investment cannot materialize unless sufficient saving is accumulated in the form of bank deposits (McKinnon, 1973). Also, Shaw (1973) has postulated that financial intermediaries promote investment and raise output growth through borrowing and lending. The result of such financial liberalization, Ang (2007) argues, will lead to increased output growth.

The capital market is no doubt pivotal to the level of development and growth of the economy. Chinwuba & Amos, (2011) note that capital market is one of the major institutions that act in propelling a prostate economy through sustainable investments for growth and development. It is a complex institution imbued with inherent mechanism through which long-term funds of the surplus sectors of the economy are mobilized, harnessed and made available to deficit sectors of the economy (Nyong, 1997). The market deals on medium and long term securities. Activities in the capital market are good indicators of the direction of the national economy. Efficiency and effectiveness in the performance of the market is expected to translate into buoyancy in economic development.

Osaze and Anao, (1999) assert that capital market is the cornerstone of any financial system since it provides the funds needed for financing not only business and other economic institutions, but also the programmes of government as a whole. Ilaboya and Ibrahim, (2004) document that capital market functions as an economic barometer for galvanizing economic activities. Al-Faki, (2006) summarizes that the market covers the entire schedule that facilitate the buying and selling of securities.

The studies on stock market development and economic growth in developing countries have shown controversial results. Levine and Zervos (1996) examines whether there is a strong empirical association between stock market development and long-run economic growth. The study used pooled cross-country time-series regression of forty-one countries from 1976 to 1993 to evaluate this association. The study tow the line of Demirguc-Kunt and Levine (1996) by conglomerating measures such as stock market size, liquidity, and integration with world markets, into the index of stock market development. The growth rate of Gross Domestic Product (GDP) per capita was regressed on a variety of variables designed to control for initial conditions, political stability, investment in human capital, and macroeconomic conditions; and then include the conglomerated index of stock market development. The finding was that a strong correlation between overall stock market development and long-run economic growth exist. This means that the result is consistent with the theories that imply a positive relationship between stock market development and economic growth.

The study of Mahtadi and Agarwal (2001) covers many emerging markets over 21 years and finds that this relationship exists both directly and indirectly by boosting private investment behavior. In a similar study, Caporale and Soliman (2004) observe that an organized and managed stock market stimulate investment opportunities by recognizing and financing productive projects that lead to improved economic activity, mobilize domestic savings, capital allocation proficiency, and help to diversify risks, and facilitate the exchange of goods and services. Stock markets are expected to increase economic growth by increasing the liquidity of financial assets, make global and domestic risk diversification possible, promote wiser investment decisions and positively influence corporate governance practices by increasing shareholders' interest value.

Ted Arzarmi et al. (2005) examined the empirical association between stock market development and economic growth in India. The authors found no evidence of the association between the Indian stock market development and economic growth in the entire period they studied. Whereas the authors found support for the relevance of stock market development in economic development during pre-liberalization, they discovered a negative relationship between stock market development and economic development for the post-liberalization period.

Enisan and Olufisayo (2009) through autoregressive distributed lag (ARDL), evaluate the long-run relationship between stock market development and economic growth in seven of the Sub-Saharan African countries. The results indicate that stock market has a positive and significant impact on growth. Causality results indicate unidirectional causality from stock market development to economic growth for both South Africa and Egypt. While

Cote D'Ivoire, Kenya, Morocco and Zimbabwe indicate bidirectional causality, Nigeria on the other hand shows weak evidence that growth causes the finance. Finally, Osinubi (1998) examines whether stock market promotes economic growth in Nigeria between the period 1980 and 2000. The study employed the Ordinary Least Squares (OLS) regression technique as the method of data estimation. The regression results confirm that there exist a positive relationship between the economic growth and the measures statistically insignificant. This in essence means that the effect of the stock market on economic growth is weak and insignificant considering the stock market development used. However, these relationships are statistically insignificant. This in essence means that the effect of the stock market on economic growth is weak and insignificant.

3.0 Analytical framework

In investigating the relationship between stock market performance and economic growth, we made use of the Neo=Classical Growth model, where rate of economic growth depends on the growth rate of (i) Capital Stock, K; (ii) Labour Supply, L; and (iii) Technological Progress over Time, (Dwivedi, 2008). The relationship between the national output and these variables are expressed in the form of a production function, thus:

$Y = f(K, L, T)$ ....(01)

The application of this model is however modified to represent the variables in our study and is accordingly specified as follows:

EG= f (SMP, TVS, TLE, FID, MTR, NMD, INT) .... (02)

Where, EG (Economic Growth) is Gross Domestic Product (GDP), Stock Market Performance (SMP), Total Value of Shares Traded (TVS), Total Listing on the Exchange (TLE), Financial Development (FID), Monetization Ratio (MTR), Narrow Money Diversification (NMD), and Interest Rate (INT). We consider capital market variables as SMP, TVS and TLE; while, financial deepening variables as FID, MTR, NMD, and INT.
Rearranging equation 2 in line with the model, we have:
$GDP= \beta 0 + \beta 1MCAP + \beta 2TVS + \beta 3TLE + \beta 4FID + \beta 5MTR + \beta 6\text{NMD} + \beta 7INT + \mu$...... (03)

Equation (3) is designed to measure the relationship that exists between Gross Domestic Product and other independent variables. This is to see how those explanatory variables influence Economic Growth in the economy. In line with a priori expectations, the expected signs of the coefficients are: $\beta 1 > 0$; $\beta 2 > 0$; $\beta 3 > 0$; $\beta 4 > 0$; $\beta 5 > 0$; $\beta 6 > 0$; $\beta 7 < 0$. The above sign (> 0) implies a positive relationship between GDP and the coefficients of the independent variable while (< 0) connotes a negative relationship.

Our Model for analysis is derived from equation (3) above. The Model contains GDP, Capital Market variables (MCAP, TVS and TLE) and Financial Deepening variables (FID, MTR, NMD and INT). Note that capital market variables are clear as specified since the figures for them can be obtained directly over the years. However, the financial deepening variables require further definitional analysis as follows:

Financial development (FID):
It is a measure of the increase in the volume of financial services of the banks, financial intermediaries, financial institutions and financial market, as demonstrated by credit to the private sector of the economy. Augusto de la Torre et al. (2006) noted that stock market development under globalization; whether the gain from reforms. The trio used F.D as one of the independent variables that determine G.D.P growth in the economy. They found that the financial development leads to growth.

FID = Credit to Private Sector/GDP... (04)
Where, FID = Financial Development and GDP = Gross Domestic Product

Monetization ratio (MTR):
This ratio is computed as M2 divided by nominal GDP. It is sometimes referred to as the Broad Money Velocity was used by King and Levine (1993). It reflects the depth of the financial market relative to the overall economy. Increases in this ratio indicate further expansion in the financial sector relative to the rest of the economy. Thus:

MTR = M2/GDP.. (05)
Where, MTR = Monetization Ratio, M2 = Total Monetary Liability (Broad Money), and GDP = Gross Domestic Product

Narrow money diversification (NMD):

This is the ratio of demand deposits to the narrow money stock. Vogel and Buser (1976) argue that this measure represents the complexity, or sophistication of the financial market (primarily banks). The increase in this ratio implies a higher degree of diversification of financial institutions and greater availability or use of non-currency balances (bank deposits) in the transaction process. In this paper, we adopted narrow money stock denoted as M1. Therefore;

NMD = DD/M1.. (06)

Where, NMD = Narrow Money Diversification, DD = Demand Deposit, and M1 = Money Supply.

Interest Rate (INT):
The annualized cost of credit or debt-capital and is computed as the percentage ratio of interest to the principal. The Monetary Authority determines it. In Nigeria, the interest rate which is determined by the Monetary Authority is referred to as the Monetary Policy Rate.

Given the variables definitions, it must be mentioned that the figures for GDP, MCAP, TVS and TLE are obtained in Millions while figures for FID, MTR, NMD and INT are in rates. Therefore, to obtain realistic results for our model of analysis, we would transform the model by taking logarithm of the variables in Millions. Therefore, our equation 3 becomes transformed to equation seven below:

$LogGDP = \alpha_0 + \alpha_1 LogMCAP + \alpha_2 LogTVS + \alpha_3 LogTLE + \alpha_4 FID + \alpha_5 MTR + \alpha_6 NMD + \alpha_7 INT + \mu$ .... (07)

4.0 Results and analysis

4.01 Estimation strategy

The estimation technique consists of four steps procedures. The first step is the unit root test which involves the determination of the stationarity property of the time series variables, using the Augmented Dickey-Fuller (ADF) test statistics for unit root (Dickey & Fuller, 1979). The second is impact estimation, using Least Squares multiple regression methods (including a constant term) is run over the sample period 1981-2011. The third is cointegration test to establish whether the time series variables have long-run equilibrium relationship. The fourth step involves testing for Error Correction Mechanism. If the cointegration test shows that the variables have long-run equilibrium relationship, then, it is a sufficient condition for an ECM formulation. If variables are non-stationary at level, but cointegrated, their dynamic relationships will be specified correctly by an error correction model (Granger and Engle, 1987).

4.02 Unit root test

The unit root test is necessary because research has shown that non-stationary data leads to spurious regression, which may affect in determining the cointegration relation in the long run. A summary of the results of the tests is presented in Table 1 below.

From the ADF test statistics, the results in Table 1 show that LOGGDP, LOGMCAP, LOGTVS, LOGTLE, FID, MTR, NMD and INT were integrated at order one, that is I(1), or they became stationary at first difference. Comparing the variables levels with their first difference (the ADF unit root test statistic) and various probabilities, the test statistics show that the variables are integrated at order of one. All the variables were statistically significant at 1%, 5% and 10% critical values in first difference.

Table 01: ADF Fisher unit root test result

Variables	I()*	ADF T-Stat	Max Lag
D(LOGGDP)	I(1)	-4.697***	1
D(LOGMCAP)	I(1)	-4.342***	1
D(LOGTVS)	I(1)	-4.665***	1
D(LOGTLE)	I(1)	-5.398***	1
FID	I(1)	-4.657***	1
MTR	I(1)	-6.258***	1
NMD	I(1)	-4.914***	1
INT	I(1)	-8.796***	1

Note: ***, **, and * referrers significance at 1%, 5%, and 10% respectively.

4.03 The estimated model

The regression equation of 07 was designed to measure the relationship that exists between Gross Domestic Product and other independent variables. This is to see how those explanatory variables influence Economic Growth in the economy. In line with a priori expectations, the expected signs of the coefficients are: B1 < 0; B2< 0; B3> 0; B4> 0; B5 > 0. The above sign (> 0) implies a positive relationship between GDPR and the coefficients of the independent variables.

Table 02: Result of multiple regression

Variable	βi	Std. Error	t-Statistic	Prob.
α	5.793	2.539	2.282	0.032
LOGMCAP	0.670	0.118	5.679	0.000
LOGTVS	0.134	0.074	1.803	0.084
LOGTLE	-0.133	0.482	-0.275	0.786
FID	-3.180	2.011	-1.581	0.127
MTR	3.050	1.641	1.859	0.075
NMD	-2.399	0.756	-3.171	0.004
INT	2.462	0.888	2.772	0.011
R-squared	0.896	Mean dependent var		14.246
Adjusted R-squared	0.845	S.D. dependent var		2.319
S.E. of regression	0.171	Akaike info criterion		-0.478
Durbin-Watson stat	1.948	Schwarz criterion		-0.112

Thus, the estimated models can be written as:

LOGGDP = 5.793276416 + 0.6696874623*LOGMCAP + 0.1340924895*LOGTVS - 0.1326147752*LOGTLE - 3.179804231*FID + 3.049844749*MTR - 2.398620918*NMD + 2.462058429*INT .... (08)

A quick view of the result in table 2 shows that GDP is positively related to LOGMCAP, LOGTVS, MTR AND INT while LOGTLE, FID and NMD are negatively related to LOGGDP. The R-squared and Adjusted R-squared indicated a good fit. About 89% of the variation in GDP is explained by the variation in the independent variables.

From the estimated result, it is obvious that if Log of Market Capitalisation (LOGMCAP), Log of Total Value of Shares Traded (LOGTVS), Monetisation Ratio (MTR) and Interest Rate (INT) are increased by 1%, GDP will increase by 0.66%, 0.13%, 3.05%, and 2.46% respectively. The result also shows that if Log of Total Listing of Equity (LOGTLE), Financial Development (FID), and Narrow Money Diversification (NMD) are increased by 1%, GDP will decrease by 13%, 3.18% and 2.40% respectively.

To test our hypothesis we used the probability (p-value) of observing the t-statistic given that the coefficient is equal to zero. Only three independent variables are statistically significant in explaining the variation in GDP at 5% and 1% levels of significance. The variables are Log of Market Capitalisation (LOGMCAP), Narrow money Diversification (NMD) and Interest Rate (INT).

The variable with the strongest significant impact on GDP is Interest Rate with a positive coefficient of 2.46. This is closely followed by Narrow Money Diversification (NMD) with a negative coefficient of 2.40. NMD refers to credit advanced to Private Sector by Banks in the economy. With negative and positive coefficients of 3.17 and 3.05 Financial Development and Monetisation Ratio indicates very strong relationship with GDP while noting that the coefficients are statistically insignificant. The variable with the weakest and most-insignificant impact on GDP is Log of Total number of securities listed on an exchange (TLE). The value of Durbin-Watson Statistic (1.95) indicates the absence of autocorrelation in the analyzed data. The value of F-Statistic is 808.14. An analysis of the probability value for F-Statistic (Prob F-Stat = 0.0000) indicates that entire regression equation is significant at both 1% and 5% levels of significance. The model is a good fit.

To effectively test the joint significance of both financial deepening variables and capital market variables in explaining the variation in GDP we employed Wald Coefficient test statistic referenced in Appendix 1. From the result, we observe that the combined impact of the financial deepening variables showed that F-Statistic of 7.95 and Chi-Square statistic showed 28.84. But the Probability results showed 0.007 indicating that the combined impact of Financial deepening variables (FIN, MTR, NMD and INT) on GDP during the period of analysis are statistically significant (at both 5% and 1%). The Wald test result on capital market variables (LOGMCAP, LOGTVS and LOGTLE) shows that F-statistic is 626.71, and Chi-Square is 1880.13. However, the Probability results showed 0.000

indicating that the combined impact of Capital Market variables LOGGDP during the period of analysis are statistically significant (at both 5% and 1%).

4.04 Cointegration test

The unit root test earlier conducted showed that the variables are stationary at first difference. Stationarity of the residuals is potent evidence that there is evidence of convergence to long-run equilibrium among the integrated variables. Now we wish to test whether the variables are cointegrated over the sample period and if so, what the cointegrating relation is. To determine the number of significant co integration relationships, we use the Johansen's co-integration test that yields the log likelihood estimates for the unconstrained co-integration vectors.

Table 03: Johansen cointegration test

Hypothesized No. of CE(s)	Eigenvalue	Trace Statistic	Critical Value	Prob.**
None *	0.921	303.181	187.470	0.000
At most 1 *	0.884	226.750	150.558	0.000
At most 2 *	0.787	162.001	117.708	0.000
At most 3 *	0.781	115.477	88.803	0.000
At most 4 *	0.636	69.844	63.876	0.014
At most 5	0.433	39.461	42.915	0.106
At most 6	0.323	22.415	25.872	0.126
At most 7	0.299	10.691	12.517	0.099

Note: Trace test indicates 5 cointegrating eqn(s) at the 0.05 level. * denotes rejection of the hypothesis at the 0.05 level; **MacKinnon-Haug-Michelis (1999) p-values

The results of the co-integration in table 3 confirmed that there are five co-integration relationships among the variables included in the model. Specifically, the result of the co-integration test suggests that the variables have long-run equilibrium relationship with each other. This evidence of co-integration among the variables rules out spurious correlations and applies that five directions of influence can be established among the variables. It is important to note that the existence of co-integration vectors among a group of variables may not imply that there is causal influence between pairs of variables in the model of co-integration test. The presence of a co-integrating relation forms the basis of the error correction specification. The cointegration term is known as an error correction term since the deviation from long-run equilibrium is corrected gradually through a series of partial short-run adjustments Granger and Engle (1987).

4.05 Error correction model and long-run behavior of the model

A vector error correction (VEC) model is a restricted VAR designed for use with non-stationary series that are known to be cointegrated. The VEC has cointegration relations built into the specification so that it restricts the long-run behavior of the endogenous variables to converge to their cointegrating relationships while allowing for short-run adjustment dynamics. Our analysis of table 1 shows that since the variables are non-stationary at levels but become stationary after first difference, the variables in the model are cointegrated. Given the situation, their dynamic relationships must be specified by the error correction model (ECM) in order to capture both the short-run and long-run relationships. The Error Correction for the long run Economic Growth equation is written below:

$$\begin{aligned} D(LOGGDP) = {} & -0.217*(LOGGDP(-1) - 8.915 - 0.219*LOGMCAP(-1) + 0.400*LOGTVS(-1) \\ & + 0.768*LOGTLE(-1) + 3.615*FID(-1) - 6.605MTR(-1) + 0.699*NMD(-1) \\ & - 5.708*INT(-1)) \quad \ldots\ldots (09) \end{aligned}$$

The equation above depicts the Error Correction Mechanism (ECM) of our Model (see Appendix 2). It implies that the long run adjustment coefficient of the dependent variable (LOGGDP) is – 0.22. The value is negative and statistically significant in conformity with an effective error correction model. It indicates that the speed of annual (short-run) adjustments of LOGGDP is 22% to long run deviations from equilibrium. The long-run intercept term for the model is negative with 8.92. The Error Correction Equation also depicts that the coefficients of LOGMCAP, MTR and INT are negative in adjusting to the long run disequilibrium given by the ECM value (-0.58). The coefficients of LOGTVS, LOGTLE, FID and NMD are positive in serving the same purpose. However, the result shows that LOGMCAP, LOGTVS and INT are statistically significant, therefore, more meaningful in our analysis while trying to determine the growth rate of LOGGDP in the long run.

5.0 Policy recommendation for Nigeria

This research study attempts to investigate the relationship between capital market, financial deepening and economic growth. The deductions that could be made from the empirical findings are predicted on the sizes and magnitude of the slope coefficient. It was revealed that Market Capitalisation, Narrow Money Diversification (credit to a private sector) and Interest Rate significantly impacted the promotion of economic growth of the country during the period of study. Though, other measures of liquidity represented by Financial Development (FID) and Monetisation Ratio (MTR) were not significant in explaining the trend in economic growth, they exhibited very strong coefficients in the process. Overall, the Wald Coefficient Test revealed that jointly, the proxies for both Capital Market and Financial Deepening (separated) are significant in explaining the trend in economic growth.

In the light of the above, the Government and other stakeholders in the economy should put measures that are directed at: *First*, improve liquidity of the economy and further expand the financial services sector. Specific measures along this line would involve further monetization of the economy to involve the huge sector that does not utilize the financial services provided by the money and capital markets. The process may require more enlightenment of the middle and lower cadre of the Nigerian people and spread of Branches of financial institutions in the country to areas without access to banking services. *Second*, the role of credit to the growth of the economy is well-exhibited by the significant impact of narrow money diversification (NMD) on economic growth (GDP) in our analysis. It means that a further advancement of properly structured loans and advances to the key producing sectors of that would improve the size of the country's GDP. *Third*, improvements in capital market activities. This can be handled by improving the enabling environment to make the Nigerian stock market globally competitive and improve the architecture to enhance hitch free trading and reporting. Regulatory activities for trading should also be properly supervised while emphasizing professionalism on the part of market operators and stock brokers. Government policies should also be geared towards increasing money supply and improving the liquidity of the capital market as this will enhance overall economic efficiency and increase investor confidence in capital market activities.

6.0 Conclusion

The broad focus of this paper was to identify, within an empirical framework, the proportionality relationship between economic growth and proxies for capital market and financial deepening of the Nigerian economy. We developed a multiple regression equation model, which focuses explicitly on the impact of capital market and financial deepening proxies on the country's economic growth. The econometric model that is adopted was used to regress the impact of these factors on Nigeria's economic growth that is proxied by GDP. The results and analysis of our research findings are predicated on the values of the different parameters of dependent variables.

This paper provided evidence showing that activities in the Nigeria's Capital Market have impact on the Country's economic growth. Financial deepening variables also have impacted on the Country's GDP. Specifically, GDP is significantly impacted by Growth in Market Capitalisation (MCAP), Narrow Money Diversification (NMD) and interest rate (INT). The paper recommends that Government and stake holders in the economy should come up with measures to improve liquidity in the economy. Expansion of financial services to deficient locations is emphasized along with the extension of credit facilities to key producing sectors of the economy. The paper also recommends that there should be concrete improvements in the activities of the Nigerian capital market. Laws should be enacted to make the Nigerian stock market more globally competitive, and there should be proper regulation of the activities of market operators.

References

Al-FakI, M. 2006. The Nigerian capital market and socioeconomic development. 4th Distinguished Faculty of Social Science Public Lecture, 9-16.

Ang, J. B., & McKibbin, W. J. 2007. Financial liberalization, financial sector development and growth: evidence from Malaysia. Journal of Development Economics, 84(1): 215-233. http://dx.doi.org/10.1016/j.jdeveco.2006.11.006

Caporale, G. M., Howells, P. G., & Soliman, A. M. 2004. Stock market development and economic growth: the causal linkage. Journal of Economic Development, 29(1): 33-50.

Chinwuba, O., & Amos, O. A. 2011. Stimulating Economic Development through the Capital Market. The Nigerian Experience. JORIND, 9(2).

De la Torre, A., Gozzi, J. C., & Schmukler, S. L. 2007. Stock market development under globalization: Whither the gains from reforms?. Journal of Banking & Finance, 31(6): 1731-1754. http://dx.doi.org/10.1016/j.jbankfin.2006.11.008

Demirgue Kunt, A. and R. Levine 1996. Stock market, corporate finance and economic growth: an overview. The World Bank Review, 10(2): 223-239. http://dx.doi.org/10.1093/wber/10.2.223

Dwivedi, D.N 2008. Managerial Economics; New Delhi: Vikas Publishing House

Efina.org, http://www.efina.org.ng/about-us/financial-inclusion/

Engle, R.F. and C.W.J. Granger 1987. Cointegration and error correction: representation, estimation and testing. Econometrica, 55: 251-276. http://dx.doi.org/10.2307/1913236

Enisan, A. A. and A.O Olufisayo 2009. Stock market development and economic growth: evidence from seven sub-Sahara African countries. Journal of Economics and Business, 61: 162-171. http://dx.doi.org/10.1016/j.jeconbus.2008.05.001

Goldsmith, R.W. 1969. Financial Structure, and Development, Yale University Press: New Haven.

Gurley J.G and E.S Shaw 1955. Financial aspects of economic development. American Economic Review, 45:515-538

Hicks, J.A 1969. A theory of economic history, Oxford: Clarendon Press

Ilaboya, O.J. and Ibrahim, S. 2004. Impact of stock market performance on the level of economic activities: Evidence from Nigerian stock market. Nigerian journal of business administration, Vol.6 No 1.

King R.G and R. Levine, 1993. Finance and growth: Schumpeter might be right. Quarterly Journal of Economics, 108:715-735. http://dx.doi.org/10.2307/2118406

Levine and Zervos 1996. Stock market development and long-run growth. The World Bank Economic Review, 10(3): 323 – 339.

Mahtadi, H. and Agarwal, S., 2001. Stock market development and economic growth: evidence from developing countries. http://www.articlesbase.com /finance- articles/stock-market-developmentandeconomic-growth-evidence-from- underdevelopednation- Nepal-1096815.html

McKinnon, R., 1973. Money and capital in economic development, Washington, D.C.: Brookings Institution

Nnanna, J. & Dogo, M., 1999. Structural reform, monetary policy and financial deepening: the Nigeria experience: Mimeo

Nyong, M. O. 1997. Capital market development and long-run economic growth: theory, evidence and analysis. First Bank Review :13-38.

Oloyede, A., 1998. The financial system's role in resource mobilization and investment: an analysis of financial deepening in Nigeria's financial sector. In the Dynamics of Managing the Nigerian Financial System in the 21st Century. A Publication of the Central Bank of Nigeria.

Osaze, B.E. & Anao, A.R., 1999. Managerial Finance. Benin City: UNIBEN Press.

Osinubi, Tokunbo S., 1998. Stock market development and long-run growth in Nigeria. Unpublished M.Sc. Economics Dissertation, University of Ibadan Nigeria. Presented at 3rd Distinguished Faculty of Social Science Public Lecture Series, University of Ibadan

Schumpeter, J.A, 1911. The theory of economic development. Oxford: Oxford University Press

Shaw, E., 1973. Financial deepening in economic development. Oxford: Oxford University Press Journal of Development Economics, September/October, 1-24

Ted, A., Lazar, D., & Jeyapaul, J., 2005. Is the Indian stock market a casino?. Journal of Business and Economic Research, 3(4): 63-72.

Ukeje EU, Kama U, Eluemunor, 2007. A review of the Nigerian capital market in capital market dynamics in Nigeria: structure, transaction cost and efficiency 1980- 2006. A Publication of the Central Bank of Nigeria.

Vogel R. and S. Buser 1976. Inflation, financial repression, and capital formation in Latin America in Money and Finance in Economic Growth and Development. Ed, R. McKinnon, New York: Marcel Dekker, Inc.

Yartey C.O. and Adjasi C.K., 2007. Stock market development in sub Saharan Africa: critical issues and challenges. International Monetary Fund working paper No. wp/07/209.

Appendix 01: Wald coefficient test

CAPITAL MARKET VARIABLES					FINANCIAL DEPEENING VARIABLES				
Test Statistic		Value	df	Prob.	Test Statistic		Value	df	Prob.
F-statistic		626.71	(3, 24)	0.000	F-statistic		7.948	(3, 24)	0.007
Chi-square		1880.13	3	0.000	Chi-square		23.844	3	0.000
Null Hypothesis Summary									
Normalized Restriction (= 0)		Value	Std. Err.		Normalized Restriction (= 0)		Value	Std. Err.	
C(2)	LOGMCAP	0.669	0.117		C(5)	FID	-3.179	2.010	
C(3)	LOGTVS	0.134	0.074		C(6)	MTR	3.049	1.640	
C(4)	LOG TLE	-0.132	0.482		C(7)	NMD	-2.398	0.756	
					C(8)	INT	2.462	0.888	

Note: Restrictions are linear in coefficients.

Appendix 02: Vector error correction estimates

D(LOGGDP) = C(1)*(LOGGDP(-1) - 0.2191144118*LOGMCAP(-1) - 0.4003384731*LOGTRADG(-1) + 0.7684554124*LOGTLE(-1) + 3.614986651*FID(-1) - 6.604877693*MTR(-1) + 0.6994782486 *NMD(-1) - 5.708437143*INT(-1) - 8.914839977) + C(2) *D(LOGGDP(-1)) + C(3)*D(LOGMCAP(-1)) + C(4) *D(LOGTVS(-1)) + C(5)*D(LOGTLE(-1)) + C(6)*D(FID(-1)) + C(7)*D(MTR(-1)) + C(8)*D(NMD(-1)) + C(9)*D(INT(-1)) + C(10)

Dependent Variable: (LOGGDP)	Coefficient	Std. Error	t-Statistic	Prob.
C(1)	-0.217368	0.120047	1.810690	0.0352
C(2)	0.020220	0.252239	0.080163	0.9369
C(3)	0.537295	0.164253	3.271142	0.0038
C(4)	-0.237335	0.078401	-3.027192	0.0067
C(5)	0.458186	0.479631	0.955289	0.3508
C(6)	2.438575	2.178629	1.119316	0.2763
C(7)	-0.034211	1.957491	-0.017477	0.9862
C(8)	-1.047194	0.638638	-1.639730	0.1167
C(9)	1.888486	0.783177	2.411316	0.0256
C(10)	0.159350	0.056058	2.842604	0.0101
R-squared	0.571499	Mean dependent var		0.223897
Adjusted R-squared	0.378673	S.D. dependent var		0.174152
S.E. of regression	0.137274	Akaike info criterion		-0.872477
Log likelihood	23.08716	Durbin-Watson stat		2.109284

7

Determinants of effective tax rates for firms listed on Chinese stock market: Panel models with two-sided censors

Yong-Ching Chiou[a*], Yao-Chih Hsieh[b], Wenyi Lin[c]

[a] Department of Insurance and Finance , National Taichung University of Science and Technology, Taiwan.
[b] Department of Public Finance, Feng Chia University, Taiwan. E-mail: ychsieh@fcu.edu.tw
[c] Graduate Institute of Financial and Economic Law, Feng Chia University, Taiwan. E-mail: wylin@fcu.edu.tw
[*] Corresponding author's email address: yvonne@nutc.edu.tw

HIGHLIGHTS:

1. This paper highlights the role of tax preferences within set effective tax rates between 0 and 1.
2. This paper attempts to use the panel models with two-sided censoring suggested by Alan, Honor´e, and Leth-Petersen (2014) to study the determinants of ETRs for the listed on China stock markets.
3. This article adopts four definitions of ETR and the empirical results demonstrate fruitful conclusions.
4. Our findings suggest this model can add more observations especially the observations with tax preferences

Article History

Keywords:
Effective tax rate;
Political power (cost) hypothesis;
Tax preference;
Two-sided censoring.

ABSTRACT

This paper is to investigate the determinants effective tax rate for the firms listed on China's stock markets. The panel data consists of 481 firms from 2007 to 2009 as our empirical data. In order to illustrate a country's tax policies on firms' real tax burdens, the dependent variable, ETR, is left-censored at 0 and right-censored at 1, the estimation for panel data model with two-sided censoring suggested by Alan, Honor´e, and Leth-Petersen (2014) is implemented in this paper. There are two important findings are obtained: first, this model can add more observations especially the observations with tax preferences. Second, theories suggest that ETR reflects outcomes of tax preference and this paper is the first time to consider the effective tax rates set between 0 and 1 and this range is more meaningful for the ETRs.

1.0 Introduction

Due to its convenience for measuring the tax burdens of corporate, effective tax rates (ETRs) have long been used by policy makers and interest groups in tax reform rebates, especially those related to corporate tax provisions. Success in the political process normally leads to future changes in effective tax rates. Tax preferences include all special exemptions from taxable income, deductions in excess of normal amounts, and deferrals of taxable income that enabled some individuals or corporations with substantial income to pay little or no tax while other taxpayers with less income have been required to pay a relative higher percentage of their income in taxes.

Empirically, studies on the relation between ETRs and firm size have produced conflicting results. Zimmerman (1983) observes a positive association between ETRs and firm size while Porcano (1986) observes a negative association. No association between ETRs and firm size is found in Stickney and McGee (1982) and Shevlin and Porter (1992). Subsequent studies have tried to reconcile the conflicting results by using modified proxies, period, time, term, data basis, and methodologies (e.g., Kern and Morris,1992; Wilkie and Limberg,1990; Holland, 1998; Kim and Limpaphayom, 1998; Derashid and Zhang, 2003). All studies are based on OLS model and firms with negative ETR are eliminated from the sample. Some previous articles, in order to correct the specification, panel data models have been used to overcome the problem of model mis-specification in studies on determinants of ETRs (e.g. Gupta and Newberry, 1997; Harris and Feeny, 2003; Liu and Cao, 2007). Besides, Gupta and Newberry (1997) suggest that because ETRs concerns firms with tax refunds, negative income and measurement issue, they constrained the ETR of their sample firms to lie between zero and one. This is the characteristic of censored sample. However, the censoring characteristic of ETRs is not considered in existing literature. The effective tax rate for the current empirical research and cannot fully explain the role of tax preferences. Because of tax incentives has led many companies and therefore not subject to tax, to remove these samples clearly unreasonable. Therefore, the effective tax rate of less than 0 is set to 0 will be able to comply with the real situation. Besides, Derashid (2003) point out the effective tax rate of a firm may be greater than one for a number of reasons. One reason is that, in the process of consolidation within a group of firms, subsidiaries/associated firms with net operating profit are combined with those subsidiaries/associated firms with net operating loss. Thus, this article will be an effective tax rate is set to 1.

In our sample, there are more than 13 % of firms with zero ETRs. It is well known that the regression estimators are biased and inconsistent if the existence of censoring in dependent variable is neglected. Therefore, this paper attempts to use the panel data models with two-sided censoring suggested by Alan, Honor´e, and Leth-Petersen (2014) to study the determinants of ETRs for the listed on China stock markets.

The remaining of this paper is organized as follows. Section 2 introduces the estimation of panel data models with two-sided censoring suggested by Honor´e and Leth-Petersen (2014). Empirical studies are investigated in section 3. Conclusions are presented in the last section.

2.0 Panel data models with two-sided censoring

Since the effective tax rates are between 0 and 1 with a significant number of observations on either of the limits. In panel data setting, the specific model is

$$y_{it}^* = \mathcal{X}_{it}'\beta + \epsilon_{it} \qquad \text{Eq. (01)}$$

$$y_{it} = \begin{cases} a \text{ if } y_{it}^* < a \\ y_{it}^* \text{ if } a \le y_{it}^* \le b \\ b \text{ if } y_{it}^* > b \end{cases} \qquad \text{Eq. (01. A)}$$

Where ϵ_{it} is stationary conditional on$(\mathcal{X}_{i1}, \dots, \mathcal{X}_{iT})$. The derivation of estimator for β suggested by Alan, Honor´e, and Leth-Petersen (2014) is briefly summarized as follows. Define, for $a \le b$,

$$\text{ma mi}\ \{a, y, b\} = \begin{cases} a \text{ if } y < a \\ y \text{ if } a \le y \le b \\ b \text{ if } y > b \end{cases} \qquad \text{Eq. (01. B)}$$

So Eq. (01) can be written as

$$y_{it} = \text{ma mi}\{a, \mathcal{X}_{it}'\beta + \epsilon_{it}, b\} \qquad \text{Eq. (02)}$$

Consider an individual, i, in two-time periods, t and s. The distribution of $(y_{it} - \mathcal{X}_{it}'\beta)$ will be the same as that of ϵ_{it} except that the former is censored from below at $a - \mathcal{X}_{it}'\beta$ and from above at $(b - \mathcal{X}_{it}'\beta)$. The dotted line depicts the distribution of ϵ_{it}, while the solid line gives the distribution of $b - \mathcal{X}_{it}'\beta$, which typically has point mass at $a - \mathcal{X}_{it}'\beta$ and $b - \mathcal{X}_{it}'\beta$ (illustrated by the fatter vertical lines). Since $\mathcal{X}_{it}'\beta$ will typically differ from $\mathcal{X}_{is}'\beta$, the distributions of $y_{it} - \mathcal{X}_{it}'\beta$ and $y_{is} - \mathcal{X}_{is}'\beta$ (given $(x_{it}\ x_{is})$) will differ even if $\{\epsilon_{it}\}$ is stationary. However, it is clear that one could obtain identically distributed "residuals" by artificially censoring $y_{it} - \mathcal{X}_{it}'\beta$ and $y_{it} - \mathcal{X}_{is}'\beta$ from below at max $\{a - \mathcal{X}_{it}'\beta, a - \mathcal{X}_{is}'\beta\}$ and from above at $\min\{b - \mathcal{X}_{it}'\beta, b - \mathcal{X}_{is}'\beta\}$. One can then form moment conditions from the fact that the difference in these "re-censored" residuals will be orthogonal to functions of $(\mathcal{X}_{it}, \mathcal{X}_{is})$.

Also define functions $u_1(y_{it},.)$ and $u_2(y_{is},.)$ over the interval −(b−a) to (b−a) as follows

$$u_1(y_{it}, d) = \begin{cases} \max\{y_{it} - d, a\} \text{ for } b - a \ge d \ge 0 \\ \min\{y_{it}, b + d\} \text{ for } 0 \ge d \ge -(b - a) \end{cases}$$

and

$$u_2(y_{is}, d) = \begin{cases} \max\{y_{is}, b - d\} \text{ for } b - a \ge d \ge 0 \\ \min\{y_{is} + d, a\} \text{ for } 0 \ge d \ge -(b - a) \end{cases}$$

With these definitions, $u_1(y_{it}, \mathcal{X}_{it}'\beta - \mathcal{X}_{is}'\beta) - u_2(y_{is}, \mathcal{X}_{it}'\beta - \mathcal{X}_{is}'\beta)$ will give the difference in the re-censored residuals by artificially censoring $y_{it} - \mathcal{X}_{it}'\beta$ and $y_{is} - \mathcal{X}_{is}'\beta$ from below atmax $\{a - \mathcal{X}_{it}'\beta, a - \mathcal{X}_{is}'\beta\}$ and from above at min $\{b - \mathcal{X}_{it}'\beta, b - \mathcal{X}_{is}'\beta\}$.

Let the functions $r_1(y_{it},.)$ and $r_2(y_{is},.)$ are defined over the interval $-(\mathrm{b}-\mathrm{a})$ *to* $(\mathrm{b}-\mathrm{a})$ as

$$r_1(y_{it},d) = \begin{cases} db + \frac{1}{2}d^2 + \frac{1}{2}(y_{it}-b)^2 \ for \ d \le y_1 - b \\ dy_{it} \ for \ y_{it} - b \le d \le \mathrm{a} \\ dy_{it} - \frac{1}{2}d^2 \ for \ \mathrm{a} \le d \le y_{it} - \mathrm{a} \\ \mathrm{da} + \frac{1}{2}(y_{it}-\mathrm{a})^2 \ for \ y_{it} - \mathrm{a} \le d \end{cases}$$

and

$$r_2(y_{is},d) = \begin{cases} \mathrm{da} + \frac{1}{2}d^2 + \frac{1}{2}(y_{is}-\mathrm{a})^2 \ for \ d \le -(y_{is}-\mathrm{a}) \\ \frac{1}{2}d^2 + dy_{is} \ for \ -(y_{is}-\mathrm{a}) \le d \le \mathrm{a} \\ dy_{is} \ for \ 0 \le d \le b - y_{is} \\ db - \frac{1}{2}d^2 - \frac{1}{2}(y_{is}-b)^2 \ for \ b - y_{is} \le d \end{cases}$$

The functions $r_1(y_{it},.)$ and $r_{12}(y_{is},.)$ are constructed, so their derivatives are $u_1(y_{it},.)$ and $u_2(y_{is},.)$, respectively. Finally, define

$$R(y_{it},y_{is},d) = r_1(y_{it},d) - r_2(y_{is},d).$$

Alan, Honor´e, and Leth-Petersen (2014) show that

$$\frac{\partial}{\partial d} R(y_{it},y_{is},d) = r_1(y_{it},d) - r_2(y_{is},d)$$

Suppose that

$$\mathrm{y_{it}} = \mathrm{mami}\{\mathrm{a}, \delta + \epsilon_{\mathrm{it}}, \mathrm{b}\}$$

and

$$\mathrm{y_{is}} = \mathrm{mami}\{\mathrm{a}, \epsilon_{\mathrm{is}}, \mathrm{b}\}$$

Where ϵ_{it} and ϵ_{is} are identically distributed random variables with support on the whole real line. Then Alan, Honor´e and Leth-Petersen (2014) prove that

$$\arg \min_{\mathrm{d} \in [-(\mathrm{b}-\mathrm{a}),(\mathrm{b}-\mathrm{a})]} \mathrm{E}[\mathrm{R}(\mathrm{y_{it}},\mathrm{y_{is}},\mathrm{d})] = \begin{cases} -(\mathrm{b}-\mathrm{a}) \text{ if } \delta \le -(\mathrm{b}-\mathrm{a}) \\ \delta \text{ if } -(\mathrm{b}-\mathrm{a}) < \delta < (\mathrm{b}-\mathrm{a}) \\ (\mathrm{b}-\mathrm{a}) \text{ if } \delta \ge (\mathrm{b}-\mathrm{a}) \end{cases}$$

If ϵ_{it} is stationary conditional on $(\mathcal{X}_{\mathrm{it}},\mathcal{X}_{\mathrm{is}})$ with support on the whole real line, then the set of solutions to

$$\max_{\mathrm{b}} \mathrm{E}\,[\mathrm{R}(\mathrm{y_{it}},\mathrm{y_{is}},)\mathrm{mami}\{-(\mathrm{b}-\mathrm{a}),(\mathrm{x_{it}}-\mathrm{x_{is}})'\mathrm{b},(\mathrm{b}-\mathrm{a})\}]$$

is

$$\{\mathrm{b} : \mathrm{P}[\mathrm{mami}\{-(\mathrm{b}-\mathrm{a}),(\mathrm{x_{it}}-\mathrm{x_{is}})'\mathrm{b},(\mathrm{b}-\mathrm{a})\} = \mathrm{mami}\,\{-(\mathrm{b}-\mathrm{a}),(\mathrm{x_{it}}-\mathrm{x_{is}})'\beta,(\mathrm{b}-\mathrm{a})\}] = 1.\}$$

Therefore, when the censoring points are a and b, the sample analog estimator is

$$\widehat{\beta_{\mathrm{n}}} = \arg \max_{\mathrm{b}} \textstyle\sum_{i=1}^{n} \sum_{1\le s\le t\le T_i} \mathrm{w_{i,t-s}} \mathrm{R}[\mathrm{y_{is}},\mathrm{y_{it}}\mathrm{mami}\{-(\mathrm{b}-\mathrm{a}),1,(\mathrm{x_{is}}-\mathrm{x_{it}})'\mathrm{b},(\mathrm{b}-\mathrm{a})\}]$$

where the $\mathrm{w'_{i,t-s}}$s are exogenous weights and $\mathrm{T_i}$ is the number of observations for the ith individual. $\mathrm{w_{i,t-s}} = 1/\mathrm{T_i}$ is a trivial choice.

It is proved by Alan, Honor´e and Leth-Petersen (2014) that $\widehat{\beta_{\mathrm{n}}}$ is consistent and asymptotically normal under appropriately conditions. Under random sampling

$$\sqrt{\mathrm{n}}(\widehat{\beta_{\mathrm{n}}} - \beta) \to_{\mathrm{d}} \mathrm{N}(0, \Gamma^{-1}\mathrm{V} + \Gamma^{-1}),$$

Where

$$\begin{aligned}\Gamma = \mathrm{E}[\textstyle\sum_{s<t} \mathrm{w_{i,t-s}} 1\{-(\mathrm{b}-\mathrm{a}) < (\mathrm{x_{is}}-\mathrm{x_{it}})'\beta < (\mathrm{b}-\mathrm{a})\} \\ (1\{-(\mathrm{b}-\mathrm{a}) < (\mathrm{x_{is}}-\mathrm{x_{it}})'\beta < \mathrm{y_{is}}-\mathrm{b}\} - 1\{-(\mathrm{b}-\mathrm{a}) < (\mathrm{x_{is}}-\mathrm{x_{it}})'\beta < \mathrm{y_{is}}-\mathrm{a}\}) \\ -1\{\mathrm{a}-\mathrm{y_{it}} < (\mathrm{x_{is}}-\mathrm{x_{it}})'\beta < \mathrm{a}\} + 1\{\mathrm{b}-\mathrm{y_{it}} < (\mathrm{x_{is}}-\mathrm{x_{it}})'\beta < (\mathrm{b}-\mathrm{a})\} \\ (\mathrm{x_{it}}-\mathrm{x_{is}})(\mathrm{x_{it}}-\mathrm{x_{is}})']\end{aligned}$$

and

$$\mathrm{V} = \mathrm{E}[\upsilon_{\mathrm{i}}\, \upsilon'_{\mathrm{i}}]$$

With

$$\begin{aligned}\upsilon_{\mathrm{i}} = \frac{1}{\mathrm{T_i}} \textstyle\sum_{s<t} \mathrm{w_{i,t-s}} 1\{-(\mathrm{b}-\mathrm{a}) < (\mathrm{x_{is}}-\mathrm{x_{it}})'\beta < (\mathrm{b}-\mathrm{a})\} \\ (\mu_1(\mathrm{y_{is}},(\mathrm{x_{it}}-\mathrm{x_{is}})'\beta) - \mu_2(\mathrm{y_{it}},(\mathrm{x_{is}}-\mathrm{x_{it}})'\beta))(\mathrm{x_{is}}-\mathrm{x_{it}}).\end{aligned}$$

Following standard arguments, these are consistently estimated by

$$\begin{aligned}\widehat{\Gamma_{\mathrm{n}}} = \frac{1}{\mathrm{n}} \textstyle\sum_{i=1}^{n} [\sum_{s<t} \mathrm{w_{i,t-s}}\, 1\{-(\mathrm{b}-\mathrm{a}) < (\mathrm{x_{is}}-\mathrm{x_{it}})'\,\widehat{\beta_{\mathrm{n}}} < (\mathrm{b}-\mathrm{a})\} \\ (1\{-(\mathrm{b}-\mathrm{a}) < (\mathrm{x_{is}}-\mathrm{x_{it}})'\widehat{\beta_{\mathrm{n}}} < \mathrm{y_i}-\mathrm{b}\} - 1\{-(\mathrm{b}-\mathrm{a}) < (\mathrm{x_{is}}-\mathrm{x_{it}})'\widehat{\beta_{\mathrm{n}}} < \mathrm{y_i}-\mathrm{a}\})\end{aligned}$$

$$-1\{a - y_{it} < (\chi_{is} - \chi_{it})'\widehat{\beta_n} < a\} + 1\{b - y_{it} < (\chi_{is} - \chi_{it})'\widehat{\beta_n} < (b - a)\}$$
$$(\chi_{is} - \chi_{it})(\chi_{is} - \chi_{it})']$$

and

$$\widehat{V_n} = \frac{1}{n}\Sigma - i = 1^n \widehat{\upsilon_i}\,\widehat{\upsilon_i'}$$

With

$$\widehat{\upsilon_i} = \frac{1}{T_i}\Sigma_{s<t}\, w_{i,t-s}\, 1\{-(b-a) < (\chi_{is} - \chi_{it})'\,\widehat{\beta_n} < (b-a)\}$$
$$(\mu_1(y_{is}, (\chi_{it} - \chi_{is})'\widehat{\beta_n}) - \mu_2(y_{it}, (\chi_{is} - \chi_{it})'\widehat{\beta_n}))(\chi_{is} - \chi_{it}).$$

3.0 Empirical studies

The sample data used in this study is collected from the Taiwan Economic Journal (TEJ) database. It consists of 481 firms each year listed on China's stock market from 2007 to 2009. The ETR is measured as four different ETRs measures are used. We follow the approach used by Porcano (1986), ETR1 is defined as (tax expenses - deferred tax expenses) divided by (profit before interest and tax paid) and ETR2 is another version of the measure used by Porcano (1986): (tax expenses)/ (profit before interest and tax). ETR 3 is a measure used by Stickney and McGee (1982) and is given as (tax expenses)/ (pre-tax profit– (deferred tax expenses/statutory tax rate)). ETR4 is the measure used by Shevlin (1987) and is calculated as (tax expenses–deferred tax expenses)/ (pre-tax profit – (changes in deferred tax/statutory tax rate)). Whenever firms report, negative income is eliminated from the sample. Negative numerator (tax refunds) will be included in the sample because of considering tax preferences. It is worthy to mention that the negative ETRs are replaced with zeros and one for those larger than one. There are, totally, 72, 101, 114 and 86 firms with zero ETR for definitions of ETR1, ETR2, ETR3 and ETR4. For the right censoring, there are 0, 0, 16 and eight firms with ETR equal to one in ETR1, ETR2, ETR3, and ETR4, respectively.

To explore the marginal effect of firm size on ETRs, the following firm-specific characteristics are taken as control variables: leverage (total liabilities divided by total asset value, denoted as "LEV"), capital intensity (net fixed assets divided by total assets, denoted as "CI"), inventory intensity (inventory divided by total assets, denoted as "II"), and return on assets (pre-tax profits divided by total assets, denoted as "ROA"), firm size (denoted as "SIZE") is measured as the natural logarithm of total asset value. The state ownership variable is defined as the ratio of state-owned shares over total outstanding shares and denoted as S1. The reasons behind to choose these variables are based on previous studies (e.g., Porcano (1986), Gupta and Newberry (1997), Derashid and Zhang (2003), Liu and Cao (2007)). To account for the factors discussed above, the empirical results are presented in table 01.

The coefficients for S1, government equity, do not appear to be statistically different from zero, except ETR2. These results suggest that the effects of government ownership may draw different conclusions because of the definitions of ETR. The coefficients for capital intensity are all statistically insignificant for all ETR measures. These evidences do not support the notion that higher capital investment and the resultant higher depreciable costs lead to a lower ETR. The coefficient for inventory intensity, on the other hand, is statistically different from zero under all ETR measures. The coefficient for leverage is negative and statistically significant when ETR is measured as ETR1. The coefficients are not statistically different from zero under ETR2, ETR3, and ETR4. Thus, there are evidences to support the intuitive notion that debt financing can be used as a tax shield for China's firms. The coefficients for inventory intensity are all statistically different from zero under all ETR measures. The coefficients of ROA, the measure for efficiency in performance, are all positive significant when ETR is measured as ETR1, ETR2, ETR3, ETR4. These results suggest that more efficient firms pay more effective tax in China. Moreover, these results are consistent to previous studies. The coefficients for firm size are positive and statistically significant when ETR is measured as ETR1, ETR3, and ETR4. Thus, we can accept the political cost hypothesis when ETR is defined as ETR1, ETR3, and ETR4. Finally, all the coefficients of year dummies for each of the four ETR measures are negative and statistically significant.

Table 01: Estimated results for panel data model with two-side censoring

	ETR1	ETR2	ETR3	ETR4
α	-0.045	0.091*	0.026	-0.001
	(0.052)	(0.050)	(0.073)	(0.060)
S1	-0.005	0.029*	0.038	-0.001
	(0.016)	(0.015)	(0.024)	(0.019)
CI	-0.013	-0.004	0.030	0.021
	(0.025)	(0.024)	(0.036)	(0.029)
II	0.105***	0.096***	0.111**	0.153***
	(0.033)	(0.032)	(0.048)	(0.039)
LEV	-0.137***	-0.055	-0.024	-0.059
	(0.043)	(0.040)	(0.064)	(0.051)
ROA	0.127***	0.192***	0.209***	0.144***
	(0.048)	(0.048)	(0.069)	(0.054)

SIZE	0.013*** (0.004)	0.002 (0.003)	0.009* (0.005)	0.011*** (0.004)
Y2008	-0.013** (0.006)	-0.029*** (0.006)	-0.054*** (0.010)	-0.031*** (0.007)
Y2009	-0.028*** (0.007)	-0.022*** (0.006)	-0.017* (0.011)	-0.028*** (0.008)

4.0 Conclusions

To demonstrate a national real tax preferences policy, ETRs concerns firms with a tax refund, negative income and measurement issue, not like previous research; this paper adopts two-sided censoring model to investigate the determinants of ETRs for the firms listed on China's stock markets. Since the dependent variable, ETRs, is left-censored at zero and right-censored at 1, the estimation for panel data model with two-sided censoring suggested by Honor´e and Leth-Petersen (2014) is implemented in this paper. Several contributions are obtained: first, this model can add more observations especially the observations with tax preferences which are the essence of a country's tax policies. Second, at our best knowledge, this paper is the first time to consider the effective tax rates set between 0 and 1 and this range is more meaningful for the ETRs. Third, for a comparison with previous research, this article adopts four definitions of ETR and the empirical results demonstrate fruitful conclusions.

References

Alan, S., and S. Leth-Petersen, 2006. Tax incentives and household portfolios: A panel data analysis. Center for Applied Microeconometrics, University of Copenhagen, Working paper number 2006-13.

Alan, S., Bo E. Honor'e, and S. Leth-Petersen, 2014. Estimation of panel data models with two-sided censoring or truncation. Journal of Econometric Methods, 3(1): 1-20. http://dx.doi.org/10.1515/jem-2012-0012

Callihan, D.S., 1994. Corporate effective tax rates: A synthesis of the literature. Journal of Accounting Literature, 13(1): 1–43.

Derashid, Check, and Hao Zhang, 2003. Effective tax rates and the industrial policy hypothesis: evidence from Malaysia. Journal of International Accounting Auditing and Taxation, 12(1): 45–62. http://dx.doi.org/10.1016/S1061-9518(03)00003-X

Gupta, S., and K. Newberry, 1997. Determinants of the variability of corporate effective tax rates: evidence from longitudinal Data. Journal of Accounting and Public Policy, 16(1): 1–34. http://dx.doi.org/10.1016/S0278-4254(96)00055-5

Harris, M. N. and S. Feeny, 2003. Habit persistence in effect tax rates. Applied Economics, 35(8): 951–958. http://dx.doi.org/10.1080/0003684032000050577

Holland, K., 1998. Accounting policy choice: The relationship between corporate tax burdens and company Size. Journal of Business Finance and Accounting, 25(3-4): 265–288. http://dx.doi.org/10.1111/1468-5957.00187

Kim, K.A., and P. Limpaphayom, 1998. Tax and firm size in Pacific-Basin emerging economies. Journal of International Accounting Auditing and Taxation, 7(1): 47–63. http://dx.doi.org/10.1016/S1061-9518(98)90005-2

Kern, B. B. and M. H. Morris, 1992. Taxes and firm Size: The effect of tax legislation during the 1980s. Journal of the American Taxation Association, 14(1): 80–96.

Liu, Xing and Shujun Cao, 2007. Determinants of corporate effective tax rates: evidence from listed companies in china. The Chinese Economy, 40(6): 49–67. http://dx.doi.org/10.2753/CES1097-1475400603

Porcano, T., 1986. Corporate Tax Rates: Progressive, proportional, or regressive. Journal of the American Taxation Association, 7(2): 17–31.

Powell, J.L., 1984. Least absolute deviations estimation for the censored regression model. Journal of Econometrics, 25(3): 303–325. http://dx.doi.org/10.1016/0304-4076(84)90004-6

Powell, J.L., 1986. Censored regression quintiles. Journal of Econometrics, 32(1): 143–155. http://dx.doi.org/10.1016/0304-4076(86)90016-3

Shevlin, T., 1987. Taxes and off-balance-sheet financing: research and development limited partnership. The Accounting Review, 62(3):480–509.

Shelvin, T., and S. Porter, 1992. The Corporate tax comeback in 1987: Some further evidence. Journal of American Taxation Association, 14(1): 58–79.

Stickney, C., and V. McGee, 1982. Effective corporate tax rates: The effect of size, capital intensity, leverage, and other factors. Journal of accounting and public policy, 1(2): 125–52. http://dx.doi.org/10.1016/S0278-4254(82)80004-5

Wilkie, P., 1988. Corporate average effective tax rates and inferences about the relative tax preference. Journal of the American Taxation Association, 10(1): 75–88.

Wilkie, P.J., and S.T. Limberg, 1990. The relationship between firm size and effective tax rate: A reconciliation of Zimmerman (1983) and Porcano (1986). Journal of American Taxation Association, 11(2): 76–91.

Zimmerman, J., 1983. Tax and firm size. Journal of Accounting and Economics, 5(2):119-149. http://dx.doi.org/10.1016/0165-4101(83)90008-3

Evaluation of relationship marketing in Islamic banks in the UAE: Empirical evidence based on sensitivity analysis algorithm

Chris I. Enyinda [a*]

[a] Department of Marketing and International Business, Canadian University of Dubai, UAE.
* Corresponding author's email: christian@cud.ac.ae

HIGHLIGHTS:

1. Leveraging AHP-based sensitivity analysis to test relationship marketing tactics robustness
2. Performance sensitivity analysis
3. Growing imperatives of relationship marketing in financial and banking sectors
4. Relationship marketing strategy is key for Islamic banks to maintain a long-term relationship
5. Factors accounting for relationship marketing success

Article History

Keywords:
AHP;
Customer loyalty;
Islamic banks;
Relationship marketing;
Sensitivity analysis.

ABSTRACT

The recorded success of a number of Islamic banks during the recent global financial crisis has indeed attracted the attention of a number of conventional commercial banks. Because these conventional banks are now operating Islamic windows, Islamic banks must focus their efforts on building relationship marketing that is grounded in the principles of Shariah to retain and attract prospective customers. This paper proposes the analytic hierarchy process (AHP) sensitivity analysis methodology to test the stability or robustness of the priority ranking of relationship marketing tactics. It used AHP-based questionnaire survey to evaluate the relative importance of factors accounting for relationship marketing success of Islamic banks. Relationship managers consider customer loyalty as the most important end-result of relationship marketing, followed by competitive advantage, customer satisfaction, and financial performance. Based on the performance sensitivity analysis, the overall priority of the alternative course actions accounting for relationship marketing success was robust (stable) to the changes in the importance of all the major objectives.

1.0 Introduction

The increasing success of a number of Islamic banks around the world has attracted a number of conventional commercial banks to adopt Islamic windows. As a result, Islamic banks are not only facing competition from the Islamic windows of conventional commercial banks, but also from other Islamic banks (Hassan et al., 2008). Therefore, the marketing strategy of an Islamic bank must be concerned with its ability to establish and gain competitive advantage (Hassan et al., 2008). However, for the Islamic banks to establish and sustain strong competitive position they must know how to meet customers' value expectations and manage customer relationships. Per American Marketing Association, "marketing is an organizational function and a set of processes for creating, communicating, and delivering value to customers and for managing customer relationships in ways that benefit the organization and its stakeholders." From the Islamic perspective, Hussnain (2011) considers

Islamic marketing as the process of identifying and implementing value maximization strategies for the welfare of both the stakeholders and the society in accordance with Quran and Sunnah general guidelines. Both definitions underscore the imperative of customer relationship building and the need to create and deliver value that serve the welfare of the society, stakeholders, and the firm.

The growing imperative of relationship marketing in banks, Islamic banks in particular has become prominent since the recent global financial crisis. The need for Islamic banking industry to differentiate itself from the conventional banking industry cannot be overemphasized. One way to achieve such a differentiation is to leverage aggressive implementation of customer relationship marketing tactics grounded in the principles of Islamic Shariah. Indeed, "this essential difference, resulting from the implementation of the Islamic *Shari'ah* principles, provides the incentive for Islamic bankers to search for different products/services to offer" (Hassan et al., 2008) through leveraging acceptable relationship marketing tactics. This involves the "process of identifying and establishing, maintaining, enhancing, and when necessary terminating relationships with customers and other stakeholders, at a profit, so that the objectives of all parties involved are met, where this is done by a mutual giving and fulfillment of promises" (Gronroos, 1997, p. 407).

This paper proposed the analytic hierarchy (AHP)-based sensitivity analysis (SA) model developed by Saaty (1980) to evaluate relationship marketing of Islamic banks within the UAE. SA checks the responsiveness of model results to possible variations in parameter values, and thus offers valuable and insightful information for evaluating the alternative courses of action. Samson (1988) suggests that SA is an important part of decision-making process thinking in real time and generally entails checking the effects of the model assumptions on the model solution. SA technique helps to examine potential changes and their influence on conclusions drawn from the model (Pannell, 1997). SA can provide decision makers with information regarding the robustness of the ranking of the alternative course of action. Per Fiacco (1983), SA determines the effect of local perturbation over results and stability analysis as the effect of finite perturbation over results behavior. According to Min (1994), "...the sensitivity analyses are necessary because changing the importance of criteria requires different levels of resource commitment ..."

The AHP encompasses three basic functions, including structuring complexity, measuring on a ratio scale, and synthesizing. It is useful in structuring complex multi-attribute problems or decisions in many fields such as marketing, project management, operations/supply chain management, and economics. The AHP merits are the reliance on easily derived expert opinion data, ability to reconcile differences (inconsistencies) in expert judgments and perceptions, and the existence of Expert Choice Software to implement the AHP (Calantone et al., 1989).

This paper is bifurcated into the following sections. The second section presents the relevant literature review, including satisfaction, customer loyalty and service quality; relationship marketing; and relationship marketing in the banking sector. Third section discusses the research methodology. Fourth section details the data collection and analysis. Final section discusses the conclusion and managerial implications.

2.0 Literature review

2.01 Relationship marketing

The express motivation for business is to acquire and retain customers. Therefore, relationship marketing is an important marketing strategy firms can use to acquire and retain customers, and sustain loyalty. Although there is no one best definition of relationship marketing, a number of definitions have graced the marketing literature (e.g., Berry, 1983; Gummesson, 1994 & 1997; Sheth, 1994; Morgan and Hunt, 1994; Sheth and Parvatiyar, 1995; Gronroos, 1996; Aijo, 1996; Panda, 2003; Hunt et al., 2006). Sheth and Parvatiyar (2000, p. 9) assert that relationship marketing "is the ongoing process of engaging in cooperative and collaborative activities and programs with immediate and end-user customers to create or enhance mutual economic value at reduced cost."

Morgan and Hunt (1994, p. 22) contend that relationship marketing is a process where all marketing activities are directed at establishing, developing, and maintaining successful long-term relational exchanges. Finally, it is the process of "attracting, maintaining, and—in multi-service organizations—enhancing customer relationships" (Berry, 1983, p. 25). Relationship marketing is consist of three important elements, namely planning and controlling of customer satisfaction, building and maintaining customer loyalty, and customer value management (Doyle, 2002). Any firm that adopts purposeful relationship marketing tactics will achieve customer satisfaction, customer loyalty, customer retention, and competitive advantage.

Customer satisfaction is one of the important results of purposeful marketing activity (Mick and Fournier, 1999; Spreng et al, 1996; Surprenant and Churchill). Forward thinking firms leverage relationship marketing to develop and cultivate long-term mutual and beneficial customer relationships (Hunt et al. 2006; Garbarino and Johnson, 1999; Barnes, 1997; Morgan and Hunt; 1994 Ganesan, 1994; Dwer et al. 1987).

Customer satisfaction encompasses overall consumer fulfillment and experience about a firm's product or service (Oliver 1997, 1999). It is one of the important determinants of long-term customer relationship (Oliver, 1980; Zeithaml et al., 1996; Athanassopoulos et al., 2001; Fornel, 1992; Levesque and McDougall, 1996). Based on the preceding, Hog and Amin (2010) suggest that enhancing customer satisfaction should be a key relationship marketing strategy for Islamic banks to maintain a long-term relationship with their customers. Customer loyalty entails customer's commitment to a repeat business that can lead to enhanced competitive advantage and financial performance in the long-term (Chu, 2009; Oliver, 1997; Hayes, 2008).

2.02 Relationship marketing in banking sector

A number of authors (e.g., Aldlaigan and Buttle, 2005; Pont and McQuilken, 2005; Baumann et al., 2005; Carson et al., 2004; Yavas et al, 2004; Farquhar, 2004; O'Loughlin et al., 2004; Lang and Colgate, 2003; Madill, et al., 2002; Jamal and Naser, 2002; Colgate and Hedge, 2001; Ennew and Binks, 1999; Barnes and Howlett, 1998; Paulin et al., 1998; Bloemer et al., 1998; Clark, 1997; Ketner, 1995) have investigated the imperatives of relationship marketing in the financial/banking sector. Relationship marketing is a new paradigm shift in marketing theory and practice (Gronroos, 1994) use in a number of industries such as in services to acquire and retain customers and most importantly to build and maintain customer relationship and loyalty. The banking industry traditionally offers products and services that are simply commodities. Essentially, there are little or no differentiations in products and services banks offer to their customers.

However, where there is no differentiation, there is no competition. Panda (2003) asserts that because most of the core products and services banks offer to customers are commodities, it is difficult for them to compete. To differentiate their products and services, build long-term relationships, and gain competitive edge banks must embrace customer relationship marketing strategy. Thus, these needs can lead to growth in the implementation of relationship marketing in banks and in financial services (Heffernan, 2010; Ennew and Bink, 2006; Musa, 2009; 2006; Modirghomi and Sarshar, 2005; Moriarty, 2003; Juhl, 2002; Abratt and Russel, 2000; Alexander and Colgate, 2000; Hocker and Wilmott, 1999). Sharpe (2007) emphasize that long-term relationship is an important source of marketing strategy firms can deploy to ward of competition and sustain profitability margins in the long run.

The banking sector can also use a relationship banking orientation strategy to create unique differentiation relative to rivals (Boot and Thakor, 2000). Moriarty (2003, p. 4) posits that relationship banking "...includes an acknowledge perception of mutual interdependence between and the customer [where] both parties is often based on mutual trust and openness, shared objectives [or vision], and a commitment to doing business with each other on long-term basis." Ratnayake (n. d) attests that "when a bank claims to be practicing relationship marketing, it signifies that they have undertaken an organization wide strategy to manage and nurture their interaction with [customers] and sales prospects."

Dibb and Meadows (2001) assert for a relationship marketing strategy to be successful a number of issues must be tackled, e.g., the role of sales-force and their training in relationship development must be taken into account, align the bank's organization structure to fit the decentralized structure required in relationship strategy. In today's hypercompetitive environment decision makers must understand the various aspects of relationship marketing as they are imperative for the effective relationship development between the firm and the customer (Ward and Dagger, 2007) and for implementing effective relationship marketing strategies (El Hinnawi, 2011). Kazi (2011) points out that an increase in a retail bank's quality service resulted in an increased customer loyalty and retention. Both product and service quality are essential for customer satisfaction and retention. Jamal and Nasser (2002) study of retail banking sector in UAE found that service quality dimensions are important drivers for customer satisfaction, where core and relational dimensions of service quality are causal antecedents of customer satisfaction.

3.0 Research methodology

The proposed AHP allows decision-makers to model a complex problem in a hierarchical structure, showing the relationships of the overall goal, criteria (objectives), and alternatives. Due to its usefulness, the AHP has been widely used in research. Some studies that have used AHP include supply chain management (e.g., Gaudesi and Borghesi, 2006; Enyinda et al., 2010; Enyinda et al., 2013) and marketing (e.g., Dyer and Forman, 1992; Enyinda, et al., 2014).

3.01 Sensitivity analysis

Sensitivity analysis (SA) is a means of investigating the impact of reasonable changes in base-case assumptions (Eschenbach, 1992) or an approach which allows decision makers to explore the impact on the optimal decision(s) of potential changes in any of the problem variables (Trueman, 1974). Some of the uses of SA include determining the impact on the ranking of alternatives of changes in various model assumptions, making better decisions, deciding which data estimates should be refined before making a decision, and enabling management to focus attention on the most critical elements during decision implementation (Kirkwood, 1997; Eschenbach, 1992). Because of SA's importance in decision-making, it has applied in a number of areas including the pharmaceuticals, medicine, civil engineering, political science and computer science (Steenland and Greenland, 2004; Blake et al., 1988; Castillo et al., 2006).

In discussing the imperatives of subjecting models to SA, Arnoff and Netzorg (1965) emphasized "the use of operations research is especially important and advantageous in that ... one can assess the sensitivity (response) of the system to a wide variety of conditions – without requiring either the time, expense, or risks associated with experimenting with system itself. [Thus,] hidden relationship can be brought to light and brought to bear upon decisions and control of activity."

3.02 Application of AHP to relationship marketing in Islamic banks

The following steps are used. First, define an unstructured problem and determine the overall goal. According to Simon (1960), the methodology of decision-making process encompasses identifying the problem, generating and evaluating alternatives, designing, and obtaining actionable intelligence. Second, build the hierarchy from the top through the intermediate levels (criteria on which subsequent levels depend on) to the lowest level contains the list of alternatives.

The overall goal of the focal firm is in the first level of the hierarchy, shown in Figure 01. We used a multi-criteria analysis by way of a three-level AHP.

Level 1 contains the ultimate goal the decision maker intends to achieve – determinants of relationship marketing success. Level 2 has the relationship marketing factors (the major decision objectives or criteria) derived from the literature reviewed. They are as follows: 1. Customer loyalty (CL) – the possibility the customer will provide the firm with an advantage or benefits in the exchange process because of their relational bonds. 2) Financial performance (FP) – comes when a firm or a bank leverages purposeful relationship-based strategies. 3) Customer satisfaction (CS) – entails customer's affective state toward a relationship. 4) Competitive advantage (CA) – competitive position gained due to customer satisfaction and loyalty, relationship commitment and trust, relationship quality, and service quality (the quality of relational bonds that exist between the customer and the bank exchange). 6) Decreased uncertainty (DU) – exists when there is transparency in information sharing between the customer and the bank. 7) Decreased switching - shifting of goodwill to rival banks tends to decline when the customer is happy with the quality of the relationship and service, commitment and trust.

Level 3 represents the factors accounting for relationship marketing success (Hunt et al., 2002), referred to as alternative course of actions or options, including Resource-Based (RESB): any tangible or intangible resources available to the bank that helps it to provide or offer products or services that have value for customers.

Figure 01: The decision hierarchy for relationship marketing

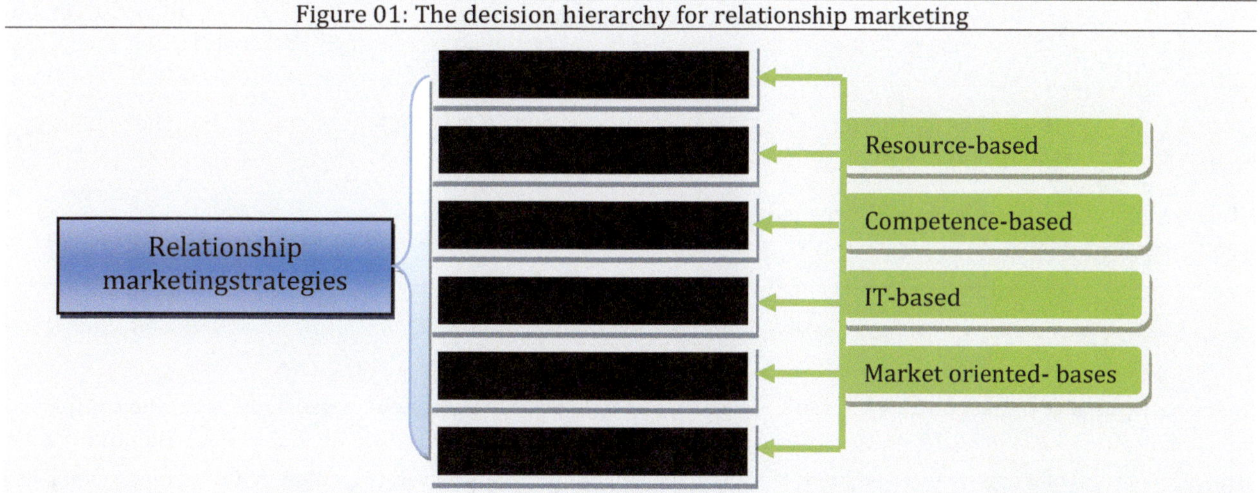

Differences in the performance of banks can be viewed as being determined mainly by differences in the types of resources they own or have access to (e.g., talents, managerial know how, information technology). Relational-Based (RELB): consists of trust, commitment, cooperation, keeping promises, shared values, communication, an effective conflict handling, and experience. Competence-Based (COMB): the ability a bank possesses to sustain the coordinated use of assets in a manner that enables it to achieve its goals. Competences are associated with a bank's sustainable competitive advantages.

A bank developing a customer-relating competency that makes customer retention a priority and gives employees, as an overall willingness to treat customers differently, wide latitude to satisfy them. It processes for personalizing product or service offerings, and its incentives for building relationships. IT-Based (ITBA): A well integrated information and communication infrastructures as well as CRM programs to manage efficiently and effectively customer relationships. Marketing Offering-Based (MAOB): a bank's blends of tangible and intangible attributes offered. They may include product or service quality, innovativeness, and customization.

Third, construct a set of pair-wise comparison matrices for each of the lower levels. The pair-wise comparison is made such that the attribute in row i ($i = 1, 2, 3, 4...n$) is ranked relative to each of the attributes represented by n columns. The pair-wise comparisons are done in terms of which element dominates another (i.e. based on the relative importance of each elements). The integer values of 1 to 9 captures the expert's judgments. Where $a_{ij}= 1$ means that i and j are equally important; $a_{ij}= 3$ signifies that i is moderately more important than j; $a_{ij} = 5$ suggests that i is strongly more important than j; $a_{ij} = 7$ indicates that i is very strongly more important than j; $a_{ij} = 9$ signifies that i is extremely more important than j.

3.02 Establishment of pair-wise comparison matrix A

The pair-wise comparisons are accomplished in terms of which element dominates or influences the order. To quantify the opinions that can be represented in an *n-by-n* matrix as follows:

$$A=[a_{ij}]=w_i/w_j=\begin{bmatrix} w_1/w_2 & w_1/w_2 & \cdots & w_1/w_n \\ w_2/w_1 & w_2/w_2 & \cdots & w_2/w_n \\ \cdot & \cdot & \cdot & \cdot \\ \cdot & \cdot & \cdot & \cdot \\ \cdot & \cdot & \cdot & \cdot \\ w_n/w_1 & w_n/w_2 & \cdots & w_n/w_n \end{bmatrix} \quad \text{Eq. (01)}$$

3.03 Eigenvalue and eigenvector

Saaty (1990) recommended that the maximum eigenvalue, λ_{max}, can be determined as

$$\lambda_{max} = \sum_{j=1}^{n} a_{ij} \; W_j/W_i. \quad \text{Eq. (02)}$$

Where λ_{max} is the principal or maximum eigenvalue of positive real values in judgment matrix, W_j is the weight of jth factor, and W_i is the weight of ith factor.

If A represents consistency matrix, eigenvector X can be determined as

$$(A - \lambda_{max}I)X = 0 \quad \text{Eq. (03)}$$

3.04 Consistency test

Consistency index (CI) and consistency ratio (CR) areused to check for consistency associated with the comparison matrix. A matrix is assumed to be consistent if and only if $a_{ij} * a_{jk} = a_{jk} \forall_{i\,jk}$ (for all $i, j,$ *and* k). When a positive reciprocal matrix of order n is consistent, the principal eigenvalue possesses the value n. Conversely, when it is inconsistent, the principal eigenvalue is greater than n and its difference will serve as a measure of CI. Therefore, to ascertain that the priority of elements is consistent, the maximum eigenvector or relative weights/λ_{max} can be determined. Specifically, CI for each matrix order n is determined by using Eq. (03):

$CI = (\lambda_{max} - n)/n - 1.$ Eq. (04)

Where n is the matrix size or the number of items to be compared in the matrix. Based on (3), the consistency ratio (CR) can be determined as:

$CR = CI/RI = [(\lambda_{max} - n)/n - 1]/RI.$ Eq. (05)

Where RI represents average consistency index over a number of random entries of same order reciprocal matrices shown in Table 1. The CR is acceptable, if its value is less than or equal to 0.10. If it is greater than 0.10, the judgment matrix will be considered inconsistent. To rectify a judgment matrix that is inconsistent, decision-makers' judgments should be reviewed and improved.

Table 01: Average RI for different numbers of n

N	2	3	4	5	6	7	8	9	10
RI	0.00	0.58	0.90	1.12	1.24	1.32	1.41	1.45	1.49

3.05 Synthesized matrix

For the priorities of the alternative a_i, the priorities then are aggregated as follows:

$P(a_i) = \sum_k w_k P_k(a_i).$ Eq. (06)

Where w_k is the local priority of the element k and $P_k(a_i)$ is the priority of alternative a_i with respect to element k of the upper level.

4.0 The case study and data collection

The Islamic banks within the UAE are the interest of this paper. We used a case study methodology to achieve an in depth knowledge of the determinants of Bank relationship marketing success in Islamic Banks. Yin (1994) popularized the use of case study methodology. According to Oke and Gopalakrishnan (2009), a case study is also relevant "where existing knowledge is limited because it generates in-depth contextual information which may result in a superior level of understanding."

The data collection period spanned February 2013 – March 2013. We assembled the data through literature review and validated by interviews with the focal Islamic banks to determine customer relationship marketing tactics. Essentially, we used the questionnaire to collect data in order to evaluate the order of preference associated with determinants of relationship marketing success. Specifically, the developed questionnaire from the hierarchy tree assisted in facilitating pair-wise comparisons between all the major objectives and the alternatives at each level in the hierarchy using Saaty's 1-9 scale.

Table 02: Pair-wise comparison matrix for the six relationship marketing objectives

	CL	FP	CS	CA	DS	DU	Priority
Customer loyalty (CL)	1	2	1	3	2	2	0.2780
Financial performance (FP)	1/2	1	1	1/2	2	2	0.1486
Customer satisfaction (CS)	1	1	1	1	2	2	0.1875
Competitive advantage (CA)	1/3	2	1	1	3	3	0.2097
switching (DS)	1/2	½	1/2	1/3	1	1	0.0882
Decreased uncertainty (DU)	1/2	½	1/2	1/3	1	1	0.0882

Finally, banks' relationship managers of the focal firms responded to several pair-wise comparisons with respect to the goal. We then used the survey questionnaire results as input for the AHP. It took 15 judgments (i.e., (6(6-1)/2) to complete the pair-wise comparisons associated with the major objectives in Table 02, while it took 10 judgments (i.e., 5(5-1)/2) to complete the pair-wise comparisons of the alternative course of actions reported in Table 03.

The objective priorities in the last columns of Tables 02-03 can be determined either automatically (i.e., using the AHP Expert Choice Software 11.5) or manually using the following steps. 1) Add the elements in each column and divide each element of the matrix by its column total. 2) Synthesize the pair-wise comparison matrix in Table 02. 3) Determine the priority vector for each relationship marketing factors. 4) Determine the consistency ratio. 5) Determine λ_{max}. 6) Determine the consistency index (CI). 7) Choose an appropriate value of the random consistency ratio in Table 01. 7) Check the consistency of the pair-wise comparison matrix to check whether the decision makers' comparisons are consistent or not.

Table 03: Pair-wise comparison matrix for the five alternative course of actions						
	RESB	RELB	COMB	ITBA	MAOB	Priority
Resource-based (RESB)	1	1/5	1	1	1/2	0.1176
Relational-based (RELB)	5	1	5	5	5	0.4476
Competence-based (COMB)	1	1	1	1	1/2	0.1123
IT-based (ITBA)	1	1/5	1	1	1/2	0.0986
Marketing offering-based (MAOB)	2	1/5	2	2	1	0.2239

5.0 Empirical results and discussion

The data were analyzed utilizing Expert Choice Software, an application that implements the AHP-based SA algorithms. Table 04 depicts the priority scores associated with the respect to the relationship marketing objectives. Relationship managers consider customer loyalty (0.2780) as the most important, followed by competitive advantage (0.2097), customer satisfaction (0.1875), and financial performance (0.1486), respectively.

Table 04 also reports the overall priority scores of the alternative course of actions that drive relationship marketing success.

With respect to the overall priority scores of the alternatives, relational-based is the most preferred option, followed by marketing offering-based, resource-based, and competence-based, respectively. That is relational-based (1) > marketing offering-based (2) > resource-based (3) > competence-based (4) > information technology-based. Thus, relational-based alternative is judge as the overall best strategic course of action that drives relationship marketing success.

Table 04: Overall priority scores								
	CL	FP	CS	CA	DS	DU	Priority	Rank
	0.2780	0.1486	0.1875	0.2097	0.0882	0.0882		
RESB	0.0940	0.0996	0.0864	0.1068	0.1096	0.2730	0.1176	3
RELB	0.5520	0.3674	0.5493	0.4142	0.3734	0.3678	0.4476	1
COMB	0.0940	0.1093	0.0922	0.1400	0.1383	0.1000	0.1123	4
ITBA	0.0940	0.1194	0.0922	0.1068	0.0967	0.6665	0.0986	5
MAOB	0.1661	0.3043	0.1799	0.2343	0.2820	0.1927	0.2239	2
C.I	0.01	0.01	0.02	0.04	0.02	0.04		

5.01 AHP-based sensitivity analysis

If the decision makers such as the customer relationship managers believe that a criterion might be more or less important than originally indicated, that criterion's bar can be dragged to the right (increase) or left (decrease) to observe the impact on the ranking of the alternatives.

Therefore, the objective of SA in this paper is to determine how small changes (perturbation) in input parameters, such as the four most important relationship marketing tactics (i.e., customer loyalty, competitive advantage, customer satisfaction, and financial performance) will influence the ranking of the alternative course of actions (i.e., resource, relational, competence, information technology, and marketing offering-based factors.

Figure 2 shows the performance SA of the alternative priorities with respect to the four most important criteria. The left vertical axis indicates the major objective's priorities with respect to goal, while the right vertical axis shows the priorities of the relationship marketing alternatives.

A series of SA was performed using AHP-based Expert Choice Software to investigate the impact of changing the priority of the major objectives on the ranking of the alternative course of actions (factors) accounting for relationship marketing success. Chang et al (2007) posit "... sensitivity analysis can be performed based on scenarios that reflect alternative future developments or different views on the relative importance of the criteria."

Figure 02: Original performance sensitivity analysis graph

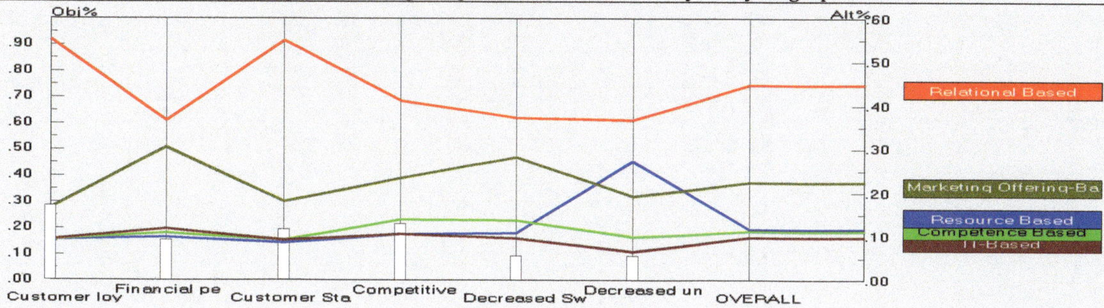

Objectives Names

Customer loy	Customer loyalty
Financial pe	Financial performance
Customer Sta	Customer Statisfaction
Competitive	Competitive Advantage
Decreased Sw	Decreased Switching
Decreased un	Decreased uncertainty

Alternatives Names

Resource Bas	Resource Based
Relational B	Relational Based
Competence B	Competence Based
IT-Based	IT-Based
Marketing Of	Marketing Offering-Based

Figure 02 reports the original performance sensitivity analysis. It shows the major relationship marketing objectives and the associated ranking of the alternatives course of actions (relational-based > marketing offering-based > resource-based > competence-based> information technology-based.

Figures 03-06 show the customer loyalty (27.8%), competitive advantage (21%), customer satisfaction (18.7%), and financial performance (14.9) SA, respectively. For example, increasing the customer loyalty priority by 10% from 27.8% to 36% in Figure 03 did not change the ranking of the alternative course of actions. Thus, the original ranking after the small changes remained stable or robust). Similarly, increasing the competitive advantage (Figure 04), customer satisfaction (Figure 05), and financial performance (Figure 06) by 10%, respectively did not change the original ranking of the alternatives. Essentially, each scenario is stable or robust.

Figure 03. Performance SA graph for customer loyalty

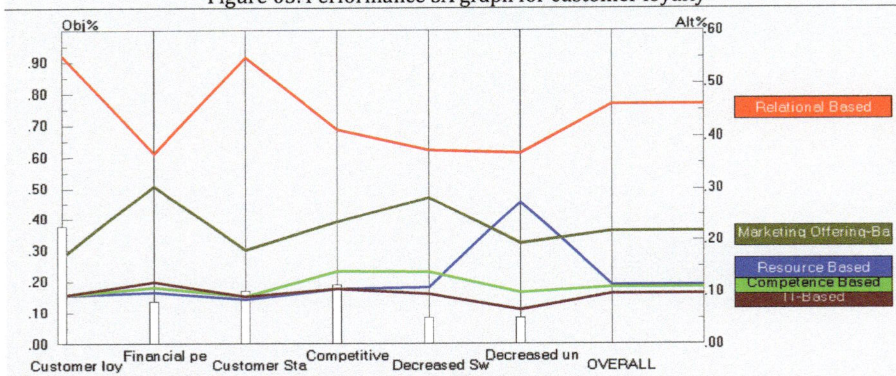

Figure 04. Performance SA graph for competitive advantage

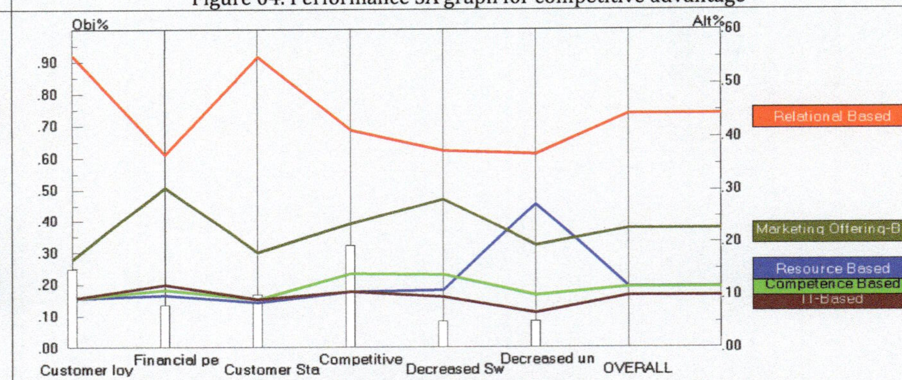

Figure 05. Performance SA graph for customer satisfaction

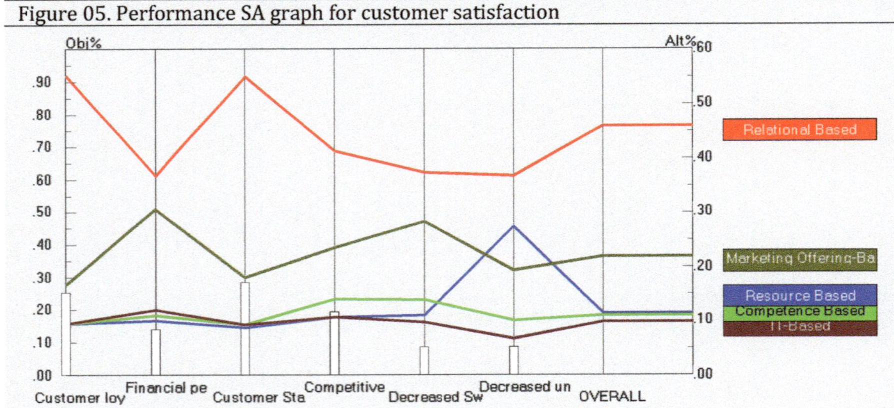

Figure 06. Performance SA graph for financial performance

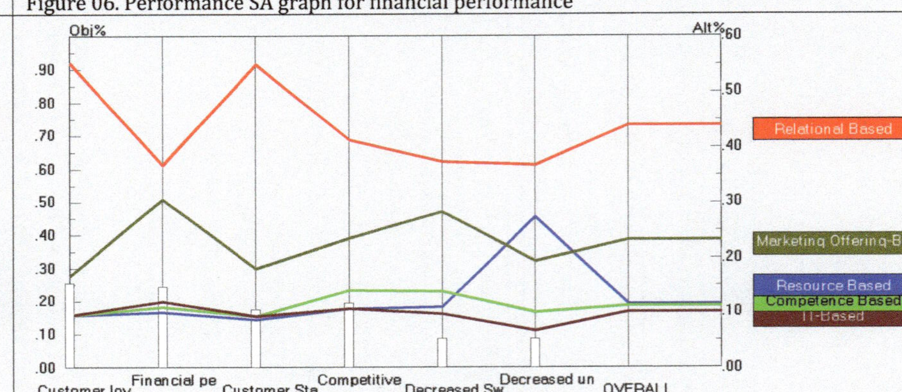

Based on the entire performance SA, the overall priority of the factors (alternative course of actions) accounting for relationship marketing success is robust or stable to changes in the importance of all the attributes. However, if the ranking becomes highly sensitive to small perturbation in the priorities of the objectives, a review of the priorities will be recommended.

6.0 Conclusion and policy implications

Given that today's conventional banks are opening up Islamic windows, Islamic banks must focus significant attention on relationship marketing in order to retain and attract prospective customers. Hence, Islamic banks that ignore customer relationship marketing implementation do so at their peril. Islamic banks must become more consumer-centric if they have to survive and prosper. Retaining existing customers is imperative because to acquire new customers is costly and inefficient. Arguably, a purposeful marketing activity that results in customer satisfaction will in turn enhance a bank's competitive advantage and financial performance in an already crowed industry. To thrive and prosper, Islamic banks must focus their efforts in attracting and maintaining loyal customer base through the purposeful use of customer relationship marketing strategies. Furthermore, to gain competitive advantage and enhance financial performance in today's competitive banking environment, it is more than ever vital for Islamic banks to offer products and services that can meet and exceed customer value expectations and in turn lead to customer satisfaction and loyalty.

The use of AHP methodology supported the performance sensitivity analysis of the banks' major objectives. For Islamic banks to prosper, they must focus on customer-centric strategy, relationship building in particular. Relationship building is an important strategy that can lead to achieving customer loyalty, customer satisfaction, competitive advantage, and financial performance. Based on the performance SA for customer loyalty, customer satisfaction, competitive advantage, and financial performance respectively, the overall priority of the factors (alternative course of actions) accounting for relationship marketing success is robust or stable to changes in the importance of all the attributes. That is, relational-based > marketing offering-based > resource-based > competence-based > information technology-based. The robustness of relational-based and marketing offering-based are particularly important factors for attaining relationship marketing success. However, if the ranking becomes highly sensitive to small perturbation in the priorities of the objectives, a review of the priorities will become necessary.

References

Abratt, R. and Russell, J. 2000. Relationship marketing in private banking in South Africa.The International Journal of Bank Marketing, 17(1): 5-19.

Aijo, T. S. 1996. The theoretical and philosophical underpinnings of relationship marketing: environmental factors behind the changing marketing paradigm. European Journal of Marketing, 30(2): 8-18.

Aldlaigan, A. and Buttle, F. 2005. Beyond satisfaction: customer attachment to retail banks. International Journal of Bank Marketing, 23(4): 349-359.

Ali, M. 1994. Marketing Strategy for Islamic Banks. Paper Presented at the 1st Global Convention on Retail Financial Services "Visions of the 21st Century" 7-11 November, London.

Anthanassopoulos, A., Gounaris, S. and Sathakopoulos, V. 2001. Behavioral responses to customer satisfaction: an empirical study, European. Journal of Marketing, 35(5/6): 687-707.

Alexander, N. and Colgate, M. 2000. Retail financial services: From transactions to relationship marketing. Journal of Retailing, 73(1): 15 - 37.

Barnes, J. G. 1997. Closeness, strength and satisfaction: examining the nature of relationships between providers of financial services and their retail customers. Psychology and Marketing, 14: 765-90.

Baumann, C., Burton, S. and Elliott, G. 2005.Determinants of customer loyalty and share of wallet in retail banking. Journal of Financial Services Marketing, 9(3): 231-248.

Berry, L. L. 1983. Relationship marketing, in Berry, L. L., Shostack, and G. L. Upah, G. D. (Eds), Emerging Perspectives on Services Marketing. American Marketing Association, Chicago, IL, 25-8.

Berry, L. L. and Parasuraman, A. 1991.Marketing services.The Free Press, New York, NY.

Bloemer, J., Ruyter, K. D., and Peeters, P. 1998. Investigating drivers of bank loyalty: the complex relationships between image, service quality satisfaction. International Journal of Bank Marketing, 16(7): 276-286.

Boot, J.M. and Thakor, J.G. 2000.The importance of customer satisfaction in explaining brand and dealer loyalty.Journal of Marketing Management, 8: 351-64.

Chu, K. M. 2009. The construction model of customer trust, perceived value and customer loyalty. Journal of American Academy Business, Cambridge, 14(2): 98-103.

Colgate, M. and Hedge, R. 2001.An investigation into the switching process in retail banking services. International Journal of Bank Marketing, 19(5): 201-212.

Doyle, F. 2002. Developing buyer-seller relationships. Journal of Marketing, Vol. 51 No 1, pp. 11-27.

Dwyer, R., Schurr, P. H. and Oh, S. 1987. Developing buyer – seller relationship, Journal of Marketing, 51(2): 11-27.

El Hinnawi, R. S. 2011. The impact of relationship marketing underpinnings on customer's Loyalty: Case Study – Bank of Palestine. MS Degree Thesis, The Islamic University-Gaza.

Ennew, C.T. and Binks, M.R. 1996. Good and bad customers: the benefits of participating in the banking relationship. International Journal of Bank Marketing, 14(2): 5-13.

Ennew, C. T. and Bink, M. R. 2006. Impact of participative service relationships on quality, satisfaction and retention: An exploratory study. Journal of business research, 46(2): 121-132.
Enyinda, C. I.,Ogbuehi, A. O. and Hamouri, S.2014.Pharmaceutical Relationship Marketing Tactics and the Impact of Social Media: An Analytic Hierarchy Process and Sensitivity Analysis. International Journal of Strategic Management (forthcoming).
Enyinda, C. I., Mbah, C. H., and Ogbuehi, A. January/February 2010. An Empirical Analysis of Risk Mitigation in the Pharmaceutical Industry Supply Chain: A Developing Country Perspective." Thunderbird International Business Review, 52(1): 45-54.
Enyinda, C. I., Gebremikael, F. and Backhar, K. 2013.Decision Support Model for Managing Disruptive Influences in Global Supply Chain Operations: A Sensitivity Analysis Insight. In Proceedings of the Decision Sciences Institute 44th Conference, Baltimore, MD, USA, November 16-19.
Farquhar, J.D. 2004. Customer retention in retail financial services: an employee perspective. International Journal of Bank Marketing, 22(2): 86-99.
Fornell, C. 1992. A national customer satisfaction barometer: the Swedish experience. Journal of Marketing, 56: 6-21.
Hassan, A. Chachi, A., and Latiff, S. A. 2008.Islamic marketing ethics and its impact on customer satisfaction in the Islamic banking industry.J.KAU: Islamic Econ., 21(1): 23-40.
Hayes B. E. 2008.The true test of loyalty. Quality Progress, 41(6): 20- 26
Heffernan, Y. 2010. Relationship marketing: The impact of emotional intelligence and trust on bank performance. Journal of the Academy of Marketing Science, 29: 3-13.
Hocker, R. and Wilmott, J. 1999.Relationship marketing in private banking in South Africa. International Journal of Bank Marketing, 17(1): 5-19.
Hog, M. Z. and Amin, M. September 2010. The role of customer satisfaction to enhance customer loyalty. African Journal of Business Management, 4(12): 2385-2392.
Hussnain, S. A. November 2011. What is Islamic marketing? Global Journal of Management and Business Research, 11(11): Online ISSN: 2249-4588 & Print ISSN: 0975-5853.
Hunt, S. D., Lambe, C. J. and Wittmann, C. M. 2002. A Theory and Model of Business Alliance Success. Journal of Relationship Marketing, 1(1):17-35.
Hunt, S. D., Arnett, D. B., and Madhavaram, S. 2006. The Explanatory Foundations of Relationship Marketing Theory. Journal of Business and Industrial Marketing, 21(2): 72-87.
Ganesan, S. 1994. Determinants of long term orientation in buyer-seller relationship. Journal of Marketing, 58:1-19.
Garbarino, E. and Johnson, M. S. 1999. The different roles of satisfaction, trust and commitment in customer relationships.Journal of Marketing, 63: 70-87.
Grönroos, C. 1994. From marketing mix to relationship marketing: Towards a paradigm shift in marketing. Management Decision, 32(2): 4–20.
Grönroos, C. 1997. Value-driven relational marketing: From products to resources and competencies. Journal of Marketing Management, 13(4): 407–419.
Gummesson, E. 1994.Making relationship marketing operational. International Journal of Service Industry Management, 5(5): 5-20.
Gummession, E. 1997. Relationship marketing as a paradigm shift: some conclusions from the 30 R approach. Management Decision, 35(4): 267-272. http://www.shahfoundationbd.org/hannan/article10.html. Islamic Banking: Problems and Prospects
Jamal A. and Naser, K. 2002. Customer satisfaction and retail banking: an assessment of some of the key antecedents of customer satisfaction in retail banking. International Journal of Bank Marketing, 20(4): 146-160.
Juhl, B. 2002. Relationship banking and competitive advantage: Evidence from the U.S. and Germany. California Management Review, 37(4): 45-72.
Kazi, O. S. 2011. The drivers of customer loyalty to retail banks: An empirical study in Bangladesh. Industrial Engineering Letters. 1(1): ISSN 2224-6096 (print) ISSN 2225-0581.
Keltner, B. 1995. Relationship Banking and Competitive Advantage: Evidence from the U.S. and Germany. California Management Review, 37(4): 45-72.
Lang, B. and Colgate M. 2003.Relationship Quality, On-line Banking and the Information Technology Gap. International Journal of Bank Marketing, 21(1): 29-37.
Levesque, T. and McDougall, G.H.G. 1996.Determinants of customer satisfaction in retail banking. International Journal of Bank Marketing, 14(7): 12-20.
Madill, J.J., Feeney, L., Riding, A. and Haines, G.H.J. 2002. Determinants of SME owners' satisfaction with their banking relationships: a Canadian study. International Journal of Bank Marketing, 20(2): 86-98.
Mick, D. and Fournier, S. 1999.Rediscovering satisfaction. Journal of Marketing, 63(4): 5-23.
Morgan, R. and Hunt, S. D. 1994. The commitment–trust theory of relationship marketing. Journal of Marketing, 58(3): 20-38.
Modirghomi, D. and Sarshar, S. 2005. Balancing transaction and relationship marketing in retail banking. Journal of Marketing Management, 20(3/4): 431-455.
Moriarty, R. 2003. The management of corporate banking relationships. Sloan Management Review, 24: 3 – 15.

Musa, N. 2009.The Impact of relationship marketing on customer's loyalty in the banking sector in Malaysia. Journal of Marketing, 58: 111-124.

Ndubisi, N. O. 2004. Understanding the salience of cultural dimensions on relationship marketing, its underpinnings and aftermaths.Cross Cultural Management, 11(3): 70–89.

Ndubisi, N. O. 2007. Relationship marketing and customer loyalty.Marketing Intelligence and Planning, 25(1): 98-106.

Oliver, R. L. 1980. A cognitive model of the antecedent and consequences of satisfaction decisions. Journal of Marketing, 17(10): 460-469.

Oliver, R. L. 1997. Satisfaction: A behavioral perspective on the consumer. New York: McGraw Hill.

Oliver, R. L. 1999. When consumer loyalty? Journal of Marketing, 63:33-44.

O'Loughlin, D., Szmigin, I. and Turnbull, P. 2004. From Relationships to Experiences in Retail Financial Services. International Journal of Bank Marketing, 22(7): 522-539.

Panda, A. 2003.Defining Relationship Marketing: An International Perspective. Management Decision, 35(4): 319-21.

Paulin, M., Perrien, J., Ferguson, R.J., Salazar, A.M.A. and Seruya, L.M. 1998. Relational norms and client retention: external effectiveness of commercial banking in Canada and Mexico. International Journal of Bank Marketing, 16(1): 24-31.

Pont, M. and McQuilken, L. 2005. An empirical investigation of customer satisfaction and loyalty across two divergent bank segments. Journal of Financial Services Marketing, 9(4): 344-359.

Ratnayake, D. n. d. Importance of relationship marketing to the banking industry. Retrieved from http://www.cimaglobal.com/Thought-leadership/Newsletters/Regional/The-CIMA-Edge-South-Asia-and-Middle-East/20111/January--February-2011/Relationship-marketing-/

Sharpe, J. 2007. The effects of organizational differences and trust on the effectiveness of selling partner relationships. Journal of Marketing, 61(1): 3–22.

Sheth, J. N. 1994. The domain of relationship marketing. The 2nd Research Conference on Relationship Marketing, Emory University, Atlanta, GA, June 9-11.

Sheth, J. N. and Parvatiyar, A. 1995. The evolution of relationship marketing. International Business Review, 4(4): 397–418.

Sheth, J. N. and Parvatiyar, A. 2000. Handbook of relationship marketing. Thousand Oaks, California: Sage Publications, Inc.

Spreng, R. A., Mackenzie, S. B. and Olshavsky, R. W. July 1996. A re-examination of the determinants of consumer satisfaction.Journal of Marketing, 60(3): 15-32.

Surprenant, C. and Churchill, G. 1982. An investigation into the determinants of customer Satisfaction. Journal of Marketing Research, 19(4): 491-504.

Yavas, U., Benkenstein, M. and Sthuldreier, U. 2004. Relationships between service quality and behavioral outcomes: A study of private bank customers in Germany. International Journal of Bank Marketing, 22(2): 144-157.

Zeithaml, V. A; Berry, L. L., Parasuraman, A. 1996.The behavioural consequences of service quality. Journal of Marketing, 60(2):31-46.

9

Bank failures and mergers in Turkey: 1992-2014

Meral Varish Kiefer[a b*]

[a] Department of Economics, Cornell University, Ithaca, NY 14850, US.
[b] Faculty of Management, Sabanci University, Istanbul, Turkey
*Corresponding author's email: meral999@aol.com

HIGHLIGHTS:

1. This study examines the process of bank failures and mergers and acquisitions in Turkey.
2. The study finds that pre-crisis reforms in Turkish banking regulation were effective.
3. In Turkey bank's default probabilities are declining nonlinearly with capitalization for the sample dataset.
4. A semi-parametric survival model is applied to Turkish banking data to confirm the findings.

Article History

Keywords:
Bank crisis;
Bank policy making;
Capitalization;
Duration model;
Mergers & acquisitions (M&A).

ABSTRACT

The Turkish banking system went through a period of crisis in 1999-2001. As a result, reforms were instituted and the banking system was consolidated. The system was then only mildly affected by the global crisis in 2008. This study examines the process of bank failures and mergers and acquisitions during this period in Turkey. A proportional hazard is used to determine the bank-specific accounting ratios that predict bank defaults and mergers and acquisitions in Turkey. The focus is on capitalization, a key regulatory tool. Capitalization decreases the failure rate, as expected, and does so at a decreasing rate. This is consistent with regulatory policy that focuses on capitalization. For banks at risk, income is a good short-run predictor of default. The results for mergers and acquisitions imply that under-capitalized banks are more likely to be acquired. Finally, the implied "frontier" for the trade-off between return and equity and default risk is calculated.

1.0 Introduction

The world of financial institutions is changing rapidly as new risk management techniques are developed and as supervisors worldwide manage the transition to the Basel II and Basel III supervisory standards and subsequent revisions. In this paper, we build an econometric bank default prediction model based on bank specific financial ratios during 1992-2014. A duration model is used to determine the financial ratios that are associated with bank failures and mergers in the Turkish financial markets.

We examine the banking system during the pre-crisis period, crises and subsequent recovery period with emphasis on the implications of banking reforms on the recovery. The time to bank failure event is investigated by analyzing bank indicators in determining the process of bank defaults and mergers. We also examine the impact of bank policy to determine the likelihood with which banks exited through failure, merger, or acquisition under the SDIF[1] banks during 1992-2014. Using a comprehensive data set, we apply a duration

[1] The Turkish analog of the FDIC in the US.

model to link bank-specific data with each bank's risk of failure. While there were 68 private commercial banks in 1999, this number decreased to 18 commercial banks as the results of failures or mergers and acquisitions by 2003. SDIF took over 19 banks, 12 banks merged, 5 banks sold, 3 banks' license withdrew and 3 banks under legal procedure and 9 banks were under SDIF at the end of 2003. As of February 2014, there are 48 banks in total; 31 commercial banks, 13 investment banks and 4 participation banks.[2]

Our aim is to develop a model capable of identifying potential problem banks and vulnerabilities of the banking system, and which could be used by supervisory authorities to inform policy. Since banking crises can generate serious disruptions of economic activities, a main concern of policy makers and regulators is to ensure the safety and soundness of the banking system and prevent the occurrence of banking crises. The role of market discipline in ensuring financial stability is becoming so prominent that the New Basel Capital Accord developed by the Basel Committee on Banking Supervision in 2004. It has included market discipline as one of the three pillars. Although there is extensive literature on the forecasting of banking crises using balance sheet information of banks as well as macroeconomic indicators, studies on prediction of banks defaults using duration model are still novel.

Semi parametric methods are used in this study which allows measuring the effect of bank specific explanatory variables bank failure or default process with duration dependence effects. The capitalization ratio and profitability ratio are the major indicators for measuring banks performance. At the same time, the Basel Committee Accord (Basel Committee on Banking Supervision 2004) requires that banks and supervisory and regulatory authorities consider the capital ratio of the banks they regulate and impose minimum requirements.

A hazard rate and survival model provides a good statistical and econometric tool for banks default and failure prediction in emerging markets. Cox (1972), Kiefer (1988) and Lancaster (1990) developed the semi parametric proportional hazards model. Kiefer (1988) and Lancaster (1990) used duration models in labor economics. Lane & Ansley (1986), Weelock & Wilson (2000), and Whalen (1991) are applied duration models to detect financial distress in US banking sector. Barr & Siems (1994) studied the link between bank management quality and bank failures. Maggiolini (2005) used survival analysis to study the probability of defaults for the novo cooperative credit banks in Italy during 1990-2000. Andersen (2008) investigated the risk index for Norwegian banks. Gepp & Kumar (2008) used survival analysis to predict business failures. Arena (2008) investigated bank failures for Latin America and East Asia during the nineties. Mannasoo & Mayes (2009) searched macroeconomic and structural indicators to explain bank failures in Eastern Europe during 1995-2004.

There have been a few studies that investigated time to bank failure using duration models after financial distress in emerging countries. Gonzalez-Hermosillo et Al (1996, 1997) modeled bank failures after the Mexican crisis in 1994. Peek (1995) and Molina (2002) applied a proportional-hazard model to explain time to bank failure during the 1994-1995 Venezuelan banking crisis. Carree (2003) did a hazard rate analysis of Russian commercial banks in 1994-1997 crises. DeYoung (2003) applied hazard and logit on bank distressed in the US in 1980-1985. Canbas (2005) used parametric models with another parametric approach, principal component analysis.

Estrella & Peristiani (2000) and Van den Heuvel (2004) showed that capital ratio is a major risk indicator for financial firms during crises times. Gomez-Gonzalez & Kiefer (2009) found the capitalization ratio played a crucial role as a explanatory variable to detect the failure of financial institutions in Columbia's economy. Tatom & Houston (2011) applied to predict the bank failures by using the CAMEL method during 2006-2010 and 1988 and 1994. Avkiran & Cai (2012) used a DEA logit with a fully specified CAMELS besides financial market information as credit rating. They identified distressed banks up to two years ahead. Cole & White (2012) reported that large banks have been found less likely to fail than smaller banks. Fiordelisi & Mare (2013) focused on the contribution of efficiency to cooperative bank probability of default and the survival analysis.

We proceed by giving a brief overview of the banking sector and its dramatic reform in the three decades following the 1999 crisis in sections 2-4. Section 5 briefly reviews merger activity and the effects of foreign direct investment. Section 6 notes the effects of the Basel international capital accord. Section 7 introduces the data, the methods of analysis, summary statistics including survivor functions, and the final estimation results. Implications for the tradeoff between return on investment and default risk are presented in section 8. Section 9 concludes.

2.0 Banking crisis and restructuring

---

[2] Participation banks collect funds through participation accounts and make loans.

Turkey went through a banking crisis 1999-2001. This led to restructuring and a series of reforms which strengthened the system. As a result, Turkish banking was only mildly affected by the global financial crisis of 2008-2009. We review these reforms briefly.

2.01 Banking in the 1990s

For the banking sector in Turkey, the pre-crisis period was characterized by weak transparency, supervision and risk management. The Undersecretary of the Treasury (the Turkish Treasury) and the Central Bank of Turkey were the supervisory authorities under the 3182 Bank Act. The Saving Deposits and Insurance Fund (SDIF) was the Turkish version of the FDIC and took over problem bank management. There was a weak monitoring program and a watch list on problematic banks. Permanent examiners were appointed to evaluate closely the risk assessments of the potential risky banks. During this period, the supervisory authorities were not independent, well structured or encouraged by the governments to take serious steps against the problem banks.

In 1994, a minor banking crisis occurred as a result of macro economic instabilities and banking sector problems[3]. Bank runs happened due to the loss of confidence caused by a sharp depreciation of Turkish Lira versus US Dollars from 0.0144 in 1993 to 0.0384 in 1994. Banks continued to operate in a very risky environment and take high risks to make profits. Banks faced substantial risks in their interest rate exposures with maturity mismatches. They had problems in high foreign exchange position, liquidity and potential loan losses. For instance, within 1994, total loans and receivables to total assets fell by 28 percent and shareholders equity declined by 35 percent. Shareholders equity to total assets ratio downed to 8.5 percent in 1994 from 9.4 in 1993. Net working capital to total assets plunged from 2.2 percent in 1993 to 0.5 in 1994. Non-interest income to non-interest expenses ratio diminished from 15 to -11.3 percent. However, the banking sector recovered quickly after three risky banks[4] were taken over by SDIF. The Government implemented insurance scheme was applied to all savings deposit holders to stop the panic within the banking system.

In the pre-crisis period, under pressure from the IMF as well as public demand and potential EU membership preparation, the 4398 Bank Act was enacted in June 1999 by the Parliament. This Act partially applied international standards; providing full independence to the Banking Regulation and Supervisory Agency, transferring the authority for licensing, regulating and auditing of banks to the Agency, tightening the related group loans-capital relationship, and accelerating the procedure to deal with financially trouble banks. Based on the 4398 Bank Act, the Banking Regulation and Supervision Agency(BRSA), the Turkish version of the US Office of Comptroller Currency(OCC), was established legally in 1999 and started its activities in 2000. Like the US OCC, the BRSA's goals are safety and soundness.

In August 1999, a catastrophic earthquake hit Adapazari, near Istanbul, 15,000 people dead. The earthquake absorbed the attention and resources of the government. This combined with weak Ecevit's coalition governments[5] slowed the structural reforms and solving macroeconomic problems; high inflation with 70 percent, high government deficit and high external and internal debts. Therefore, the banking system struggled with the problems of inadequate capitalization, poor asset quality, extreme exposure to market risk, high level of credit risk and operational risk and lack of risk management, responsible corporate governance, independent auditing, transparency, and extensive fraud and corruption.

The most important reason for the high level of risks was the bad influence of the macro economic imbalances on both economic activity and behaviors of economic units[6]. The public sector borrowing requirements caused the real interest rates for short maturities to rise up to 30 percent. This situation caused the losses of the state-owned banks to reach record levels, and the cash flow and liquidity of the banks weakened. Turkish Lira depreciated over 150 percent against US Dollar.

2.2 Banking and Economic Crises: November 2000 and February 2001

The banking and economic crises happened in November 2000 and February 2001. Market confidence disappeared. Interest rates dramatically rose. The crises occurred as a result of macroeconomic and political instability[7] as well as banking sector's structural problems. In particular, state banks domination

[3] Inflation rate was 121 percent in 2014, GNP declined by 26 percent. Capital outflow reached to 4 billion US Dollar.

[4] These banks were Marmara Bank, Impexbank and TYT Bank operated as commercial banks.

[5] The coalition consisted of the Democratic Left Party(DSP) of Bulent Ecevit as Prime Minister with Motherland Party(ANAP) of Mesut Yılmaz and the Nationalist Movement Party(MHP) of Devlet Bahçeli.

[6] Interest rates on domestic borrowing increased owing to the rise in the public sector's borrowing requirement since external borrowing remained limited in result of the low country rating. Together with the contraction in economic activity reducing demand for loans, the high and chronic inflation effect on the financial condition was seen in the second half of 1998.

[7] The inflation rate (CPI, annual average) was 64.9 percent in 1999, 54.9 percent in 2000 and 54.4 percent in 2001. Interest rate for

caused the market distortion in the sector. The mag- nitude of these crises forced the Ecevit coalition government to face Turkey's economic problems, including fiscal mismanagement, and the need to undertake structural reforms in many sectors including banking.

As of the end of 1999, there were total 81 banks operating in the Turkish banking sector. Of these, 62 were commercial banks, and 19 were development and investment banks. Of the commercial banks, 4 were state-owned, 31 were privately-owned, 19 were foreign banks, and 8 were banks in the SDIF. Of the development and investment banks, 3 are state-owned banks, 13 are privately-owned banks, and 3 are foreign banks.

During 1992-2000, the capital ratios figures[8] in the banking sector shows that there was a clear deterioration in the financial conditions of the banks. Capital ratios plunged from 9.34 percent to 8.39 percent in 1994 owing to financial meltdown in 1994 mainly caused by short liquidity and foreign exchange exposures as well as fundamental economic problems. Capitalization of banks was corrected to 8.92 percent relatively again in 1996. However, it worsen to 5.87 in 1999, 7.32 in 2000. It back to 9.0 percent at the end of 2001. Net working capital to total assets ratio decreased from 2.34 in 1996 to -0.71 in 1999, -1.23 in 2000 and -3.6 in 2001. Foreign currency as a fraction of shareholders' equity increased dramatically from 50.60 percent in 1996 to 362.73 in 1999 and realized at 212.23 in 2000. This ratio that showed the foreign currency exposure became more risky. Assets in Turkish currency fell from 61.8 percent in 1993 to 54.8 in 1994. However, assets in foreign currency increased from 38.2 in 1993 to 45.2 percent during 1994 mini crises. The ratio for foreign currency liabilities jumped from 37 percent in 1992 to 46.8 in 1994 as TC liabilities decreased from 63.0 percent in 1992 to 53.2 in 1994. While non-performing loan(NPL)s as a ratio of total loans was at around 2 percent in 1996 and subsequent years, it increased continuously from more than 7 percent in 1998 to 10.72 in 1999 and to 11.52 in 2000 and 19.9 percent in 2001.

3.0 Banking restructuring and rehabilitation

The Banking Regulation and Supervision Agency(BRSA) had been tested with these crises and had managed to clean up the sector and recover banking sector confidence. Under the established rules, BRSA went into banking restructuring and rehabilitation. The program consisted of four levels; namely, the restructuring of state banks, the resolution of banks in receivership, the strengthening of private banks and implementation of the new legal and regulatory requirements under the Basel, IMF Program and EU requirements throughout whole banking system.

The first step was to restructure the state banks and adopt a program to eliminate short term funding needs. Overnight liabilities of the state banks were decreased, foreign currency open positions were reduced and new capital was provided to state banks by the Treasury. For example, as a state bank, Emlak bank[9] was a mortgage bank, which built and sold houses to public at reasonable prices. Since there was no private mortgage financing in the economy, the governments supported low and middle incomes home buyers through Emlak Bank. Emlakbank was politicized, mismanaged and corrupted over time so that increasing losses became a real problem in the banking sector. Emlakbank was transferred to Ziraat bank, the biggest agricultural state bank as of May 31, 2001.

3.01 Bank intervention and resolution

The most dramatic intervention is receivership; a complete takeover by the SDIF after referral from the BRSA, like the US OCC handing a problem bank to the FDIC. After the restructuring and strengthening of the state banks, full attention was given to the private banks. First, BRSA forced all banks to stop a number of unsound practices immediately. The BRSA established a comprehensive monitoring and auditing system for all private banks especially focusing on of the control of their exposures to liquidity and interest rates risks. SDIF took over 20 private banks between 2001 and 2003. By 2002, only 2 banks were left in the hands of the SDIF. SDIF banks' overnight liabilities which were USD 5.2 billion decreased to USD 0.8 billion within two months. Some of SDIF banks were sold or merged with more solvent bank(s) or forced into liquidation. All defaulted or bad assets of SDIF banks were transferred to the collection department. The number of commercial banks declined from 81 in 1990 to 53 in April 2003. The total asset size of the mergers and acquisitions that took place in the sector is around 26 billion dollars.

Treasury Bills and Bonds was 104.6 percent in 1999, 38.2 percent in 2000 and 99.6 percent in 2001.

[8] Appendices Table 1

[9] Emlak-Eytam Bankası was founded in 1926 and its name was changed to" Emlak Kredi Bankası" on September 1, 1946. It merged with Anadolu Bankası on January 8, 1988. The bank name was changed to Türkiye Emlak Bankası". After the restructuring process by Act (No 4603) in 2000, it was transferred to"T.C. Ziraat Bankası" with all assets and liabilities as of July 6, 2001. As of July 9, 2001, the headquarter as well as all the branches of T. Emlak Bankası continued their banking activities under the name of Ziraat Bankası. Then, 96 branches of T. Emlak Bank, together with balance sheets and staff were transferred to T. Halk Bankasi on November 12, 2001.

3.02 The strengthening of private banks

Each private bank submitted a restructuring business plan covering capital injection, ratio- nalization of branches and personnel, cost reduction and structuring concentrated credits. These were actively followed up on the implementation of such plans within the time limit by BRSA. For instance, Imarbank[10] was an example of the combination of operational risk[11] in terms of fraud activities and credit risk[12] for bad loans defaulted. Imarbank which was a small size commercial bank belonged to the Uzanlar group mostly gave the bank loans to Uzanlar group's companies. The problems of the bank were compounded by differences between reported and non-reported deposit amounts, illegal bond operations and off-shore deposits transferred to domestic deposits.

3.03 The implementation of the new regulations and accounting rules

The Capital Strengthening Program encouraged small banks to effect commercially justified mergers and acquisitions. Private commercial banks with an asset market share below 1 percent as of September 2001 could apply for a Tier 1 capital contribution by the SDIF, provided that they meet this threshold through approved mergers or acquisitions. Banks with an asset market share above 1 percent had to apply to the BRSA for approval of mergers or acquisitions by April 30, 2002.

Tax withholding rates on Turkish Lira(TL) deposit accounts were brought down to 14 percent for maturities from 3 to 6 months, to 10 percent for from 6 to 12 months and to 6 percent for those exceeding 12 months. Withholding tax rate on Foreign Exchanges deposit accounts having maturities above one year did not change, but the rate on the accounts with a less than one year maturity was raised from 16 to 18 percent. For repurchase agreements(repo) earnings, the rate was raised from 16 to 20 percent. In fact, many banks survived after restructuring or merging, so public losses were limited. With the changes in the accounting system, banks could prepare balance sheets in line with International Accounting Standards.[13].

4.0 Post crisis bank performance (2002-2012)

After the 2001 banking crisis, banks performance recover dramatically[14]. Non performing loans came under control, reduced as a fraction of total loans from 19.9 in 2001 to 6.6 in 2002, 1.4 in 2003 and continuously decreased to 0.7 in 2004 and 0.3 in 2006. It slightly increased again to 0.7 in 2008 and 0.8 in 2009 due to the global credit crisis. It is realized as 0.5 percent as of June 2012.

Returns on assets improved from -6.6 in 2001 to 1.1 in 2002 and 2.2 in 2003 subsequently; slightly down to 1.4 in 2005 due to the impact of short term international turmoil and recovered to 2.6 in 2007. As of the end of 2007 and 2008, the Turkish banking system felt deeply the negative effects of the global credit crisis in spite of domestic macro economic stability. Return on assets deceased to 1.8 in 2008 and recovered relatively to 2.4 in 2009 and back to 2.2 in normal range for banking industry. ROE decreased to 1.6 in 2011 and it is realized 0.9 as of September 2012. The non-performing loans are under control, reduced dramatically as a fraction of the total assets since the crises. Banking supervisory authorities are stricter and general provision is over 80 in average. Hence, net non-performing loans are almost insignificant.

Table 01: Percentile (1999-2012)

Banks	Percentile		
	25	50	75

[10] T. Imar Bankasi was founded as a privately owned deposit bank in 1928. The license of T. Imar Bankasi to perform banking activities and accept deposits was revoked upon the Resolution (No.1085) of BRSA, on July 3, 2003, pursuant to Article 14/3 of the Banks' Act No. 4389, due to the fact that the Bank could not timely fulfill its obligations, that it did not take the required measures, and that continuation of its banking activities would have posed a danger to depositors' rights as well as the safety and soundness of the financial system. The Court decided the bank to bankruptcy on June 8, 2005.

[11] Operational risk is a new risk category under Basel II. It is defined rather imprecisely as BCBS (2006) para644; the risk of loss resulting from inadequate or failed internal processes, people and systems or from external events.

[12] Credit risk is a form of financial risk that is economic loss from default on a loan.

[13] The preparation of consolidated financial statements is related to International Accounting Standards (IAS27). The application of consolidated prudential supervision/reporting requirements based on the models from developed markets. One of the major difficulties faced Turkish banks in preparing consolidated financial statements was the accounting policy differences between banks and non-bank financial institutions. To identify significant inconsistencies between the current accounting policies for banks and non-bank financial institutions(particularly brokerage firms, insurance companies financial leasing companies and factoring companies). To bring the existing consolidation rules for banks in line with International Accounting Standard 27 (IAS27 Consolidated Financial Statements and Accounting for Investments in Subsidiaries), an analysis was performed of the discrepancies between IAS27 consolidation requirements and current consolidation rules for banks.

[14] See Appendices Table 2.

Cap	10.07	14.58	32.84
Income	0.16	1.08	2.25
Loan	17.72	40.73	51.64
Obs	104.85	199.71	357.28
Size	3.42	13.28	82.88

Net income to total asset called "Income" is shown by quartile over time in Figure 1. There is a convergence in performance as uniform standards spread through the sector. The convergence occurs as the industry recovered from 2000-2001 crisis. The smaller distance between quartiles indicates probably increasing competition and efficiency in banking.

Capitalization (Cap) is defined here as the shareholder's equity over total assets and is graphed in Figure 2. It shows that capitalization at the low side gradually increasing over the period. The lowest quartile is over 10 percent. The median reached 17 or 18 percent after the recovery of 2000-2001.The capital ratio was nearly 14 percent in 2008, 17 percent 2009, 16 percent in 2010 and decreased to 14 in 2011 and 2012. The upper quartile varies considerably showing that this distribution has a long and changing upper tail.

Figure 1: Net income to total assets

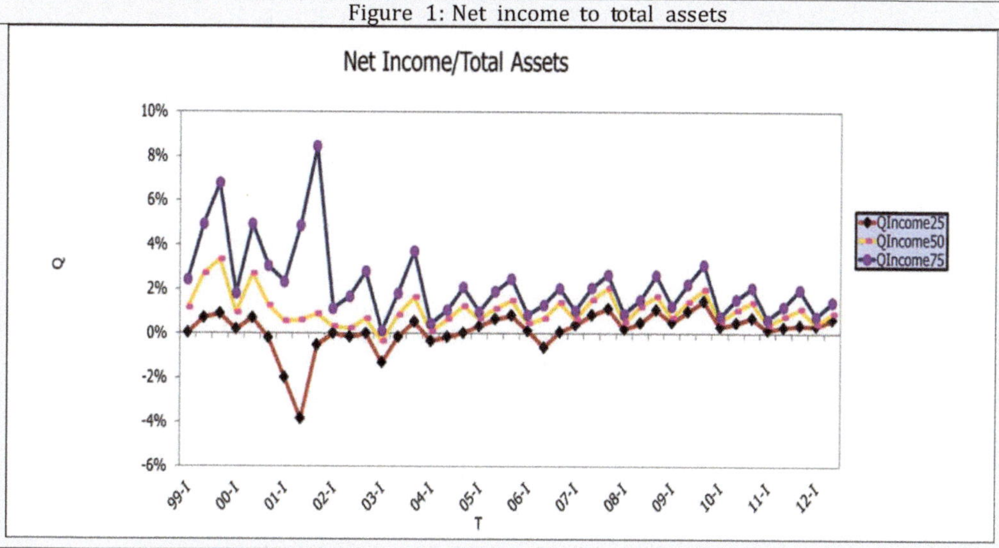

The capital ratio was nearly 20.55 percent in 2001, 48 percent in 2003. 39 percent in 2008, 42 percent in 2009. It realized 29 percent in 2011 and 25 percent as of June 2012. Therefore, there is some convergence since 2009 as overcapitalized banks reenter the markets.

Figure 2: Shareholder's equity to total assets

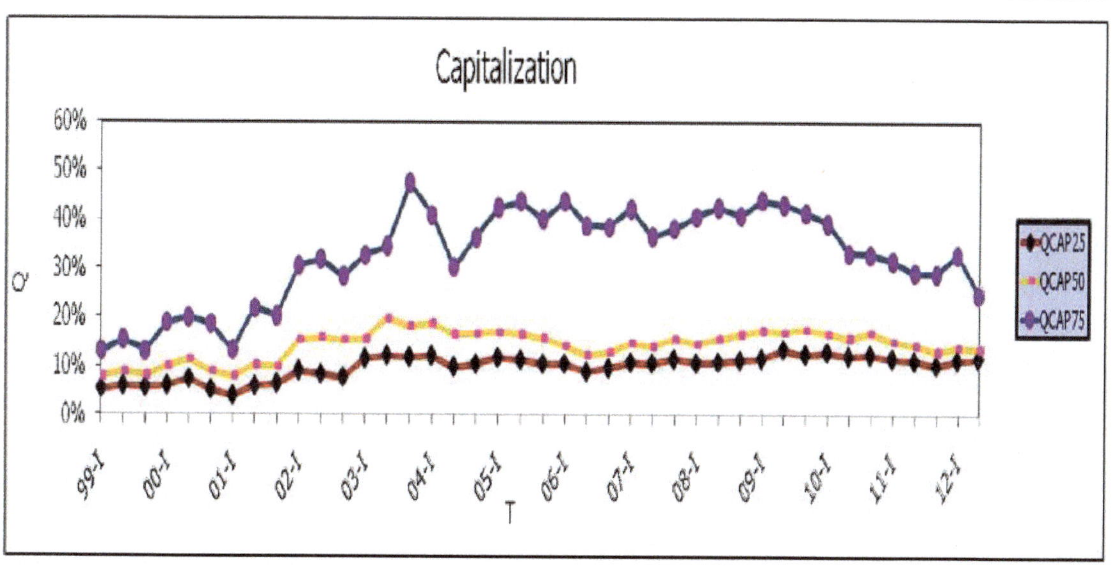

Higher capital could help enhance banks' soundness and stability. However, high capital ratios may imply some weaknesses in their earning capacities. If this happens, then it may take a long time for banks to regain their competitiveness. This prospect may then undermine their soundness and hence weaken their competitiveness further. This competitive disadvantage could become more serious if financial markets are opened up while the financial sector restructuring is in progress.

Figure 3: Total loans to total assets

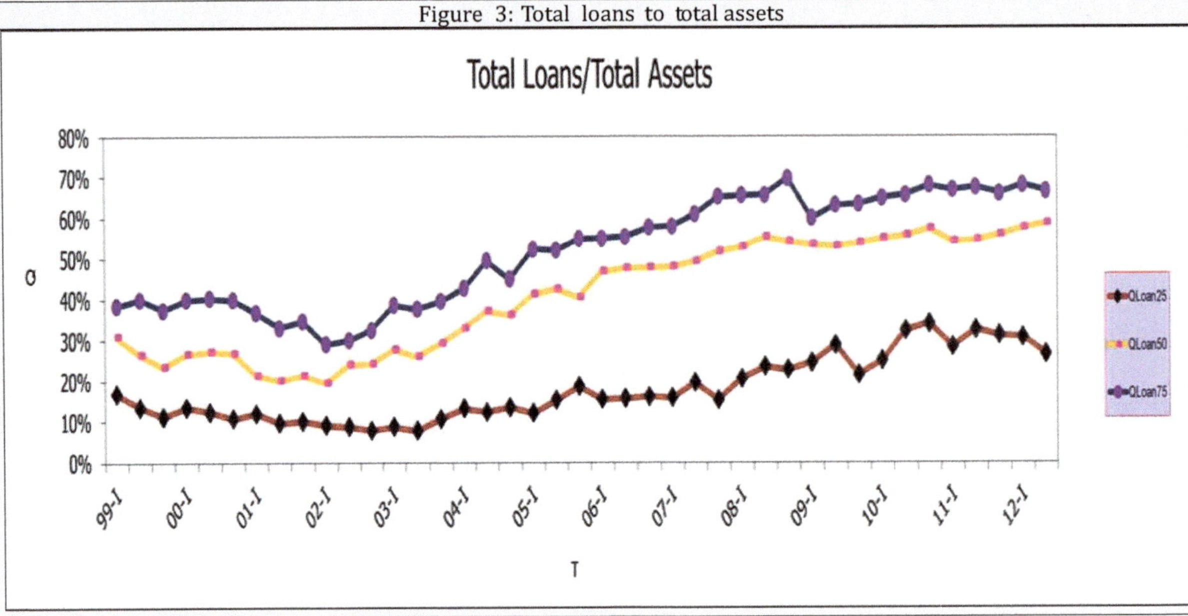

Loans to total assets(Loan) is a crude measure of exposure to credit risk. The quartile graph is Figure 3. This distribution shows a long lower tail; the distance between first and median is much bigger than median and third quartile. It is more spread on the long end; probably some banks do not make loans. Banks are generally increasing their loan activity since 2002. It indicates that banks focus on doing real banking activities that is good for the economy. It can be interpreted that other profit centers such as trading are less associated with the real economic activity.

Figure 0 4: Off-balance sheet transactions to total assets

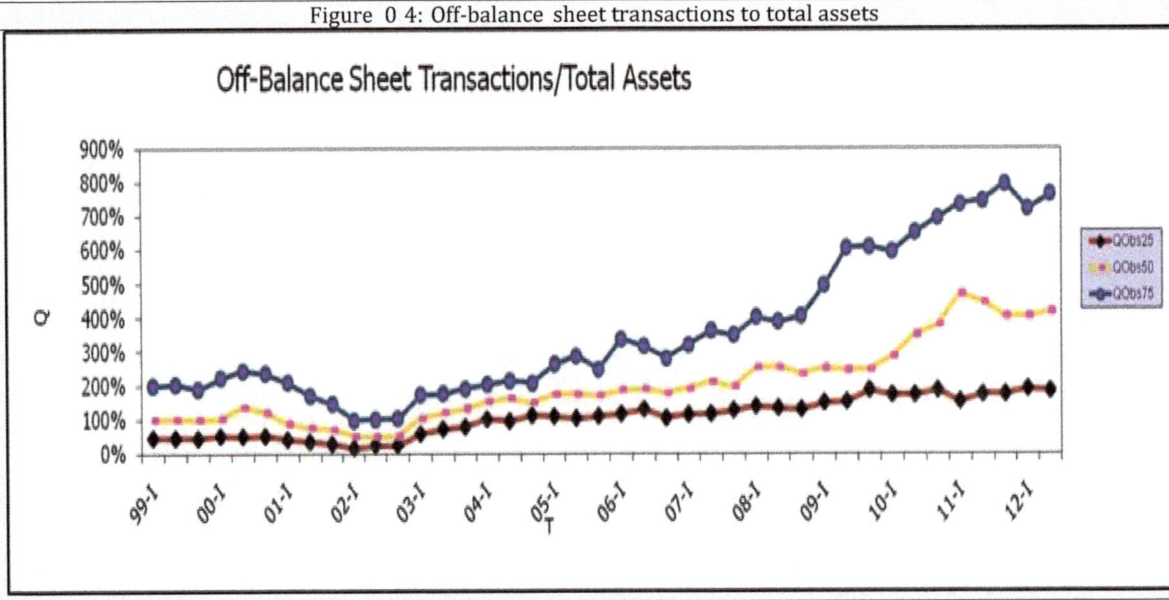

Off balance sheet transactions to total assets is shown in Figure 4, by quartiles. The whole distribution has been shifting up since 2003, probably reflecting increasing hedging and increased foreign currency denominated international activities. It is plausible whether this variable represents increased risk, because of the lack of capital requirements for off- balance sheet activities or decreased risk arising from effective hedging with derivatives.

Size defined as the total assets of the bank divided by by a common number to scale the variable. As shown in Figure 5, these are a small number of large banks and more smaller banks.

Figure 0 5 : Size of the firms

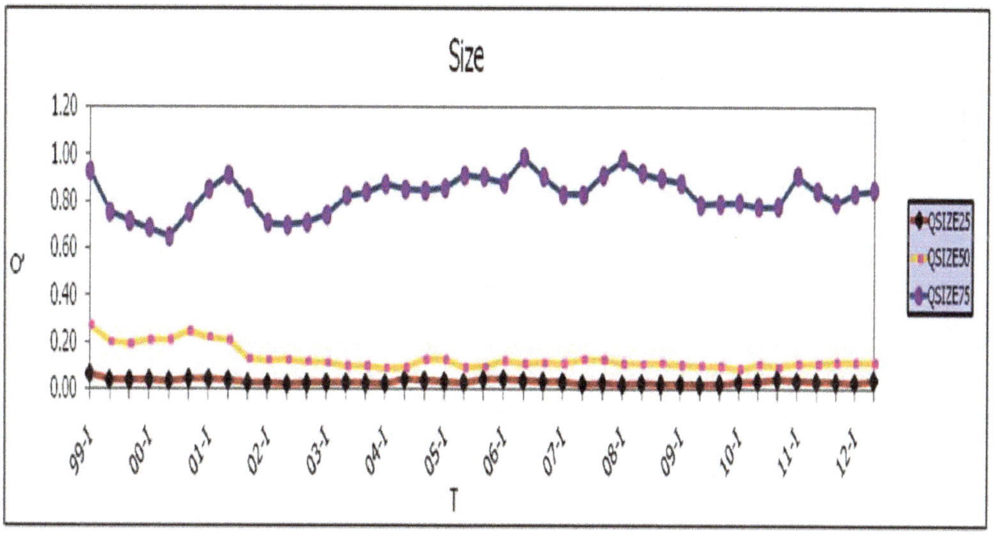

5.0 Merger and acquisition (MA) and foreign direct investment (FDI)

Since 2002, banks have been operating in a considerably less risky environment.[15] Turkey has achieved macroeconomic stability by following tight monetary and fiscal policies in cooperation with the IMF guidelines. Further, it completed privatization programs and cleaning up the banking sector. Improvement in the banking sector made investments in Turkey more appealing to the international market. Foreign direct investments increased since the recovery. Foreign direct investments soared to 10 billion dollar in 2005, 20.2 billion in 2006, 22 billion in 2007, 19.5 billion in 2008 and plunged to 8.4 billion in 2009 and 9 billion. FDIs reached to 16 billion dollar in 2011 and 12.4 billion US dollars in 2012.

It is clear that the smooth operation of the banking system under the new regulations and risk management contributed significantly to the recovery and to the inflow of international capital. Foreign investors' interest intensified. Table 3 shows the major deals of mergers and acquisitions. The financial institution has the highest level of foreign direct investments with the peaked level to 12 billion in 2007, 6 billion in 2008 and 6 billion dollar in 2011.

6.0 Basel standards and EU directives

The Banking Regulatory and Supervisory Agency(BRSA) in 2005 announced the implemen- tation of EU directives and Basel standards[16]. As of July 2011, BRSA accelerated again the adoption Basel II and European Union's standards. In particular, the Basel II process in Turkey has been started as of July 1, 2011[17]. However, many biggest commercial banks have been implemented these standards voluntarily to adapt international standards. The standard approach and basic standard approach realized for capital adequacy ratio and calculations of credit risks in 2012. The Advanced Approach have been harmonized by 2013. However, EU's full implementation of Basel II for all member states have been by 2012 for credit risk and market risk. The Advanced approach to operational risk; basic and standardized approach have been implemented as of 2012. After the 2008 global financial crisis, new Basel III regulation has taken placed for strengthen capital requirements and liquidity. Basel Committee on Banking Supervision (2012) focuses on safety and sound supervisory systems in international financial system.

---

[15] Turkey completed successfully a three year 10 billion dollars lending accord with the IMF which improved the economy significantly and established strong growth after the 2001 financial crisis. The first AKP(Justice and Development Party(JDP) government in 2003, using all advantages of the economic reform agenda inherited from the Ecevit-Yilmaz and Bahceli coalition government, and the good global economic environment, applied a successful tight fiscal and economic program, making reforms for starting EU accession, accelerating privatization and so attracting foreign direct investments to the country.

[16] The Basel II agreement categorized mainly three pillars for capital determination. These are minimum capital requirements; supervisory review, and transparency, leading to market discipline. The minimum capital requirements include three major types of risk: credit risk, market risk, and operational risk.

[17] Like EU authorities, BRSA also declared the postponing of previous 2005 road map due to the negative effects of the 2008 and 2009. global credit crisis on the Turkish banking system.

7.0 Analysis

A duration model is used in this study to analyze the time to banks failures and mergers and acquisition in Turkey. This model generalizes the more common binary response logit or probit analysis by modeling the occurrence of failure or merger or acquisition and the time to failure or MA jointly, allowing for covariates and not restricting (much) the duration dependence.

7.01 Data

We collected time dependent bank-specific data[18] between 1992-2014 (quarterly and annually reports) for private and state-owned depository commercial banks, development and investment banks[19] and foreign banks operated in Turkey between March 1992 and January 2014. We examined financial statements including balance sheets, income statements and statement of cash flows. In line with the literature, we selected bank performance measurement ratios as quarterly time-dependent covariates. We focused on capitalization ratio, loans to total assets, net income to total assets and contingencies to total assets and each banks size ratio(total assets to mean of total assets).

Failure is the event in which a bank is liquidated, either by the decision of BRSA or SDIF or by the decision of the bank management. The moment in which the bank fails is defined as the time in which the bank is liquidated formally; that is, the moment at which the bank stops reporting its financial statements to the BRSA and SDIF. Although this is not a exact measure of the moment in which a bank fails, it appears to be the best possible approximation. Banks that have made decision to merge or were acquired by other financial institution while financially healthy are not considered as failures in this study. It is a failure if it was under a serious financial distress, transfer, merged and sold by BRSA or SDIF to another bank.

Overall, there are 88 banks in the sample, of which 30 banks failed between March 1992 and March 2003 based on the research fails criteria. Of these 30, 25 were commercial banks and 5 investment banks. There were no further bank failures and mergers in 2003-2014. We collected mergers and acquisitions data from the various reports of BRSA, SDIF and Turkish Banking Association and banks official resources. Mergers and acquisitions sample consists of total 67 mergers or acquisitions events between March 1992 and January 2014. Most of the mergers and acquisitions deals were observed as a foreign bank acquisition as which the acquirer is a bank holding company, commercial bank or investment bank or financial institutions, at the same time target Turkish bank is a commercial bank or a investment bank or a bank holding financial services company. We excluded MA deals if a bank was liquidated by SDIF Fund or under the fund management or fails based on the BRSA regulations discussed in above. We also excluded if a foreign seized the operations in Turkey with associated of the any reason. Besides, the sample did not include any mergers and acquisitions deals were not approved or were canceled by BRSA.

Figure 0 6: Survivor function: TR bank failures

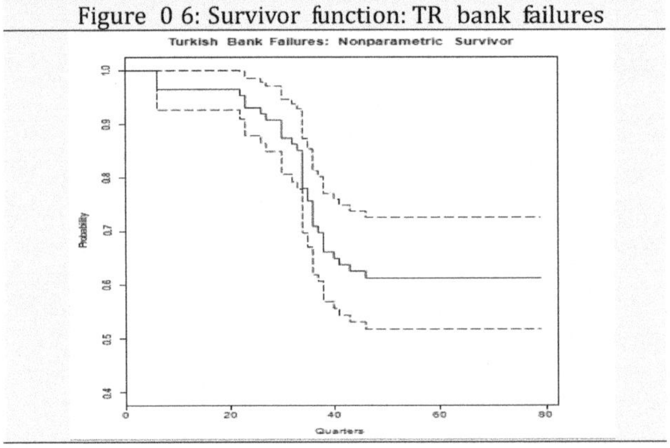

[18] Data Sources: Bank Association of Turkey (BAT) and Banking Regulatory and Supervisory Board (BRSA).

[19] Banks in Turkey are classified into two main groups: commercial banks and investment and development banks. By owners, each group can be put into three subcategories: private-owned, state-owned and foreign banks. Commercial banks operate as universal banks providing traditional depository and lending services, financing foreign trade activities and sustaining capital market services as well as investment bank activities. The major differences between commercial banks and investment banks are based on capital, liability composition and size. Investment banks are non- depository financial intermediaries. However, commercial banks accept deposits from customers and also make consumer and commercial loans. Mostly commercial banks' loans are held on the bank's balance sheet as an asset of the bank.

Figure 6 shows the raw survivor functions (non-covariates). Most of the bank failures occur between 1999-2003. The survivor function does not have a exponential distribution which is against using a general model like logit. The dotted lines are the 95% confident intervals for the estimated survival function. This paper emphasizes some major accounting ratios that are considered in the explana- tion of time to failure and mergers of banks.

Cap: Capitalization defined as the ratio of shareholder's equity to total assets

Cap^2: Quadratic function(non-linearity) square of the capitalization ratio.

Loan: Loans given by total loans over total assets

Obs: Off-balance sheet transactions defined as the ratio of totaloff-balance sheet trans- actions to total assets

Profit: Income given by the ratio of annualized net income to total assets

InvBank: It is a dummy variable covers only non deposit financial institutions, Invest- ment Banks

Fail : An insolvent bank is liquidated by supervisory or regulatory authority.

Since capitalization is a key ratio for regulators, typically with a minimum regulatory capital requirement, we are particularly interested in this variable. We look for non-linearity, suspecting that the marginal effect of capital is more crucial in reducing default risk when capital is low than when it is high. This would seem to be the logic underlying most regulation. Note that our measure of capital is not quite that used by regulators, who typically use more than equity in the numerator and adjust the denominator for riskiness of different assets. With our data attempting to adjust for riskiness would just add noise. Note that the non-weighted asset figure is that used in calculating leverage limits by some regulators. Further, note in interpreting the results that the risk-weighted capital ratio will be larger than our capital ratio. To account for a non-linearity of capitalization, we added a variable Cap-squared Cap^2.

Table 0 2: Summary statistics

Variable	Mean	sd	Median
Cap	19.28	21.08	11.35
Loan	36.04	32.36	34.54
Obs	3657.0	44208	177.1
Profit	3.00	27.85	1.48
InvBank	0.29	-	-
Fail	0.0068	-	-

Table 2 gives the summary statistics. We have also considered other accounting and financial ratios, but these are our focus. The difference between the mean and median in Obs indicated that Obs is concentrated in a few banks, probably specialists in foreign exchange activities. The failure rate is low since the data are reorganized so that each bank/period is an observation. This is to allow time-varying covariates. It is the bank failure probability in a particular period every quarter which is quite small.

7.02 Survival analysis

Duration models are widely used to study the time to the occurrence of an event. In the case of bank failure or default, duration is the time that it takes for a bank to fail or mergers and acquisitions activities after the occurrence of a banking crisis that might affect the whole financial system. The Kaplan Meier estimates of the survivor function for the raw data (unadjusted for explanatory variables) is given in Figure 6. The survivor function does not exhibit the geo-metric decline characteristic of the exponential indicating caution in specifying a functional form is appropriate. It is difficult to make a real inference without adjusting for covariates.

7.03 Explanatory variables and proportional hazard regression

Our main aim in this empirical study is to understand how bank-specific accounting and financial covariates influenced the conditional probability of default and time to failure and mergers and acquisitions after the crises in the banking system. In ordinary regression models, explanatory variables involve the dependent variable by moving its mean. In duration models, it is not straightforward to see how explanatory variables influence duration and the interpretation of the coefficients in these types of models depends on the particular specification of the model.However, proportional hazard regression is a semi-parametric model that assumes a parametric form for the effects of the explanatory variables but allows an unspecified form for the underlying hazard function with minimal assumptions. The specification for the hazard function (the default probability at the conditional time on survived to time t and covariates x is:

$\lambda(t, x, \beta, \lambda_0) = \varphi(x, \beta)\lambda_0(t)$ (01)

Where λ_0 is the baseline hazard. Time-varying covariates enter in an index form ($X_i(t)\beta$). Note that the effect of time on the hazard rate is captured completely through the baseline hazard. One common specifications for the function φ, which is followed, is $\varphi(x, \beta) = \exp(x'\beta)$ where x is a vector of covariates and β is the coefficient vector. A partial likelihood approach similar to Cox's can be used and the baseline hazard can be estimated. This requires that data have units of observation bank/quarter - so failure is a rare event.

Under this specification for all k.

$$\frac{\partial \log(\lambda(.))}{\partial x_k} = \beta$$

Therefore, the coefficients can be interpreted as the constant, proportional effect of the corresponding covariate on the conditional probability of completing a spell. In the particular case of bank default, completing a spell is associated with the moment in which a bank is liquidated or SDIF intervened to the problem bank or the authority revoke the license of the bank. The index form is potentially restrictive although we explore nonlinear effects by ap- propriate regressors, in particular the square of capitalization. Since the baseline hazard is unrestricted, the model is semi-parametric in that regressors enter as parametric but the un- derlying duration distribution is completely unrestricted. This is very general specification. With the small of data for the low failure rate more general models are not indeed feasible.

7.04 Maximum likelihood estimation

We estimated the proportional hazard model using maximum partial likelihood. We use the survivor package Therneau & Lumley (2008)[20].

7.4.1 Estimation result for failure

We begin by reporting a fit of a linear probability model, noting that this is not an adequate model for this problem; however, that is nevertheless a common first approach, showing that things make sense and providing an easily understood summary of some elementary relationships in the data. We experimented with several specifications and report the simple regression of a binary survive or fail variable on capitalization, net income to assets and dummy variables as investment banks. As expected, capitalization has a negative effect on the failure rate. The net income to assets has a negative effect, puzzling if this variable is interpreted as measuring exposure to credit risk. Perhaps healthier banks make more or better loans.

Figure 0 7: Bank Failures: nonparametric survivor

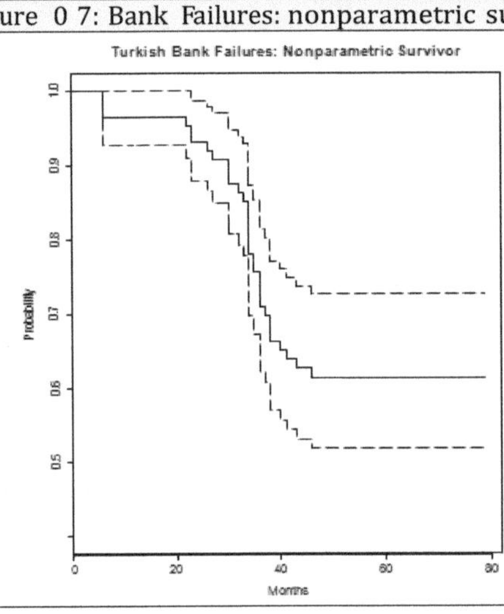

Note that most failures occur during 25-45 quarters period which is corresponding be- tween 1999 to 2003. This survivor function is far from the exponential form which is only suggestive as there is no control for covariates.

---

20 Original by Terry Therneau and ported by Thomas Lumley (2008) in R.

Table 0 3- Linear model results

Variables	Coefficient	Standard Error
Intercept	1.632e-02	2.325e-03
Cap	-1.061e-03	1.971e-04
Cap^2	1.141e-05	2.317e-06
Profit	-8.764e-05	4.127e-05
InvBank	4.772e-03	3.027e-03
F Statictics	8.236 on 4 and 4395 DF, p=1.295e-06	
Multiple R Squared	0.006537	

The linear model is included only for completeness. Nevertheless, the results are signifi- cant and suggestive; capitalization decreases the failure rate, with a nonlinear effect, namely capital increases are more effective when capitalization is low. It is obvious that profitable banks are less likely to fail.

Table 0 4: Cox proportional hazard model results

Variables	Coefficient	Standard Error
Cap	-0.1214867	0.0333819
Cap^2	0.0012487	0.0003634
Profit	-0.0965066	0.0211373
InvBank	0.5088305	0.5485916
Log-likelihood test	44.39 on 4 df, p=5.332e-09	
Wald test	50.52 on 4 df, p=2.807e-10	
Score(logrank)test	57.22 on 4 df, p=1.114e-11	
R-squared	0.01 (max possible= 0.046)	
n	4400	

Note that the data are set up in a format with observation equal to bank/time period in order to accommodate time-varying covariates. Consequently the great bulk of observation has no failure and R^2 is a highly misleading statistics since there is a little variation around the mean. Therefore, the F and Log-likelihood statistics are more relevant. Turning to the rather more reliable proportional hazard results, we find that the negative effect of capitalization on failure holds up. We also find a non-linearity - under capitalized banks gain more from an increase in capital than well-capitalized banks. The results are not substantially changed for neighboring values. There is a clear non linearity, as shown by the significance of the capitalization variable (these are robust standard errors). Experimentation with a number of other financial ratios and a dummy variable iden- tifying investment banks did not substantially change the results so the simplest model is reported(almost). The loans to total assets variable is insignificant; dropping it does not substantially change the results. It is included since it seems economically compelling as a measure of exposure, thought clearly it could also be a measure of the banks' financial health.

The results from the nonlinear specification show convincingly that the effect of capitalization on the default probability is larger for low values of capitalization (higher default probabilities) and much smaller for higher capitalization. This is consistent with most regulatory policy. The baseline survivor function from the proportional hazard model is given in Figure 8 together with the 95 percentconfidence interval. This is not very precisely estimated, so a variety of functional forms would probably fit equally well. It does not seem to exhibit geometric decline, so the exponential model (underlying some logit analyses) is not likely to be appropriate. Our results, because of the semi parametric formulation with the unspecified baseline hazard, do not depend on a functional form assumption here, but do give significant results on the variables of interest.

Figure 0 8- Baseline Survivor(Fail)CPH-Covariates; Cap, profit	Figure 0 9- Baseline Survivor(Fail) CPH-Covariates; Cap, profit, deposit

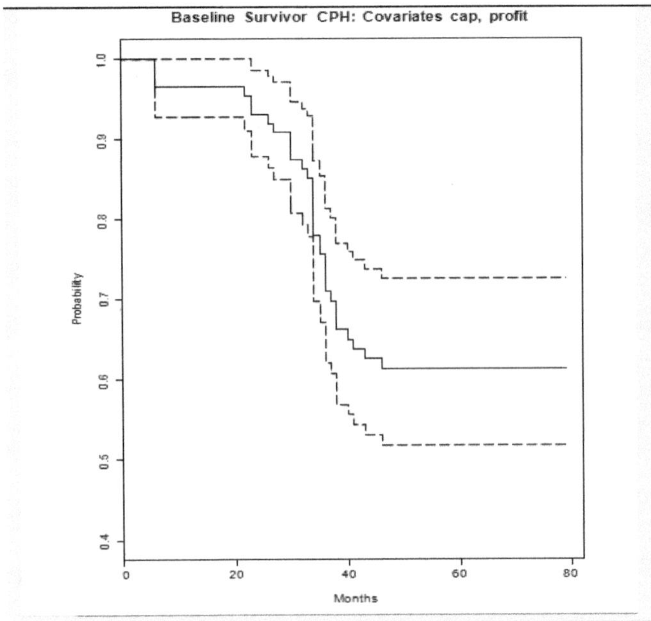

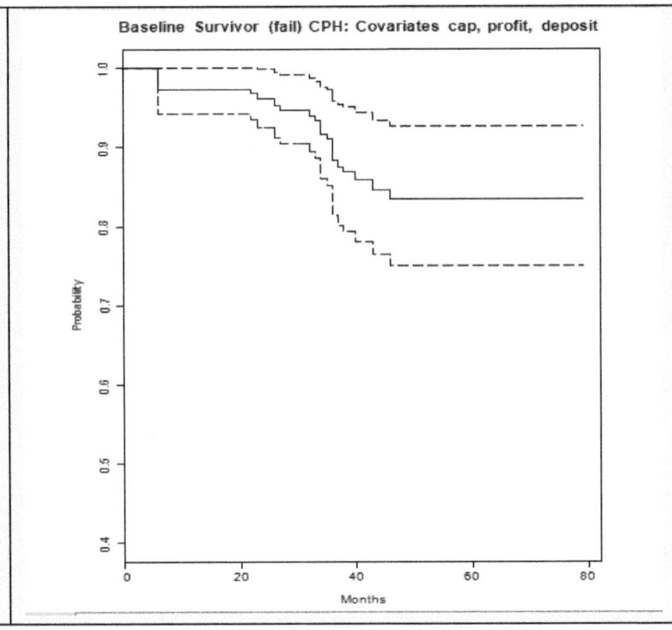

7.4.2 Estimation result for MA

There were a large number of mergers and acquisitions following the banking reforms as banks came into compliance with the new requirements. These consisted of both domestic and foreign acquisitions.. Our results show that undercapitalized banks were more likely to be acquired. This is not an obvious result: overcapitalized banks might be seen as a profit source and a way to improve capitalization in the merged bank. In fact, undercapitalized banks in this period were often also unprofitable, indicating probably a problem with management.

Table 0 5: Mergers and acquisitions in Turkish banking

Year	Acquirer	Target	Shares (%)	Value (US$ M)
2001	HSBC	Demirbank	100	350
2004	BNP-Paripas	TEB	50	217
2004	Unicredito	Kocbank	57.42	1,484
2004	RIBO-JSC(2006)	Sekerbank	37	90
2005	Fortis	Disbank	89.34	1136
2005	GE Financial	Garantibank	25.5	1,556
2005	Unicredito-Koc	YKB	57.4	1,500
2006	Dexia	Denizbank	99.85	3,253
2006	Merrill Lynch	Tatbank	75	6
2006	NBG	Finansbank	46	2,774
2007	Citigroup	Akbank	20	3,078
2007	ING	Oyakbank-ING	100	2,673
2007	Deutche Bank	Garantibank	100	115
2009	NBG	Finansbank	9	700
2010	Credit Europe Bank	Millenium Bank	95	85
2011	GE Capital	Adabank	100	75
2012	Sberbank	Denizbank(Dexia)	99.85	3,504

As seen Table 5, most of mergers and acquisitions began right after the 2001 crises and intensified until 2007[21].

[21] The biggest examples are as follows: Demirbank was transferred to SDIF Fund and sold to HSBC Bank in Turkey. Fortis Bank acquired 89.34 percent of Türk Dış Ticaret Bankası, Türk Ekonomi Bankası(TEB) took over Fortis Bank with all assets and liabilities on January 25, 2011. BNP Paribas indirectly acquired 42.125 percent shares of Türk Ekonomi Bankası on February 10, 2005. Finans Bank signed an agreement to sell 46 percent shares to National Bank of Greece April 3, 2006. National Bank of Greece acquired all shares Koc Bank. Koç Financial Services wentthe 50/50 jointventure between Unicredit and KoçGroup. The joint venture acquired 57.4 percent share by Yapı ve Kredi Bankası held by the Çukurova Group and SDIF fund.

Figure 10- Nonparametric Survivor(MA)

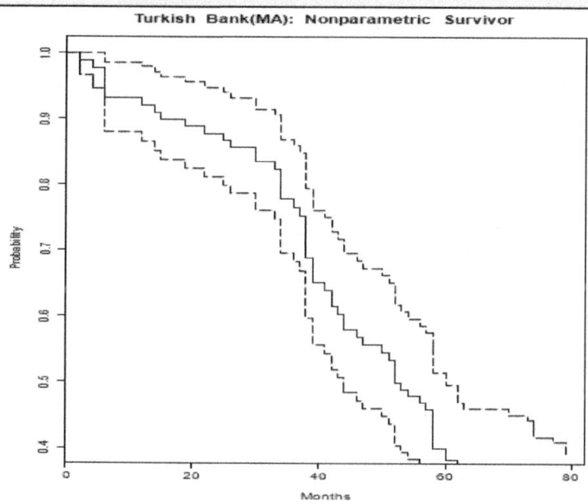

Figure 11- Baseline Survivor(MA) CHP: Covariates Cap, Profit

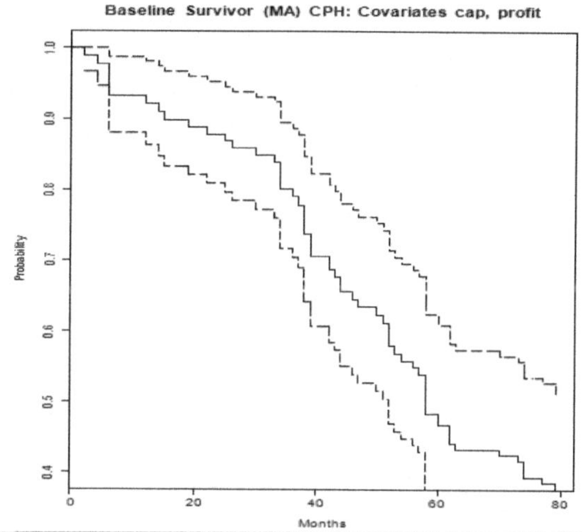

Investment banks works for MA, and is also significant variable. We suppose this means people like to acquire investment banks in Turkey. That makes sense for an expanding institution; commercial banks provide a stable source of funds.

Table 0 6: Linear model (MA) result

Variables	Coefficient	Standard Error
Intercept	1.608e-02	3.739e-03
Cap	1.527e-04	3.171e-04
Cap^2	4.561e-07	3.726e-06
Profit	-6.575e-05	6.637e-05
InvBank	-1.682e-02	
F Statictics	3.63 on 4 and 4395 DF, p= 0.005863	
Multiple R Squared	0.002385	
F Statictics	3.63 on 4 and 4395 DF, p= 0.005863	

Table 0 7: Cox Proportional Hazard Model Results (MA)

Variables	Coefficient	Standard Error
Cap	-0.0139890	0.0230438
Cap^2	0.0002429	0.0002603
Profit	-0.0351064	0.0189241
InvBank	-1.6617096	0.5172117
Log-likelihood test	20.73 on 4 df, p=0.0003576	
Wald test	14.96 on 4 df, p=0.00479	
Score(logrank)test	14.01 on 4 df, p=0.007251	
R-squared	0.005 (max possible= 0.11)	
N	4400	

These coefficients make sense; under capitalized banks are more likely to be acquired, as are unprofitable banks (an unprofitable bank can perhaps be acquired a good terms). Specification checks based on Schoenfeld residuals are reported in the appendices and do not indicate problems with the proportional hazard specification.

8.0 Implications

Figure 12 shows the nonlinear effect of capitalization on the one-quarter ahead default probability as estimated with the extended Cox proportional hazard model. Increasing capitalization decreases the default probability at a decreasing rate. Current values of capitalization are around 13 percent, indicated on the figure, and the historical regulatory value was 8 percent.

The estimated-quarterly values are converted to annual values in that the default probability is equal to the expected value about 0.07 for annual default. We used various Cap at the estimated coefficients to calculate the new default probabilities. This shows the estimated relation between capitalization and the annual default rate. The default probabilities are probably too high for the current economy – recall they are based on the cluster of defaults in the 99-02 period. It is that group of defaults, however, that allows estimation of a significant nonlinear relation between defaults and capitalization. The shape of the graph is likely to be still relevant, although the actual plotted rates may be higher than currently relevant.

The key is that the default rate is decreasing in capitalization, and in fact decreasing at a decreasing rate. Thus, the benefits of additional capitalization are higher at lower levels of capital. This is consistent with regulatory policy.

Figure 13 shows a return on equity by capitalization that is an approximation by calculation of ROE. Return on equity is income over equity. The calculation adjust the fraction of assets earning at risk free rate and the rest of capital earned the average return on equity in the sample. Therefore, increasing capitalization decreases the ROE in two ways; 1-By increasing equity by decreasing income 2-Two curves are given in this Figure 13. First (upper high) is ignoring default risk. The second(lower down) curve takes into account of the default risk.

Increasing capitalization decreases the default rate but also decreases the return on equity. We have done an approximate (very approximate!) calculation of ROE (income/equity) by capitalization. This calculation simply adjusts the fraction of assets earning the risk-free rate (assumed zero for this calculation). The rest of capital earns the average ROE. Increasing capitalization thus decreases ROE by increasing equity and decreasing income. There are two curves, one ignores default risk, the other (lower) takes into account that risk with default resulting in a 100 percent loss.

There is an interesting offsetting effect here: at lower capitalization the 1)ROE is higher because of the higher leverage, 2) default risk is higher (from the previous graph), and 3)loss given default is reduced, since the equity is lower and losses are limited to equity since banks are corporations. The total effect is given by the red curve.

A social optimum requires balancing these effects. One hundred percent reserves would eliminate (most) failures, but would be an ineffective social allocation of capital, as capital is buying too much failure protection. Note that all corporations face a failure risk and indeed this is encouraged by the existence of the corporate limited liability form. As a first approximation, we can use our results to examine the return on equity cost of increased capitalization. We take as base values return on equity of 13 percent and return on assets of 2) percent (roughly consistent with recent values). We suppose that increasing equity increases the fraction of assets earning the risk-free rate–assumed to be zero– and decreases the fraction earning the return on risky assets. Obviously there are a lot of approximations here and the results are speculative, but interesting. For example, decreasing equity would doubtless increase the cost of the bank's bond financing, but this is not taken into account at this level of approximation. With these qualifications in mind, Figure 13 gives plots of the return on equity versus the capitalization. One curve (the higher) shows the ROE assuming non- default. This is relevant potentially as there is some speculation that agents under emphasize or ignore very small probabilities. The lower curve plots expected return taking account of the possibility of default and sub- sequent loss of all equity. Both curves show that considerations only of ROE will lead to as low a capitalization as possible. This illustrates the need for regulation, as the investors have only their equity at risk, while society has more through deposit insurance. Our results help policymakers think about the menu of choices available.

As a final summary, we plot the expected ROE vs the failure rate in Figure 14. It shows a kind of menu as ROE and Default Rate pairs that is available by choosing different values of capitalization. This figure combines the cap-failure and ROE-Failure graphs to eliminate failure. This gives the "menu" of ROE-default rate pairs available to a bank. ROE takes account of default. Note again all the approximations involved – so the actual numbers should not be taken too seriously. But the shape is sound. This figure is tricky to interpret. Here are some of the considerations:

First, this is the tradeoff from the point of view of the bank. The social trade-off, relevant to regulators, is different. In particular, the social loss given default is larger for society than for the bank. To see this, note that the corporate form (designed to encourage risk taking) limits losses to shareholders. They can lose their equity and no more. On the other hand, if a commercial bank fails, depositors will lose some fraction of their deposits. This is a social loss. This is true whether it is covered by deposit insurance or not: the point is, someone incurs a loss, perhaps depositors, perhaps taxpayers, perhaps the population of bank customers if losses are covered by insurance paid for by all banks as in the US.

Second, ROE, of interest to some investors and some regulators, is not the same as the present value of the stream of income associated with the investment. If a bank fails, ROE is −100 percent during the period of failure. Income attributable to that equity goes to zero and remains at zero for all future periods. So, focusing on ROE may understate the actual value of the losses to shareholders, depending on their investment horizon. Third, when one bank fails in isolation, the figure is relevant (subject to the warnings above). When many banks fail the losses are compounded as the financial system is com- promised. This is a concern of regulators, not the individual bank.) But what does the figure say?

Figure 12- Annual default probability by capitalization

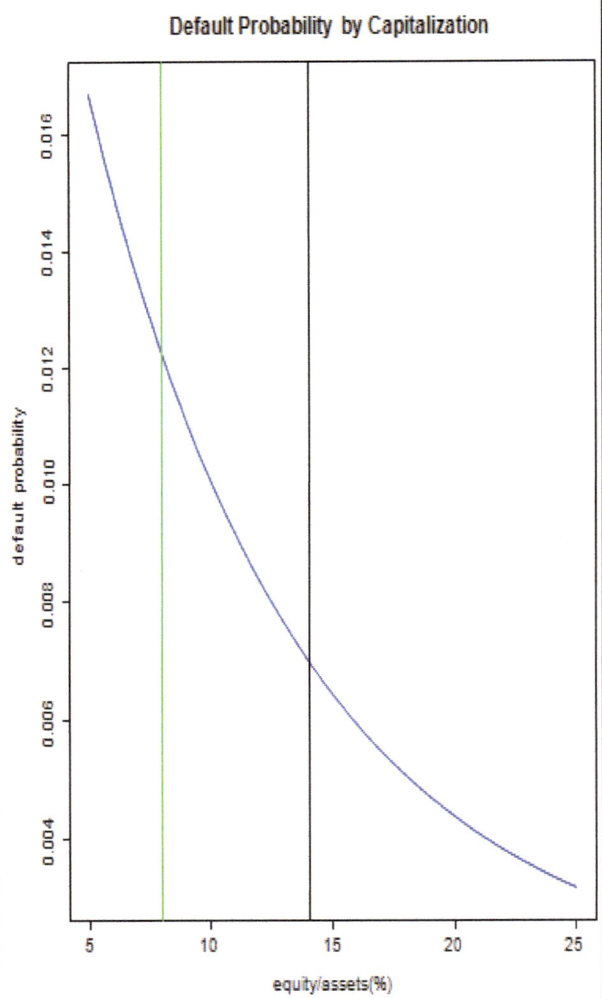

Figure 13- Return on equity by capitalization

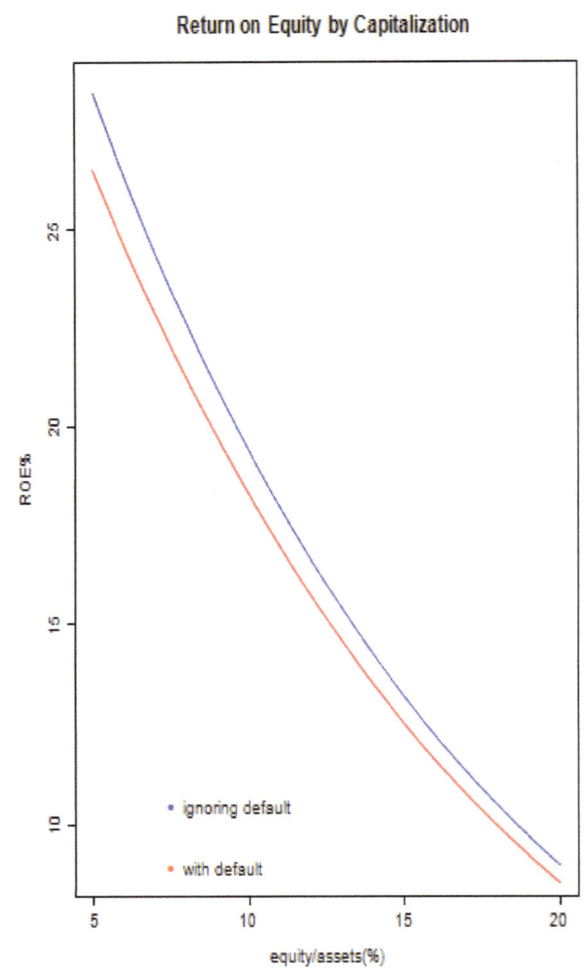

Figure 14- Return on Equity vs Failure

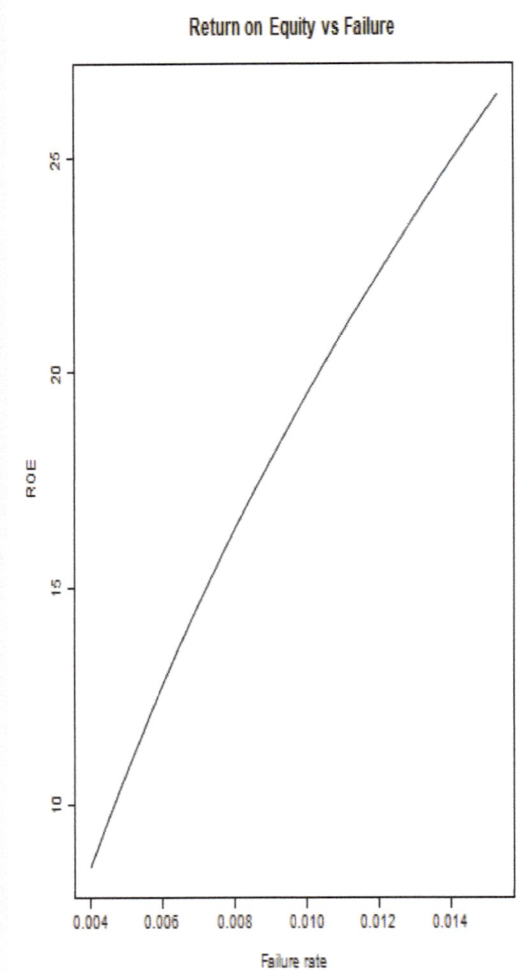

From the bank's point of view, risk taking is attractive, due in large part to corporate limited liability, which shifts risk away from the bank and to depositors and other counterparties. Hence, regulation is necessary from a social point of view. From the regulators point of view, allowing additional default risk decreases the amount of capital necessary to support the financial system, thus releasing capital for other productive uses. On the other hand, the additional default risk could lead to more frequent crises than a highly capitalized system. A richer country can afford more safety and Turkey is now "buying" more safety. Choosing the right point on the tradeoff is tricky. But calculations like these can help guide the discussion.

9.0 Conclusions

We have studied the default rate in the Turkish banking system during the tumultuous period of 1992-2012. Our focus was on estimating the effect of capitalization, the principle regulatory tool, on failure. We use a semi-parametric model for estimation so that the conclusions on capitalization will not be affected by potential specification error in duration dependence. Our results provide evidence against the exponential failure model implicitly underlying a number of specifications previously implemented. We find that, at low levels of capitalization, increasing capitalization substantially reduces the risk of default. At higher levels of capitalization, the marginal effects of capitalization on defaults are much smaller and not statistically significant. Thus, minimum capital requirements seem to be a sensible tool. Too little capital is associated with a higher default risk. At high levels, increasing capital does not change the (low) default rate but will, of course, reduce profitability. This is the tradeoff that must be managed by banking authorities. Our examination of MA show that under-capitalized institutions are less profitable and these banks are more likely to be acquired. This is not an obvious result: over-capitalized banks will be less profitable typically and therefore ripe for acquisition and new management. Finally, we make a rather speculative calculation of the implied tradeoff between the default rate and the return on capital. This relationship is increasing in the relevant range, as expected, but we are able to add empirical content to the social choice problem.

References

Andersen, H., 2008. Failure prediction of Norwegian banks: A logit approach. Norges Bank Working Paper 2.

Arena, M., 2008. Bank failures and bank fundamentals: A comparative analysis of Latin America and East Asia during the nineties using bank-level data. Journal of Banking & Finance, 32: 299-310.

Avkiran, N. K. & Cai, L. C., 2012. Predicting bank financial distress prior to crises. Working Paper.

Barr, R. S.; Seifors, L. M. & Siems, T. F., 1994. Forecasting bank failure: A non-parametric frontier estimation approach. Working Paper.

Basel Committee on Banking Supervision 2004. International convergence of capital mea- surement and capital standards: A revised framework, Technical report, Bank for International Settlements.

Basel Committee on Banking Supervision 2012. Core principles for banking supervision, Technical report, Bank for International Settlements.

Canbas, S., & Cabuk, K., 2005. Prediction of commercial bank failure via multivariate statistical analysis of financial structures: The Turkish case. European Journal of Operational Research, 166(2): 528–546.

Carree, M., 2003. A hazard rate analysis of Russian commercial banks in the period 1994-1997. Economic Systems, 255–269.

Cole, R. A., & White, L., 2012. Deja vu all over again: The causes of US commercial bank failures this time around. Journal of Financial Services Research, 42: 5–29.

Cox, D., 1972. Regression models and life-tables. Journal of the Royal Statistical Society, B34: 187–220.

DeYoung, R., 2003. De novo bank exit. Journal of Money, Credit, and Banking, 35(5): 711–728.

Estrella, A.S.P., & Peristiani, S., 2000. Capital ratios as predictors of bank failure. Economic Policy Review, 6: 33–52.

Fiordelisi, F., & Mare, D.S., 2013. Probability of default and efficiency in cooperative banking. Journal of International Financial Markets, Institutions and Money, 26:30–45.

Gepp, A., & Kumar, K., 2008. The role of survival analysis in financial distress prediction. International Research Journal of Finance and Economics, Issue 16: 13–34.

Gomez-Gonzalez, J., & Kiefer, N.M., 2009. Bank failure: Evidence from the Colombian financial crisis. The International Journal of Business and Finance Research, 3: 15–31.

Gonzalez-Hermosillo, B., Pazarbasioglu, C., and Billings, R., 1996. Banking system fragility: Likelihood versus timing of failure: an application to the Mexican financial crisis. IMF Working Paper.

Gonzalez-Hermosillo, B., Pazarbaşioglu, C. and Billings, R., 1997. Determinants of Banking System Fragility: A Case Study of Mexico. Staff Papers - International Monetary Fund 44: 295-314.

Kiefer, N. M., 1988. Economic duration data and hazard functions. Journal of Economic Literature, XXVI: 646–679.

Lancaster, T., 1990. The Econometric Analysis of Transition Data. Cambridge University Press.

Lane, W. S. L., & Wansley, J., 1986. An application of the cox proportional hazards model to bank failure. Journal of Banking and Finance, 10: 511–531.

Maggiolini, P., & Mistrulli, P. E., 2005. A survival analysis of de novo co-operative credit banks. Empirical Economics, 30: 359–378.

Mannasoo, K., & Mayes, D. G., 2009. Explaining bank distress in Eastern European transition economies. Journal of Banking & Finance, 33(2): 244–253.

Molina, C., 2002. Predicting bank failures using a hazard model: The Venezuelan banking crisis. Emerging Markets Review, 3: 31–50.

Peek, J., Rosengren, E., 1995. Bank regulation and the credit crunch. Journal of Banking and Finance, 19: 679–692.

Schoenfeld, D., 1982. Partial residuals for the proportional hazards regression model. Biometrika, 69(1): 239–241.

Tatom, J., & Houston, R., 2011. Predicting failure in the commercial banking industry. Networks Financial Institute, Working Paper No. 2011/27.

Therneau, T., & Lumley, T., (2008) S original survival: Survival analysis, including penalised likelihood, R package version 2.

Van den Heuvel, S., 2004. The Bank Capital Channel of Monetary Policy. Wharton School University of Pennsylvania.

Weelock, D., & Wilson, P., 2000. Why do banks disappear? The determinants of U.S. bank failures and acquisitions. The Review of Economics and Statistics, 1: 127–138.

Whalen, G., 1991. A proportional hazards model of bank failure: An examination of its usefulness as an early warning tool. Economic Review, 27: 21–30.

10

Will the unemployment rate fall with a robust forecast for the U.S. current account balance?

Mehdi Hojjat [a*]

[a] Professor, Neumann University, Aston, PA, USA.
[*] Corresponding author's e-mail: hojjatm@neumann.edu

HIGHLIGHTS:

1. The U.S. current account improvement generates higher level of employment. There two are statistically correlated.
2. The employment created by the improvement in the current account is mostly in the export sector.
3. More higher-paying jobs can be created if the U.S. provides incentive for manufacturers to use local contents in their products.
4. Regional trade agreements neither help U.S. current account balance nor its employment.

Article History

Keywords:
Balance of payment;
Current account balance:
US trade deficit.

ABSTRACT

This paper investigates the relationship between the U.S. current account balance and the U.S. rate of unemployment. Would the improvement in the current account balance cause a fall in the unemployment rate? Although previous researchers argued that U.S. current account balance does not influence U.S. unemployment rate, this article shows that these two are statistically correlated. This article also suggests policy recommendations that benefit both the employment level and the U.S. current account balance.

1.0 Introduction

The current account balance consists of four categories: balance on goods trade, balance on service, balance on income receipts and payment, and unilateral trade balance. On a theoretical basis, when a country reports a current account surplus or an improvement in the current account, it is an indicative of more exports or more income receipts compared to imports and payments to foreigners. More exports mean more jobs and almost certainly higher paying jobs in manufacturing and production sectors. Therefore, improvement in the balance of payment is always good news for the main street. It is good for you, your neighbor, your town and your country. It is a sign of strengthening of the U.S. international competitiveness, therefore, it is the reason that you should care about the status of the U.S. current account balance.

One of the most volatile economic consequences of the global financial crisis was a decline in the U.S. trade deficit in 2009 and subsequent improvement in the U.S. current account balance. After 2009, creation of new natural gas industry not only significantly reduced the U.S. import of energy products but also created thousands well-paying jobs in this industry.

At the same time, rising demand for U.S. exports to emerging markets such as the BRICK countries (Brazil, Russia, India, China and Korea) means higher demand for the U.S. dollar which maintains its value as the most important reserve currency in the world. This article examines recent data on the U.S. current account to see it diverges from the old declining pattern. The article, using the forecasted trend in the U.S. current account balance, shows its impact on the U.S. unemployment rate.

2.0 Literature review

In 1998, Daniel Griswold from the Cato Institute[1] wrote an article about the U.S. trade deficit. He wrote that article two years after the 1996 Asian financial turmoil. As he was projecting a deeper and deeper deficit for the U.S. current account balance, one of the main points of the article was the following: the U.S. trade deficit has no relationship with the U.S. unemployment rate. This point is still valid. In recent years, inflection points appear in all trade data that make many of the previous trade analysis erroneous.

In 2014, five years after the global financial crisis, this article broadens Griswold's research from a mere trade balance to the U.S. current account balance and comes up with a very different conclusion. Let us first examine the most recent data and present an analysis of the current account. In 2007, Doug Karmin (2007) asserted that the U.S. trade deficit was one of the largest deficits in the U.S. history. He projected that $800 billion deficit in 2007 was more than 6% of the U.S. Gross National Income. At that time, there were legitimate reasons to be concerned about the economic impact of such enormous trade imbalances. Despite the litany of reports and assumptions to the contrary, however, the threat of rampant job loss is not one of them. However, Karmin (2007) mistakenly concludes that there was no proven link between trade deficits and rising unemployment[2]

Another research, James Moreland (2014), recently stated that the U.S. trade policy basically induce firms to take their productions to other countries and do not penalize them for exporting the same product back to the U.S. consumers. This policy which is continuing has cost U.S. millions of good paying manufacturing jobs. The U.S. Department of Commerce estimates that for 5000 jobs are created for every billion dollar exported goods. The reality is that this calculation works both ways and for every billion dollar replacement imports, 9000 jobs are destroyed, according to the data from the Economic Policy Institute shows.[3] According to Moreland, "Free" trade has not been free at all, but has cost America millions of jobs. Unfortunately Moreland does not provide any statistical analysis to prove his point.

Jonathan Eaton, Samuel Kortum and Brent Neimann (2013) studied unemployment rate in Europe between 2007 and 2011. In this period, this rate increased substantially during the same period that a number of European countries experienced large decline in their trade deficits. The three researchers use a general equilibrium, thirty-four country Ricardian model with potential wage inflexibility to explore the relationships among external adjustment, relative GDP, and unemployment over the period. Their analysis provides decomposition between how increased unemployment and relative wage declines bore the burden of adjustment to lower external deficit. [4]

Houseman (2014) focuses her attention on globalization's effects on workers. While many are concerned that the rapid growth of trade has harmed job growth in the United States, the Great Recession and weak jobs recovery since 2009 has encourage the U.S. Administration to turn into export promotion policies to increase exports to boost employment. The indirect foreign labor contents of U.S. manufactured goods has risen substantially since the mid-1990s, underscoring the importance of accounting for imported intermediates in estimating the domestic employment effects of export promotion policies.[5] It appears that proving incentives for manufacturing firms to use domestic contents, as the expenses of foreign contents, can be an effective tool in generating employment. Given that the export sector of the economy is 12 percent of GDP and the manufacturing sector is several times that size, this tool can be a more potent in lowing employment rate than export promotion policies.

Yuan (2014) examined the U.S. trade deficit with China and concluded that the U.S. trade deficit with has little to do with trade in China and the U.S. unemployment rate. This is hard to believe because U.S. is the largest trade partner and over-sea market of China and China is the largest trade deficit source of the U.S. In 2013, the deficit with China constitutes forty three percent of total U.S. trade deficit.[6] United States blames this deficit on China's exports and

---

[1] Griswold, Daniel, T. (1998), America's Maligned and Misunderstood Trade Deficit. Retrieved from www.ciaonet.org

[2] Karmin, Douglas. (2007). "The Facts on Trade", Progressive Policy Institute. Retrieved from http://www.dlc.org/documents/TradeJobs100107.pdf

[3] Moreland, James. (2014). "U.S. Trade Deficit Fosters Unemployment", American Economy Report, February 2, 2014.

[4] Eaton, J, Kortum, S and Neimann, B. (2013). "On Deficit and unemployment". Based on Eaton's keynote address at the meeting of Association Francaise de Science Economique on July 3, 2012.

[5] Houseman, Susan (2014). "Trade, Competitiveness and Employment in the Global Economy", Employment Research Newsletter, Upjohn Institute, Volume 21, Number 1, 2014.

[6] Hojjat, Mehdi (2014). "Do Multinational Trade Agreements Help or Hinder Improvement in the U.S. Current Account Balance?", Global Journal of Business Research, Volume 8, Number 4, September 2014.

exchange rate of RMB, and tries to contribute them to the U.S. unemployment rate. Yuan states that even when there are no China's exports the U.S. trade deficit will not disappear. The U.S. trade deficit with China is an excuse, which the U.S. takes to suppress China's economic advantage.[7]

These points are valid but less important since in recent years we are observing inflection points in all trade data that make much of the previous trade analysis erroneous. In this article, I am expanding the scope of previous researches by connecting the unemployment rate not just to trade deficit but to a broader measure of U.S. external trade which is the U.S. current account. Furthermore, this research uses the latest forecast in the U.S. current account balance that shown an inflection point missed in previous researches.

3.0 Data and methodology

In July 2014, the U.S. Department of Commerce reported that the U.S. trade deficit narrowed as exports reached to a yet another record high, and at the same time, the U.S. unemployment rate dropped to its lowest level in six years.[8] In this report, the Commerce Department stated that the trade deficit declined 5.6 percent to $44.4 billion. The recent improvement in U.S. exports suggests a much brighter outlook for the employment picture in the U.S., as more export creates more jobs. The U.S. current-account deficit; which is a combined balance on trade in goods and services, income, and net unilateral current transfers, declined to $98.9 billion in the second quarter of 2013 from $104.9 billion in the first quarter of 2013. The decrease in the current account deficit was accounted for by a decline in the deficit on imported goods, a rise in the surplus on income, and a surge in the surplus on services.

3.01 Projection of the current account balance

Throughout the 1980s and 1990s, the current account deficit created worry about "unfair" foreign trade practices, loss of U.S. jobs, and the U.S. ability to compete in the global marketplace. However, the argument of this section will show that none of these statements is true. In early 1990s, annual U.S. trade deficits reached unprecedented levels. After three decades of surpluses, the U.S. current account deficit reached a record of $800 billion in 2007, as a percentage of GDP; it approached the unprecedented level of 6% (see Figure 2). In the aftermath of the global financial crisis, the current account deficit started to shrink. By 2009, the account trade deficit was cut in half to less than $400 billion, which shattered all doom and gloom projections in this area.

In 2014, five years after the global financial crisis, I broaden previous researches from just a trade balance to the U.S. current account balance and examine the most recent data and analyze the current account in a relationship to the recent unemployment rates.

Figure 01: The U.S. current account balance ($Millions)

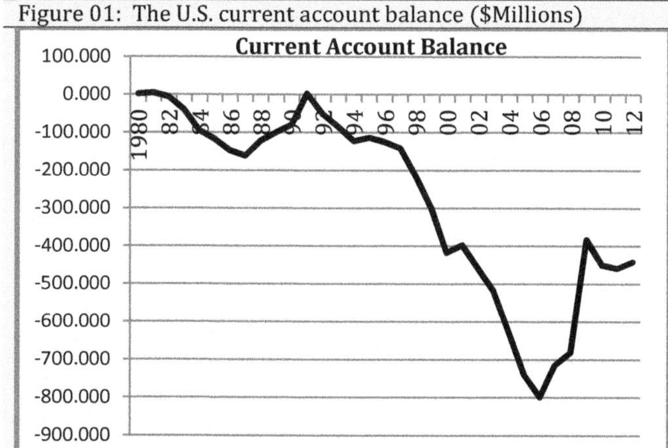

Figure 1 shows quarterly data of the U.S. current account balance from 1980 through 2013. The inflection point took place in the last quarter of 2006 and the improvement is continuing.
Source of Data:
U.S. Bureau of Census and Federal Reserve Economic Data. Retrieved from http://research.stlouisfed.org/fred2

Figure 02: The U.S. current account balance as percentage of GDP

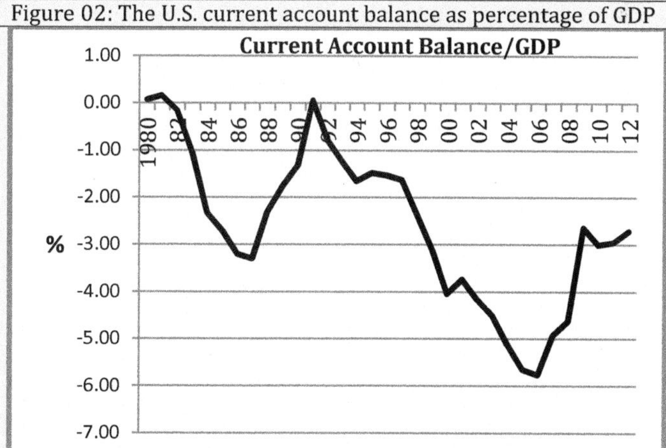

Figure 2 shown the U.S. current account balance as a percentage of U.S.GDP. Again inflection point happens in 2006 and the improvement is continuing.
Source of Data:
U.S. Bureau of Census and Federal Reserve Bank of St. Louis. Retrieved from http://research.stlouisfed.org/fred2

Figure 3 – Projected U.S. current account balance ($b)

[7] Yuan, Tao (2014) "The U.S. Trade Deficit with China: An Excuse", On China's Trade Surplus, pp77-94
[8] VOA News, "US Trade Deficit Narrows as Exports Hit Record High", July 3, 2014.

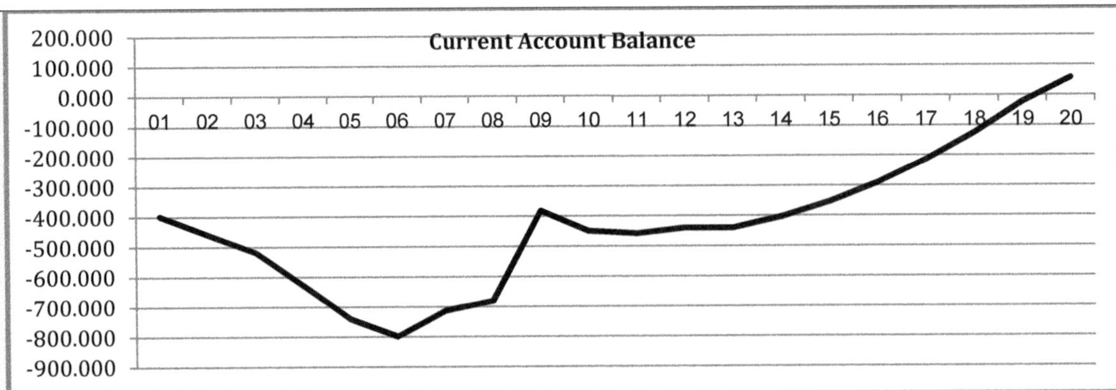

Figure 3 is the projection of the U.S. current account balance based on cross-sectional analysis of trade and service accounts of the U.S. balance of payments account. The assumptions include 4 percent increase in the service account, four percent decline on petroleum imports and a gradual increase in LNG exports from Louisiana and Maryland LNG ports. For more information see Hojjat (2014): "Cross-Sectional and Time Series Forecast of the U.S. Current Account Balance

Hojjat (2014) demonstrated that the U.S. Current Account balance will reach equilibrium by 2020.[9] Figure 3 demonstrates this projection which is based on the following three assumptions: (1) Four percent improvement of trade in services per year, (2) Increase in export of LNG from 1 billion cubic feet (CF) in 2014 to 6 billion CF by 2020, and (3) reduction of 4 percent in imports of petroleum products, including crude oil. Hojjat confirmed this cross-sectional projection by also conducting a time series forecast.

Table 01 is the numerical presentation of the above graph, showing a positive balance by 2020. Both time series and cross section projections display a rather robust outlook for the U.S. current account balances. Both are projecting that by 2020 the U.S. will have a current account surplus.

Since the focus of this research is to show the relationship between the U.S. current account and employment, readers can review the projection in the above referenced citation.

Table 01: Projected U.S. current account balance ($b)

2014	-193.22
2015	-149.36
2016	-105.5
2017	-61.64
2018	-17.78
2019	26.08
2020	69.94

Table 1 presents the projection of the U.S. current account balance, equilibrium will be achieved by 2018 and for the first time in 4 decades U.S. will have a surplus in the current account balance by 2020.

4.0 U.S. unemployment rate and current account

There is a debate among economists about the effect of higher trade and current account deficits on the rate of unemployment. Some blame globalization and outsourcing as the main reasons for both a higher rate of employment and the trade deficit. The relationship seems to be obvious: more outsourcing results in loss of jobs and more imports results a higher trade deficit. A 1997 study by the Institute for Policy Studies asserted that a large trade deficit caused by the East Asian financial meltdown cost the U.S. economy more than 1 million jobs.[10] The U.S. Department Commerce estimates that for every $1 billion of exports, 20,000 jobs are created. That's 3.5 million American workers who would have good manufacturing jobs if U.S. simply closes its trade imbalance.

On the other hand, Griswold (1998)[11] believes that all these estimates are based on a basic misunderstanding between the relationship of trade deficit and employment rate. He stated that the total number of jobs in the United States is largely determined by fundamentally macroeconomic factors such as labor-supply growth and monetary

[9] Hojjat, M. (2014), "Cross sectional and Time Series Forecast of the U.S. Current Account Balance", Journal of International Business and Economics, American Research Institute for Policy Development (www.aripd.org/jibe).
[10] Quoted in Wayne Leighton, "Playing with the Numbers: Why Protectionists Are Wrong about Trade," Issue Analysis, Citizens for a Sound Economy Foundation, Washington, September 18, 1997, p. 1. Buchanan made his remark on CNN on March 3, 1996.
[11] Griswold, Daniel, T. (1998), America's Maligned and Misunderstood Trade Deficit.

policy, therefore, trade with other nations does not affect the number of jobs created or lost in the United States. Trade lowers demand for jobs in one sector and increases demand for jobs in other sectors. For example, trade allows the United States to export more Boeing jetliners, pharmaceuticals, software, and financial services for export creating more jobs in these sectors. And at the same time, trade may mean that U.S. produces fewer shoes and t-shirts, hence, losing jobs in these sectors. Meanwhile, total output and employment keep growing.

He showed that larger trade deficits can correlate positively with falling unemployment. Using recent data on the current account, the above hypothesis can be tested. A linear regression was run on the data: unemployment rate as a dependent variable and current account deficit as percentage of GDP as an independent variable. Here is the regression equation between these two variables:

$$Y = 12.38 + 1.366\,X \qquad (1)$$

t- statistics (14.3)

R^2 0.8313

Where Y presents the U.S. unemployment rate and X presents the U.S. current account deficit as percentage of GDP, t-statistics is 14.3 which provide 98% confidence interval. R^2 is .8313, it represents the goodness of fit which means that 83.13 percentage of variations in Y can be explained by independent variable, X. The following table presents the full regression results between these two variables.

Regression results show a significant relationship between these two variables, as the U.S. current account improves, its unemployment rate falls. Figure 4 illustrates how closely the unemployment rate corresponds with changes in the current account deficit. [12]\

Table 2: Regression results

Y = Current Account Deficit as % of GDP X = Unemployment Rate

Multiple R	0.911797007				
R Square	0.831373782				
Adjusted R Square	0.812637536				
Standard Error	0.830419211				
Observations	11				

	df	SS	MS	F	Significance F
Regression	1	30.59908995	30.59909	44.37248	9.25379E-05
Residual	9	6.206364594	0.689596		
Total	10	36.80545455			

	Coefficients	Stand. Error	t Stat	P-value	Lower 95%
Intercept	12.38330898	0.865624021	14.30564	1.7E-07	10.4251314
X Variable 1	1.366940458	0.205207264	6.661267	9.25E-05	0.902729376

Figure 04: Current account as % of GDP (Left) and unemployment rate (right scale)

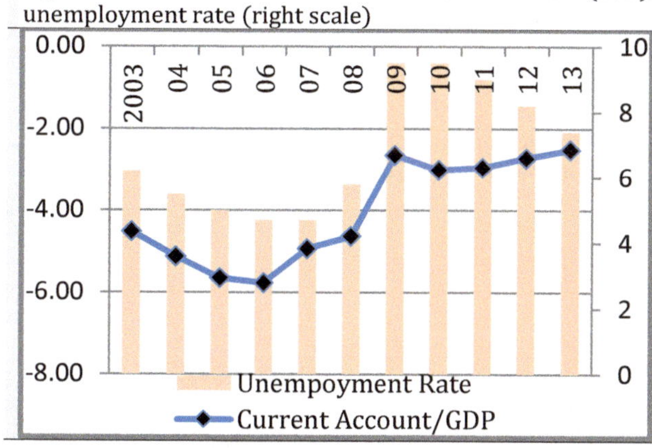

Figure 05: Correlation between current account deficit/GDP and unemployment rate

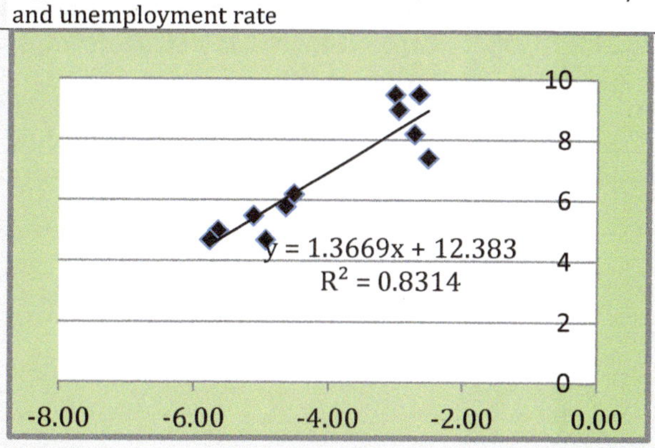

[12] Source of data: Bureau of Labor Statistics (unemployment rate for the year is represented by the rate in July of that year) and Bureau of Economic Analysis (current account deficit as a percentage of GDP for 2013 is estimated)

The current account deficit is now shrinking, and the unemployment rate is falling. As the deficit shrank during the period of 2009-2013, the unemployment rate steadily declined. But the unemployment also declined when the deficit expanded in the 2003-2006 period. As the trade deficit declined in the 2007-2009 period, the unemployment rate rose. Overall, there seems to be very little relationship between the current account deficit and the unemployment rate. However, in recent years, improvement in the unemployment rate is positively associated with an improvement in the current account balance.

5.0 Conclusion and policy implications

Recent current account data indicates that U.S. is nearing an inflection point in the projection of its current account deficit. This article estimated that by 2020, the U.S. will post current account surpluses, thanks mostly to the improvement in the U.S. trade balance. Higher exports, especially the export of energy products and lower imports of energy will make this happen. The current account will also receive a boost from higher surpluses in the service and income accounts. The article also showed that unlike many previous projections, there is a positive relationship between improvement in the current account balance and improvement in the unemployment rate, although using quarterly data might make this relationship more statistically significant.

Some of the policy implications from this article include the following: (a) export promotion policies should be continued with more vigor to encourage small and medium size firm start exporting, (b) policies should be developed to encourage the use of local content in manufactured goods, such as using steel poured in the U.S. for infrastructure projects, (c) regional trade agreement does not help the U.S. current account, hence they do not help employment, therefore, policy makers should not pursue them, and (d) the U..S trade policy should be focused on reducing trade barriers by discussing them at the World trade Organization (WTO), rather than by taking unilateral and bilateral actions. It provides a better trade outlook for U.S. when the world is open for business rather than country or a region.

References

Eaton, J, Kortum, S and Neimann, B. 2013. On deficit and unemployment. Based on Eaton's keynote address at the meeting of Association Francaise de Science Economique on July 3, 2012. Retrieved from http://faculty.chicagobooth.edu/brent.neiman/research/EKN.pdf

Griswold, Daniel, T. 1998. America's maligned and misunderstood trade deficit. Retrieved from www.ciaonet.org

Hojjat, Mehdi. 2014. Cross-sectional and time series forecast of the U.S. current account balance. Journal of International Business and Economics, American Research Institute for Policy Development (www.aripd.org/jibe).

Hojjat, Mehdi. 2014. Do multinational trade agreements help or hinder improvement in the U.S. current account balance? , Global Journal of Business Research , Volume 8, Number 4. September 2014.

Houseman, Susan. 2014. Trade, competitiveness and employment in the global economy, Employment Research Newsletter, Upjohn Institute, Volume 21, Number 1, 2014. Retrieved from http://research.upjohn.org/cgi/viewcontent.cgi?article=1216&context=empl_research&sei-redir=1&referer=http%3A%2F%2Fscholar.google.com.ezproxy.neumann.edu%2Fscholar%3Fas_ylo%3D20

Karmin, Douglas. 2007. The facts on trade. Progressive Policy Institute. Retrieved from http://www.dlc.org/documents/TradeJobs100107.pdf

Moreland, James. 2014. U.S. trade deficit fosters unemployment. American Economy Report, February 2, 2014. Retrieved from http://economyincrisis.org/content/lack-jobs-due-our-massive-trade-deficit

Nir, J and Taylor L. 2013, Economic growth in foreign regions and U.S. export growth. Economic Review, Federal Reserve Bank of Kansas City.

VOA News, US trade deficit narrows as exports hit record high, July 3, 2014. Retrieved from http://www.voanews.com/content/reu-trade-deficit-narrows-as-export-hit-record-high/1949981.html

Yuan, Tao, 2014. The U.S. trade deficit with china: an excuse. On China's Trade Surplus, pp77-94

11

Implications of the US-South Korea free trade agreement on agricultural exports from the US✧

Srinivasa Konduru[a*], Tae Hun Kim[b], Mechel Paggi[c]

[a] Assistant Professor, Dept. of Agricultural Business, California State University, USA.
[b] Department of Agricultural Development Research, Korea Rural Economic Institute (KREI), South Korea.
[c] Director, Center for Agribusiness, California State University Fresno, Fresno, CA. Email: mpaggi@csufresno.edu
* Corresponding author email: skonduru@csufresno.edu

HIGHLIGHTS:

1. We study the impact of S. Korea – US Free Trade agreement (KORUS) on California's agricultural exports.
2. Import demand estimation methodology is appropriate for an ex-post analysis is utilized in this study.
3. KORUS has implications on market access in S. Korea for agricultural products from various other countries.
4. Results reveal that California's agricultural exports will now become more competitive in S. Korea.

Article History

Keywords:
Free trade agreement;
KORUS;
Market access.

ABSTRACT

The United States-S. Korea Free Trade Agreement (KORUS FTA) became effective in 2012 and is expected to create new opportunities and improve access for one another's markets. It is expected to benefit the US agricultural sector particularly as S. Korea maintains high trade barriers for agricultural imports. This paper analyses the impact of KORUS FTA on the agricultural exports from the US with an example of table grapes. The results obtained by using the Import demand estimation method show that table grape exports will become more competitive in S. Korea due to the KORUS FTA. The paper also calculates preference indices for various agricultural imports from the US and rest of the world before and after the free trade agreement in S. Korean agricultural markets. This will help in understanding the implications of KORUS FTA not only on the US-S. Korean agricultural trade, but also between S. Korea and the rest of the world.

1.0 Introduction

The United States has Free Trade Agreements (FTAs) in force with as many as twenty countries since its first FTA with Israel in 1985. A free trade agreement (FTA) is an agreement between the countries party to that agreement to remove trade barriers such as tariffs and import quotas (Urata, 2002). Along with the elimination of trade barriers, some of the recent FTAs also incorporated rules governing foreign direct investment, intellectual property rights protection, environmental and labor issues, etc., in their agreements (Cooper, 2014). The FTAs not only help in the expansion of the markets but also aid in creating greater competition leading to more efficiency and better growth of the economies of the participating countries (Urata, 2002). There have been many studies that analyzed the impact of FTAs on their member countries. It has been found that on average, an FTA approximately doubles two

✧ A working paper version of this manuscript was first made available at
http://www.fresnostate.edu/jcast/cab/documents/Implications%20of%20the%20South%20Korea.pdf

countries bilateral trade after ten years (Baier and Bergstrand, 2006). Many other studies also found a significant effect of economic integration on trade flows among member countries (Abramis, 1980; Brada and Mendez, 1985).

Out of all the FTAs that the US has signed, the North American Free Trade Agreement (NAFTA) in 1994 has created the largest FTA in the world. Due to this agreement, the U.S. agricultural exports to NAFTA countries increased by an annual average of 9.5 percent compared to a 2.8 percent annual increase to its non-NAFTA partners between 1993 and 1998 (Burfisher, Robinson and Thierfelder, 2001). Later, the US signed the Central American Free Trade Agreement (CAFTA) in 2004 with five countries among many other FTAs with countries as Australia, Peru, Chile, etc. The latest one that the US signed was with South Korea, which was called as United States-Korea Free Trade Agreement (KORUS FTA) and was signed on June 30, 2007. The agreement became effective on March 15, 2012 creating new opportunities to many sectors in S. Korea and the US by improving access to one another's markets. S. Korea is already the seventh largest trading partner for the US since 2004, and its position is bound to strengthen much further because of the KORUS FTA. In 2012, the total US exports to S. Korea stood at $42b whereas imports are $62b, thereby having an overall trade deficit with S. Korea. However if we take only the food and agricultural sectors, the US has a trade surplus of about $5.9b before the KORUS FTA came into existence (US Census Bureau, 2014). In this context, although the KORUS FTA will lower the trade barriers between the two countries in all sectors of trade, the US agricultural sector is expected to benefit significantly as S. Korea maintained high trade barriers for agricultural imports. According to the US International trade Commission, KORUS FTA is estimated to increase the US agricultural exports to Korea by minimum $1.9 billion upon full implementation of the agreement.

This paper analyses the impact of KORUS FTA on the agricultural exports from the state of California in the United States. The paper explains the schedule for removing tariffs on major agricultural exports from California and how it may benefit California exporters in S. Korean markets. The paper uses the example of Table grapes and analyses the impact of KORUS FTA on both the US and S. Korea. The second section explains the relevance of KORUS FTA for California agriculture and types of market access it will get in S. Korea. The third section explains the methodology for determining preferential indices for US agricultural products before and after KORUS FTA. The fourth section analyzes the results of that analysis. The paper concludes with the table grape sector and how it is impacted in both S. Korea and the US due to KORUS FTA.

1.01 Importance of KORUS FTA

Before KORUS FTA was signed, the US had Free Trade Agreements with 11 countries, whereas S. Korea has FTAs with six countries and is a member of the ASEAN group of nations. According to the U.S. Department of Commerce, the KORUS FTA is estimated to increase US merchandise exports by nearly $11 billion annually. It is also expected to improve the US market share in the S. Korean market, currently the third largest import supplier. U.S. exports face an average 6.2 percent tariff on goods they export to S. Korea. Following the KORUS FTA, tariffs will be eliminated on over 95 percent of US exports of consumer and industrial products within five years. Elimination of tariffs took place immediately for two-thirds of agricultural goods after the agreement was implemented (USTR, 2012). The U.S. exported about $6.9 billion worth agricultural products to S. Korea in 2011. The major products include the red meat products, food and feed grains and fruits and fruit preparations. The value of selected agricultural product imports by S. Korea and the share of the U.S. and other competitors are given in the below table 01.

The KORUS agreement is expected to have a positive impact for California as many of the products produced in the state are exported to S. Korea. The agreement is expected to open up new markets for key sectors of California like computers and electronic products, agricultural products, machinery manufacturing and transportation equipment. The KORUS FTA will eliminate tariffs and other barriers on a range of California's agricultural products, including dairy, beef, vegetables, fruits and tree nuts. S. Korea agricultural exports to US may be less effected by of the KORUS FTA, but it is expected to have a positive impact for other sectors such as automobiles and other machinery goods.

Table 01: Value of S. Korean imports and shares of US and other competitors, 2011

Commodity	S. Korea's Imports ($m)	Share of U.S. (%)	Other Competitors and their share (%)
Beef and Products	1522	39	Australia (51), ROW (10)
Dairy	610	26	EU (26), New Zealand (16), ROW (32)
Cotton	855	47	Brazil(34), Australia (14), ROW (5)
Wine	132	8	EU (58), Chile (22), ROW (12)
Oranges	170	95	Chile (3), ROW (2)
Table Grapes	115	13	Chile (87)
Rice	124	32	NA
Almonds(Shelled)	85	99	Chile (1)
Walnuts (Shelled)	81	100	-
Orange Juice	66	25	Brazil (62), ROW (13)

Cherries	48	95	New Zealand (3), ROW (2)
Tomatoes, processed	35	34	China (34), EU (23), ROW (9)
Grape Juice	11	92	Israel (8)
Raisins	10	94	Chile (4), ROW (2)
Lemons	10	85	Chile (14), ROW (1)
Source: WTO database, 2013			

In 2011, the total value of agricultural exports from California to S. Korea was about $781 million (See table 2). S. Korea is the sixth largest destination for California exports, constituting about five percent of total exports in 2011. Agricultural exports from California to S. Korea increased by 35 percent in 2011 compared to 2010. Among all the agricultural exports from California to S. Korea, oranges and orange products ranked first followed by rice, beef, almonds and walnuts respectively (other products can be seen in the table 2 below.) Agricultural exports, which have shown very high growth rates, over 60 percent in 2011 over the previous year, include rice, dairy products, cotton, pistachios, prunes and strawberries. The value of the exports of each of the above products is more than $2 million.

Table 02: Agricultural Exports from California to S. Korea, 2011

Commodity	Exports ($m)	Growth over previous year (%)	Rank among all destinations*
Total	781.4	35	6
Oranges and products[3]	153.0	33	23
Rice	123.9	68	14
Beef and products[5]	97.4	28	27
Almonds	84.3	32	-
Walnuts	84.2	27	8
Dairy and products[2]	66.7	67	-
Cotton[2]	46.1	80	11
Hay	34.4	-4	17
Table Grapes	13.8	59	-
Tomatoes, Processed	12.1	-10	-
Raisins	10.0	20	-
Wine	9.9	1	-
Cherries	9.3	-11	9
Lemons	8.6	40	-
Pistachios	7.2	109	-
Prunes	4.8	125	-
Grape Juice	4.3	-36	11
Strawberry	2.4	195	-

*Ranks were given where they were available
Source: CDFA Statistics

Lee and Sumner (2011) have categorized how the KORUS FTA creates more market access for agricultural products. They identified four mechanisms: *(1) the immediate opening of certain markets without restrictions (2) the phase-out of tariffs over a specified number of years (3) the expansion of tariff rate quotas with the phase out of over quota tariffs and (4) the imposition of safeguard measures.* Safe guard measures are basically a quantity or price triggers, which once reached, additional duties are imposed to give protection to domestic farmers. The table 3 shows the base tariff levels and number of years it takes for them to go to zero for major agricultural exports from California to S. Korea. With the advent of KORUS FTA, the agricultural product exporters in California may also overcome some of the competition from Chile, which has had a FTA with S. Korea (Lee and Sumner, 2009). It may also improve the competitiveness of US exporters compared to S. Korean domestic producers especially in table grapes and rice, where import barriers were quite high.

2.0 Materials and methods

The most important provisions in KORUS FTA are those that increase market access. The farmers in California will be better able to sell into markets that reduce barriers, and S. Korea will have greater access to California markets and as well as markets of other states of US. Along with tariff cuts there are other aspects of market access such as relaxation of tariff rate quotas where they exist and other conditions that affect the cost of selling into a foreign market or that influence the costs of others selling into domestic markets.

The impact of an FTA is in essence to change the tariff heading for goods coming from a particular country. In the simplest example, consider a country with a two-part tariff schedule: one 'column' for preferred partners, say in a free trade area, and one for all other WTO members (MFN schedule). Entry into a free-trade area with a country moves the applicable tariff from the MFN column into the tariff-free column. The impact of that on market access will depend on (a) how competitive the newly preferred supplier is relative to other suppliers, both preferred and non-preferred; (b) how great the degree of preference implied by the free trade area is; and (c) how much export capacity the newly-preferred country has. With a high degree of preference, only the low cost suppliers will be able to make use of the new market opportunities.

To understand the impact on potential imports into the US can be best judged by comparing access for S. Korea before and after the KORUS FTA. But, for this potential impact to be realized, there has to be capacity in S. Korea to expand exports. To conduct an analysis would require detailed investigation of the possibilities for investment and expansion in these sectors and the competitiveness of such new production. Such an analysis is beyond the scope of this study.

With respect to market access in S. Korea, the goods from the U.S. gain preference relative to those countries that do not have a free trade arrangement with S. Korea. This means that the competitiveness will be a function of the current trade agreements that S. Korea has with other countries. The California suppliers, along with those in other states, would move (over a transition period) from supplying at MFN tariffs to having duty-free access. The advantage of this depends on which other suppliers already enjoy such privileges and whether the US more competitive than the other suppliers.

The effective impact of KORUS FTA in providing additional export market opportunities for California agricultural products will be a change in the additional preferences that California gains for its exports to S. Korea relative to its competitors. In general terms, the gains in preference that will result from KORUS FTA can be illustrated in terms of where US goods will fit in the basic tariff access structure currently in place. For example, the three major categories used to describe the level of access afforded to exporting countries to S. Korea, in order of preference, are (1) duty free, where imports enter S. Korea with zero tariff (2) preferred access, where imports enter S. Korea with a tariff less than those of other countries and (3) most favored nation status, where imports enter S. Korea with tariffs equal to those of all other countries not included in the first two categories. In this format the potential benefits for California agricultural products will be where they shift to a higher preference category.

In order to gain a more precise understanding of what benefits may accrue to California agricultural product exporters, as a result, of KORUS FTA, a detailed analysis of the specific changes in tariffs currently in place for those products is necessary. This paper follows the methodology followed by Paggi, et al. (2005) in calculating the impact of Central America Free Trade Agreement (CAFTA) on US agricultural trade. The methodology calculates preference indices for three countries with different types of market access. It assumes that three exporters serve one import market. Let us consider the case of KORUS FTA by considering three countries: Country A, United States, and Rest of the World (ROW). Country A has a free trade agreement with S. Korea and faces zero tariff rates; the United States faces an MFN rate before the free trade agreement ($TAus^0$) but free trade access after KORUS FTA ($TAus^1$), and the ROW faces the MFN tariff levels.

A detailed derivation of the preference indices for the three types of countries relative to one another is given in Appendix A. From the results of the derivation, before the KORUS FTA, preference index for the US relative to country A ($\Theta us^0 a$) and the ROW ($\Theta us^0 row$) is expressed as the following:

$$\Theta us^0 a = \frac{Mus^0 a}{Nus^0} = Pd\left(\frac{1}{1+TAus^0} - 1\right) * \left(\frac{1+TAus^0}{Pd}\right) = -TAus^0 \text{ .... Eq. 1}$$

$$\Theta us^0 row = \frac{Mus^0 row}{Nus^0} = Pd\left(\frac{1}{1+TAus^0} - \frac{1}{1+TArow}\right) * \left(\frac{1+TAus^0}{Pd}\right) = 0 \text{ .... Eq. 2}$$

After KORUS FTA, they are:

$$\Theta us^1 a = \frac{Mus^1 a}{Nus^1} = \left(\frac{Pd - Pd}{Pd}\right) \text{ .... Eq. 3}$$

$$\Theta us^1 row = \frac{Mus^1 row}{Nus^1} = \left(1 - \frac{1}{1 + TArow}\right) \text{ .... Eq. 4}$$

The above four indices are used to examine the preferences of the United States relative to other exporters for some of the California Agricultural products. An example is calculated in the footnote below[1] for Table grapes imported by S. Korea from Chile and the US. In the case of table grapes, KORUS FTA brings positive changes in the preferential index for the US by 45 percent relative to Chile, which has a duty free access with S. Korea due to FTA, and by 31 percent relative to those other exporters who face MFN tariff level. The results for the other commodities selected

---

[1] For example, S. Korea import table grapes with MFN rate of 45 percent. So, before KORUS FTA, the preference index for the US relative to country A with zero tariff ($\Theta us^0 a$) and the ROW, which faces an MFA rate ($\Theta us^0 row$), is expressed as the following:
$\Theta us^0 a = \frac{Mus^0 a}{Nus^0} = Pd\left(\frac{1}{1+0.45} - 1\right) * \left(\frac{1+0.45}{Pd}\right) = -0.45 = -TAus^0$ and $\Theta us^0 row = \frac{Mus^0 row}{Nus^0} = 0$, since $TAus^0 = TArow$`
After KORUS FTA they are $\Theta us^1 a = \frac{Mus^1 a}{Nus^1} = \left(\frac{Pd-Pd}{Pd}\right) = 0$ and $\Theta us^1 row = \frac{Mus^1 row}{Nus^1} = \left(1 - \frac{1}{1+0.45}\right) = 0.31$

for analysis are presented in table 3. The preferential index of US/MFN after KORUS agreement is implemented shows that the US exporters enjoy a considerable advantage over other exporters with MFN tariffs.

Table 03: Estimated Preference Indices for the Imports of Selected California Agricultural Products by S. Korea.

			Before KORUS		After KORUS	
Commodity	Base Tariff before KORUS FTA (%)	Number of years for complete tariff phase out	Index US/ Free	Index US /MFN	Index US/ Free	Index /MFN US
Beef and Products	40	15	-40	0	0	28.6
Dairy - Butter	89	TRQ	-89	0	0	47.1
Dairy -Cheese	36	TRQ	-36	0	0	26.5
Cotton	0	Immediate	0	0	0	0.0
Wine	15	Immediate	-15	0	0	13.0
Oranges	50	TRQ (In season); 6 (Off season)	-50	0	0	33.3
Table Grapes	45	17 (In season); 4 (Off season)	-45	0	0	31.0
Almonds(Shelled)	8	Immediate	-8	0	0	7.4
Walnuts (Shelled)	30	6	-30	0	0	23.1
Orange Juice	54	5	-54	0	0	35.1
Cherries	24	Immediate	-24	0	0	19.4
Tomatoes, processed	8	Immediate	-8	0	0	7.4
Grape Juice	50	Immediate	-50	0	0	33.3
Raisins	21	Immediate	-21	0	0	17.4
Lemons	30	2	-30	0	0	23.1
Pistachios(Shelled)	30	Immediate	-30	0	0	23.1

Source for Tariff values: USTR tariff schedule

In order to analyze the impact of KORUS FTA on table grape exports from the US, this paper uses the model of import demand estimation. The details of the model are explained in the next section.

3.0 Results and discussion

Among all the agricultural products that California exports to S. Korea, table grapes ranks among the top ten. Though it is small in terms of value compared to other major agricultural products, imports in the table grape constitute only a small percent of total consumption in S. Korea. Thus the potential for an increasing role for imports resulting from changes in existing trade barriers should be robust. In 2011, the table grape imports constituted only 16 percent of the domestic consumption (See figure 1). As the size of the domestic table grape sector is quite significant, S. Korea imposed a two-tier tariff structure for table grape imports. The tariff on 'in-season' grapes (May 1- Oct 15) is phased out over a period of 17 years, whereas the tariff on 'off-season' grapes (Oct 16- Apr 30) is phased out in 4 years (USTR Tariff Schedule, 2012). The tariff imposed on off-season grapes from Chile will be phased out completely by 2014 as the FTA with Chile started in 2003. The tariff on off-season grapes from Peru would be phased out by 2015, but the share of Peru is very little compared to that of from Chile and the US. With regard to the US, the tariff on in-season grapes will get phased out in 2028 and that of off-season grapes in 2016.

Figure 01: Domestic production and imports of table grapes in S. Korea (1000 MT)

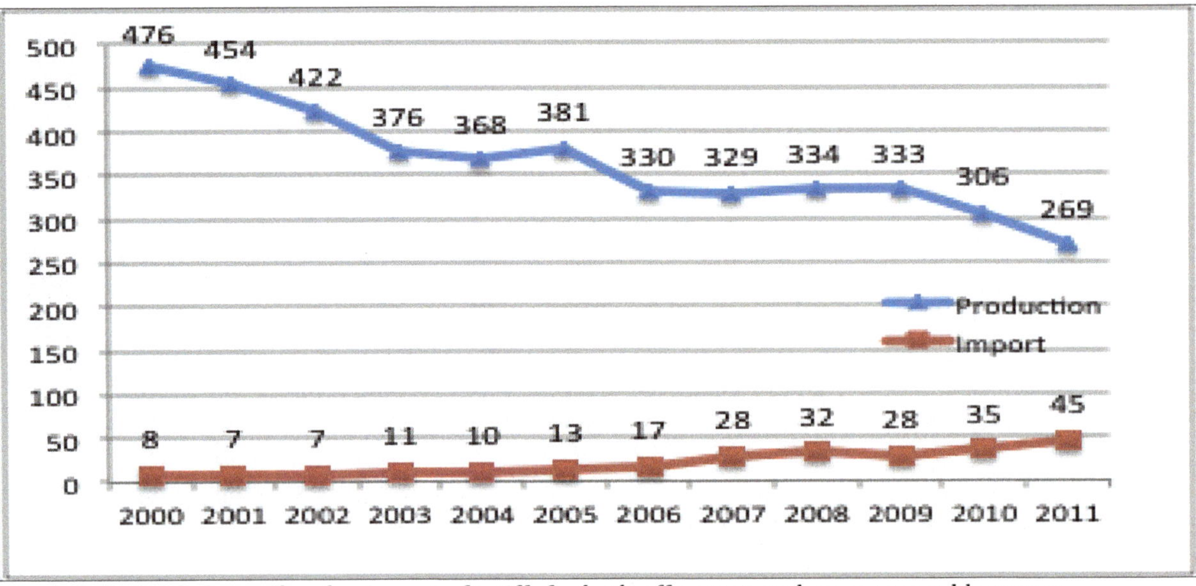

The graph in figure 2 shows the phasing out of tariffs for both off-season and on-season table grapes.

Figure 02: Tariffs imposed by S. Korea on table grape imports from various countries

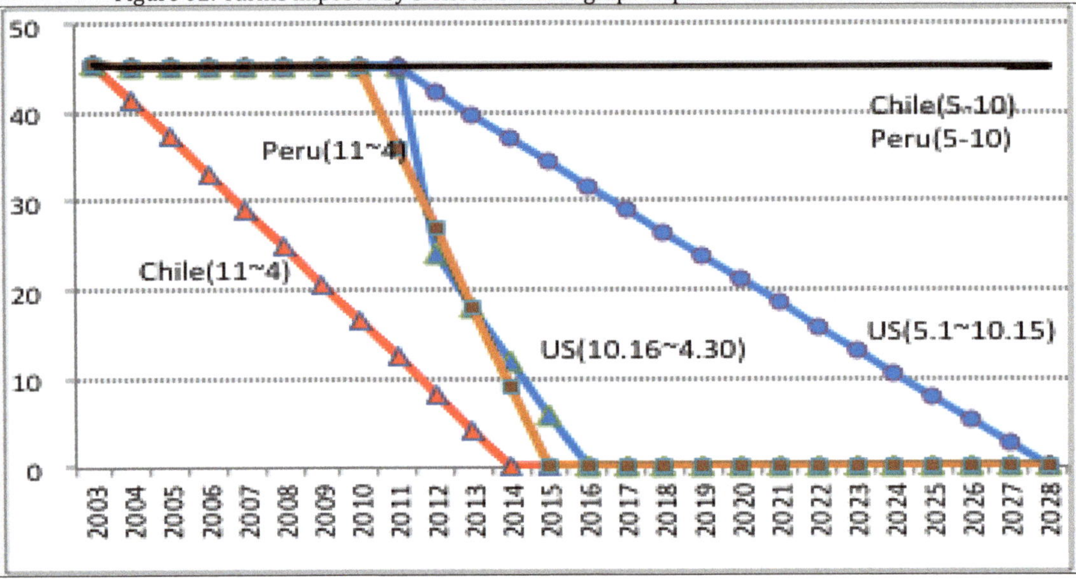

The tariff on in-season grapes from Chile and Peru will not phased out as the two countries do not export much during the in-season period of S. Korea. As shown in Figure 3, the exports of table grapes from the US peak in the months of September to November. But, that is also the time, when higher amount of tariffs are imposed compared to other months. Taking the advantage of their location in the southern hemisphere, Chile captures the S. Korean market during the off-season period, leading the US in terms of total grape exports to S. Korea. In total, Chile captured 87 percent of the import market compared to only 13 percent by the US in 2011. Peru just started exporting grapes to S. Korea in 2011.

Within this context, this paper analyzes the impact of KORUS FTA on the table grape sectors of both S. Korea and the US. In order to measure the impact of FTA we generally use CGE model, gravity model, and import demand function approach (Heng and Suu, 2009).

Figure 03: Average monthly table grape imports from the US 2003-12 (MT)

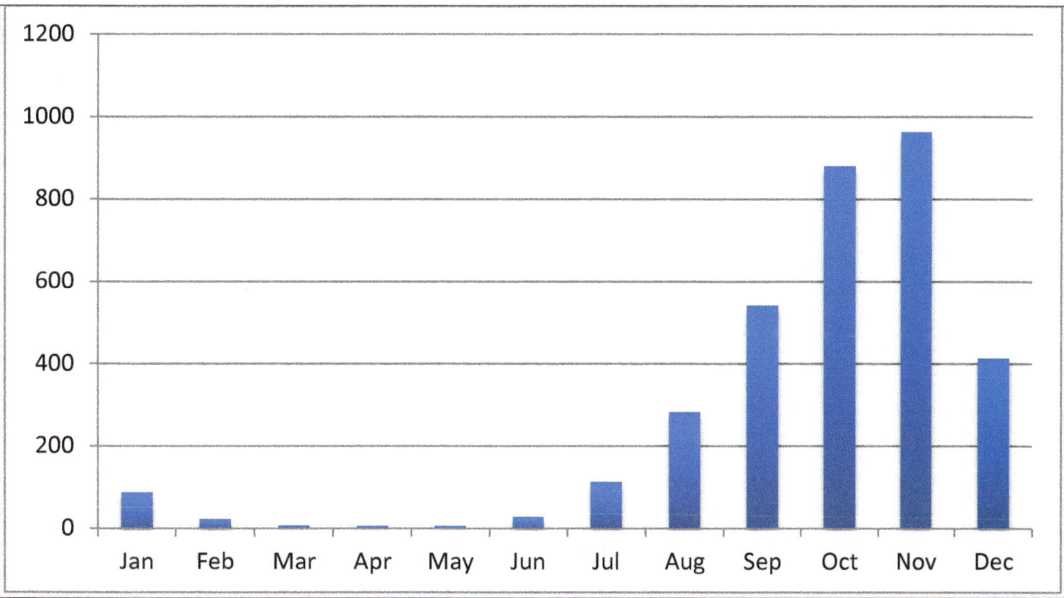

Using a CGE model is not appropriate in our case here, as CGE model requires large amount of data due to large number of parameter requirements. On the other hand, the gravity model involves regressing trade flows on a series of explanatory variables, but Heng and Suu (2009) observe that there is not conclusive evidence as to what explanatory variables should be included in the gravity model based on economic theory. The third method and the one that will be used in this paper is the method using import demand functions to study the impact of KORUS FTA. The major advantage of this method is that extensive research has been done to specify the key determinants of import demand. Also, this method is more appropriate for an ex-post analysis as that of our study and also it requires lot less data compared to CGE model (Heng and Suu, 2009). In the case of KORUS FTA, as it is being implemented only in the last one year, there is lack of sufficient number of data points. So, the model of import demand estimation is highly suitable to follow in our study.

In this study the methodology for estimating the impacts of KORUS FTA on table grapes is revised from the approach followed by Choi, et al., (2009) and Kim and Choi (2007). The model assumes that the quantity of imports of the table grapes from the US (Q^f) is a function of price of US table grapes (P^f) price of grapes from rest of the world (P^{rw}), Price of domestic (S. Korea) grapes (P^d), price of substitute products (P^{rd}) and income of the country (M).

$$Q^f = f(P^f, P^{rw}, P^d, P^{rd}, M) \ldots\ldots\ldots\ldots\ldots Eq. 5$$

A detailed theoretical derivation of the demand, supply and cross price elasticity formulas and further derivation of the formulas for estimating price and quantity changes and the associated changes in value of imports are given in Appendix II. The results of the theoretical derivation are given below. The new equilibrium price and equilibrium quantity due to KORUS FTA are as follows

$$\Delta Q^d = \frac{1}{\eta^d}\Delta Q^d + \Delta TP^d = \left(\frac{\varepsilon^d\eta^d}{\eta^d-\varepsilon^d}\right)\frac{1}{\delta_d^f}\left[\delta_f^f\left(\frac{t}{1+t}\right)\Delta t\right] \ldots\ldots\ldots\ldots Eq.\ 6$$

$$\Delta P^d = \frac{1}{\varepsilon^d}\Delta Q^d = \frac{1}{\varepsilon^d}\left(\frac{\varepsilon^d\eta^d}{\eta^d-\varepsilon^d}\right)\frac{1}{\delta_d^f}\left[\delta_f^f\left(\frac{t}{1+t}\right)\Delta t\right] \ldots\ldots\ldots\ldots.. Eq.\ 7$$

The data for the estimation of impact of KORUS FTA is obtained from the database of Korea Agricultural Trade Information (KATI, 2013) and all the prices and GDP data were deflated by consumer price index (CPI). Some information on tariff profiles is also obtained from World Trade Organization's database on tariffs. The price elasticity of US imports and cross price elasticity are obtained from our own estimation results. The available estimates of domestic grape demand elasticity and domestic grape supply elasticity were incorporated in the estimation process. The estimation results and all the elasticity values are given in table 4 (a) and 4 (b) respectively.

Table 4(a): Results of the S. Korean Table Grape Import Demand Estimation

	Coeff.	t-value	P>t
Domestic Grape price	0.52	0.28	0.78
US Grape Price	-0.23	-2.69	0.01

Other Grape Price	0.19	2.22	0.03
Domestic other price	5.43	1.46	0.15
GDP	0.01	2.31	0.03
Constant	-2583.91	-1.69	0.1
R square = 0.34; No of observations = 45			

Table 4 (b): Elasticity estimates

	Values
Price elasticity of US imports	-2.11
Cross price elasticity	0.14
Domestic demand elasticity	-0.51
Domestic supply elasticity	0.62

By using the above elasticity values and the formulas obtained from the theoretical derivation, we have estimated the impact of KORUS FTA on grape imports by S. Korea. It is estimated that in 2012, the grape imports have increased by 14 percent and the grape production in S. Korea decreased by 7.8 percent due to KORUS FTA. The results also show that in 2013 as the in-season and off-season tariffs get reduced to around 40 percent and 18 percent respectively, the imports from US may increase by 9.7 percent and production in S. Korea may decrease by 5.3 percent over previous year. The results confirm the expectations of the impact of KORUS FTA on US agricultural exports. As the tariffs get reduced to much lower levels in future, the impact is expected to be much higher than what our results show. Due to reduction in barriers, the table grape sector in S. Korea may initially face a negative impact leading to a reduction in production, but in the long term it is bound to perform well as it will become more efficient due to the global competition it faces.

4.0 Conclusion and policy implications

The results show that the KORUS FTA definitely creates opportunities for exporters of agricultural products from California. The lower barriers and eventual phasing out of tariffs on most products will create a very lucrative market for California agriculture. Along with the reduction of the tariffs, the relaxation of non-tariff barriers by means of simplification of rules and regulations, better and faster administrative procedures will also lead to increased exports from the US. Our analysis has also shown that the S. Korean grape sector will be decreasing its production due to more imports from the US, which may happen with many other agricultural products as well. This may be due to that the S. Korean agriculture is much smaller and much more protected and dependent on government support compared to that of US agriculture. But, by reducing the tariffs and other barriers as well, the S. Korean agriculture may become more competitive and more efficient than before. In order to understand the impact of KORUS FTA more effectively, similar analysis can be done on all major products after few more years of its implementation, as more data will be generated by that time.

The other major finding of this study is the advantage that the U.S. exporters may obtain due to the degree of preference that will be given to them compared to exporters from other countries. But, it difficult to quantify this advantage as it also depends on the marketing strategies of the exporters and not just on trade policies of the exporting countries.

It is expected that the success of KORUS FTA would definitely motivate countries to fast track free trade negotiations between Pacific Rim nations towards a much bigger multilateral free trade agreement called Trans-Pacific Partnership (TPP) and between the US and the European Union towards developing Transatlantic Trade and Investment Partnership (TTIP). Already, the US is pushing forward negotiations on these two free trade agreements, as they will lead to more interdependence between countries and integrated markets around the world.

References

Aitken, N., D., 1973. The Effect of the EEC and EFTA on European Trade: A Temporal Cross-Section Analysis, American Economic Review, 5(Dec), 881-892.

Baier, S.L., and Bergstrand, J.H., 2007. Do free trade agreements actually increase members' international trade?, Journal of International Economics, 71, 72-95.

Brada, J.C., and Mendez, J.A., 1985. Economic Integration among Developed, Developing and Centrally Planned Economies: A Comparative Analysis, Review of Economics and Statistics, 67(4), 549-556.

Burfisher, M.E., Robinson, S., Thierfelder, K., 2001. The Impact of NAFTA on the United States, The Journal of Economic Perspectives, 15(1), 125-144.

Choi, S.K., Kim, T.H., and Chung, D.H., 2009. Evaluation of compensation measures and impacts of implemented FTAs on agricultural sector, R597, Korea Rural Economic Institute.

Cooper, W.H., 2014. Free Trade Agreements: Impact on U.S. Trade and Implications for U.S. Trade Policy, Congressional Research Service Report 7-5700, U. S. Congress Research Service, Washington, D.C.
Heng, T. M., and Suu, K. Y., 2009. Impact of Selected Bilateral FTAs on Singapore's Exports & Imports, Singapore Economic Review Conference, Singapore.
Kim, Y. S. and Choi, S.K., 2007. Ex Post Evaluation of the Korea-Chile FTA in terms of Demand Side: Application to Chilean Grapes, Korean Journal of Agricultural Economics, 48(1), 81-98.
Korea Agricultural Trade Information (KATI). 2013. www.kati.net. Accessed June 2013.
Lee, H. and Sumner, D. A., 2009. The prospective Free Trade Agreement with Korea: Background, Analysis and Perspectives for California Agriculture, University of California Giannini Foundation Information Series 09-2, Davis, CA.
Lee, H. and Sumner, D. A., 2011. South Korea – U.S. Free Trade Agreement Will Lower Export Barriers for California Products, California Agriculture, 65(2).
Paggi, M., Yamazaki, F., and Josling, T., 2005. The Central American Free Trade Agreement: What's at Stake for California Agriculture, CATI Publication 50402, Center of Agribusiness, California State University, Fresno, CA.
Urata, S., 2002. Globalization and the Growth in Free Trade Agreements, Asia Pacific Review, 9(1), 20-32.
US Census Bureau, 2014. U.S. International Trade Data, Accessed in April 2014. http://www.census.gov/foreign-trade/balance/c5800.html
USTR Tariff Schedule- Korea, 2012. United States Trade Representative Office, Accessed in July 2012. http://www.ustr.gov/trade-agreements/free-trade-agreements/korus-fta/final-text
World Bank, 2004. Beyond Economic Growth, Published by World Bank, Washington, D. C. http://www.worldbank.org/depweb/english/beyond/global/intro.html
World Tariff Profiles, 2012. Accessed in January 2014. www.wto.org/statistics
World Trade Law 2013. Bilateral and Regional Trade Agreements Notified to WTO, Accessed July, 2013 http://www.worldtradelaw.net/fta/ftadatabase/ftas.asp

Appendix A

Derivation of Preference indices for three countries with different market access

In practice, a tariff is a tax on imports; the price a domestic purchaser pays for imported goods exceeds the amount the foreign exporter receives by the amount of tariff payment. For the simplest case of a specific tariff, the domestic price of importer (Pd) is expressed as Pd=N + T where N is the foreign price of some good (or net price) and T is the specific tariff levied upon it. Assume three exporters serve one import market. Exporter A has tariff free access, exporter B faces a reduced tariff (on a transition path to free access or with a preferential tariff rate) and C faces the MFN tariff levels.

If the domestic price in the importing country is Pd for all three suppliers, and the specific tariffs are Ta, Tb and Tc, then the net price (N) for the exporters is

$$Na = Pd - Ta = Pd$$
$$Nb = Pd - Tb$$
$$Nc = Pd - Tc$$

Thus the preference margins (where Mab is the margin for A relative to B) are

$$Mab = Na - Nb = Tb$$
$$Mac = Na - Nc = Tc$$
$$Mbc = Nb - Nc = (Pd - Tb) - (Pd - Tc) = Tc - Tb$$

As a proportion of net price, these are

$$Mab/Na = Tb/Pd$$
$$Mac/Na = Tc/Pd$$
$$Mbc/Nb = (Tc - Tb)/(Pd - Tb)$$

Alternatively, tariffs are often ad-valorem (TA) – a specified percentage of the price paid to the foreign exporter. In this case domestic price is: Pd = N (1+ TA), thus Pd consists of the payment to the foreigner, N, plus the import tax N*TA. When a tariff is ad-valorem, above expressions are changed to

$$Na = \frac{Pd}{(1+TAa)} = Pd$$
$$Nb = \frac{Pd}{(1+TAb)}$$
$$Nc = \frac{Pd}{(1+TAc)}$$

And the percentage margins are expressed as the following:

$$Mab = Na - Nb = Pd - \frac{Pd}{1+TAb} = Pd\left(1 - \frac{1}{1+TAb}\right)$$

$$Mac = Na - Nc = Pd - \frac{Pd}{1+TAc} = Pd\left(1 - \frac{1}{1+TAc}\right)$$

$$Mbc = Nb - Nc = \frac{Pd}{1+TAb} - \frac{Pd}{1+TAc}$$

As a proportion of net price, these are

$$Mab/Na = \left(1 - \frac{1}{1+TAb}\right)$$

$$Mac/Na = \left(1 - \frac{1}{1+TAc}\right)$$

$$\frac{Mbc}{Nb} = Pd\left(\frac{1}{1+TAb} - \frac{1}{1+TAc}\right) * \frac{1+TAb}{Pd} = 1 - \frac{1+TAb}{1+TAc}$$

These margins can be interpreted either as higher prices (more profits) for the preferred exporter or higher costs that would be offset by the preference (or combination of both). Similarly, a negative preference is the amount by which costs in B have to be less than in A to allow them to be competitive, or lower profit in that market. In this analysis we do not try to distinguish between the cost and profit interpretations. Thus the preference index would be the margin as a proportion (or percent) of the net price. This would vary by commodity and over time, and could in principle be calculated for nay pair of countries.

Let us denote the preference index as Θ then

$$\Theta ab = Mab/Na = \left(1 - \frac{1}{1+TAb}\right)$$

$$\Theta ac = Mac/Na = \left(1 - \frac{1}{1+TAc}\right)$$

$$\Theta bc = \frac{Mbc}{Nb} = Pd\left(\frac{1}{1+TAb} - \frac{1}{1+TAc}\right) * \frac{1+TAb}{Pd} = 1 - \frac{1+TAb}{1+TAc}$$

Let us consider the case of KORUS FTA by considering three countries: A, United States, and Rest of the World (ROW). Country A has a free trade agreement with S. Korea and faces zero tariff rate; the United States faces an MFN rate before the free trade agreement ($TAus^0$) but free trade access after KORUS FTA ($TAus^1$), and the ROW faces the MFN tariff levels. Thus, before the KORUS FTA, preference index for the US relative to country A ($\Theta us^0 a$) and the ROW ($\Theta us^0 row$) is expressed as the following:

$$\Theta us^0 a = \frac{Mus^0 a}{Nus^0} = Pd\left(\frac{1}{1+TAus^0} - 1\right) * \left(\frac{1+TAus^0}{Pd}\right) = -TAus^0 \ldots\ldots\ldots\ldots\ldots\ldots\ldots \text{Eq A 1.1}$$

$$\Theta us^0 row = \frac{Mus^0 row}{Nus^0} = Pd\left(\frac{1}{1+TAus^0} - \frac{1}{1+TArow}\right) * \left(\frac{1+TAus^0}{Pd}\right) = 0 \ldots\ldots\ldots\ldots\ldots\ldots\ldots \text{Eq A 1.2}$$

Since ($TAus^0$=TArow)

After KORUS FTA, they are

$$\Theta us^1 a = \frac{Mus^1 a}{Nus^1} = \left(\frac{Pd - Pd}{Pd}\right) \ldots\ldots\ldots\ldots\ldots\ldots \text{Eq. A1.3}$$

$$\Theta us^1 row = \frac{Mus^1 row}{Nus^1} = \left(1 - \frac{1}{1+TArow}\right) \ldots\ldots\ldots\ldots \text{Eq. A1.4}$$

Appendix B

Theoretical derivation of elasticities and price and quantity changes

In this study, the methodology for estimating impacts of KORUS FTA on table grapes is revised from Choi, et.al.(2009)'s approach. Suppose an import demand function of Korea from the US is denoted as

$$Q^f = f(P^f, P^{rw}, P^d, P^{rd}, M) \ldots\ldots\ldots\ldots\ldots \text{Eq. A2.1}$$

Where Q^f=import quantity from the US, P^f= US price, P^{rw}=other country price, P^d= Korean domestic price, P^{rd}=Korean domestic substitute price, M =income (GDP)

By total derivative, we get

$$dQ^f = \frac{\partial Q^f}{\partial P^f} dP^f + \frac{\partial Q^f}{\partial P^{rw}} dP^{rw} + \frac{\partial Q^f}{\partial P^d} dP^d + \frac{\partial Q^f}{\partial P^{rd}} dP^{rd} + \frac{\partial Q^f}{\partial M} dM \text{.... .... Eq. A2.2}$$

It can be re-written in terms of the rate of change as follows

$$\frac{dQ^f}{Q^f} = \frac{\partial Q^f}{\partial P^f}\frac{dP^f}{Q^f} + \frac{\partial Q^f}{\partial P^{rw}}\frac{dP^{rw}}{Q^f} + \frac{\partial Q^f}{\partial P^d}\frac{dP^d}{Q^f} + \frac{\partial Q^f}{\partial P^{rd}}\frac{dP^{rd}}{Q^f} + \frac{\partial Q^f}{\partial M}\frac{dM}{Q^f} \text{.......... Eq. A2.3}$$

$$\Rightarrow \frac{dQ^f}{Q^f} = \frac{\partial Q^f}{\partial P^f}\frac{P^f}{Q^f}\frac{dP^f}{P^f} + \frac{\partial Q^f}{\partial P^{rw}}\frac{P^{rw}}{Q^f}\frac{dP^{rw}}{P^{rw}} + \frac{\partial Q^f}{\partial P^d}\frac{P^d}{Q^f}\frac{dP^d}{P^d} + \frac{\partial Q^f}{\partial P^{rd}}\frac{P^{rd}}{Q^f}\frac{dP^{rd}}{P^{rd}} + \frac{\partial Q^f}{\partial M}\frac{M}{Q^f}\frac{dM}{M} \text{................ Eq. A2.4}$$

$$\Rightarrow \Delta Q^f = \delta_f^f \Delta P^f + \delta_{rw}^f \Delta P^{rw} + \delta_d^f \Delta P^d + \delta_{rd}^f \Delta P^{rd} + \delta_M^f \Delta M \text{.......... Eq. A 2.5}$$

Where δ_f^f= own price elasticity of imports from US by a change of import price of the US,
δ_{rw}^f=cross elasticity of imports from US by the change of other country import price,
δ_d^f= cross elasticity of imports from US by the change of Korean domestic price,
δ_{rd}^f=cross elasticity of imports from US by change of Korean domestic substitute price,
δ_M^f=income elasticity of imports from US by the change of Korean domestic income,
Δ = rate of change.
The prices can be expressed with tariff or without tariff

$$P_0^f = (1+t)P^f \text{ with tariff(t) .... Eq A2.6}$$

$$P_1^f = P^f \text{ without tariff(full elimination of tariff)}$$

When the tariff is fully eliminated, the change in the import price of table grapes from the US in Korea is as follows,

$$\frac{(P_1^f - P_0^f)}{P_0^f} = -\frac{t}{(1+t)} \text{... Eq. A2.7}$$

So, the change in import volume due to change in tariff is

$$\Delta TQ^f = \delta_f^f \left[\left(\frac{t}{1+t}\right)\Delta t\right] \text{... Eq. A2.8}$$

If other things are constant, Korean domestic price will be affected by the change in import volumes from the US. The change can be depicted as

$$\Delta TP^d = \frac{\Delta TQ^f}{\delta_d^f} = \frac{1}{\delta_d^f}\left[\delta_f^f\left(\frac{t}{1+t}\right)\Delta t\right] \quad \because \; \delta_d^f = \frac{\Delta TQ^f}{\Delta TP^d} \text{..... Eq. A2.9}$$

The change in imports also affects the domestic supply and demand in Korea.
Change in demand: $\Delta P^d = \frac{1}{\eta^d}\Delta Q^d + \Delta TP^d = \frac{1}{\eta^d}\Delta Q^d + \frac{1}{\delta_d^f}\left[\delta_f^f\left(\frac{t}{1+t}\right)\Delta t\right]$
Change in supply: $\Delta P^d = \frac{1}{\varepsilon^d}\Delta Q^d$
Where
η^d= own price elasticity of Korean domestic demand
ε^d=Korean domestic supply elasticity

The change in imports causes a shift in demand curve so that we can get a new equilibrium price and quantity, which are shown as:

$$\frac{1}{\varepsilon^d}\Delta Q^d = \frac{1}{\eta^d}\Delta Q^d + \frac{1}{\delta_d^f}\left[\delta_f^f\left(\frac{t}{1+t}\right)\Delta t\right] \text{...... Eq. A 2.10}$$

$$\Rightarrow \Delta Q^d = \frac{1}{\eta^d}\Delta Q^d + \Delta TP^d = \left(\frac{\varepsilon^d\eta^d}{\eta^d - \varepsilon^d}\right)\frac{1}{\delta_d^f}\left[\delta_f^f\left(\frac{t}{1+t}\right)\Delta t\right] \text{...... Eq. A2.11}$$

$$\Delta P^d = \frac{1}{\varepsilon^d}\Delta Q^d = \frac{1}{\varepsilon^d}\left(\frac{\varepsilon^d\eta^d}{\eta^d-\varepsilon^d}\right)\frac{1}{\delta_d^f}\left[\delta_f^f\left(\frac{t}{1+t}\right)\Delta t\right] = \left(\frac{\eta^d}{\eta^d-\varepsilon^d}\right)\frac{1}{\delta_d^f}\left[\delta_f^f\left(\frac{t}{1+t}\right)\Delta t\right] \text{........... } Eq. A2.12$$

From the change in Quantity and Price, we obtain the change in value of production

$$\Delta(Q^dP^d) = \Delta P^d + \Delta Q^d = \left(\frac{\eta^d}{\eta^d-\varepsilon^d}\right)\frac{1}{\delta_d^f}\left[\delta_f^f\left(\frac{t}{1+t}\right)\Delta t\right] + \left(\frac{\varepsilon^d\eta^d}{\eta^d-\varepsilon^d}\right)\frac{1}{\delta_d^f}\left[\delta_f^f\left(\frac{t}{1+t}\right)\Delta t\right] \text{..... } Eq\ A2.13 \quad = (1+\varepsilon^d)\left(\frac{\eta^d}{\eta^d-\varepsilon^d}\right)\frac{1}{\delta_d^f}\left[\delta_f^f\left(\frac{t}{1+t}\right)\Delta t\right] = (1+\varepsilon^d)\,\Delta P^d$$

In actual calculation, we directly estimated price elasticity of US imports and cross price elasticity and used Korean domestic demand elasticity and Korean domestic supply elasticity from Choi, et.al. (2009).

Evidences of investors' risk tolerance in Nairobi securities exchange: Does education or specialization matter?

Tobias Olweny [a*]

[a] Department of Finance and Accounting, Jomo Kenyatta University of Agriculture and Technology, Kenya.
* Corresponding author's email: toolweny@yahoo.com or tolweny@jkuat.ac.ke

HIGHLIGHTS:

1. The study tests the effect of education or specialization influence risk tolerance.
2. The sample of 500 investors includes investors trading at Nairobi Securities Exchange.
3. Result suggests that education level positively increases risk tolerance, while specialization reduces.

Article History

Keywords:
Heuristics;
Logistic regression;
Risk tolerance;
Specialization.

ABSTRACT

The main objective of the study is to evaluate the extent to which investors' education level or specialization in finance or accounting determines investor risk tolerance at the Nairobi Securities Exchange using a total of 500 individual investors out of 9,32,510 investors holding CDS accounts. Data is collected through questionnaires comprising 13-item risk tolerance instrument and demographic attributes that determine individual investors' risk tolerance. Analytical framework included ordinal logistic regression model, as well as an analysis of variance and Wolfowitz Wald test at $\alpha=0.05$. The key findings are that investor education level are significant in the determination of risk tolerance only at below the high school level with a positive impact of 1.831 log of odd for every unit increase in risk tolerance. Specialization in finance or accounting discipline also influenced investor risk tolerance at a significance level of 0.022 with a negative impact of -0.389.

1.0 Introduction

Investor risk tolerance is an important aspect in investment decision making. Rigorous theoretical analyses relating risk tolerance to optimal portfolios are based on the economic concept of risk aversion. The first trial at conceptualizing the investors risk aversion belongs to Friedman and Savage (1948), who explained investment behavior using the returns of risky financial investments behavior, and that of risky financial investments utility functions. They argued that the main factor that changes the investor's attitude towards risk is the size of their wealth. Further studies have shown that there are also other factors with direct impact over the attitude towards risk, which include economic growth forecast of a market, the level of training and experience gained, fluctuations of the exchange market and psychological factors among others. In an effort to understand the factors that influence the degree of risk aversion, Arrow and Pratt (1965), observed that investors with high risk aversion are less willing to take those risks, since the price for the given risk (risk premium) is much higher. In their approach, the main factors of risk aversion were the wealth of investors and the utility measure of the investors risk aversions. There are two major indicators that reflect an investors' risk tolerance: risk tolerance attitude and behavior; which are synthesized as above to develop utility function of the investor. Risk tolerance; a person's attitude towards taking risk, is a complex psychological concept. Jackson et al (1992), contend that risk tolerance has four dimensions: financial, physical, social and ethical.

Irwin (1993) classifies the predisposing factors into two categories: environmental and bio-psychosocial factors. Environmental factors here include measurable individual and family financial attributes, such as income, net worth, and home ownership status. He defines bio-psychosocial factors to include characteristics such as age, gender, personality traits, birth order and ethnicity, which one has little or no control of. Other factors that appear to influence a person's financial risk tolerance include environmental factors such as financial knowledge, and family situation. Roszkowski (1999) and Sulloway (1997) contend that birth order is a significant factor influencing risk tolerance level of individuals. Haynes (2001) also found that factors such as age, race and net worth affect risk attitudes and behavior.

Friend and Blume (1975), estimated risk aversion by analyzing household portfolios and other decisions under risk. However, it is necessary here to assume that a household behaves with all information and rationality in order for such empirical analysis to reveal risk aversion. Risk tolerance can be operationalized as the inverse of relative risk aversion (Some researchers have proposed that risk tolerance is the inverse of risk aversion Brennan and Kraus (1976); Barsky, Juster, Kimball and Shappiro (1997). Grabble (2000), however they stated that financial risk tolerance is the maximum amount of uncertainty that someone is willing to accept, when making a financial decision. Risk tolerance is therefore an important concept that has implications for both financial services providers and consumers. Despite its importance in the financial services industry, there still remain some questions with respect to the 'determinants' of risk tolerance. The current theoretical review on risk tolerance and aversion determination is directed towards heuristics or rule of thumb. Investment decision making literature referring to heuristics defines the concept as a set of processes that assist with complex decision making and which are unproven, untested and may result in systematic biases. Shefrin (2001) defines heuristics as "rule of the thumb". Baker and Nosfinger (2002), in their review of behavioral finance, contend that heuristics are common investment decisions with cognitive and emotional biases leading to sub-optimal decision for investors

Many Kenyans rarely consult investment advisors licensed by the CMA whenever they intend to invest in the stock market (CMA, 2010). These advisors also tend to avoid provision of services to individual investors because of their low income level; they prefer dealing with institutional investors, who have regular income to pay advisory charges rather than erratic fee from individual investors. Brokerage firms and investment banks have played advisory roles to investors in Kenya from its independence to date (CMA, 2010). The advice however, is rarely objective because their principal aim is to convince the investors to open an account for their custody and earn commissions or brokerage fees. They seldom evaluate a person's investment policy for relevant decision making. In Kenya, individual investors are mainly guided by stock brokerage firms and investment bankers when selecting their optimal portfolio and setting their investment policy. The firms rarely evaluate formal factors influencing investor's risk tolerance and aversion level. As alluded to in the background of the study, the core competence of the firms is security trading rather than research and guidance on investor's portfolio management.

The paper reviews literature on the effect of education and specialization on risk tolerance from other countries to develop the hypotheses of study. Data is then collected and collated, relevant descriptive statistics are used to present the data. Ordinal Logistic Regression is applied as a model to determine the hypothesis and finally the findings are discussed for development of proposed policy implications.

2.0 Literature review and hypotheses development

Paun et al (2007), takes into account the demographic characteristics of Romanians, when estimating their risk aversion levels. Ajmi (2008), also applied a questionnaire on demographically segregated respondents in Bahrain, similarly Yuen and Chen (2008), employed a psychometric instrument to determine risk tolerance level in Hong Kong. Education is thought to increase a person's capacity to evaluate risks inherent to the investment process and therefore endow them with a higher financial risk tolerance (see Baker and Haslem, 1974; Sung and Hanna, 1996). Shaw (1996) derives a model which suggests an element of circularity in this argument however, as the relative risk aversion of an individual is shown to determine the rate of human capital acquisition. While testing the efficacy of demographics on risk tolerance, Grabble and Lytton (1998), took 2626 respondents in United States of America. They used discriminate analysis to separate, discriminate, estimate and classify investors. They concluded that whites were more tolerant than blacks. Equally, by heuristics they agree that individuals with higher levels of education are proportionately more likely to have higher risk tolerance than individuals with lower educational levels.

Schooley and Worden (1996), constituted a sample of 3143 households in America. They concluded that investors make their portfolio allocation based on their time horizon and risk tolerance. About half of them or less reported that they were not willing to take financial risks, whereas only a quarter of investors with time horizon of 10 years or more were not willing to take risk. Investors with post-secondary education held higher percentage of their assets in securities, while couples held a large percentage on equity. Using the 1989 SCF sponsored by the United States Federal Reserve Board, the researchers gathered detailed information on all assets and liabilities of households, as well as demographic characteristics of households to measure their attributes about the economy, financial planning and savings, as well as risk taking for investments.

Individuals with higher level of education are found to take more risk, Sung and Hanna (1996), however it could be argued that financial knowledge is more important than general education achievement influencing risk taking attitude for example an investor with a master's degree in history may be less tolerant than an individual with a diploma in financial management. Grable and Joo (2004), argue that financial education may have influence on an individual's risk tolerance /aversion determination. They recommend a further study to test the hypothesis of whether business /financial education background or specialization would significantly influence an individual's risk tolerance level.

While some researchers have found that people with higher education usually show more risk tolerance behavior compared to others, contrary findings also exist. The former researchers argue that with increase in the level of education, people become capable of assessing the risk and benefits more carefully than those who are with less education. There is evidence to suggest that higher education encourages people to take more financial risks and a person who is more educated is more risk tolerant than a person with lower level of education (Grable & Lytton, 1999; Grable, 2000 and Al-Ajmi, 2008). In contrast Faff et al (2004) found that education was not a significant determinant of a person's risk tolerance behavior. However, these findings have created an increased interest in including „education" as a variable that explain financial risk tolerance. From the above review it is therefore necessary to test the influence of the above variables on the determination of risk tolerance. The research hypotheses were therefore formulated as follows:

H_1: Education level does not affect investor risk tolerance
H_2: Specialization in finance or accounting does not affect investor risk tolerance

3.0 Data and methodology

3.01 Research design

This study adopted a complex descriptive approach to evaluate the determinants of an individual investor's risk tolerance. Investor attributes such as bio-psychological, financial and sociocultural were hypothesized to influence an individual's inclination towards risk. Data on the said attributes which include investor's age, financial literacy, income, household status, home ownership as well as racial/ethnic orientation were obtained through a questionnaire.

Target population:
The population of investors from whom a sample for assessing individual risk tolerance in Kenya, comprised of all investors holding accounts with the Central Depository Systems Corporation (CDSC), was drawn. The total number of investors was 932,510 as at 30th September 2010 (CMA, 2010). The CDSC was created by the Central Depository Act 2000 to establish and operate a system for a central handling of securities in Kenya, provide immobilization and eventual dematerialization of, and dealings in securities deposited there with in the country and for connected purposes; such securities are immobilized or dematerialized and dealings in respect of those securities are affected by means of entries in securities accounts without physical necessity of certificates. The CDSC provides a reliable source of demand for investments in the Kenyan capital market. The system has created a databank which is ideal for a framework for establishing whether investment managers, advisors and individuals assess their risk tolerance levels before selecting an investment portfolio given limited resources.

Sampling frame and technique:
Since the population variance with respect to the dependent variable is unknown and also because a large portion of the predictor and criterion variables are measured as categorical and not continuous variables, the sample size estimate follows the recommendations by Bartlett et al. (2001) and Sekaran (2011), in the form shown below:

$$n_0 = \frac{(t)^2 * p * q}{(d)^2} = \frac{(2.58)^2 * 0.75 * 0.25q}{(.05)^2} = 499.23 = 500 \text{ (approx.)}$$

Where n_o is the sample size, "t" = the value for the selected alpha level of 1% in each tail to increase precision, hence 2.58; (p) (q) =estimates of variance; where "d" is the acceptable margin of error for the proportion being estimated, that is error researcher is willing to accept = 5%. The selected sample size, of 500, is further informed by three factors: the desire to reduce the sampling error, many respondents may not fill all the details and lowering the number of valid responses, and the fact that the target population is expected to be highly heterogeneous with respect to a number of the internal variables under study. A random sample of 500 individual investors was selected from 22 investment banks and 3 stock brokers which represent the entire licensed brokerage firms by the

CMA as at 31 December 2011. A simple random sample was drawn from all the account holders in each investment bank and stock broker, which is considered manageable in terms of costs and representative of all custodians in contact with individual investors.

3.02 Analysis tools

Descriptive statistics cross tabulation; ordinal logistic regression and correlation analysis was employed to analyze the data. Histogram of risk tolerance and mean, median score and standard deviations forms descriptive statistics, which were further analyzed through statistical package for social sciences (SPSS 20) to determine various coefficients, standard error, regression equations tests, Wolfowitz Wald test, one way as well as paired Analyses of variance (ANOVA) was performed on the data. Ordinal logistic regression was applied to test the implication of individual variable in the determination of an individual's risk tolerance in relation to other variables that have specific ordered characteristics. The log of odds for increase or decrease was obtained for each coefficient of the variables holding others variables constant as explained in the section below. Each value of the independent components was obtained in the questionnaire and a score ranging to a scale of 47 using a 13-item risk tolerance measurement questionnaire (Grable and Lyton, 1999).

An ordinal logistic regression analysis was preferred, since risk tolerance is deemed to be a function of these selected variables of education level and specialization of an individual; which had been categorized into ordered responses. Investor education level was classified into five main categories such as below high school, high school, college and first degree, postgraduate diploma and masters' degree as well as doctorate and above. Financial knowledge of an investor was determined by specialization in professional accountancy or finance on full or partial level. The maximum possible score was 47. A score of 33 and above categorized as very high risk tolerances, 29-32; Above average risk tolerance, 23-28 average risk tolerance ; 19-22 below average while 0-18 low risk tolerance. The equations for this model are as follows:

$$\text{logit}(p) = \log[p / (1-p)] = \ln[p / (1-p)] \quad \text{.................(01)}$$

$$\text{Logit } p = \frac{p}{1-p} = \beta o + \beta eE + \beta sS \quad \text{..........................(02)}$$

Where p is the probability of risk tolerance of an investor

$$p = \frac{e^{\beta o + \beta eE + \beta sS}}{1 + e^{\beta o + \beta eE + \beta sS}} \quad \text{...(03)}$$

Where,

β_o= coefficient of the constant variable

β_{eE}=coefficient of investor level of education

β_e s=coefficient of specialization/qualification in accounting or finance

έί is the error term.

P-represents the logit of risk tolerance; it's the log of odds in which risk tolerance occurs. The risk tolerance score was ordered in to 5 levels; very high score 33 and above, above average 29-32, average score 23-28, below average 19-22 and very low 0-18.

4.0 Results and discussion

4.01 Education and risk tolerance scores

Very high score of risk tolerance was not reported among those with less than high school education; 22 investors with between high school and college had very high risk tolerance, 12 with first degrees; 40 with post graduate diploma and masters; 3 doctorate and above level of education out of a total of 137 respondents. Above average score had a total of 161 including 27 high schools to college, 77 first degrees; 54 post graduate and masters' level and 3 with doctorate and above. Those with below average risk tolerance were 2 college, 13 first degree, 9 post graduate diploma average risk tolerance was reported with 4 less than high school, 36 high school college , 81 first degree 42 post graduate diploma-master and 4 doctorate and above. There were 2 people with low risk tolerance at high school college levels, postgraduate diploma and first degree. Table 01 presents the cross tabulation results.

Table 01: RTS * Education level Cross tabulation

	Education level					
	Less than high school	High school - college	First degree	Postgraduate diploma-Master degree	Doctorate and above	Total
Risk Tolerance Scores Very high	0	22	72	40	3	137

Above average	0	27	77	54	3	161
Average	4	36	81	42	4	167
Below average	2	4	13	9	0	28
Low risk tolerance	0	2	2	2	1	7
Total	6	91	245	147	11	500

Exact chi square test on correlation was observed to have a P value of 0.078, and therefore at α=7.8% Education levels would singly contribute to risk tolerance; Likelihood ratio had a P value of 0.164. All levels of education beginning from less than high school to doctorate level of education had average score of risk tolerance, except those with post graduate diploma and masters' degree, who had scored above average risk tolerance. This result could have been expected for those with doctorate degree except that the numbers of the doctorate degree holders in the sample were fewer relative to the others in the category. It may therefore be concluded that risk tolerance generally increases with the level of education, since education provides new experiences and exposure to individuals. The figure below shows details of the levels of risk tolerance for each of the categories of investor education.

Any qualification in accounting or finance:
Of those who had full or partial qualification in accounting or finance 83 had very high risk tolerance scores 100 below average, 82 average, 14 below average and 1 low risk while; among those without qualification, 55 had very high risk tolerance, 63 above average, 85 average, 15 below and 6 low risk tolerance. Those with qualification or specialization in finance or accounting had above average risk tolerance while those without specialization scored average risk tolerance. Those who were specialized would be willing to take more risk other things being equal; this could be due to the understanding of the finance discipline or financial literacy of the expectations of financial instruments. This variable was quite significant on its own in the determination of risk tolerance level of the investors. The Pearson chi had a P value of 0.020 while the likelihood ratio recorded a P value of 0.017. Table 02 presents cross tabulation results between risk tolerance and specialization in accounting or finance.

Table 02: Any qualification in accounting/finance and risk tolerance

Risk tolerance	Any qualification in accounting/finance		Total
	No	Yes	
Very high	83	55	138
Above average	100	63	163
Average	82	85	167
Below average	14	15	29
Low risk tolerance	1	6	7
Total	280	224	504

One way analysis of variance was performed for the two variables on risk tolerance. It was established that the level of education and specialization contributed highly to the risk tolerance of each of the individuals interviewed. Education recorded a significance with a P value of 0.049 as seen in table 02, which is below α=5% at 95% confidence interval while specialization or qualification showed a significance with a P value of 0.005 as shown in table 03 below. Specialization contributed heavily in determining the risk tolerance level of investors because of financial knowledge exposure among these individuals. Financial literacy is thus more important than general education; however education per se would still influence an individual's risk tolerance level.

Table 03: RTS and Specialization ANOVA

	Sum of Squares	Df	Mean Square	F	Sig.
Between Groups	7.232	1	7.232	8.003	.005
Within Groups	453.625	502	.904		
Total	460.857	503			

Table 04: RTS and education ANOVA

	Sum of Squares	Df	Mean Square	F	Sig.
Between Groups	202.535	4	50.634	2.401	.049
Within Groups	10439.857	495	21.091		
Total	10642.392	499			

4.02 Ordinal logistic regression model (OLRM)

SPPS ordinal procedure (Polytomous Universal Model -PLUM) was used to analyze the data to preserve the natural ordering of data. This is an extension of general regression model to logistic ordinal of general categories. Table 04 provides the summary statistics of the model. It's a combination of parameter into probabilities of the dependent variable occurring. The risk tolerance score was ordered in to 5 levels; very high score 33 and above, above average 29-32, average score 23-28, below average 19-22 and very low 0-18. The model fitted at P=0.006 which is less than P=0.050, as shown on the table 05 below.

Table 05: model fitting

Model	-2 Log Likelihood	Chi-Square	df	Sig.
Intercept Only	149.204			
Final	133.049	16.155	5	.006
Link function: Logit.				

The parameter estimates indicated in table 07 below, were computed with SPSS calculating standard error and a Wald test which is a variant of z test was performed through the program. Education below high school level was found to be considerably significant in determination of risk tolerance with P=0.053 almost equivalent to α=5%. Those with less than high school education are therefore influential to risk tolerance. For each unit increase in education level from below high school level, the expected ordered log of odds of risk tolerance increased by 1.831, for each unit increase in education level between high school and college the expected log of odds of risk tolerance reduced by 0.102 while for each unit increase in education level from first degree the expected log of odds of risk tolerance reduced by 0.261 and for each unit increase of education level from masters the expected log of odds of risk tolerance reduced by 0.353 as the threshold for risk tolerance rises holding other factors constant.

The risk tolerance scores increases with the level of education, below high school level respondents had an average RTS less than 25. The scores increased to 30 from high school level to doctorate level of education as shown in the appendix. The study reveals that level of education influences an individual's willingness to take investment risk and that higher levels of attained education are associated with increased levels of risk tolerance, because education plays an important role in the level of understanding of risks inherent to the financial investment and therefore higher education encourages taking more financial risk. Therefore this research concurs with Grable and Lytton (1998). Grable and Lytton (1999), Grable (2000), Grable and Joo (2004) and Al-Ajmi (2008) who found that individuals with higher attained education were more risk tolerant than individuals with lower attained educational levels, although it contradicts Faff et al. (2004) found that education was not a significant determinant of an individual's attitude towards risk.

Table 06: Logistic regression case processing summary

		N	Marginal Percentage
RTS	Very high	136	27.3%
	Above average	161	32.3%
	Average	167	33.5%
	Below average	28	5.6%
	Low risk tolerance	7	1.4%
Education level	Less than high school	6	1.2%
	High school - college	91	18.2%
	First degree	244	48.9%
	Postgraduate diploma- Master degree	147	29.5%
	Doctorate and above	11	2.2%
Any qualification in accounting/finance	Yes	277	55.5%
	No	222	44.5%
Valid		499	100.0%
Missing		7	
Total		506	

Qualification or specialization in finance or accounting was found to be significant in determination of risk tolerance at P= 0.022 which is Greater than 0.050 therefore the null hypothesis that specialization does not influence an investor's risk tolerance was rejected. For every single unit increase in specialization or qualification in accounting or finance, the expected ordered log of odds of risk tolerance reduced by 0.389 as the threshold of risk tolerance rises holding other variables constant.

Figure 01: Education and risk tolerance

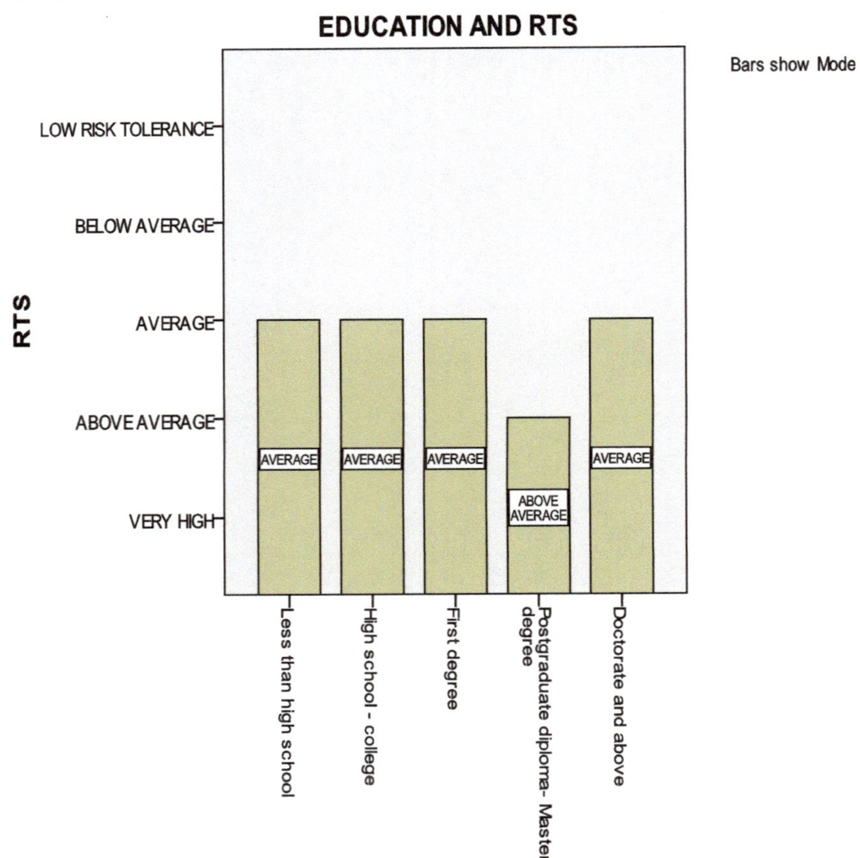

Figure 02: Specialization and risk tolerance

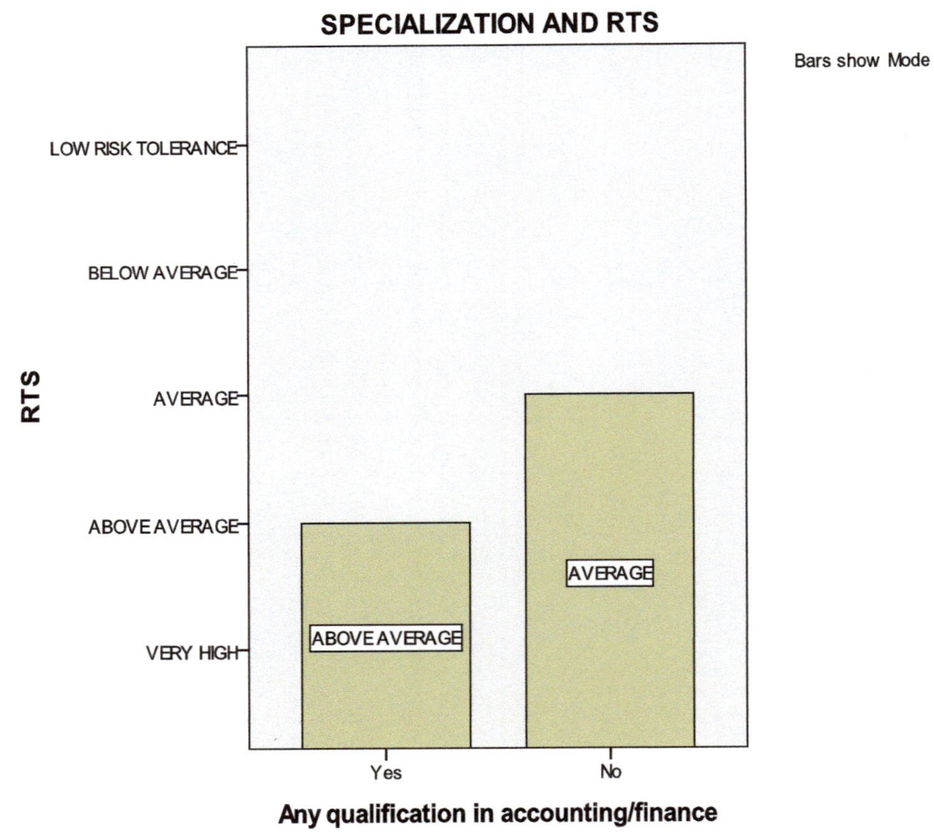

RTS = Risk tolerance score

This implied that those who had partial or full qualification in accounting and or finance had higher average score of risk tolerance compared to those without qualification or specializations as indicated in the appendix. Grable and Joo (2004) argued that financial education may have influence on an individual's risk tolerance determination. They recommend a further study to test the hypothesis of whether business /financial education background or specialization would significantly influence an individual's risk tolerance level.

Table 07: Ordinal logistic regression parameter estimates

		Estimate	Std. Error	Wald	Deg of freedom	Sig.
Threshold	[RTS = 1]	-1.454	.568	6.542	1	.011
	[RTS = 2]	-.059	.564	.011	1	.916
	[RTS = 3]	2.208	.583	14.352	1	.000
	[RTS = 4]	3.897	.675	33.316	1	.000
Location	[Var1_Quez6_Education_level=1]	1.831	.948	3.730	1	.053
	[Var1_Quez6_Education_level=2]	-.102	.584	.030	1	.862
	[Var1_Quez6_Education_level=3]	-.261	.562	.215	1	.643
	[Var1_Quez6_Education_level=4]	-.353	.572	.382	1	.537
	[Var1_Quez6_Education_level=5]	0[a]	.	.	0	.
	[Var1_Quez7_AnyQualification_accounting_finance=1]	-.389	.170	5.257	1	.022
	[Var1_Quez7_AnyQualification_accounting_finance=2]	0[a]	.	.	0	.

Link function: Logit.

a. This parameter is set to zero because it is redundant.

5.0 Conclusion and policy implication

Investors with higher levels of education were more risk tolerant than those with lower level of education, thus risk tolerance was positively related to education level, however the education level was more significant at below high school level compare to other levels therefore it is necessary for stock market investors to complete high school. The significance level increased as the level of education increased to doctorate level this may be associated to the level of reasoning before accepting to tolerate risk. Those with accounting and/or finance qualification were more risk tolerant than non-specialist in these thematic areas therefore the inclination towards risk is influenced by specialization.

Capital Market Authority should design more elaborate investor education plans that can reduce the significant challenge of very low risk tolerance as exposed in the research for those investors with less than high school education. As the Nairobi Securities Exchange (NSE) becomes more vibrant, it would also be appropriate for part of school curriculum at primary level of education to highlight on securities offered at the securities exchange and the role of the market in the economy as indicated in Kenya vision 2030 economic pillar. Investor education can also be promoted at the country level with appropriate county budget to enable many Kenyans understand their risk tolerance level.

Although specialization or lack of specialization is an individual's volition, the government as well as fund managers should make conscious efforts to provide basic understanding of the available security instruments at the securities market to enable investors select portfolio of assets that are equivalent to their risk profiles. The NSE and CMA should develop a standard investment profiling questionnaire that incorporates basic attributes such as financial education and financial knowledge to guide Kenyan investors.

References

Al-Ajmi, J.Y., 2008. Risk tolerance of individual investors in an emerging market. International Research Journal of Finance and Economics, 17: 15-26.

Arrow, J. & Pratt J.W. 1965. Risk aversion in the small and in the large Econometrica, 32: 122-136.

Baker, H. K., & Haslem, J. A., 1974. The impact of investor socioeconomic characteristics on risk and return preferences. Journal of Business Research, 2(4): 469-476. http://dx.doi.org/10.1016/0148-2963(74)90032-0

Barsky, R. B., Kimball, M. S., Juster, F. T., & Shapiro, M. D., 1997. Preference parameters and behavioral heterogeneity: an experimental approach in the health and retirement survey (No. w5213). National Bureau of Economic Research.

Bartlett, J. E. II., JW Kotrlik, & CC Higgins, 2001. Organizational Research: Determining Appropriate Sample Size in Survey Research. Information Technology, Learning, and Performance Journal, 19(1).

Brennan, M. J., & Kraus, A., 1976. The geometry of separation and myopia. Journal of Financial and Quantitative Analysis, 11(02): 171-193. http://dx.doi.org/10.2307/2979048

CMA (2010) Quarterly Statistical Bulletin, Quarter Ended September 2010.Issue 5/2010 Capital Markets Authority 2010

Hallahan, T. A., Faff, R. W., & McKenzie, M. D., 2004. An empirical investigation of personal financial risk tolerance. Financial Services Review, 13(1): 57-78.

Faff, R., Mulino, D., & Chai, D., 2008. On the linkage between financial risk tolerance and risk aversion. Journal of Financial Research, 31(1); 1-23. http://dx.doi.org/10.1111/j.1475-6803.2008.00229.x

Friedman, M., & Savage, L. J., 1948. The utility analysis of choices involving risk. The Journal of Political Economy, 279-304. http://dx.doi.org/10.1086/256692

Friend, I., & Blume, M.E., 1975. The demand for risky assets. American Economic Review, 75: 900 -922.

Grable, J. E., & Lytton, R. H., 1994. Assessing financial risk tolerance: Do demographic, socioeconomic, and attitudinal factors work. Family Relations and Human Development/Family Economics and Resource Management Biennial, 3: 80-88. http://dx.doi.org/10.1023/A:1022994314982

Grable, J. E., 2000. Financial risk tolerance and additional factors that affect risk taking in everyday money matters. Journal of Business and Psychology, 14(4): 625-630.

Grable, J. E., & Joo, S., 1997. Determinants of risk preference: Implications for family and consumer science professionals. Family Economics and Resource Management Biennial, 2: 19-24.

Grable, J. E. and Lytton, 1998. Investor's risk tolerance: testing the efficacy of demographics as differentiating and classifying factors. Association for Financial Counseling and Planning, 9(1): 61-74.

Grable, J. E., & Joo, S. H., 1999. Factors related to risk tolerance: A further examination. Consumer Interests Annual, 45: 53-58.

Grable, J. E., & Joo, S. H., 2004. Environmental and Biophysical Factors Associated with Financial Risk Tolerance. Journal of Financial Counseling and Planning, 15(1):73-82.

Grable, J., Lytton, R. H., O'neill, B., Joo, S. H., & Klock, D., 2006. Risk Tolerance, Projection Bias, Vividness, and Equity Prices. The journal of investing, 15(2): 68-74. http://dx.doi.org/10.3905/joi.2006.635632

Hanna, S. D., & Lindamood, S., 2005. Risk tolerance of married couples. Proceeding of the Academy of Financial Services, 13 (4).

Hanna, S., & Chen, P., 1997. Subjective and objective risk tolerance: Implications for optimal portfolios. Financial Counseling and Planning, 8(2): 17-26.

Irwin, C.E, 1993. Adolescence and Risk Taking: How are they Related? In J. Bell & R.W Bell (eds) Adolescent risk taking Newsbury, park C.A: Sage

Jackson, D. N., Hourany, L., & Vidmar, N. J., 1972. A four-dimensional interpretation of risk taking1. Journal of Personality, 40(3): 483-501. http://dx.doi.org/10.1111/j.1467-6494.1972.tb00075.x

Nofsinger, J., & Baker, 2002. Investment, Prentice Hall, New Jersey.

Paun, C Radu , M, Lulian, B., 2007. Empirical evidence of risk aversion for individual Romanian capital market investors. MPRA , 6842, 22

Roszkowski, M.J., 1999. Risk tolerance and risk aversion. Financial Planning, 213-225.

Roszkowski, M.J., 1993. Risk–tolerance in financial decisions. In R.M. Crowe Hughes (Eds).Fundamentals of Financial Planning (2nd Ed.) Bryn Mawr. PA The American College.

Roszkowski, M., & Grable, J., 2005. Estimating risk tolerance: The degree of accuracy and the paramorphic representations of the estimate. Journal of Financial Counseling and Planning, 16(2).

Sekaran,U.,(2011) Research methods: A skill building approach. 4th Edition John Wiley & Sons

Schooley, D. K., & Worden, D. D., 1996. Risk aversion measures: Comparing attitudes and asset allocation. Financial services review, 5(2): 87-99. http://dx.doi.org/10.1016/S1057-0810(96)90003-7

Shaw, K. L., 1996. An empirical analysis of risk aversion and income growth. Journal of Labor Economics, 626-653. http://dx.doi.org/10.1086/209825

Shefrin, H., 2001. Behavioral corporate finance. Journal of Applied Corporate Finance, 14(3):113-126. http://dx.doi.org/10.1111/j.1745-6622.2001.tb00443.x

Sulloway, F.J, 1997. Born to rebel: Birth order, family dynamics and creative lives. Boston Pantheon.

Sung, J., & Hanna, S., 1996. Factors related to risk tolerance. Financial Counseling and Planning, 7, 11-20.

Wang, C., & Hanna, S. D., 2007. Racial/ethnic disparities in stock ownership: A decomposition analysis. Consumer Interests Annual, 53.

Wang, C., & Hanna, S. D., 2007. The risk tolerance and stock ownership of business owning households. Financial Counseling and Planning, 18(2): 3-18.

Xiao, J. J., Alhabeeb, M. J., HONG, G. S., & Haynes, G. W., 2001. Attitude toward Risk and Risk-Taking Behavior of Business-Owning Families. Journal of Consumer Affairs, 35(2): 307-325. http://dx.doi.org/10.1111/j.1745-6606.2001.tb00116.x

Yuen, W.,T & Chen.,C.W., 2008. Investor risk tolerance: A survey of Hong Kong. Working Paper Series. Economics Department Hong Kong University.

13

Defragmenting the effect of major news announcements on financial markets

Ikhlaas Gurrib [a*]

[a] Coordinator, MBA (Finance) program, Canadian University of Dubai, Dubai, United Arab Emirates.
* Corresponding author e-mail: ikhlaas@cud.ac.ae.

HIGHLIGHTS:

1. The effects of major announcements released by the Central Bank on major currency pairs, all paired against the US Dollar, have been investigated.
2. Effect of the major announcement on three major currency pairs were calculated using a 1 minute analysis post announcement data.
3. Announcements to affect local currency relatively more than foreign currencies.
4. Stability diagnostic tests between the changes in EUR/USD against AUD/USD following news announcements do not reveal the presence of significant breakpoint tests.

Article History

Keywords:
Cash rate;
Minimum bid rate;
News announcements;
Official bank rate.

ABSTRACT

The issue of High Frequency Trading (HFT) and its impact on financial markets is hitting the headlines hard nowadays. This paper looks at the effects of three major news announcements on two major currency pairs namely the Australian dollar against the US dollar and the Euro against the US dollar. The three major news announcements are the cash rate from the Reserve Bank of Australia, the minimum bid rate from European Central Bank (ECB) and the official bank rate from the Bank of England. A one minute data interval analysis is used over a time period of four years. Findings suggest the effects of the specific news under analysis to be insignificant for a trader to benefit from the fluctuations in the two major currency markets. The use of other macroeconomic news or higher frequency data is warranted to defragment the effects of major news announcements further.

1.0 Introduction

The advancement in globalization has increased with the help of financial markets by allowing investors to invest their money across any industry in the globe through financial markets in the form of public equity or debt infrastructures. Extensive literature exists regarding the importance of financial markets to any economy. Agenor and Pereira da Silva (2012) presented reviews on arguments for and against attributing an explicit financial stability objective to monetary policy. The reviews were in the context where regulations can be made to prevent disruptive and costly financial crisis. Essentially, financial markets are places in which people and entities can trade financial securities, commodities, and other fungible items of value at low transaction costs and at prices that reflect supply and demand. They trade financial instruments which include mainly securities and derivatives. The key risk determinants of these securities are volatility of the market, performance of the organizations or institutions issuing these securities and individual risks. Financial derivatives being derived from the financial securities provide the advantage of leverage and hence have higher expected returns than securities but the corresponding risk is also higher with key risk determinants as volatility of market and efficiency of the leverage strategy adopted (Darskuviene, 2010). There are many factors that affect the stock price movements in the financial markets. These include the performance of the company, economic position, demand and supply in the industry, product response among the public among others. Along with these key economic variables, politics, events occurring in the industry or market or in the company also play a major role in stock price movements of the company. Any good or bad news about the company, any major policy change in the nation or economy or industry, any change in the corporate governance structure of the organization among other news would lead to immediate effects on the stock prices. Gurrib (2008), using recursive estimates, found major economic events in the 1990s to have no significant effects on hedgers' and speculators' trading decisions and risk attitude. While Laïdi (2008) findings support that market events have significant impact on the stock price movements, Gurrib (2010) showed that in major US futures markets, hedger and speculator volatilities have shown a tendency to decay over time in response to shocks, supporting the belief that both players are informed and react well to news volatility. Similarly, Poterba and Summers (1988) showed that a significant impact of volatility on the stock prices can only take place if shocks to volatility persists over a long time.

As discussed above, market events and industry changes tend to have some impacts, significant or not, on the financial markets. Major news announcements made by the Central banks of various nations or economic policy changes affecting the inflation rates, employment rate and other economic parameters would have a significant impact on the financial markets and their price movements. Savor and Wilson (2013) observed that the average returns of the financial stock markets of Unites States of America were performing higher on those days where economic parameters or macroeconomic variables were declared to the public. These factors include consumer price index, employment rate and statistics, decisions made by Federal committee on financial markets among others. Statistically, it is observed that 60% of the overall returns from the financial markets are earned just on 13% of the trading days.

This paper discusses the effects of major news announcements from three different sources, the Reserve Bank of Australia, the Bank of England, and the European Central Bank. Since there are many variables that affect financial markets globally, the scope of this paper will discuss one economic announcement from each source that usually has a high impact on the financial markets. This paper discusses the Cash Rate by the Reserve Bank of Australia whose currency is the Australian Dollar (hereinafter known as AUD); the Official Bank Rate by the Bank of England whose currency is the Pound Sterling (hereinafter known as GBP); the Minimum Bid Rate by the European Central Bank whose currency is the Euro (hereinafter known as EUR). The announcements taken into consideration in this paper are those that were made by the central banks of the relative currencies.

There are several ways to measure the effects of major news announcements in financial markets, and this paper will focus mainly on the foreign exchange rate between AUD and the United States Dollar (hereinafter known as USD), and between the EUR and the USD. The measurement will be in percentage change and it will be a comparison between the exchange rate at the time of the announcement and the exchange rate one minute later. Extensive literature on the use of high-frequency financial data are provided by Andersen (2000) and Gouriéroux and Jasiak (2001). The findings tend to be mix, where in some cases, one minute is considered enough time to measure the reactions of the market since most of the tools used today are automated and work on algorithms and react quickly to the announcements, while in other cases, it is merely an indication of where the market is heading but is not enough time to provide information about the full reaction of the market. The one minute gap is used to be in line with more recent research using high frequency data. Currently, the fifteen most traded currencies around the globe are United States Dollar, Euro, Japanese Yen, Pound Sterling, Australian Dollar, Swiss Franc, Canadian Dollar, Mexican Peso, Chinese Yuan, New Zealand Dollar, Swedish Krona, Russian Rouble, Hong Kong Dollar, Singapore Dollar, and the Turkish Lira, respectively, while all the other currencies together form 12.2% of the daily trades in currencies (BIS, 2013).The AUD/USD and EUR/USD are chosen since they are the only two currency pairs which have grown consistently in terms of global foreign exchange market turnover, during the period 2001 to 2013 as reported in BIS (2013). The rationale behind pursuing this study is that it bridges the gap in existing literature, to be the first one, using 1 minute interval data to analyse the possible effects of significant news announcements on major currency pairs. The policy implications of this study extend toward giving added information to policy makers such as the U.S. Commodity Futures Trading Commission (CFTC), U.S. Securities Exchange Commission (SEC), and the Australian Security Investment Commission (ASIC), about whether the markets are rigged due to high frequency trading systems following releases of news announcements. Insignificant movements in major currency pairs, following global news, would add value that HFT systems do not posit harmful market activities. For instance, during the May 6 2010 "Flash Crash", the Dow Jones Industrial Average plunged about 1000 points (about 9%) only to recover those losses within minutes (Lin, 2013). As a regulatory response, the SEC and CFTC, as a joint committee, recommended that the Commissions require that the pause rules of the

Exchanges and Financial Industry Regulatory Body (FINRA) be expanded to cover all but the most inactively traded listed equity securities, ETFs, and options and single stock futures on those securities (SEC, 2010).

The presence of the fifteen most traded currencies with fifteen or more potential major news announcements might cause a clash between announcements in which more than one announcement is made at the same time, or an announcement follows another announcement very quickly, thus making it difficult to measure which announcement affected the financial market. Therefore, a one minute gap between the announcement and the measurement has been seen to be ample and measure the automatic reactions based on algorithms without involving people's different analyses into the measurement, thereby creating more of a controlled environment for measurement. All the announcements that have been chosen measure the short term interest rates of their respective monetary authorities. The reasons that they have been chosen are for their importance in currency valuation and the prediction of rates in the future. The announcements had solid values and the responses were measured accurately, which made it clearer on how traders responded to the announcements made by the respective monetary authorities. The announcements that had more than one announcement at the same time or within a one minute gap were excluded because including them may affect the integrity of the data collected and the conclusion at the end of the report. The rest of the paper provides the research methodology and data composition, the analysis section and some conclusive remarks.

2.0 Data and research methodology

The data set has been collected through secondary sources using mainly Forex Factory, established in 2004, and is currently the most viewed forex-related website (Forexfactory, 2014).The website has been used to gather the different timings of the announcements, the sources of the announcements, the frequency of the announcement, what the announcements measure, what makes them important, and the usual expected effects that the announcements might have on the market. Once the type of the announcement, its date and time of release have been established based on (GMT -8:00) Pacific Time (US & Canada), the next data source used was GAIN Capital, a company established in 1999 to provide investors with information and easy access to financial markets whose data archives go back to the 2000 period. The archives were used to determine the exchange rate between AUD/USD and EUR/USD at the dates and times of the announcements and then one minute after the announcements have been made.

3.0 Analysis

3.01 Cash rate announcements

Cash Rate is the term used in Australia for the bank rate and the rate of interest that the Reserve Bank of Australia (Central Bank) charges on overnight loans to commercial banks. This allows the Reserve Bank of Australia to adjust the interest rate in its economy. The announcement is made on the first Tuesday of every month except in January, and its usual effect is when the actual cash rate is higher than the forecasted, then it is generally better for the home currency (AUD). Short term interest is one of the most important factors in currency valuation, which helps investors to predict what will happen in the future. The main goal behind setting the Cash Rate is to keep the inflation rate stable between 2-3%, which is in line with the country's inflation targeting policies. Graph 2 and Graph 3 show the effect of the Cash Rate announcements on the financial markets and the exchange rates of AUD/USD and EUR/USD respectively; while the third graph is a bar chart taken from Forex Factory showing the actual cash rates that have been announced by the Reserve Bank of Australia.

Table 01: AUD and EUR 1 minute data post release of cash rate announcement

		AUD	AUD	AUD	EUR	EUR	EUR
Date	Time of Announcement	At Time	1 Minute Later	Change	At Time	1 Minute Later	Change
01-Feb-10	7:30pm	0.891	0.8911	0.0112%	1.3924	1.3926	0.0144%
01-Mar-10	7:30pm	0.8986	0.8991	0.0556%	1.3552	1.3555	0.0221%
05-Apr-10	8:30pm	0.9179	0.9181	0.0218%	1.3455	1.3457	0.0149%
03-May-10	8:30pm	0.9259	0.9259	0.0000%	1.3191	1.3191	0.0000%
31-May-10	8:30pm	0.842	0.8419	-0.0119%	1.226	1.2257	-0.0245%
05-Jul-10	8:30pm	0.8331	0.8336	0.0600%	1.2489	1.249	-0.0079%
02-Aug-10	8:30pm	0.9127	0.9126	-0.0110%	1.3178	1.3177	0.0152%
06-Sep-10	8:30pm	0.9139	0.9139	0.0000%	1.2809	1.2808	-0.0158%
04-Oct-10	7:30pm	0.9667	0.9671	0.0414%	1.3665	1.3666	0.0429%

01-Nov-10	7:30pm	0.9879	0.9879	0.0000%	1.3898	1.3897	0.0141%
06-Dec-10	7:30pm	0.9883	0.9882	-0.0101%	1.3287	1.3285	-0.0151%
31-Jan-11	7:30pm	0.9983	0.9983	0.0000%	1.3721	1.372	-0.0147%
28-Feb-11	7:30pm	1.0187	1.0186	-0.0098%	1.3819	1.3818	0.0000%
04-Apr-11	8:30pm	1.0344	1.0348	0.0387%	1.421	1.4211	0.0140%
02-May-11	8:30pm	1.0925	1.0927	0.0183%	1.4789	1.4789	0.0202%
06-Jun-11	8:30pm	1.073	1.0729	-0.0093%	1.4585	1.4584	-0.0205%
04-Jul-11	8:30pm	1.0722	1.0725	0.0280%	1.4524	1.4526	0.0280%
01-Aug-11	8:30pm	1.0991	1.0989	-0.0182%	1.4271	1.4268	-0.0280%
05-Sep-11	8:30pm	1.0516	1.0515	-0.0095%	1.407	1.407	0.0142%
03-Oct-11	7:30pm	0.9504	0.9499	-0.0526%	1.3181	1.3179	0.0075%
31-Oct-11	7:30pm	1.0539	1.0541	0.0190%	1.385	1.3853	0.0000%
05-Dec-11	7:30pm	1.02523	1.02545	0.0215%	1.33952	1.33962	-0.0022%
06-Feb-12	7:30pm	1.07247	1.07271	0.0224%	1.31215	1.31225	0.0060%
05-Mar-12	7:30pm	1.06817	1.06812	-0.0047%	1.32207	1.32202	-0.0287%
02-Apr-12	8:30pm	1.04227	1.04246	0.0182%	1.33315	1.33315	0.0000%
30-Apr-12	8:30pm	1.04225	1.0422	-0.0048%	1.32387	1.32389	-0.0208%
04-Jun-12	8:30pm	0.97531	0.97532	0.0010%	1.2537	1.25354	0.0088%
02-Jul-12	8:30pm	1.02493	1.02477	-0.0156%	1.25848	1.25835	0.0032%
06-Aug-12	8:30pm	1.05547	1.05548	0.0009%	1.23881	1.23871	0.0106%
03-Sep-12	8:30pm	1.0231	1.02297	-0.0127%	1.25852	1.2585	-0.0063%
01-Oct-12	8:30pm	1.03647	1.03634	-0.0125%	1.28942	1.28926	-0.0039%
05-Nov-12	7:30pm	1.03744	1.03735	-0.0087%	1.27962	1.27959	-0.0236%
03-Dec-12	7:30pm	1.04207	1.0422	0.0125%	1.30516	1.305	0.0008%
04-Feb-13	7:30pm	1.04484	1.045	0.0153%	1.35078	1.35078	-0.0044%
04-Mar-13	7:30pm	1.02154	1.02132	-0.0215%	1.30317	1.30309	-0.0031%
01-Apr-13	7:30pm	1.04342	1.04363	0.0201%	1.28455	1.28458	0.0180%
06-May-13	8:30pm	1.02411	1.02415	0.0039%	1.30708	1.30714	-0.0296%
03-Jun-13	8:30pm	0.97509	0.97519	0.0103%	1.30688	1.30695	0.0054%
01-Jul-13	8:30pm	0.92489	0.92469	-0.0216%	1.30668	1.30667	-0.0008%

Graph 1 is a historical bar chart which shows the actual changes of Cash Rate as announced by the e Reserve Bank of Australia. Towards the end of 2011, the Cash Rate has been declining and by May 2013, the Reserve Bank has decided to lower the Cash Rate further from 3.00% to 2.75%. The main decision behind the decrease was that the inflation rate was actually lower than the target and the Reserve Bankof Australia thought that it would help increase employment and economic growth in Australia since it was a little below the growth trend (Stevens, 2013).

Graph 01: Cash rate (2010-2013)

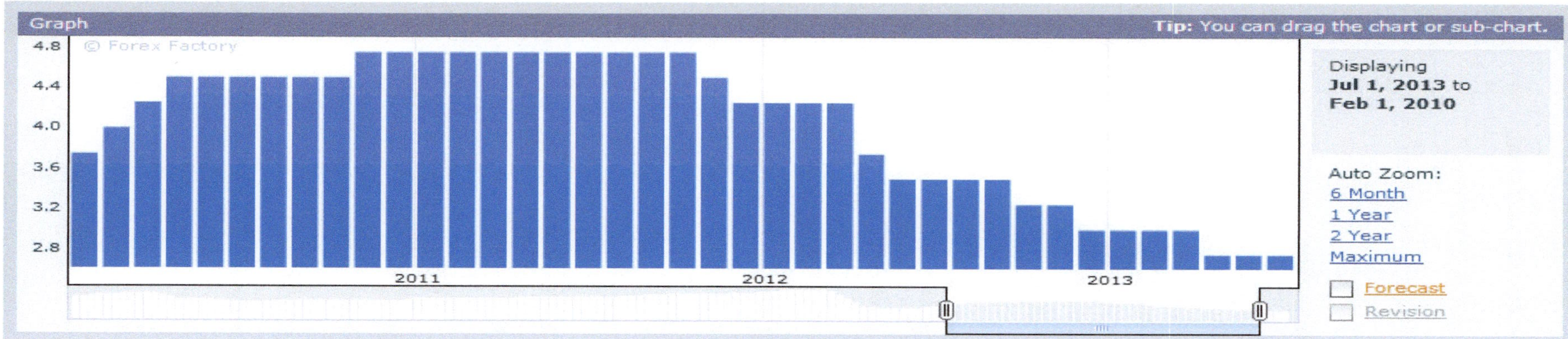

Source: Forexfactory (2014)

Graph 02: Effect of Cash Rate Announcement on AUD/USD

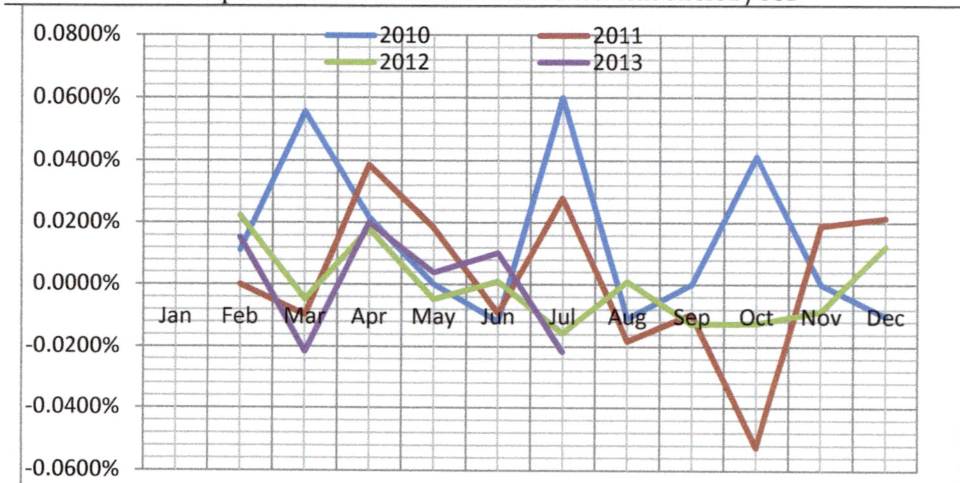

Graph 03: Effect of Cash Rate Announcement on EUR/USD

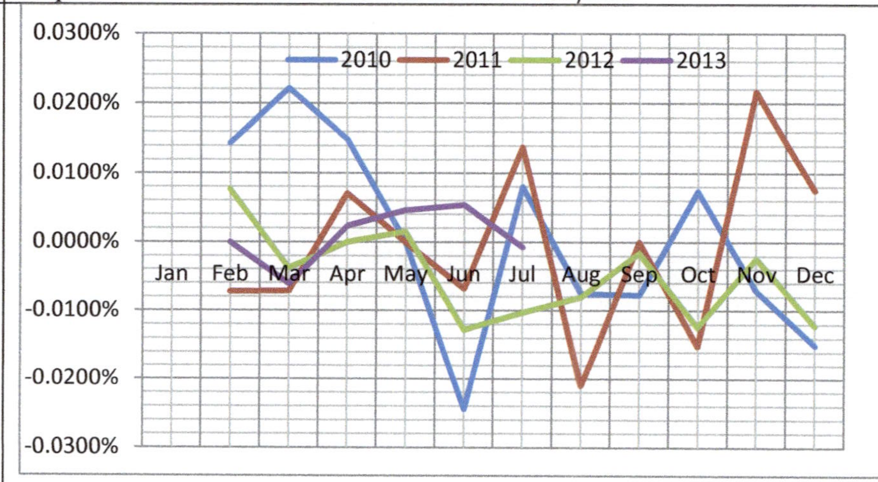

Graph 2 shows how the AUD/USD exchange rate has been affected by the Cash Rate announcements from the Reserve Bank of Australia. The graph has some sharp ups and downs, but that is mostly because the changes are very small that the percentage changes were in hundredths of a percentage, and therefore the graph had to be magnified to see the actual reaction of the market, or the affects that the announcements had on the market. Since the percentage change hovers in the range of ±0.06%, it is safe to say that the exchange rate is not significantly affected by the announcements. In line with Graph 1which shows how the Cash Rate announcements have changed over time, and even with the Cash Rates going lower since the end of 2011, it seems to not have an effect on the exchange rate. This is in line with Gurrib (2010) where the effects of news announcements tend to decay over time. While, graph 3 shows that there are minute fluctuations in the EUR/USD exchange rate. It is not critical to know whether or not the Cash Rate announcements have contributed to the percentage changes, because the changes are so small such that they can be attributed to a normal trading day without announcements.

3.02 Minimum bid rate announcements

Minimum Bid Rate is the main refinancing rate, which is the publicly visible interest rate that the European Central Bank announces.

Table 02: AUD and EUR 1 minute data post release of minimum bid rate announcement

		AUD	AUD	AUD	EUR	EUR	EUR
Date	Time of Announcement	At Time	1 Minute Later	Change	At Time	1 Minute Later	Change
14 January 2010	4:45AM	0.93	0.9299	-0.0108%	1.4522	1.4519	-0.0207%
04 February 2010	4.45AM	0.8792	0.8793	0.0114%	1.3845	1.3844	-0.0072%
03 April 2010	4.45AM	0.8997	0.8997	0.0000%	1.3653	1.3651	-0.0146%
08 April 2010	3.45AM	0.9241	0.9239	-0.0216%	1.3309	1.3297	-0.0902%
06 May 2010	3.45AM	0.9037	0.9039	0.0221%	1.2786	1.2789	0.0235%
10 June 2010	3.45AM	0.838	0.8378	-0.0239%	1.2032	1.2029	-0.0249%
08 July 2010	3.45AM	0.8731	0.873	-0.0115%	1.2641	1.2642	0.0316%
05 August 2010	3.45AM	0.9144	0.9145	0.0109%	1.3141	1.3142	0.0000%
02 September 2010	3.45AM	0.9059	0.9062	0.0331%	1.2782	1.2784	-0.0312%
07 October 2010	3.45AM	0.9897	0.9896	-0.0101%	1.3987	1.3989	-0.0072%
04 November 2010	4.45AM	1.0081	1.008	-0.0099%	1.4202	1.4202	-0.0070%
02 December 2010	4.45AM	0.9688	0.9685	-0.0310%	1.3184	1.3184	-0.0227%
13 January 2011	4.45AM	0.9962	0.9963	0.0100%	1.3157	1.3157	0.0076%
03 February 2011	4.45AM	1.0136	1.0138	0.0197%	1.378	1.3785	0.0073%
03 March 2011	4.45AM	1.0161	1.0163	0.0197%	1.3847	1.3848	0.0000%
07 April 2011	3.45AM	1.048	1.048	0.0000%	1.429	1.4288	0.0070%
05 May 2011	3.45AM	1.0717	1.0715	-0.0187%	1.489	1.489	-0.0134%
09 June 2011	3.45AM	1.0603	1.0602	-0.0094%	1.4641	1.4638	-0.0205%
05 July 2011	3.45AM	1.0689	1.0687	-0.0187%	1.4478	1.4485	0.0419%
04 August 2011	3.45AM	1.0657	1.0656	-0.0094%	1.4314	1.4316	0.0000%
08 September 2011	3.45AM	1.058	1.0582	0.0189%	1.3888	1.3886	-0.0142%
06 October 2011	3.45AM	0.9531	0.9535	0.0420%	1.3343	1.3339	0.0000%
03 November 2011	4.45AM	1.0239	1.0243	0.0391%	1.3681	1.3679	0.0146%
08 December 2011	4.45AM	1.02857	1.02838	-0.0185%	1.34058	1.34018	0.0097%
12 January 2012	4.45AM	1.03098	1.03097	-0.0010%	1.27261	1.27248	-0.0157%
09 February 2012	4.45AM	1.08225	1.0822	-0.0046%	1.32972	1.32946	-0.0128%
08 March 2012	4.45AM	1.06498	1.06523	0.0235%	1.3276	1.32763	-0.0098%
04 April 2013	3.45AM	1.02554	1.02552	-0.0020%	1.31947	1.31948	0.0008%
03 May 2012	3.45AM	1.03001	1.02999	-0.0019%	1.31525	1.3155	-0.0327%
06 June 2012	3.45AM	0.9851	0.98555	0.0457%	1.25052	1.25084	-0.0016%
05 July 2012	3.45AM	1.02633	1.02641	0.0078%	1.25226	1.25257	-0.0216%
02 August 2012	3.45AM	1.05515	1.0553	0.0142%	1.21957	1.21974	0.0310%
06 September 2012	3.45AM	1.01824	1.01825	0.0010%	1.26102	1.26125	-0.0135%
04 October 2012	3.45AM	1.02208	1.02202	-0.0059%	1.29427	1.29434	0.0247%
08 November 2012	4.45AM	1.0401	1.03985	-0.0240%	1.27318	1.27309	-0.0039%
06 December 2012	4.45AM	1.04863	1.04848	-0.0143%	1.30767	1.30755	-0.0069%
10 January 2013	4.45AM	1.0569	1.05714	0.0227%	1.30778	1.30851	-0.0214%
07 February 2013	4.45AM	1.03252	1.03243	-0.0087%	1.3565	1.35685	-0.0007%
07 March 2013	4.45AM	1.02664	1.02665	0.0010%	1.30397	1.30385	-0.0092%
04 April 2013	3.45AM	1.04152	1.04176	0.0230%	1.28184	1.28205	0.0188%
02 May 2013	3.45AM	1.02324	1.02337	0.0127%	1.31556	1.31564	0.0076%
06 June 2013	3.45AM	0.9478	0.94784	0.0042%	1.31201	1.31192	-0.0069%
04 July 2013	3.45AM	0.91355	0.91373	0.0197%	1.30024	1.30041	0.0131%

Graph 04: Minimum Bid Rate (2009-2013)

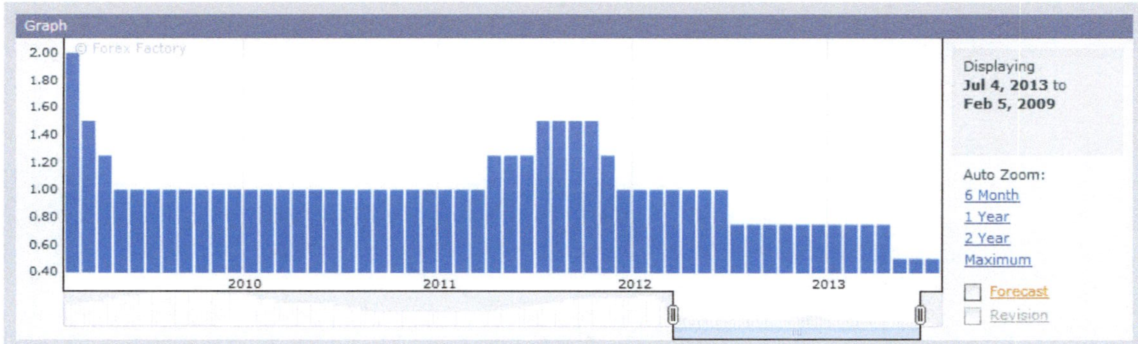

Source: Forexfactory (2014)

Graph 05: Effect of minimum bid rate on AUD/USD

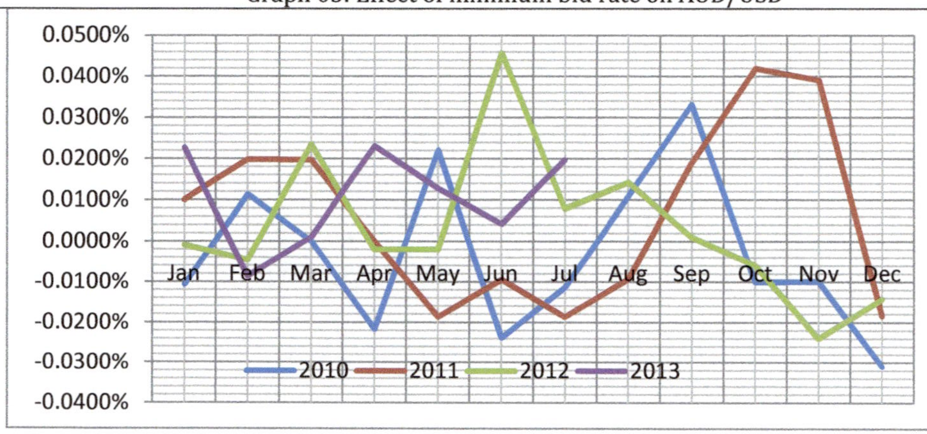

Graph 06: Effect of minimum bid rate on EUR/USD

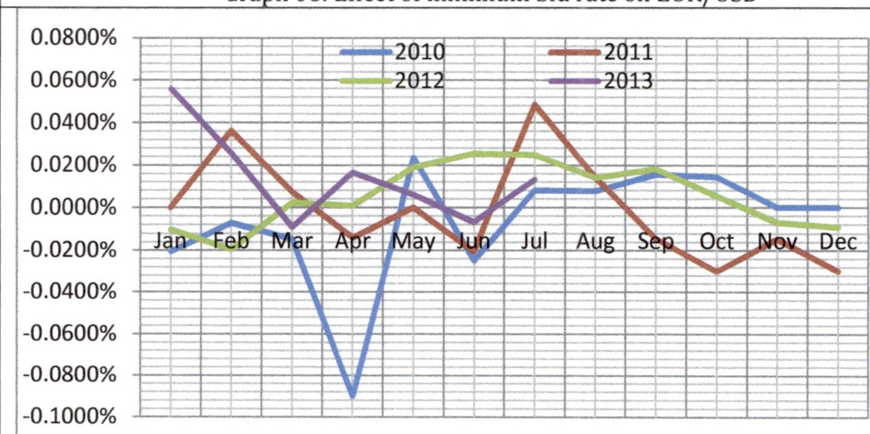

It serves as a bidding floor for refinancing loans, and refinancing operations that are the bulk of liquidity to the banking system (ECB, 2013). The announcement is scheduled monthly, and they are considered important because they measure the interest rates on short term loans, which, as stated earlier is one of the most important factors in currency valuation. It has a good effect on the currency when the actual rate is higher than the forecasted rate. The primary objective of the monetary policy of the European Central Bank is to keep inflation rate below, but close to 2% over the medium term (ECB, 2013). As seen in Graph 4, in the middle and end of 2011, the Minimum bid rate has increased gradually and then decreased gradually, which may explain the erratic behaviour in the percentage changes of the exchange rate in 2011 between the EUR/USD. Though the Minimum Bid Rate has been steadily decreasing since 2012, there is no major change in the exchange prices of EUR/USD. Graph 4 and Graph 5 show the effect of the Minimum Bid Rate announcements on the financial markets and the exchange rates of AUD/USD and EUR/USD respectively.

Graph 5 shows the percentage changes of the AUD/USD exchange rate with the announcements of the European Central Bank regarding the Minimum Bid Rate and the graph does not show any signs of significant change with the exchange rate fluctuating within the general range of ±0.03%. A small anomaly shows that the exchange rate has increased by 0.04% in June 2012, even though the Minimum Bid Rate has remained unchanged from May 2012, therefore, there might have been another announcement that has affected the exchange rate which is not reported here. Although it is still not significant, the percentage change in exchange rate was less than 0.01% in July, which is when the European Central Bank has decided to decrease the Minimum Bid Rate from 1% to 0.75%, as gathered in graph 4.

Graph 6 shows the percentage changes of the exchange rate of EUR/USD. Clearly, there is an anomaly in April 2010 where the exchange rate changed by around -0.09%.Further, findings shows no changes in the Minimum Bid Rate all year in 2010, which may mean that there are other announcements that have affected the currency and created the dip in the exchange rate, especially since the majority of the percentage changes have taken place in the range of ±0.03%.

3.03 Official bank rate

Official Bank Rate, also known as Bank of England Base Rate, is the interest rate that the Bank of England charges banks for secured overnight lending. It is the British Government's key interest rate for enacting monetary policy. The announcements are scheduled monthly and they are important because they are related to the short term interest rates which tend to be one of those factors affecting currency valuation. It is generally better for the home currency (GBP) when the actual rate is higher than the forecasted rate.

Table 03: AUD and EUR 1 minute data post release of the official bank rate announcement

		AUD	AUD	AUD	EUR	EUR	EUR
Date	Time of Announcement	At Time	1 Minute Later	Change	At Time	1 Minute Later	Change
07 January 2010	5:00am	0.9196	0.9197	0.0109%	1.4353	1.4357	0.0279%
04 February 2010	5:00am	0.8794	0.879	-0.0455%	1.3847	1.3845	-0.0144%
04 March 2010	5:00am	0.9005	0.9006	0.0111%	1.3648	1.3648	0.0000%
08 April 2010	4:00am	0.926	0.9263	0.0324%	1.3288	1.3293	0.0376%
10 May 2010	4:00am	0.9045	0.9043	-0.0221%	1.304	1.3039	-0.0077%
10 June 2010	4:00am	0.8374	0.8385	0.1312%	1.2012	1.2014	0.0167%
08 July 2010	4:00am	0.8739	0.8736	-0.0343%	1.2648	1.2647	-0.0079%
05 August 2010	4:00am	0.914	0.9141	0.0109%	1.3151	1.3153	0.0152%
09 September 2010	4:00am	0.9228	0.9228	0.0000%	1.2679	1.2677	-0.0158%
07 October 2010	4:00am	0.9905	0.9908	0.0303%	1.3982	1.3988	0.0429%
04 November 2010	5:00am	1.0085	1.0087	0.0198%	1.4206	1.4208	0.0141%
09 December 2010	5:00am	0.9841	0.9837	-0.0407%	1.3213	1.3211	-0.0151%
13 January 2011	5:00am	0.9962	0.9961	-0.0100%	1.3152	1.3147	-0.0380%
10 February 2011	5:00am	1.003	1.0032	0.0199%	1.363	1.3628	-0.0147%
10 March 2011	5:00am	1.0038	1.0038	0.0000%	1.3835	1.3835	0.0000%
07 April 2011	4:00am	1.0479	1.048	0.0095%	1.4278	1.428	0.0140%
05 May 2011	4:00am	1.0722	1.072	-0.0187%	1.4879	1.4882	0.0202%
09 June 2011	4:00am	00:52.8	01:58.4	0.0000%	1.4628	1.4625	-0.0205%
07 July 2011	4:00am	1.0736	1.0739	0.0279%	1.4298	1.4302	0.0280%
04 August 2011	4:00am	1.065	1.065	0.0000%	1.4264	1.426	-0.0280%
06 October 2011	4:00am	0.971	0.9712	0.0206%	1.4109	1.4107	-0.0142%
10 November 2011	5:00am	1.015	1.0148	-0.0197%	1.3346	1.3347	0.0075%
08 December 2011	5:00am	1.02909	1.02903	-0.0058%	1.3616	1.3616	0.0000%
12 January 2012	5:00am	1.03298	1.03292	-0.0058%	1.34025	1.34022	-0.0022%
09 February 2012	5:00am	1.08311	1.08333	0.0203%	1.27511	1.27484	-0.0212%
08 March 2012	5:00am	1.06448	1.06435	-0.0122%	1.32714	1.32722	0.0060%
05 April 2012	4:00am	1.26058	1.26056	-0.0016%	1.32198	1.3216	-0.0287%

10 May 2012	4:00am	1.01107	1.0108	-0.0267%	1.31467	1.31449	-0.0137%
07 June 2012	4:00am	0.99375	0.99387	0.0121%	1.29587	1.2956	-0.0208%
05 July 2012	4:00am	1.02632	1.02636	0.0039%	1.2546	1.25471	0.0088%
02 August 2012	4:00am	1.04835	1.04854	0.0181%	1.25229	1.25233	0.0032%
06 September 2012	4:00am	1.0243	1.02422	-0.0078%	1.226	1.22613	0.0106%
04 October 2012	4:00am	1.02227	1.02225	-0.0020%	1.26199	1.26191	-0.0063%
08 November 2012	5:00am	1.0399	1.03986	-0.0038%	1.29464	1.29459	-0.0039%
06 December 2012	5:00am	1.04861	1.04874	0.0124%	1.27326	1.27296	-0.0236%
10 January 2013	5:00am	1.05757	1.05756	-0.0009%	1.30777	1.30778	0.0008%
07 February 2013	5:00am	1.03253	1.0325	-0.0029%	1.31035	1.31035	0.0000%
07 March 2013	5:00am	1.02657	1.02658	0.0010%	1.35631	1.35625	-0.0044%
04 April 2013	4:00am	1.0411	1.04103	-0.0067%	1.30414	1.3041	-0.0031%
09 May 2013	4:00am	1.02344	1.02324	-0.0195%	1.27857	1.2788	0.0180%
06 June 2013	4:00am	0.9488	0.94916	0.0379%	1.31667	1.31628	-0.0296%
04 July 2013	4:00am	0.91012	0.91014	0.0022%	1.31177	1.31209	0.0244%

Graph 7 shows that the Official Bank Rate as announced by the Bank of England has not changed from 0.5% since at least January 2010, but once the data set is extended further back in time, it will show that in fact, the Official Bank Rate has not changed since March 2009. Graph 8 and Graph 9 show the effect of the Official Bank Rate announcements on the financial markets and the exchange rates of AUD/USD and EUR/USD respectively.

Graph 8 shows that the Official Bank Rate as announced by the Bank of England does not have a big impact on the percentage change of the exchange rate of AUD/USD, because the graph shows that the changes are within the range of ±0.03%, except in June 2010, where the change of exchange rate suddenly spiked to around 0.13%. Graph 9 shows that the Official Bank Rate has been steady at 0.5% for the whole period, which suggests that there may have been an announcement that has inflicted the change that was not related to Central Bank announcements of the currencies that have been chosen for this paper. 0.13% is not a significant change, but when compared to the other percentage changes, it seems to be higher than earlier findings.

Even though Graph 9 shows sharper spikes and dips with the changes in the exchange rate of EUR/USD than with the AUD/USD, it is important to notice that Graph 8 range is between ±0.05%, while for the AUD/USD the graph range was between -0.06% and 0.16%, which made it look smoother, but once the anomaly is covered, it will be clear that the spikes and dips are similar to that of the percentage change of the EUR/USD exchange rate.

3.04 Comparative analysis

Graph 10 provides an overview of all the three announcements and how they have affected the exchange rate of AUD/USD with time, beginning in January 2010 and ending in July 2013. It is clear from the graph that almost all the percentage changes in the exchange rate have been within the ±0.05% range, which are not significant changes, except for the 0.13% change in June 2010 with the Official Bank Rate announcement affecting the exchange rate, even though 0.13% is not a significant change, but it remains higher than the other results reported here. The highest negative percentage change of exchange rate was with the Cash Rate announcement that took place on October 2011 by the Reserve Bank of Australia. Breaks are due to the non- release of one of the three announcements during a specific time period.

Graph 7: Official Bank Rate (2010-2013)

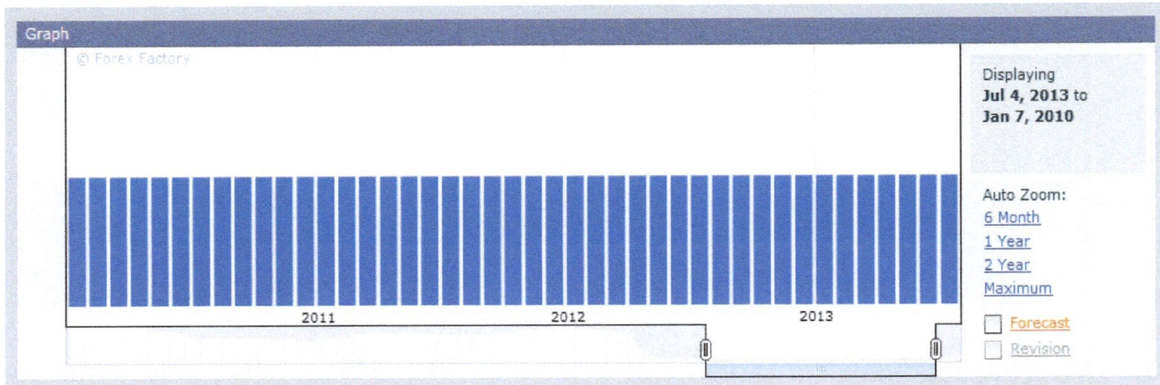

Source: Forexfactory (2014)

Graph 8: Effect of Official Bank Rate on AUD/USD

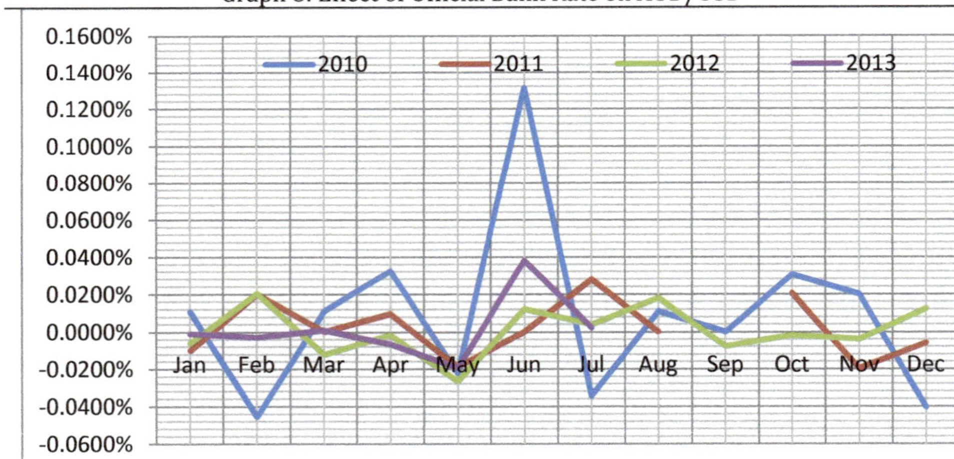

Graph 9: Effect of Official Bank Rate on EUR/USD

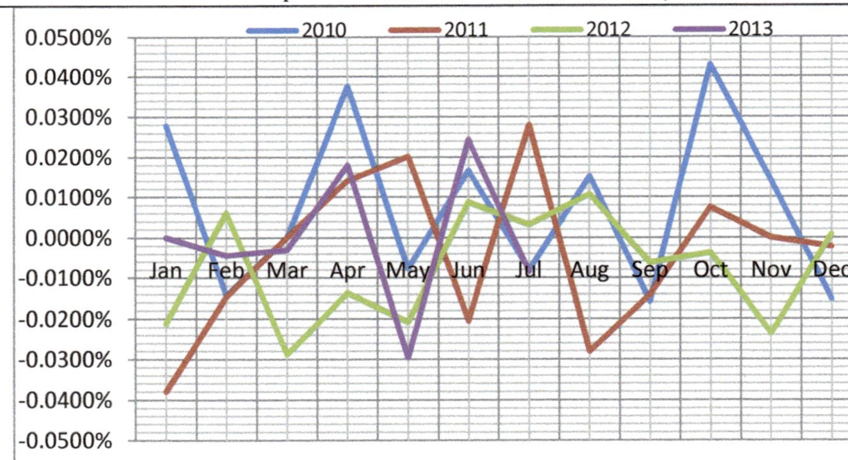

Graph 11 provides an overview of all the three announcements and how they have affected the exchange rate of EUR/USD with time. It is clear from the graph that the results are within the percentage change range of ±0.04%, which is less than the AUD/USD change, but neither changes are significant. The anomaly in the EUR/USD percentage change is the Minimum Bid Rate announcement of April 2010 which reaches around -0.09% as opposed to the other announcements and dates which stayed within the range of ±0.04%.

Graph 10: Effects of the Cash Rate, Minimum Bid Rate and Official Bank Rate on the AUD/USD

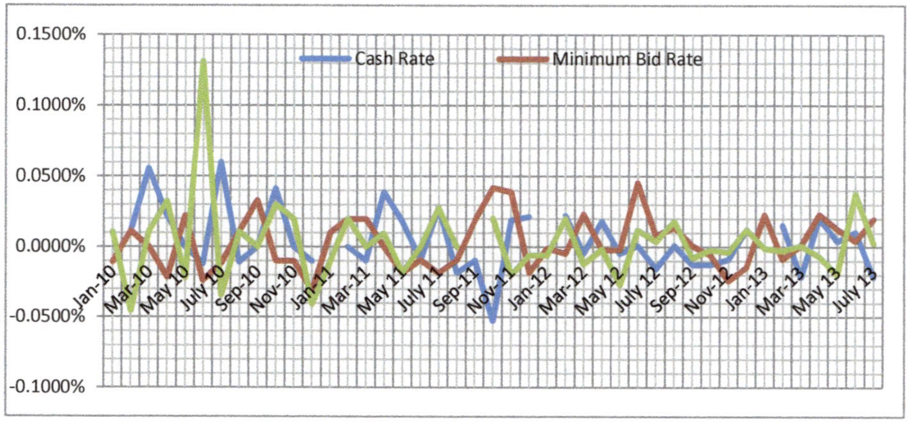

Graph 11: Effects of the Cash Rate, Minimum Bid Rate and Official Bank Rate on the EUR/USD

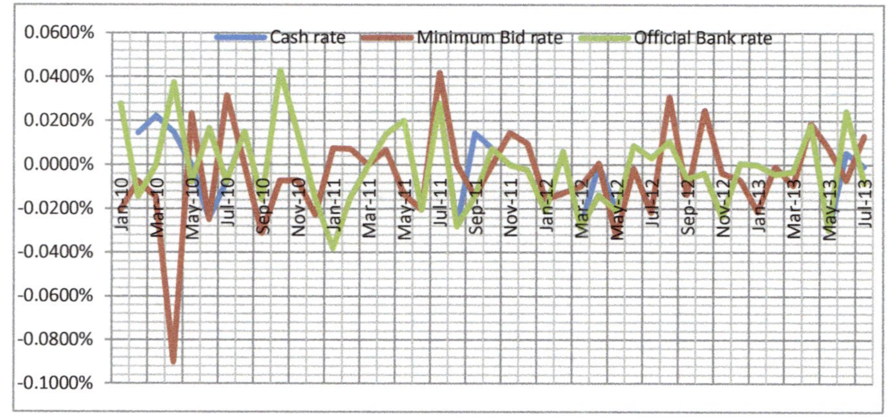

Graph 12: Average yearly percentage change in AUD/USD following announcements' releases

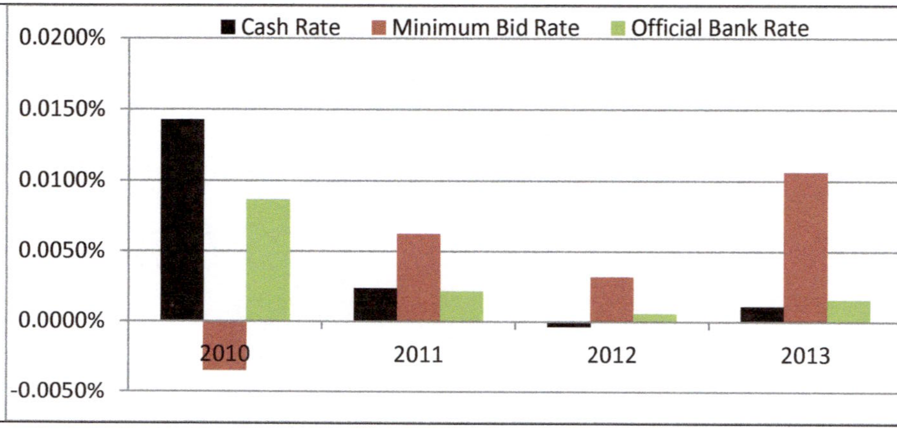

Graph 13: Average yearly percentage change in AUD/USD following announcements' releases

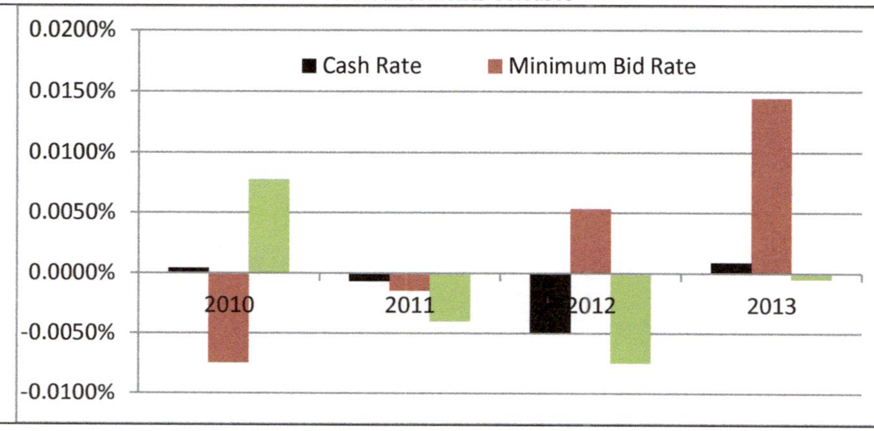

Breaks are due to the non- release of one of the three announcements during a specific time period. Due to the existence of those breaks, the comparison of the effect of the three announcements on the exchange rate becomes less obvious. An average yearly percentage change in the currency pairs is used to smooth out any possible break in the years. Graphs 12 and 13 provide the results on the AUD/USD and EUR/USD respectively.

From Graph 12, it is noticeable that the only announcements that have had an average positive change in exchange rates are those of the Official Bank Rate. The Minimum Bid Rate has had a negative average percentage change in AUD/USD exchange rates but has stayed positive since, even though all these changes are of minute significance with the highest average change having been around 0.014%. The highest negative percentage change of exchange rate was with the Minimum Bid Rate announcement that took place on April 2011 by the European Central Bank, while the highest positive percentage change of exchange rate was with the Official Bank Rate announcement in October 2010.

Graph 13 shows the average yearly percentage changes in the EUR/USD exchange rate. It is noteworthy to point out that there seems to have more negative average percentage changes than positive average percentage changes. The highest percentage change is around 0.0144%. The highest negative percentage change was around 0.007% as opposed to the highest negative percentage change of around 0.003% for the AUD/USD. Findings tend to support that currencies are more affected by the announcements made by their respective monetary authorities.

3.05 Robustness testing

A look at the change in both the AUD and EURO against the USD following cash rate announcements, show that there is some displacement in the dataset for the period ending 10/03/2011. To robust test earlier findings, the CUSUM (Cumulative Sum Control Chart) structural test is applied to test for the constancy of coefficients between the currency pairs' change and news announcements. The test is carried out both on the effect of the change in EUR/USD against the effect of the change in AUD/USD following the cash rate announcement. Essentially, the CUSUM test takes the cumulative sum of recursive residuals and plots its value against the upper [K, ±3a(T-k)1/2] and lower [K, ±a(T-k)1/2] bounds of the95% confidence interval at each point, (a=0.948 for 95% level) as per Page (1954) and (Brown, Durbin, and Evans, 1975).The CUSUM test is based on the statistic as follows:

$$W_t{}^{\mathrm{n}} = \sum_{n=k+1}^{t} \frac{\lambda_n}{\sigma}$$

for $t = n + 1, \ldots, T$, whereλ is the recursive residual, and σ is the standard deviation of the recursive residuals λ_n. If the β vector remains constant from period to period, $E(W_t) = 0$. If, however, the β coefficient changes within the data period,$W_t$will tend to diverge from the zero mean value line.

Table 4: Chow structural break test

F test of no structural break:	
Effect of EURO/USD on AUD/USD Change	0.2826
Effect of AUD/USD on EUR/USD Change	0.2210

The findings are reported in Graph 14. It can be observed that after the 10/03/2011 period, the parameters in both CUSUM graphs become more unstable, although not breaking the 5% significance level. To check for the statistical validity of the instability between the variables' relationships, the Chow test is used to check for any significant structural break in the models. As reported in Table 4, the low probabilities of 0.2826 and 0.2210 suggest there are no structural break at the 10/03/2011 period.

Graph 14: Stability diagnostic test of the recursive residuals

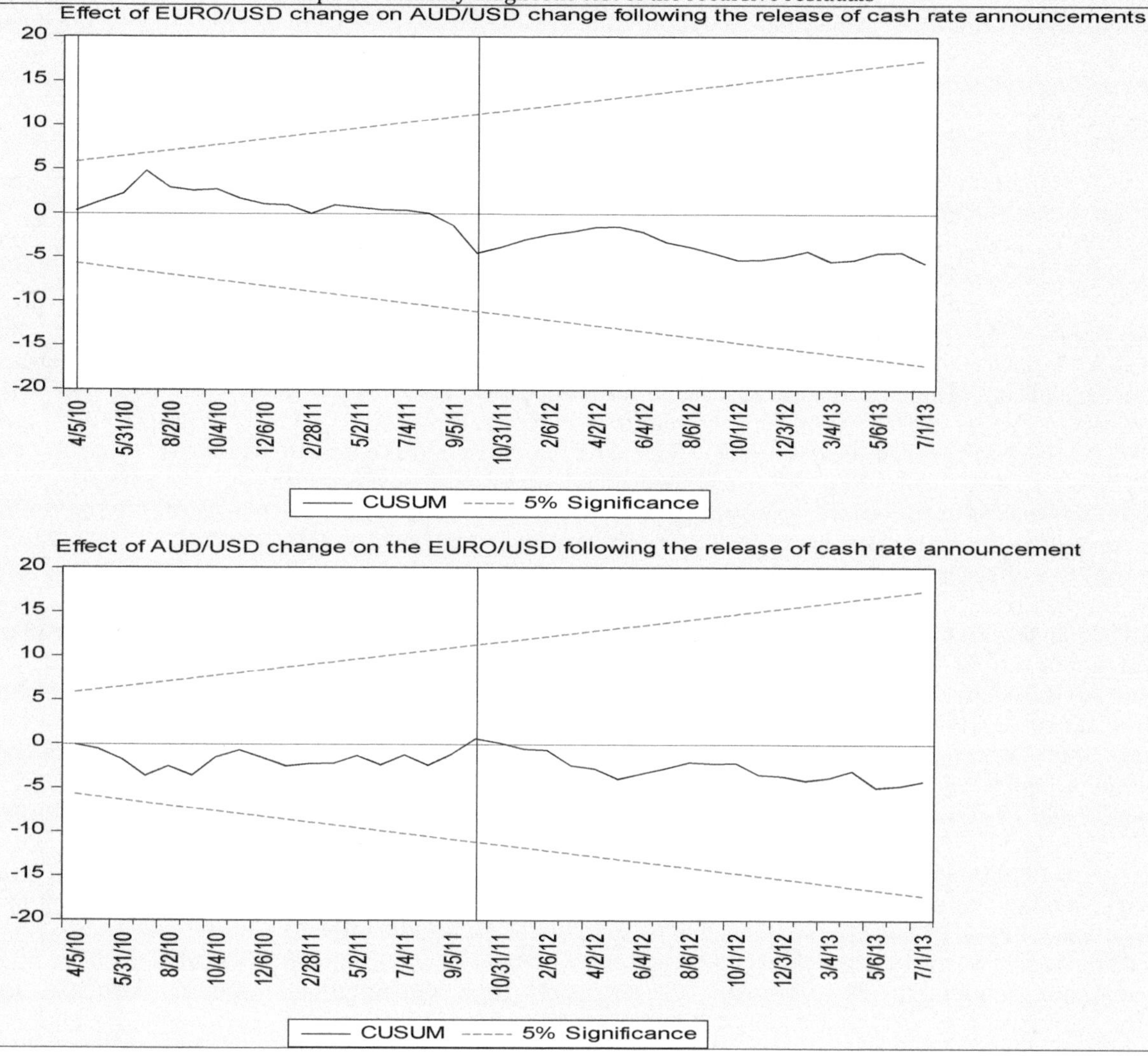

4.0 Conclusion

Findings tend to support that announcements made by the respective monetary authorities do not have a significant role in the percentage changes of the exchange rate. For a profit of one Australian Dollar on the 0.014% change in the currency exchange rate of the AUD/USD, a trader would have to sell 7,142 Australian Dollars, which may not be worthwhile for many traders and even in huge quantities, it would not be worthwhile for traders since there are transaction costs along with the purchase of sale of the currencies. There are many other factors that affect the exchange rates between currencies, some of them are apparent and measureable, while the others may seem like invisible forces that might have effects that are not accurately foreseeable, but are still measureable once they occur, such as Terms of Trade, Current Account Deficit, Public Debt, the Economic and Political Stability, Rate of Employment, Rate of Unemployment, Inflation Rate, Gross National Product, Gross Domestic Product. Future areas of research can include other currencies' comparative analysis. The Pound Sterling is the fourth more traded currency around the globe after the United States Dollar, the Euro, and the Japanese Yen. Structural breaks were tested for at some specific data period, but found no significant breakpoint to justify for the possibility of inadequate model constructions. It would be interesting to look at the currency market reactions to the announcements made by Bank of Japanand analyse how the exchange rates are affected by them. There could have been more than one announcement that was not from the Central Bank that occurred at the same time of the Central Bank announcements that affected the exchange rate, but they were not taken into consideration for analytical purposes. The gap between the time of announcement and the measurement of the value was taken at one minute after the announcement in comparison with the exchange rate at the time of the announcement to keep the results in a controlled environment, but perhaps expanding the gap between the announcement and the measurement (5-10 minutes) could help form a better view of the reaction of the financial market to the announcements made. The policy implication of this study is that findings tend to suggest that regulatory bodies such as SEC and CFTC need to revisit their stance regarding High Frequency Trading systems and all their regulatory tools such as the pause rules and the consolidated audit trails (CAT). The insignificance of one minute effect of global news over the most volatile financial markets (foreign currency markets) needs however not to be overlooked. Market Higher frequency data is definitely an area of future research to be remembered and dealt with.

References

Agenor, P. R., & Pereira da Silva, L. A., 2012. Macroeconomic stability, financial stability, and monetary policy rules. International Finance, 15: 205-224. http://dx.doi.org/10.1111/j.1468-2362.2012.01302.x

Andersen, T. G., 2000. Some reflections on analysis of high-frequency data. Journal of Business and Economic Statistics, 18(2): 146-153. http://dx.doi.org/10.2307/1392552

BIS. 2013. Triennial central bank survey, Bank of International Settlements. http://www.bis.org/publ/rpfx13.htm [Accessed on 01/02/2014]

Brown, R. L., J. Durbin, and J. M. Evans., 1975. Techniques for testing the constancy of regression relationships over time, Journal of the Royal Statistical Society, Series B, 37: 149–192.

Darskuviene, V., 2010. Financial markets. Leonardo da Vinci programme project. http://www.bcci.bg/projects/latvia/pdf/7_Financial_markets.pdf [Accessed 10/04/2014]

ECB.2013. Key ECB interest rates, European Central Bank. http://www.ecb.europa.eu/stats/monetary/rates/html/index.en.html [Accessed on 02/02/2014]

Forexfactory. 2014. Forex Factory. http://www.forexfactory.com/ [Accessed on 08/15/2013]

Gouriéroux, C. and Jasiak, J., 2001. Financial econometrics: Problems, Models and Methods. New Jersey: Princeton University Press.

Gurrib, I., 2008. Do large hedgers and speculators react to events? a stability and events analysis. Applied Financial Economics Letters, 4 (4): 259-267. http://dx.doi.org/10.1080/17446540701720501

Gurrib, I., 2010. Measuring risk for large hedgers and large speculators in major US futures markets. The Journal of Risk, 12(2): 79–103.

Laïdi, A., 2008. Currency trading and intermarket analysis: how to profit from the shifting currents in blobal markets. John Wiley & Sons.

Lin, Tom C. W.2013. The new investor, 60 UCLA Law Review 678, Temple University Legal Studies Research Paper No. 2013-45

Page, E. S., 1954.Continuous inspection scheme. Biometrika,41 (2): 100–115. http://dx.doi.org/10.2307/2333009

Poterba, J., and Summers, L., 1988. Mean reversion in stock prices: evidence and implications. Journal of Financial Economics, 22(1): 27–59. http://dx.doi.org/10.1016/0304-405X(88)90021-9

Savor, P., & Wilson, M., 2013. How much do investors care about macroeconomic risk? evidence from scheduled economic announcements. Journal of Financial and Quantitative Analysis, 48(2): 343-375. http://dx.doi.org/10.1017/S002210901300015X

SEC. 2010. Recommendations regarding regulatory responses to the market events of May 6, 2010, Summary Report of the Joint CFTC-SEC Advisory Committee on Emerging Regulatory Issues. http://http://www.sec.gov/spotlight/sec-cftcjointcommittee/021811-report.pdf [Accessed 10/04/2014]

Stevens, G., 2013. Media release, Reserve Bank of Australia. http://www.rba.gov.au/media-releases/2013/mr-13-10.html [Accessed on 11/15/2013]

A new perspective of benevolent loan, Qard Al-Hassan, using upfront payment 'Mesbah Point'

Amir Behnam Izadyar [a*], Feroza Ragnath [b]

[a] Darulmaali Financial Consulting Group, LLC, Maryland, USA.
[b] Darulmaali Financial Consulting Group, LLC, Maryland, USA. E-mail: feroz@darulmaali.com
*Corresponding author e-mail: Amir@darulmaali.com

HIGHLIGHTS:

1. This paper introduces a new method in benevolent lending using optimum amount of upfront payment.
2. Profitability of the new method in comparison with a conventional method has been addressed.
3. The finding promotes the presence of institutional investors and discusses some common misconceptions in Qrad al-hassan.
4. Recommendations for using Mebash Point as a new Islamic finance method and creating a secondary market in benevolent loan have been made.

Article History

Keywords:
Benevolent loan;
Islamic Finance;
Mesbah finance;
Microfinance;
Qard al-hasan.

ABSTRACT

Bound by religious or moral beliefs of the participants, benevolent loan, Qard al-hasan, is an interest free loan in which only the return of the capital is required during the term of the loan. Lack of institutional investor participation, as well as high administrative fees, are some of the major obstacles that have kept Qard al-hasan from gaining popularity in financial lending. This study has demonstrated a new method in Qard al-hasan lending using Mesbah Point to promote Qard al-hasan as a viable lending transaction. Based on this method the borrower initially makes an optimum amount of upfront payment to receive a zero percent interest rate, no fee loan. The distribution of remaining principal has been studied under two scenarios; Standard MP and Accelerated MP. Based on Mesbah Finance platform the Qard al-hasan lenders and the financial institutions can gain sufficient returns which may help them to cope with their accruing costs as well as earn some profit by providing Qard al-hasan. Although the rate of return in this method unsurprisingly remains below the conventional method, accelerating the monthly payments to the level of conventional monthly payments significantly improves these shortfalls and offsets the gap of return. Accelerated MP shortens the payback period especially in longer loan terms as well as increases the earnings to the level that the participation of institutional investors are possible. The institutionalization of Qard al-hasan is the ultimate aspiration in the Islamic banking system and this study meets the most challenging Islamic lending practice which is Qard al-hasan.

1.0 Introduction

Bound by religious or moral beliefs of the participants, Qard al-Hasan (benevolent loan), is an interest free loan in which only the return of the capital is required during the term of the loan. In several aspects, the application of Qard al-hasan (QH) has been scattered among underprivileged communities. It has been used in satisfying the social needs of communities in marriages, education and situations beyond the control of the applicant like prolonged delay in salaries or wages (Farook, 2007). Among community investment clubs this tool has been used as a monthly draw to determine who will get the pot of money for that month. Some companies have used QH to lend to its employees for a short period of time where the payment is directly withdrawn from the employees salaries. Savings accounts and certificates of deposits have been structured where the client provides an interest-free loan to the bank through deposits and the bank may utilize the funds for its own means (Bakar, 2008a). Charge cards and credit cards are issued by the banks to their clients based on charging fees and structured on the principles of QH (Bakar, 2008b). Berthoud & Hinton (1989) noted that credit unions possessed with co-operative financial structures, offer loans that are funded by the pool of savings from members themselves. Credit unions main objective is to act as the promoter of thrift. They believe the credit unions are not formed to make profits, rather to maximize the benefit to their members through financial gains as well as other social factors such as financial education. Mirakhor and Iqbal (2007) have reported that the QH funds in Iran consist of funds from the bank itself but also include contributions from other individuals, financial corporations, business organizations and even the government. However, the banks (mostly state-owned) collaborate with local mosques, religious organizations, and at times with professional associations to extend small consumer QH loans. The QH fund is made up of contributions by the well-off and capable individuals of society who have guarantee on their capital by the banks and they are free to withdraw their funds any time they desire. There is no interest charges involved, but some funds do charge administrative costs to the recipients.

The current view of QH has been focused on introducing QH as a financial, humanitarian, and welfare tool which would alleviate inequalities and mobilize the wealth in societies by helping impoverished and disadvantaged people (Farooq, 2010; Obaidullah &Tariqullah, 2008; Khan, 2008; Mojtahed & Hassanzadeh, 2009; Najeeb & Lahsasna, 2012). These contemporary studies have established the role of QH on amelioration of the human condition through religious avenues as well as the historical data collected from various countries in the past couple of decades. While the concept is widely used in providing microfinance by NGOs, charities, religious organizations, etc. (Khan, 2008), the results have not been satisfactory in alleviating poverty, improving conditions and gaining popularity among Muslim communities due to several reasons. According to Widiyanto, Mutamimah, & Hendar (2011) providing QH financing to the poor cannot alleviate poverty on its own and requires a more integrated approach which also involves broader aspects such as education, information and morality. Extending financing through QH has been inadequate and inefficient in alleviating poverty mainly due to the lack of ability to profit from it, high administrative and transaction costs, high risk and lack of demand from recipients (Ariffin & Adnan, 2011). To absorb losses and inject more capital to QH, several authors have recommended using charities and donations in conjunction with QH so that the issue of lack of funding can be remedied (Ahmed, 2007; Febianto & Ashany, 2012). According to Farooq (2007), one of the advantages of QH funding is that the source of financing can be originated from the local community so that the QH financing model does not rely on the government or commercial sources. Despite exciting developments in individual practices of charities and donations, there is much work remaining in terms of putting these pieces back into a holistic system to address social economic problems (Ahmed, 2007).

The lack of sufficient access to capital and despondency among institutional investor participants have prevented QH to grow in the financial cycles mainly based on the assumption that benevolent loan is only a nonprofit and "free-loan". Unfortunately, this presumption has not been sufficiently challenged or the possibilities not fully explored by scholars to provide an alternative viable QH method. Lack of institutional investor participation as well as the high administrative fees are some of the major obstacles that have kept QH gaining popularity in financial lending. In this article, the authors have addressed these issues and demonstrated a method in which QH is given a new perspective among key participants and consequently bring more liquidity to QH financial market.

2.0 Methods and analysis

In the authors' view, QH is an interest-free loan in which the same amount of principal is returned to the lender at no extra charge to the borrower. In brief, MP is the vertex point of the parabolic curve shape resulted from calculating the discounted values of the total interest paid by the borrower in each interest rate between 1%-30% at each 5,10,15,20 and 30 years term in a conventional loan. For further reading on the concept of MP, refer to the previous article (Izadyar and Ragnath 2014). Previously, the MP was discounted based on compounding monthly (n=12) in the time value of money formula (TVM).

Table 1 shows the amount of MP and associated interest rates at each term based on biannual compounding factor (n=2). The assumption is that the amount of cash flow will be invested in sukuk (Islamic bonds) where the compounding is generally in biannual frequencies. Our intent is to introduce an interest free and no fee QH lending platform in which the borrower initially makes MP upfront payment and receives a zero percent interest rate, no fee loan and pays the remaining principal during the term of the loan. The MP upfront payment as well as the remaining principal monthly cash inflows will be invested in profit bearing sukuk.

Table 01: The optimum amount of upfront payment "Mesbah Point" (MP) and associated interest rate based on 30,20,15,10 and 5 year terms

Period	Interest Rate	MP
30 years	3.875%	$ 21,908.00
20 years	6.000%	$ 22,054.76
15 years	8.000%	$ 22,204.30
10 years	12.250%	$ 22,506.76
5 years	26.250%	$ 23,462.92

Table 2 (see appendix) demonstrates the future value of invested MP and future values of monthly cash inflows on a $100,000 QH loan at the rate of return of 3.875% on a 30 years term. Based on this example, in order for the borrower to receive a $100,000 QH loan, the borrower will need to make an initial payment of $21,908 (MP) and agrees to make the monthly payments of $216.92 for the next 30 years ($100,000 - $21,908 /360). The lender at its own discretion will invest the amount of received cash inflows in the financial markets. Assuming the cash flows are invested in sukuk at the annual rate of return of 3.875% and the gains are compounded semi-annually, the total amount can reach $214,555.77. The borrower is making an initial contribution of $21,908 and total monthly payments of $78,092 ($216.92 X 360) during the term of the loan which equals $100,000, while the lender has been able to accelerate its gains by investing the upfront payment and the future cash inflows in a new investment vehicle.

The remaining principal after making the upfront payment (MP) can be distributed in a regular monthly schedule during the full term of the loan (Standard MP) or the monthly payment can be accelerated to the conventional monthly level based on the market condition in order to produce more gains to the lender (Accelerated MP). Table 3 shows the amount of future value (FV) of $100,000 loan under conventional, Standard MP and Accelerated MP at interest rates 1% to 30% during the terms 5,10,15,20 and 30 years. The rate of return has been calculated using CAGR (compounding annual growth rate). CAGR= [(ending value/beginning value) 1/n] -1 where n is the number of years. The FV of a $100,000 conventional loan is the FV of monthly received cash inflows which is invested in the market interest rate. Assuming the compounding will occur every 6 months, the formula used to determine FV is FV= C [(1+ i)n-1/ i] where C is the cash flow or the monthly payment per period (6 months), i is equal the semi-annual interest rate (annual interest rate/2) and n is twice number of the years (term x 2). The FV of Standard MP scenario is based on the FV of the cash inflows or the monthly payments per period (6months) as just discussed plus the FV of the MP in each term using the data of table 1. The monthly payment is based on ($100,000-MP)/term and FV MP = MP (1+ i)n , where i is equal the semi-annual interest rate and n is the term times 2.

The FV of Accelerated MP scenario is conducted in two stages; the first stage is to calculate the FV1 in which the FV of MP and the conventional monthly payment during M period is estimated (table 3). The value of M is calculated using M= (100,000-MP)/conventional monthly payment. M is the total of months in which the remaining principal balance will be paid and it is the period that the $100,000 QH loan will be paid off. In order to calculate FV1, the M needs to be changed to semiannual period, meaning it be divided to 6. The remaining period is term-M in which the second stage of FV2 will be calculated. In this stage, the amount of FV1 will be used as the PV (present value) in estimating FV2; FV2 = FV1 (1+i)n , where i is based on the semi-annual rate and n is (monthly term-M)/6.

By increasing the monthly payments to conventional level, not only will CAGR achieve a higher percentage (Figure 1), but also the payback period is reduced (column M in table 3) depending upon the interest rate in the market. The borrower's monthly payment will be higher as the interest rates in the market move up. Figure 1 shows the CAGR of the three lending scenarios; conventional, Standard MP and Accelerated MP at interest rates ranging from 1% to 30% in a 30 years loan. Although the rate of return in Accelerated MP is less than the rate of return in conventional method, it provides better return in comparison with Standard MP. The percentage of CAGR shortfalls in Standard and Accelerated MP have been compared with conventional method at interest rates 1% to 30% during 5,10,15,20 and 30 years terms in figure 2. The performance of the investment has a negative relationship with the term and the interest rate in the market; the shorter the term of the loan or the higher the interest rates in the market, the worse the return. Accelerated MP reduces the rate of shortfalls in each term.

Payback period is the time in which the initial principal is expected to be recovered from the cash inflows generated by the investment. It is a quick and simple tool in measuring the period that the initial capital is at risk. Generally, a lower payback period suggests lower risk. Figure 3 illustrates the payback period of $100,000 in Accelerated MP at interest rates 1%-30% during 5,10,15,20 and 30 years terms. Depending upon the market conditions, the higher the interest rate in the market, the shorter the payback period is as higher amounts of monthly payments are made (figure 3 in appendix).

3.0 Discussion

The latest financial turmoil starting in 2007 has caused irreversible regulatory consequences in the financial market in which a more conservative approach has been mapped into the structure of capitalism. The attempt is to deviate from the expectation of conceptual conventional returns and lean toward more realistic and stable returns whereby exploitation can be eliminated in society and thus prevent the accumulation of wealth in the hands of few. Meanwhile, the emergence of alternative financing such as Islamic finance and microfinance has been accelerated as new tools in combating against the societal dysfunctions such as inequalities and poverty.

The scholarly view of QH has been restricted to application of this financial tool in alleviating poverty and financial justice, although the comprehensive aspects of QH has not been fully explored and is shrouded in misunderstandings. Obscurity in profitability of QH has made many believe that QH is a non-viable financial instrument in the contemporary financial lending system. The current misconception of QH as a charity loan has prevented institutional investors to enter such a market. While QH should not be confused with charity and donation, it is a loan that should be offered to everyone; it is not just for the poor and needy but for the rich and prosperous as well. QH is an ultimate, a final financial lending destination and a benevolent loan. It is a free loan to all society members and can be funded by sources from charities and donations but is not loaned as charity or donation. In this respect, QH should not be applied to mendicants where the borrower is unable to return the original principal. The charities and donations funds should help mendicants and other destitute members in the communities such as unemployed and financially distressed families etc. In developed countries, the governments as well as non-profit organizations take responsibility in providing the basic life necessities such as shelter, food stamps where there is still much more help and funds needed. Charities, donations and volunteering for social services play a vital role in supporting such causes. However, QH covers a much broader financial field other than as a tool for charity only.

Meanwhile, the current role of banks and other QH sponsoring institutions have been a double standard; QH has been successfully promoted in consumer checking and savings accounts by the banks where there are no returns committed to depositors and the funds are being used in profit bearing practices. On the other hand, high costs in administration fees are improperly imposed on borrowers and cause higher amount of return of capital to the lender. Obviously, the whole concept of QH is based on receiving the same amount of principal from the borrower. Imposed administration or compensation fees by banks do not have religious and moral merits and is subject to exploitation and abuse. However, third party charges such as attorney fees are not part of administration fees since these charges are not paid to the banks and banks will accordingly need to distinguish their business from third party practices.

In our view, collecting additional fees to the principal is prohibited in direct-to-consumer related QH transactions. We have presented MP as an interest rate-proof value in which the borrower, regardless of interest rates in the market, can contribute a pre-determined amount of upfront payment to receive interest free, no fee QH loans (table 1). Collecting optimum amount of upfront payment will release the lender to cover all the administrative costs and fees by reinvesting the MP and the future cash flows in a profit bearing account. Reinvesting MP and the remaining monthly principal payment is performed under a separate transaction and the earned future profits are not at the expense of the borrower for the reason that the amount of principal collected is the same. The details of such transaction have been demonstrated as an example in table 2 where the borrower returns the same $100,000 QH principal during the 30 years period and the cash flows are invested in sukuk.

Based on MP platform the QH lenders and the financial institutions can gain sufficient returns which may help them to cope with their accruing costs as well as earn some profit by providing QH. Although the rate of return in MP financing still remains below the conventional method, accelerating QH remaining monthly payments to the level of conventional monthly payments significantly improve this offset in the gap of return and significantly reduces the payback period (figure 1 and 3). Figure 2 emphasizes the shortfalls in Standard and Accelerated MP in comparison with a conventional method.

Accelerated MP shortens the payback period especially in longer QH loan terms which suggests lower capital risk to the investor (figure 3), at the same time increasing the earnings to the level that the participation of institutional investors are possible. Presence of institutional investors as well as other major participants is a crucial step in making QH a viable Islamic product. On the one hand they are able to inject the required capital to the local communities, credit unions and small banks and on the other hand they can provide more liquidity through issuing QH sukuk in the secondary market. A secondary market for the QH funds demand more actions from governments and their related central banks where they need to actively promote establishing QH funds by monetary policies such as guaranteeing QH funds, tax breaks and other financial subsidies. The monetary policies should perform as a compensating factor in conjunction with the QH funds as there is a shortfall in the rate of return in QH loans in comparison with conventional lending. This way, the institutional investors are enticed to participate and take more responsibilities in this financial reform.

4.0 Conclusion

The institutionalization of QH is the ultimate aspiration in the Islamic banking system and requires a more holistic approach. Establishing a viable QH lending method, devoid of misconceptions, is the first step toward this approach. Then, participation of the regulators as well as institutional investors in creating a secondary market is crucial in providing liquidity and sufficient capital to the QH markets. Here we introduced a new platform to the most challenging Islamic lending practice which is QH that will allow financial institutions to enter the QH market with the intention of entrepreneurship. Although our concept is in its infancy and will require support through Sharia scholars in conjunction with proven practical results, this concept is rooted in consumer demand for a true interest-free, no fee product which potentially provides prosperity for the global society.

References

Ahmed, H., 2007. Waqf-based microfinance: realizing the social role Of Islamic finance. Jeddah: Islamic Development Bank

Ariffin, N.M., & Adnan, M.K., 2011. Malaysian Islamic banker's perceptions of al-qard al-hasan. Review of Islamic Economics, 15(2): 97-111.

Bakar, M., 2008a. Contracts in Islamic commercial law and their application in modern Islamic financial system. In M. Bakar & E.R. Engku Ali (Eds.), Essential Readings in Islamic Finance. CERT Publications, Kuala Lumpur, pp. 47-84.

Bakar, M., 2008b. Shari'ah approaches to product development and product enhancement in Islamic banking and finance. In M. Bakar & E.R. Engku Ali, (Eds.), Essential Readings in Islamic Finance. CERT Publications, Kuala Lumpur, pp. 113-130.

Berthoud, R., & Hinton, T., 1989. Credit Unions in the United Kingdom. UK: Policy Studies Institute, Printer Publishers Limited.

Farook, S., 2007. On corporate social responsibility of Islamic financial institutions. Islamic Economic Studies, 15(1): 31-46. http://dx.doi.org/10.1163/026805507X247563

Farooq, M.O., 2007. Stipulation of excess in understanding and misunderstanding riba: the al-jassas link. Arab Law Quarterly, 21(4): 285-316. http://dx.doi.org/10.1163/157302511X553985

Farooq, M.O., 2010. Qarḍ ḥasan, wadīʿah/amānah and bank deposits: applications and misapplications of some concepts in Islamic banking. Arab Law Quarterly, 25(2):115-146.

Febianto, I., & Ashany, A.M., 2012. The impact of qardul hasan financing using zakah funds on economic empowerment. Asian Business Review, 1(1): 15-20.

Izadyar, A.B. , & Ragnath, F., 2014. Establishing an interest-free lending platform applying optimum premium, "Mesbah Point", in amortization and time value of money. International Journal of Business and Social Research, 4(1): 1-18.

Khan, A.A., 2008. Islamic Microfinance Theory, Policy and Practice. Birmingham: Islamic Relief Worldwide.

Mirakhor, A., & Iqbal, Z., 2007. Qard hasan microfinance. New Horizon, 164(2): 18-20.

Mojtahed, A., & Hassanzadeh, A., 2009. The evaluation of Qard-al-hasan as a microfinance approch in poverty alleviation programs. Money and Economy, 5(2): 1-32.

Najeeb, S.F., & Lahsasna, A., 2012. Qard hasan: its rules and applications in Islamic finance. Sahulat, 1(2): 11-22.

Obaidullah, O., & Tariqullah, M.K., 2008. Islamic Microfinance Development Challenges and Initiative. Jeddah: Islamic Development Bank.

Widiyanto, W., Mutamimah, S., & Hendar, H., 2011. Effectiveness of Qard al-hasan financing as a poverty alleviation model. Economic Journal of Emerging Markets, 3(1): 27-42.

Appendix: A

Table 2: Future value (FV) of invested Mesbah Point (MP) and FV of monthly cash inflows on a $100,000 loan at the rate of return of 3.875% on a 30 years term.

Compound	Principal	FV		Compound	Principal	FV
1	$23,209.52	$23,633.99		31	$62,255.12	$94,316.12
2	$24,511.04	$25,393.42		32	$63,556.64	$97,445.02
3	$25,812.56	$27,186.93		33	$64,858.16	$100,634.54
4	$27,114.08	$29,015.20		34	$66,159.68	$103,885.85
5	$28,415.60	$30,878.89		35	$67,461.20	$107,200.16
6	$29,717.12	$32,778.69		36	$68,762.72	$110,578.68
7	$31,018.64	$34,715.30		37	$70,064.24	$114,022.66
8	$32,320.16	$36,689.42		38	$71,365.76	$117,533.37
9	$33,621.68	$38,701.80		39	$72,667.28	$121,112.10
10	$34,923.20	$40,753.17		40	$73,968.80	$124,760.17
11	$36,224.72	$42,844.28		41	$75,270.32	$128,478.92
12	$37,526.24	$44,975.91		42	$76,571.84	$132,269.72
13	$38,827.76	$47,148.84		43	$77,873.36	$136,133.96
14	$40,129.28	$49,363.87		44	$79,174.88	$140,073.08
15	$41,430.80	$51,621.81		45	$80,476.40	$144,088.51
16	$42,732.32	$53,923.50		46	$81,777.92	$148,181.75
17	$44,033.84	$56,269.79		47	$83,079.44	$152,354.29
18	$45,335.36	$58,661.54		48	$84,380.96	$156,607.67
19	$46,636.88	$61,099.63		49	$85,682.48	$160,943.47
20	$47,938.40	$63,584.95		50	$86,984.00	$165,363.27
21	$49,239.92	$66,118.43		51	$88,285.52	$169,868.70
22	$50,541.44	$68,701.00		52	$89,587.04	$174,461.43
23	$51,842.96	$71,333.60		53	$90,888.56	$179,143.14
24	$53,144.48	$74,017.21		54	$92,190.08	$183,915.56
25	$54,446.00	$76,752.81		55	$93,491.60	$188,780.44
26	$55,747.52	$79,541.41		56	$94,793.12	$193,739.58
27	$57,049.04	$82,384.05		57	$96,094.64	$198,794.80
28	$58,350.56	$85,281.76		58	$97,396.16	$203,947.97
29	$59,652.08	$88,235.61		59	$98,697.68	$209,200.99
30	$60,953.60	$91,246.70		**60**	**$100,000.00**	**$214,555.77**

Table 3: Future values (FV) and CAGR return of $100,000 loan under conventional, Standard MP and Accelerated MP at interest rates (I.R.) 1% to 30% during the terms 5,10,15,20 and 30 years. M is the payback period of the loan in months.

	30 years										
	Conventional			Standard MP			Accelerated MP				
I.R.	Monthly	Total payment	FV	Monthly	FV MP	CAGR	M	FV1	360-M	FV2	CAGR
1%	$321.64	$115,790.23	$134,644.79	$216.92	$120,358.63	0.62%	242.79	$113,122.16	117.21	$124,698.27	0.74%
2%	$369.62	$133,063.01	$181,120.20	$216.92	$146,095.99	1.27%	211.28	$124,157.30	148.72	$158,886.52	1.56%
3%	$421.60	$151,777.45	$243,386.91	$216.92	$178,752.64	1.95%	185.23	$133,090.26	174.77	$205,350.47	2.43%
4%	$477.42	$171,869.51	$326,699.70	$216.92	$220,322.70	2.67%	163.57	$140,104.62	196.43	$267,919.42	3.34%
5%	$536.82	$193,255.78	$438,019.36	$216.92	$273,388.18	3.41%	145.47	$145,475.21	214.53	$351,737.72	4.28%
6%	$599.55	$215,838.19	$586,552.64	$216.92	$341,292.72	4.18%	130.25	$149,496.58	229.75	$463,647.64	5.25%
7%	$665.30	$239,508.90	$784,459.04	$216.92	$428,366.49	4.97%	117.38	$152,443.24	242.62	$612,703.88	6.23%
8%	$733.76	$264,155.25	$1,047,774.80	$216.92	$540,216.81	5.78%	106.43	$154,551.98	253.57	$810,852.37	7.23%
9%	$804.62	$289,664.14	$1,397,619.61	$216.92	$684,103.69	6.62%	97.05	$156,017.48	262.95	$1,073,819.58	8.23%
10%	$877.57	$315,925.77	$1,861,770.11	$216.92	$869,424.60	7.48%	88.99	$156,994.81	271.01	$1,422,273.33	9.25%
11%	$952.32	$342,836.42	$2,476,709.58	$216.92	$1,108,339.80	8.35%	82	$157,604.81	278	$1,883,334.19	10.28%
12%	$1,028.61	$370,300.53	$3,290,294.18	$216.92	$1,416,578.43	9.24%	75.92	$157,940.22	284.08	$2,492,540.36	11.32%
13%	$1,106.20	$398,231.83	$4,365,217.12	$216.92	$1,814,476.74	10.14%	70.59	$158,071.46	289.41	$3,296,397.92	12.36%
14%	$1,184.87	$426,553.83	$5,783,503.93	$216.92	$2,328,314.22	11.06%	65.91	$158,051.57	294.09	$4,355,686.83	13.41%
15%	$1,264.44	$455,199.85	$7,652,338.38	$216.92	$2,992,031.66	12.00%	61.76	$157,920.29	298.24	$5,749,740.73	14.46%
16%	$1,344.76	$484,112.52	$10,111,604.09	$216.92	$3,849,438.63	12.94%	58.07	$157,707.28	301.93	$7,581,980.93	15.52%
17%	$1,425.68	$513,243.12	$13,343,634.99	$216.92	$4,957,047.00	13.90%	54.78	$157,434.57	305.22	$9,987,063.09	16.59%
18%	$1,507.09	$542,550.73	$17,585,806.65	$216.92	$6,387,705.33	14.86%	51.82	$157,118.55	308.18	$13,140,095.77	17.66%
19%	$1,588.89	$572,001.30	$23,146,776.98	$216.92	$8,235,256.11	15.84%	49.15	$156,771.34	310.85	$17,268,517.23	18.73%
20%	$1,671.02	$601,566.73	$30,427,409.44	$216.92	$10,620,498.46	16.83%	46.73	$156,401.93	313.27	$22,667,379.24	19.82%
21%	$1,753.40	$631,224.03	$39,947,697.37	$216.92	$13,698,815.57	17.82%	44.54	$156,016.94	315.46	$29,718,992.45	20.90%
22%	$1,835.98	$660,954.52	$52,381,371.16	$216.92	$17,669,922.76	18.82%	42.53	$155,621.27	317.47	$38,918,148.97	21.99%
23%	$1,918.73	$690,743.09	$68,600,329.45	$216.92	$22,790,314.53	19.84%	40.7	$155,218.56	319.3	$50,904,468.80	23.09%
24%	$2,001.60	$720,577.59	$89,731,618.98	$216.92	$29,389,143.58	20.86%	39.01	$154,811.45	320.99	$66,503,835.41	24.19%
25%	$2,084.58	$750,448.31	$117,230,425.46	$216.92	$37,888,459.57	21.88%	37.46	$154,401.92	322.54	$86,781,415.30	25.30%
26%	$2,167.63	$780,347.51	$152,973,470.56	$216.92	$48,828,981.21	22.92%	36.03	$153,991.41	323.97	$113,109,424.95	26.41%
27%	$2,250.75	$810,269.05	$199,378,388.78	$216.92	$62,902,884.58	23.96%	34.7	$153,580.97	325.3	$147,253,652.54	27.53%
28%	$2,333.91	$840,208.08	$259,556,144.78	$216.92	$80,995,479.80	25.01%	33.46	$153,171.38	326.54	$191,483,804.56	28.65%
29%	$2,417.11	$870,160.76	$337,505,425.67	$216.92	$104,238,137.11	26.07%	32.31	$152,763.20	327.69	$248,714,086.82	29.77%
30%	$2,500.34	$900,124.08	$438,360,302.77	$216.92	$134,075,437.64	27.13%	31.23	$152,356.84	328.77	$322,682,112.52	30.91%

	20 years			Standard MP			Accelerated MP				
	Conventional										
I.R.	Monthly	Total payment	FV	Monthly	FV MP	CAGR	M	FV1	240-M	FV2	CAGR
1%	$459.89	$110,374.63	$121,850.41	$324.77	$112,973.62	0.61%	169.49	$108,886.05	70.51	$115,459.28	0.72%
2%	$505.88	$121,412.00	$148,384.81	$324.77	$128,098.03	1.25%	154.08	$116,843.32	85.92	$134,737.28	1.50%
3%	$554.60	$133,103.42	$180,581.06	$324.77	$145,755.84	1.90%	140.54	$123,830.48	99.46	$158,492.58	2.33%
4%	$605.98	$145,435.28	$219,614.48	$324.77	$166,398.96	2.58%	128.63	$129,862.90	111.37	$187,552.72	3.19%
5%	$659.96	$158,389.38	$266,896.21	$324.77	$190,561.14	3.28%	118.11	$134,994.53	121.89	$222,934.50	4.09%
6%	$716.43	$171,943.45	$324,118.83	$324.77	$218,872.69	3.99%	108.8	$139,302.50	131.2	$265,872.60	5.01%
7%	$775.30	$186,071.74	$393,310.44	$324.77	$252,077.82	4.73%	100.54	$142,875.09	139.46	$317,856.21	5.95%
8%	$836.44	$200,745.62	$476,898.89	$324.77	$291,055.02	5.49%	93.19	$145,803.17	146.81	$380,674.04	6.91%
9%	$899.73	$215,934.23	$577,787.76	$324.77	$336,841.13	6.26%	86.63	$148,174.59	153.37	$456,468.67	7.89%
10%	$965.02	$231,605.19	$699,446.38	$324.77	$390,659.45	7.05%	80.77	$150,070.78	159.23	$547,801.47	8.88%
11%	$1,032.19	$247,725.21	$846,016.38	$324.77	$453,952.92	7.86%	75.51	$151,565.01	164.49	$657,729.77	9.88%
12%	$1,101.09	$264,260.67	$1,022,437.53	$324.77	$528,423.00	8.68%	70.79	$152,721.83	169.21	$789,898.30	10.89%
13%	$1,171.58	$281,178.17	$1,234,596.52	$324.77	$616,075.34	9.52%	66.53	$153,597.17	173.47	$948,647.29	11.91%
14%	$1,243.52	$298,444.99	$1,489,502.50	$324.77	$719,273.24	10.37%	62.68	$154,238.89	177.32	$1,139,140.06	12.94%
15%	$1,316.79	$316,029.50	$1,795,494.11	$324.77	$840,800.46	11.23%	59.19	$154,687.52	180.81	$1,367,513.45	13.97%
16%	$1,391.26	$333,901.43	$2,162,483.52	$324.77	$983,934.67	12.11%	56.03	$154,977.17	183.97	$1,641,055.00	15.02%
17%	$1,466.80	$352,032.13	$2,602,243.84	$324.77	$1,152,533.54	13.00%	53.14	$155,136.33	186.86	$1,968,411.31	16.07%
18%	$1,543.31	$370,394.77	$3,128,747.23	$324.77	$1,351,135.43	13.90%	50.51	$155,188.71	189.49	$2,359,833.19	17.12%
19%	$1,620.68	$388,964.36	$3,758,562.58	$324.77	$1,585,077.14	14.82%	48.09	$155,153.92	191.91	$2,827,463.40	18.19%
20%	$1,698.82	$407,717.91	$4,511,322.75	$324.77	$1,860,631.59	15.74%	45.88	$155,048.20	194.12	$3,385,674.55	19.26%
21%	$1,777.64	$426,634.31	$5,410,273.13	$324.77	$2,185,168.65	16.67%	43.85	$154,884.90	196.15	$4,051,465.29	20.33%
22%	$1,857.06	$445,694.38	$6,482,915.27	$324.77	$2,567,342.84	17.62%	41.97	$154,675.01	198.03	$4,844,924.66	21.41%
23%	$1,937.00	$464,880.80	$7,761,761.48	$324.77	$3,017,312.43	18.57%	40.24	$154,427.54	199.76	$5,789,775.91	22.50%
24%	$2,017.41	$484,177.96	$9,285,218.89	$324.77	$3,546,994.94	19.53%	38.64	$154,149.89	201.36	$6,914,012.84	23.59%
25%	$2,098.22	$503,571.90	$11,098,624.37	$324.77	$4,170,364.91	20.51%	37.15	$153,848.10	202.85	$8,250,644.04	24.69%
26%	$2,179.38	$523,050.21	$13,255,455.41	$324.77	$4,903,800.77	21.49%	35.76	$153,527.12	204.24	$9,838,562.46	25.79%
27%	$2,260.84	$542,601.87	$15,818,745.55	$324.77	$5,766,488.64	22.47%	34.48	$153,191.00	205.52	$11,723,560.99	26.90%
28%	$2,342.57	$562,217.15	$18,862,738.16	$324.77	$6,780,892.28	23.47%	33.27	$152,843.05	206.73	$13,959,517.54	28.01%
29%	$2,424.53	$581,887.50	$22,474,816.99	$324.77	$7,973,299.39	24.47%	32.15	$152,485.95	207.85	$16,609,777.02	29.13%
30%	$2,506.69	$601,605.40	$26,757,758.54	$324.77	$9,374,456.75	25.49%	31.09	$152,121.91	208.91	$19,748,761.91	30.25%

	15 years Conventional			Standard MP			Accelerated MP				
I.R.	Monthly	Total payment	FV	Monthly	FV MP	CAGR	M	FV1	180-M	FV2	CAGR
1%	$598.49	$107,729.01	$115,916.48	$432.20	$109,496.29	0.61%	129.99	$106,687.45	50.01	$111,216.45	0.71%
2%	$643.51	$115,831.57	$134,306.28	$432.20	$120,131.87	1.23%	120.89	$112,848.37	59.11	$124,470.33	1.47%
3%	$690.58	$124,304.70	$155,541.14	$432.20	$132,052.04	1.87%	112.65	$118,456.47	67.35	$140,003.05	2.27%
4%	$739.69	$133,143.83	$180,046.31	$432.20	$145,420.75	2.53%	105.17	$123,506.66	74.83	$158,104.26	3.10%
5%	$790.79	$142,342.85	$208,307.87	$432.20	$160,423.07	3.20%	98.38	$128,010.32	81.62	$179,114.65	3.96%
6%	$843.86	$151,894.23	$240,881.04	$432.20	$177,267.76	3.89%	92.19	$131,990.91	87.81	$203,430.20	4.85%
7%	$898.83	$161,789.09	$278,399.53	$432.20	$196,190.30	4.60%	86.55	$135,480.09	93.45	$231,507.77	5.76%
8%	$955.65	$172,017.38	$321,586.13	$432.20	$217,456.27	5.32%	81.41	$138,514.53	98.59	$263,871.92	6.68%
9%	$1,014.27	$182,567.99	$371,264.59	$432.20	$241,365.09	6.05%	76.7	$141,133.33	103.3	$301,122.93	7.63%
10%	$1,074.61	$193,428.92	$428,373.15	$432.20	$268,254.26	6.80%	72.39	$143,376.11	107.61	$343,946.06	8.58%
11%	$1,136.60	$204,587.45	$493,979.65	$432.20	$298,504.11	7.56%	68.45	$145,281.65	111.55	$393,122.24	9.56%
12%	$1,200.17	$216,030.25	$569,298.66	$432.20	$332,543.10	8.34%	64.82	$146,886.89	115.18	$449,540.12	10.54%
13%	$1,265.24	$227,743.59	$655,710.72	$432.20	$370,853.80	9.13%	61.49	$148,226.36	118.51	$514,209.79	11.53%
14%	$1,331.74	$239,713.45	$754,784.03	$432.20	$413,979.56	9.93%	58.42	$149,331.86	121.58	$588,278.24	12.54%
15%	$1,399.59	$251,925.68	$868,298.83	$432.20	$462,531.95	10.75%	55.58	$150,232.29	124.42	$673,046.84	13.55%
16%	$1,468.70	$264,366.13	$998,274.82	$432.20	$517,199.14	11.58%	52.97	$150,953.69	127.03	$769,990.89	14.58%
17%	$1,539.00	$277,020.77	$1,147,001.97	$432.20	$578,755.27	12.42%	50.55	$151,519.31	129.45	$880,781.75	15.61%
18%	$1,610.42	$289,875.79	$1,317,075.17	$432.20	$648,070.86	13.27%	48.31	$151,949.78	131.69	$1,007,311.58	16.65%
19%	$1,682.88	$302,917.69	$1,511,433.06	$432.20	$726,124.52	14.13%	46.23	$152,263.32	133.77	$1,151,721.17	17.69%
20%	$1,756.30	$316,133.37	$1,733,401.66	$432.20	$814,016.02	15.00%	44.3	$152,475.90	135.7	$1,316,431.08	18.75%
21%	$1,830.61	$329,510.21	$1,986,743.30	$432.20	$912,980.81	15.89%	42.5	$152,601.55	137.5	$1,504,176.58	19.81%
22%	$1,905.76	$343,036.08	$2,275,711.40	$432.20	$1,024,406.37	16.78%	40.82	$152,652.46	139.18	$1,718,046.81	20.87%
23%	$1,981.66	$356,699.42	$2,605,111.94	$432.20	$1,149,850.30	17.68%	39.26	$152,639.27	140.74	$1,961,528.49	21.95%
24%	$2,058.27	$370,489.26	$2,980,372.23	$432.20	$1,291,060.60	18.59%	37.8	$152,571.20	142.2	$2,238,554.98	23.03%
25%	$2,135.53	$384,395.21	$3,407,617.88	$432.20	$1,449,998.26	19.52%	36.43	$152,456.22	143.57	$2,553,560.96	24.11%
26%	$2,213.38	$398,407.51	$3,893,758.93	$432.20	$1,628,862.41	20.45%	35.15	$152,301.26	144.85	$2,911,543.68	25.20%
27%	$2,291.76	$412,517.01	$4,446,586.14	$432.20	$1,830,118.32	21.39%	33.95	$152,112.28	146.05	$3,318,131.25	26.30%
28%	$2,370.64	$426,715.16	$5,074,878.55	$432.20	$2,056,528.69	22.33%	32.82	$151,894.42	147.18	$3,779,658.96	27.40%
29%	$2,449.97	$440,994.02	$5,788,523.70	$432.20	$2,311,188.32	23.29%	31.75	$151,652.12	148.25	$4,303,254.36	28.50%
30%	$2,529.70	$455,346.21	$6,598,651.81	$432.20	$2,597,562.81	24.25%	30.75	$151,389.19	149.25	$4,896,932.19	29.62%

	10 Years Conventional			Standard MP			Accelerated MP				
I.R.	Monthly	Total payment	FV	Monthly	FV MP	CAGR	M	FV1	120-M	FV2	CAGR
1%	$876.04	$105,124.95	$110,271.42	$645.78	$106,154.60	0.60%	88.46	$104,437.20	31.54	$107,211.67	0.70%
2%	$920.13	$110,416.14	$121,562.68	$645.78	$112,778.72	1.21%	84.22	$108,633.20	35.78	$115,274.37	1.43%
3%	$965.61	$115,872.89	$133,970.31	$645.78	$119,909.74	1.83%	80.25	$112,577.67	39.75	$124,247.07	2.19%
4%	$1,012.45	$121,494.17	$147,599.43	$645.78	$127,587.96	2.47%	76.54	$116,265.20	43.46	$134,197.17	2.99%
5%	$1,060.66	$127,278.62	$162,564.44	$645.78	$135,856.86	3.11%	73.06	$119,694.67	46.94	$145,200.53	3.80%
6%	$1,110.21	$133,224.60	$178,989.75	$645.78	$144,763.33	3.77%	69.8	$122,868.53	50.2	$157,341.63	4.64%
7%	$1,161.08	$139,330.18	$197,010.65	$645.78	$154,357.91	4.44%	66.74	$125,792.19	53.26	$170,713.93	5.49%
8%	$1,213.28	$145,593.11	$216,774.16	$645.78	$164,695.07	5.12%	63.87	$128,473.39	56.13	$185,420.18	6.37%
9%	$1,266.76	$152,010.93	$238,439.96	$645.78	$175,833.53	5.81%	61.17	$130,921.63	58.83	$201,573.00	7.26%
10%	$1,321.51	$158,580.88	$262,181.41	$645.78	$187,836.53	6.51%	58.64	$133,147.73	61.36	$219,295.41	8.17%
11%	$1,377.50	$165,300.01	$288,186.67	$645.78	$200,772.21	7.22%	56.26	$135,163.39	63.74	$238,721.50	9.09%
12%	$1,434.71	$172,165.14	$316,659.82	$645.78	$214,713.96	7.94%	54.01	$136,980.83	65.99	$259,997.19	10.03%
13%	$1,493.11	$179,172.89	$347,822.13	$645.78	$229,740.78	8.67%	51.9	$138,612.50	68.1	$283,281.03	10.97%
14%	$1,552.66	$186,319.72	$381,913.44	$645.78	$245,937.74	9.42%	49.91	$140,070.86	70.09	$308,745.08	11.93%
15%	$1,613.35	$193,601.95	$419,193.53	$645.78	$263,396.37	10.17%	48.03	$141,368.17	71.97	$336,575.88	12.90%
16%	$1,675.13	$201,015.75	$459,943.77	$645.78	$282,215.19	10.93%	46.26	$142,516.36	73.74	$366,975.54	13.88%
17%	$1,737.98	$208,557.18	$504,468.68	$645.78	$302,500.17	11.70%	44.59	$143,526.91	75.41	$400,162.81	14.87%
18%	$1,801.85	$216,222.24	$553,097.78	$645.78	$324,365.30	12.49%	43.01	$144,410.78	76.99	$436,374.37	15.87%
19%	$1,866.72	$224,006.83	$606,187.48	$645.78	$347,933.15	13.28%	41.51	$145,178.37	78.49	$475,866.09	16.88%
20%	$1,932.56	$231,906.81	$664,123.11	$645.78	$373,335.49	14.08%	40.1	$145,839.46	79.9	$518,914.47	17.90%
21%	$1,999.32	$239,918.01	$727,321.14	$645.78	$400,713.97	14.89%	38.76	$146,403.22	81.24	$565,818.15	18.92%
22%	$2,066.97	$248,036.25	$796,231.50	$645.78	$430,220.78	15.71%	37.49	$146,878.21	82.51	$616,899.53	19.96%
23%	$2,135.48	$256,257.36	$871,340.10	$645.78	$462,019.47	16.54%	36.29	$147,272.38	83.71	$672,506.52	21.00%
24%	$2,204.81	$264,577.16	$953,171.54	$645.78	$496,285.66	17.37%	35.15	$147,593.07	84.85	$733,014.40	22.04%
25%	$2,274.93	$272,991.54	$1,042,291.95	$645.78	$533,208.00	18.22%	34.06	$147,847.10	85.94	$798,827.80	23.10%
26%	$2,345.80	$281,496.41	$1,139,312.09	$645.78	$572,988.97	19.07%	33.03	$148,040.69	86.97	$870,382.86	24.16%
27%	$2,417.40	$290,087.75	$1,244,890.65	$645.78	$615,845.97	19.94%	32.06	$148,179.60	87.94	$948,149.47	25.22%
28%	$2,489.68	$298,761.62	$1,359,737.74	$645.78	$662,012.26	20.81%	31.13	$148,269.08	88.87	$1,032,633.71	26.30%
29%	$2,562.62	$307,514.13	$1,484,618.65	$645.78	$711,738.11	21.68%	30.24	$148,313.95	89.76	$1,124,380.50	27.38%
30%	$2,636.18	$316,341.52	$1,620,357.91	$645.78	$765,291.99	22.57%	29.4	$148,318.59	90.6	$1,223,976.28	28.46%

	5 Years										
	Conventional			Standard MP			Accelerated MP				
I.R.	Monthly	Total payment	FV	Monthly	FV MP	CAGR	M	FV1	60-M	FV2	CAGR
1%	$1,709.37	$102,562.48	$104,901.18	$1,275.62	$102,945.14	0.58%	44.77	$102,137.60	15.23	$103,438.47	0.68%
2%	$1,752.78	$105,166.56	$110,027.49	$1,275.62	$105,992.38	1.17%	43.67	$104,207.22	16.33	$107,068.54	1.38%
3%	$1,796.87	$107,812.14	$115,388.34	$1,275.62	$109,145.18	1.77%	42.59	$106,207.45	17.41	$110,895.06	2.09%
4%	$1,841.65	$110,499.13	$120,993.47	$1,275.62	$112,407.14	2.37%	41.56	$108,137.29	18.44	$114,923.33	2.82%
5%	$1,887.12	$113,227.40	$126,852.98	$1,275.62	$115,781.93	2.97%	40.56	$109,996.08	19.44	$119,159.03	3.57%
6%	$1,933.28	$115,996.81	$132,977.34	$1,275.62	$119,273.39	3.59%	39.59	$111,783.51	20.41	$123,608.22	4.33%
7%	$1,980.12	$118,807.19	$139,377.39	$1,275.62	$122,885.42	4.21%	38.65	$113,499.54	21.35	$128,277.36	5.11%
8%	$2,027.64	$121,658.37	$146,064.34	$1,275.62	$126,622.09	4.83%	37.75	$115,144.43	22.25	$133,173.28	5.90%
9%	$2,075.84	$124,550.13	$153,049.81	$1,275.62	$130,487.56	5.47%	36.87	$116,718.69	23.13	$138,303.17	6.70%
10%	$2,124.70	$127,482.27	$160,345.83	$1,275.62	$134,486.14	6.10%	36.02	$118,223.03	23.98	$143,674.59	7.52%
11%	$2,174.24	$130,454.54	$167,964.83	$1,275.62	$138,622.26	6.75%	35.2	$119,658.39	24.8	$149,295.47	8.35%
12%	$2,224.44	$133,466.69	$175,919.70	$1,275.62	$142,900.47	7.40%	34.41	$121,025.86	25.59	$155,174.08	9.19%
13%	$2,275.31	$136,518.44	$184,223.75	$1,275.62	$147,325.50	8.06%	33.64	$122,326.68	26.36	$161,319.06	10.04%
14%	$2,326.83	$139,609.51	$192,890.75	$1,275.62	$151,902.17	8.72%	32.89	$123,562.25	27.11	$167,739.41	10.90%
15%	$2,378.99	$142,739.58	$201,934.93	$1,275.62	$156,635.50	9.39%	32.17	$124,734.06	27.83	$174,444.49	11.77%
16%	$2,431.81	$145,908.34	$211,371.03	$1,275.62	$161,530.60	10.07%	31.47	$125,843.69	28.53	$181,444.05	12.65%
17%	$2,485.26	$149,115.45	$221,214.26	$1,275.62	$166,592.79	10.75%	30.8	$126,892.80	29.2	$188,748.17	13.55%
18%	$2,539.34	$152,360.56	$231,480.33	$1,275.62	$171,827.51	11.43%	30.14	$127,883.12	29.86	$196,367.34	14.45%
19%	$2,594.06	$155,643.31	$242,185.51	$1,275.62	$177,240.38	12.13%	29.5	$128,816.42	30.5	$204,312.42	15.36%
20%	$2,649.39	$158,963.30	$253,346.56	$1,275.62	$182,837.17	12.83%	28.89	$129,694.49	31.11	$212,594.66	16.28%
21%	$2,705.34	$162,320.16	$264,980.83	$1,275.62	$188,623.83	13.53%	28.29	$130,519.16	31.71	$221,225.68	17.21%
22%	$2,761.89	$165,713.47	$277,106.22	$1,275.62	$194,606.48	14.24%	27.71	$131,292.26	32.29	$230,217.54	18.15%
23%	$2,819.05	$169,142.83	$289,741.20	$1,275.62	$200,791.43	14.96%	27.15	$132,015.64	32.85	$239,582.67	19.09%
24%	$2,876.80	$172,607.79	$302,904.85	$1,275.62	$207,185.16	15.68%	26.6	$132,691.11	33.4	$249,333.94	20.05%
25%	$2,935.13	$176,107.94	$316,616.86	$1,275.62	$213,794.34	16.41%	26.08	$133,320.50	33.92	$259,484.63	21.01%
26%	$2,994.05	$179,642.82	$330,897.56	$1,275.62	$220,625.84	17.15%	25.56	$133,905.60	34.44	$270,048.45	21.98%
27%	$3,053.53	$183,211.96	$345,767.91	$1,275.62	$227,686.72	17.89%	25.07	$134,448.18	34.93	$281,039.57	22.96%
28%	$3,113.58	$186,814.92	$361,249.53	$1,275.62	$234,984.25	18.63%	24.58	$134,949.97	35.42	$292,472.59	23.94%
29%	$3,174.19	$190,451.22	$377,364.74	$1,275.62	$242,525.89	19.39%	24.11	$135,412.70	35.89	$304,362.58	24.93%
30%	$3,235.34	$194,120.38	$394,136.54	$1,275.62	$250,319.33	20.14%	23.66	$135,838.00	36.34	$316,725.07	25.93%

Figure 1: Compounding Annual Growth Rate (CAGR) comparison between conventional, Standard and Accelerated MP at different interest rates in the market (1%-30%) in a 30 years term loan.

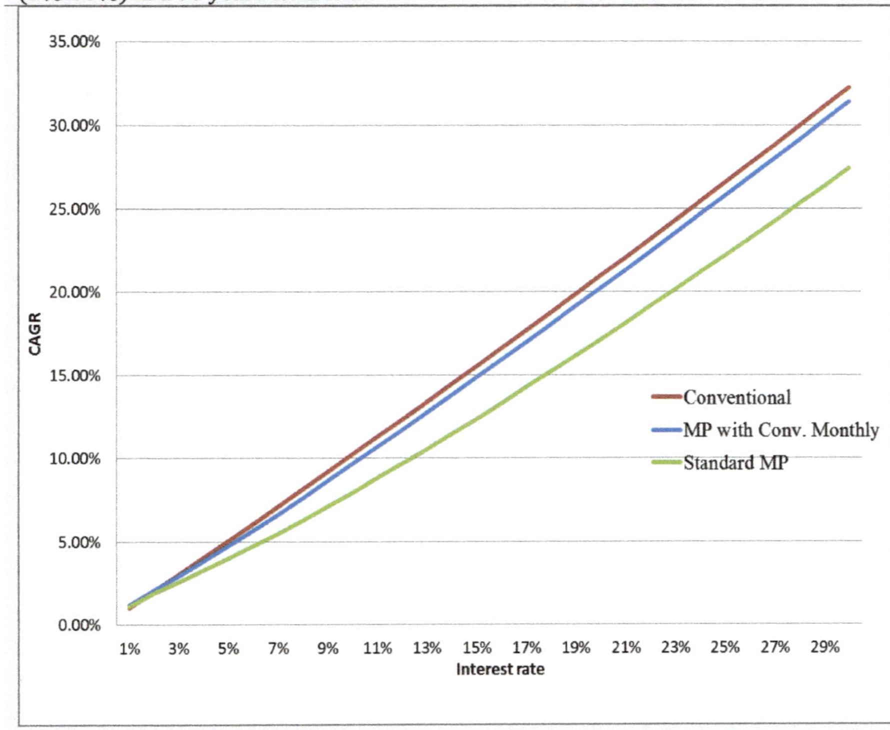

Figure 2: CAGR shortfalls in Standard MP and Accelerated MP in comparison with conventional at interest rates 1% to 30% during 5,10,15,20 and 30 years terms.

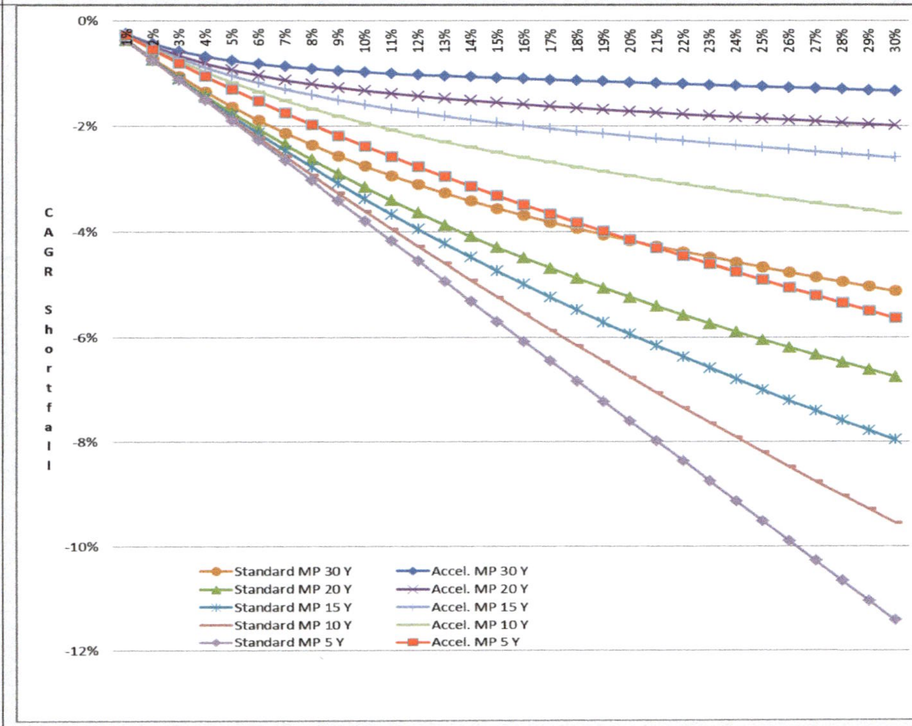

Figure 3: Payback periods in Accelerated MP at interest rates between 1% - 30% and in 5,10,15,20 and 30 years terms.

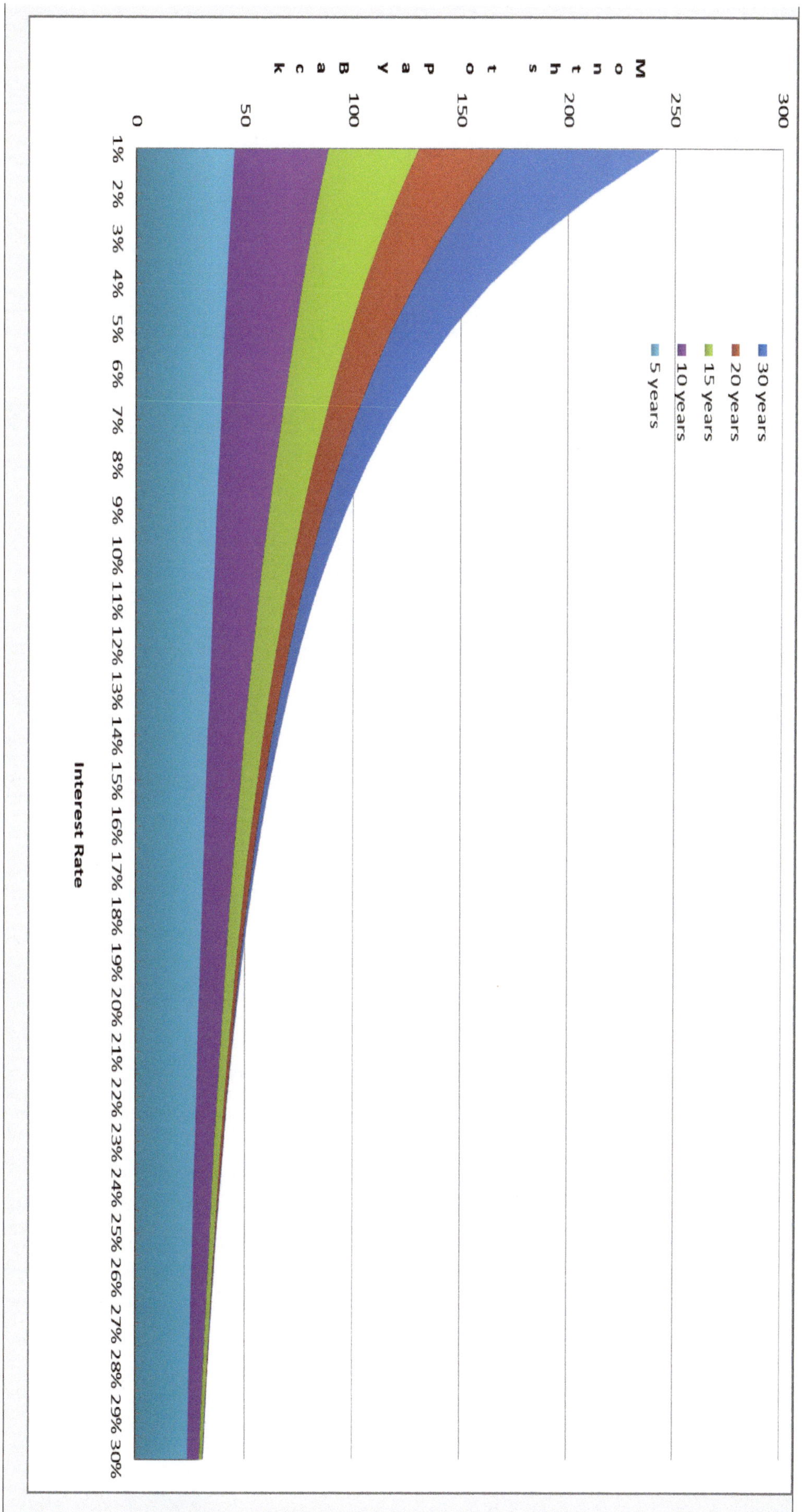
Months to Pay Back
300
250
200
150
100
50
0
30 years
20 years
15 years
10 years
5 years
1% 2% 3% 4% 5% 6% 7% 8% 9% 10% 11% 12% 13% 14% 15% 16% 17% 18% 19% 20% 21% 22% 23% 24% 25% 26% 27% 28% 29% 30%
Interest Rate

15

The arena of multiinterest, governance and fraud – A critical review of BC bailout

Ruddy Tri Santoso[a*], Hartono[a], M. Agung Prabowo[a], Guntur Riyanto[a], Sujoko Efferin[b], Yenny Tjiamudjaja[c]

[a]Faculty of Economic and Business, University of Sebelas Maret (UNS). Surakarta.
[b]Faculty of Business and Economic, University of Surabaya (UBAYA) Surabaya
[c]Editor, translator
*Corresponding author's email:ruddytri@gmail.com

HIGHLIGHTS:

1. PT. Bank Century's default in the end of 2008 was influenced internally by frauds and non-corporate governance, and externally by the global financial crisis.
2. The government of Indonesia believed that BC should be bailed out because if it was closed, it would have caused systemic impact to the entire Indonesian economy.
3. The crucial timing gave chances to the multi interests of bankers, politicians, and regulators to create a situation that politically constituted the bailout.
4. The judgement of systemic impact criteria and the decision to bail out neglected some prudential aspects.
5. The major reason of bail out was that the bank was too politically significant to fail.

Article History

Keywords:
Bank bailout;
Governance;
Fraud.

ABSTRACT

The bailout of PT. Bank Century (BC) at the end of 2008 ignites many debates. If the Indonesian Central Bank had not bailed it out, would it have been a systemic disaster for Indonesian economic? BC's total assets were not significant to the national banking asset. Why was it so important to bail BC out? This research wants to find answers to the following questions: 1) considering the internal problems of BC since 2005, was it worth to bail it out, and was the amount paid appropriate? 2) How bad was the internal problem in consideration of corporate governance theory, fraud theory, and in accordance with prudential banking principals? 3) Was the decision to bail out relevant for the national banking stabilization? 4) Was the failure of BC in 2008 a symptom of market failure, or a governance failure of BC and a regulation failure of the Indonesian Central Bank? This research uses descriptive qualitative method by in-depth analysis. The qualitative variables are classified to some significant factors which influence the decision to bail out. The result of this research shows that the historical performance, the corporate government and the fraud of the bank were not appropriately reviewed before the government decided to bail BC out. Even though the bailout was able to keep the national banking stabile at that time, the judgment of the decision was not purely economic. The non-economic factor was that the bank was too politically significant to fail.

1.0 Introduction

A bail out is an act to save a default bank by taking over 100% shares of the bank. The default can be caused by various reasons such as; an imprudent banking, a market failure, or a psychologically affected market. The important reason of a bail out is to redeem market volatility. Market volatility is dangerous because it may cause a bank rush, which in turn creates domino effect to the whole banking institution and makes the national economic instable.

BC was founded from a merger of three banks at December 6th, 2004. The banks were PT. Bank CIC International, PT. Bank Pikko, and PT. Bank Danpac. Historically, PT. Bank CIC had some fictional and high-risk transactions. The amount was up to US$25Billion. Regulation requires the bank to accumulate PPAP (Penyisihan Penghapusan Aktiva Produktif/Reserve for Loans Losses), which in turn results in a negative Capital Adequacy Ratio (CAR). Bank Pikko contained Texmaco's bad debt, which was changed to Dresdner Bank Medium Term Notes (MTN). The low quality of the MTN required the bank to accumulate a big amount of provisions in loan losses. This in turn also results in a negative Capital Adequacy Ratio (CAR). Danpac is a healthy and prudential bank. An Indonesian Central Bank report dated on October 31, 2005 shows that the CAR of BC on February 28, 2005 (two months after merger) was negative 132.5%. Due to regulations, after this report the bank should be put under special surveillance. In fact the bank was normally operating until the end of 2008 until BC failed to pay a withdrawal of a USD 1 Billion deposit. The rumor of bankruptcy ignited bank rush, and it finally caused a major liquidity crisis to the bank. The government marked PT Bank Century as a systemic risk bank which means that it should not be closed at any cost. The government put in some temporary equity to bail it out. In the end the bailout cost as much as USD 6, 7 Billion.

Researches about bank bailouts were conducted before, but it emphasized rather on bank failures caused by non-prudential conduct in normal situations. Former researches do not consider any financial crisis or the Indonesian context. This research is unique because it reviews a bank bailout in a global financial crisis and that BC was the only bank to undergo a liquidity crisis, which needed an intervention of the Indonesian government. Experts have debated over questions such as whether or not the global financial crisis affected the Indonesian economy, and did PT Bank Century really have systemic impact to the Indonesian economy, and was it appropriate to spend USD 6.7 billion to save the bank. Long before the bank was formed it already had problems which naturally climaxed when the global financial crisis happened. The quantitative data of BC shows that its internal condition was not good or systemically significant to the Indonesian economy, yet it was rescued no matter what. We come to consider that the political condition of Indonesia as the major reason of the bailout after conducted some interviews with some key persons.

This research will: a) review the financial performance of BC, b) review the financial performance ratio of BC by various financial theories to explain its condition, c) quantitatively and qualitatively analyze the application of corporate governance and fraud theory on BC. d) Use a descriptive qualitative method of the related factors and/or actors, to analyze the facts and extracted the conclusions

The case of BC is chosen because it is a national issue in Indonesian banking. The scale and complexity of the case are massive and logical. The case can be accessed by available sources, within a certain time limit. These considerations make the case both worthy and feasible to be observed.

2.0 Literature review

Former researches about the systemic impact of bank performance are using traditional financial theory. Those researches analyze bank performance from a fundamental aspect. The fundamental condition can be seen in financial reports and its ratios such as liquidity, rent ability, and solvability. Bad indicators in the financial report may mean that losses and bankruptcy is inevitable. Kaufman (1996) states that a bank bankruptcy is in fact as common as any other bankruptcy. They are caused by non-prudential regulations, inefficiency and contra productivity. Davis (1992) argues that people are more afraid of financial and banking systemic risks, than of other sectors such as automotive or real estate, because the intangible situations are more difficult to predict. Mark Flannery (1995) has a similar argumentation as Davis, bank bankruptcy costs are higher so that the banking business is unique, and it always needs financial assistance because it includes social aspect and the politic of this business is sensitive to conflict. These factors require the prudential principles of the banking industry. In the case of BC, the bank was bail out even though its fundamental data shows that the bank has had financial problem since it was founded on December 2004.

Another consideration to bail BC out was that the government believed the bank has a systematic risk to Indonesian economy. Regarding the criteria of systemically important bank (SIB), Slovick (2012) proposes a theory of systemically important bank based on the calculation of equity structure. Some banks are systemically important if they have 70% of the total assets of the banking industry in the country, calculated by weighted average of its asset to the national banking total asset. Consequently the SIBs will also have 70% of the total equity in that banking industry. In Indonesia the total number of systemically important banks consists of 15 banks, including private ones and government ones. These are: Mandiri, BRI, BCA, BNI, Danamon, CIMB Niaga, BII, Panin, Permata, BTN, OCBC

NISP, Bukopin, Mega, BTPN, and UOB Indonesia. Again, according to this theory BC was not a systematically important bank.
Research gaps emerge because classical assumption tests through the financial performance theory and the systemically important bank theory do not meet. To explain this phenomenon this research uses behavior finance theory, corporate governance, and fraud theory. Considering the impact of global crisis, BC was a bank with a systemic impact. The economic crisis in 2008-2009 was defined as an economic recession because it was short term. Brut to Domestic Product declines for six months in a row. The signs of recession are an increasing unemployment level, a stagnant salary level, and declining retail sales. The World Bank and ASEAN secretary in 2009 claimed that the global economic crisis in 2008-2009 caused a declining income per capita in countries throughout the world. This abnormal situation also explained by Widoatmodjo (2010), he researched about the systemic impact of BC by probit and logit regression to test investor behavior in BEI (Bursa Efek Indonesia) in the end of 2008. He finds that at that time, investors did not behave rationally. Negative sentiment in the market could be a dominant factor for the society to rush a bank if BC was closed.

Shleifer and Summers (1990) argue that there are two pillars in the behavior finance theory, which influence the investor's decision; limited arbitrage and investor's psychological bias. These two pillars determine buy or sell positions of a rational investor when he senses a mispricing. De Long etal. (1990), continued by Shleifer and Vishny (1997) propose that the risk of a rational investor is the arbitraged share value. That is; noise traders mislead decision when a rational investor should always decide on fundamental data. This distorted attitude happens because of a deviation in the information process and the limited ability to have the right information. Similarly, in the case of BC the customers of all the banks possibly react because of a deviation in the information process and any negative information can create a bank rush.

Corporate governance is a concept to enhance corporate performance by monitoring management performance and accountability based on a set of rules. Corporate governance builds a structure to aim at certain goals and acts as tools of performance monitoring (Dharmawati, et.al., 2004). Corporate governance will reduce agency costs and also improve corporate image and reputation (Akhtaruddin, Hossain, Hossain, and Yao, 2009). Corporate governance in banking is even more important because of some considerations. First, the bank has a dominant position as an economy growth machine (King and Levine, 1993). Second, in a country with an undeveloped equity market, a bank is the main institution of lending. Third, a bank is the prime institution to national saving mobilization. Fourth, bank liberalization by privatization and economy deregulation gives the bank's manager broader power to operate a bank.

Banking as an institution has a specific nature, which is different from non-financial institutions (Macey and O'Hara in Supriyatno, 2006). The uniqueness of this nature blends with the situation of the Asian financial crisis; leads this research to corporate governance problems (Arun and Turner in Supriyatno, 2006). The countries with deficiency in practicing corporate governance suffered most in 1997 to 1998 (Husnan, 2001). The application of corporate governance can be seen in the audited financial report of a company. Financial report is a tool for a company to inform about its condition to its stakeholders. This information has to meet quantitative and qualitative standards (fundamental concept of financial report). Information should be focused on the general needs of its stakeholders, not to cater to certain individual benefit. When a financial report is arranged for a certain need and want of a party it will create fraud risks, the report does not inform about the true condition of the company and it causes loss to the other parties. Gravitt (2006) and Nguyen (2008) say that fraud in financial reports has certain schemes: 1.) falsifying, changing, or manipulating financial material facts, supporting documents, or business transactions. 2.) Intentional negligence or misrepresentation of events, transactions, accounts, or other important information.3.) Intentional misuse of accounting principles or procedures to measure, to disclose, and to report economical events and business transactions. 4.) Intentional negligence in disclosure or improper disclosure representation.

To understand how a fraud causes loss, we need to define what fraud is. According to Badan Pemeriksa Keuangan (BPK)-Supreme Audit Board (2008)the definition of fraud is: misinterpretation of past and present, of material facts, made knowingly or recklessly, intended to make a party act, and the party suffers a detriment because of the misinterpretation. ACFE mentions three types of fraud: a) Asset misappropriation: misuse or stealing of a company's assets. This type is tangible and the value of the loss is able to be defined. b) Fraudulent statements: financial arrangements in a financial report to benefit illegally. c) Corruption: included in corruption are conflicts of interest, bribery, illegal gratitude, and economic extortion.

The link between corporate governance and fraud can be explained as follows: a.) Corporate governance includes company culture and authorization delegation, and is designed to eliminate fraud. b.) Transaction level control process by an internal auditor is a control and preventive process to ensure that only legitimate transactions takes place in the system. c.) Retrospective examination by an external auditor is aimed to detect fraud before it becomes big and dangerous for the company. d.) Investigation and remedial by a forensic audit to determine remedial acts related to size or depth of fraud. Tiscini and Donato (2004) propose that relating to CG and fraud in private and

Government Companies, accounting fraud tends to be caused by excessive power, while in a public company accounting fraud tends to be caused by performance stress. Hambrik and Mason (2004), proposes in the upper-echelon theory that the role of a TMT (Top Management Team) is a crucial issue of company performance. Top Management Team (TMT) can be an elite team of the management, or can include one or more of the owners, or a majority share holder. Finkelstein and Hambrick (1984) found that the TMT has more power than the management. In other words, the TMT has strong influence on strategic implementation, operational decisions, or internal innovation processes. The TMT has such a power that it can create major fraud to benefit illegally at the cost of other stakeholders.

In case of BC, the role of TMT by dominant shareholder (Robert Tantular/RT) strongly influenced strategic decisions. Thus, to analyze the bank's internal problem by corporate governance and fraud, it is also important to analyze the role of the TMT.

The main question of this research is, considering all those facts; did the failure of BC have a systemic impact on the Indonesian banking system? Systemic means that it affects the entire organs of a banking industry. According to the government regulation about the Jaring Pengaman System Keuangan-Social Safety Net System (JPSK) or Peraturan Pemerintah Pengganti Undang-undangJaring Pengaman Stabilitaskeuangan (PERPPU JPSK), systemic impact is:

> *'... a difficult condition caused by a bank, non bank financial institution, and/or financial market turbulence, which when it is not handled properly will cause failure to a number of banks and/or non bank financial institutions, and the people will lose trust into the financial system and the national economy.'*

In PERPPU JPSK the criteria and size of a bank with systemic impact is not clearly defined. The nature of systemic impact can be internally or externally. Internally means the problem develops from inside a bank, such as non-prudential acts, while an external cause could be a natural disaster, a global financial crisis, or a war. Thus, in such cases it is difficult to demarcate the systemic impact of the bank. A financial institution can be systemic in certain situations, but not systemic in other situations. The indicator of systemic is also not mentioned explicitly in any law code, the reason is that it would cause moral hazards and that the criteria of systemic impact are situational depends on psychological market.

The Bank of Indonesia adopts the European Union Memorandum of Understanding (MOU) framework, which says that the consideration of a systemic impact has multiple aspects: financial system, financial market, payment system, real sector, and market psychological aspect. The market psychological aspect is added to the criteria in relation to the economic crisis in 1998. At that time, the closure of 16 banks, which had only 2.3% of the banking total assets, psychologically affected the financial market. It ended up with savings withdrawals in all national banks and caused a crisis in various sectors. Further, in the era of cyber dimension, cyber gossips (Wysocki, 1998) magnify the irrational behavior of investors through various rumors spreads in the internet.

Another important factor to consider in economic decision making is Risk. As Admati says (2013);

> *'... When policymakers ignore risk, all of us may suffer in the end. A stark example was provided in Japan, where corrupted regulators and politicians colluded for years with the Tokyo Electric Power Company and ignored known safety concerns. When the earthquake and the tsunami happened in 2011, this neglect led to a nuclear disaster that was entirely preventable...'*

Admati (2013) proposes that a banking system is not difficult to understand, that all issues will move quite straightforward if it is all purely a banking consideration, without any conflict of interest from the politicians. Admati (2013) also says that the banks 'are where the money is'. Money is the main goal and source of power. To control the money, bankers are in a strong position to influence the society together with politicians and government regulations. History shows that politicians have often used banks as money machines in political interests. The phenomena of politicians, regulators, and monetary authority having various interests in making a regulation for banking, are known as 'regulatory capture'. These actors create a Political Arena in the banking system. Together, they create a situation to achieve various interests while they are 'securing national financial stabilization'. As an example, the regulation of minimum percentage of reserve requirements tends to get higher during a financial crisis. Besides the noble purpose of securing the trustworthiness of the banks, this regulation gives a chance to the government to get free loans from the central bank, because the reserve requirement is indirectly financing the government. Even though the regulation captures are not always being negative, we also need to consider the grabbing hand or helping hand theory, which says that government intervention used to be laden in corrupted interests when the intervention has neither transparency nor accountability in the process (Hopkin and Pose, 2007). The regulators of banking industry should analyze three main layers to build a healthy intervention decision: market failure, corporate governance failure, and regulation failure of the Central Bank.

This research does not discuss whether bank rush, nor capital flight, would happen if BC have been closed in 1998, but it approaches the problem of bailouts from multidisciplinary points of view: government-politics-economy. Seligman (1962: 345) proposes that the political factor needs to be related to economic and social changes in the society. Heilbroner (1977) proposes that if the economic science wants to keep relevant to modern problems, the science has to keep in pace with three areas of concern: political consideration need to be explicitly included in economic decisions, the political dimension needs to be broadened in economic decisions, and the knowledge needs a broader paradigm. Ilchman and Uphoff (1977) propose that economic decisions need to go through integrated social science of public purpose. In short, economic decision making needs to be approached multidisciplinary and to consider all relevant interests in social and political perspective.

3.0 Methodology

As a sample, this research takes BC, which operated from 2004 to 2008 along with its subsequent event data, supporting data from the Central Bank of Indonesia, depositor insurance's data, and all related data from various institutions in 2004-2008.

This research uses the time series method in an interpretative case study. The subjects are: executive officers of BC in 2004-2008, the owners of the bank Robert Tantular (RT) and Rafat Ali Rizvi (RAR), the former Vice President of the Republic of Indonesia (JusufKalla/JK), the former Government of Bank Indonesia (Budiono/BO), the former Ministry of Finance of the Republic of Indonesia (Sri Mulyani/SMI), special investigation team or Panitia Khusus (Pansus) Dewan Perwakilan Rakyat (DPR) of BC, Badan Reserse Kriminal (Bareskrim) Kepolisian Republik Indonesia, Badan Pemeriksa Keuangan (BPK) RI, officers of Lembaga Penjamin Simpanan (LPS) , officers of Komisi Pemberantasan Korupsi (KPK), former officers ofBC and all related institutions. One ofthe researchers is ex-director of PT Bank CIC (one of the banks which formed the BC) from 1998 to 2001. Information are taken by interviews/letter/e-mail, in-depth analysis and direct observation from 2010 to 2014.Primary data are taken by interviewing former decision makers in the bailout and former officers of BC. The researchers interview the former Vice President of the Republic of Indonesia (JK) face to face and interview the former Government of Bank Indonesia (BO) by letter and email. Secondary data aretaken from the PT. Bank Century annual reports from 2004 to 2008, the investigation report of the Indonesian Central Bank, the audit report of BPK, the report of Pansus DPR of BC and all the supporting data. Investigation reports of Bareskrim, Press releases through television broadcast and newspaper reports are also analyzed to enrich the in-depth analysis.

Triangulation system does data observation. Primary data are grouped in peer debriefing. Secondary data are grouped and used to check consistency in subjects' opinions. Bias is minimized by triangular model based on the content analysis of primary and secondary data. Adjustment theory of before end theory and after end theory is also used to minimize bias

4.0 Findings and discussion

Considering internal problems of BC since 2005, was it worthy to be bailed out, and was the amount to bailout appropriate? Time series data of the financial report shows that foreign exchange securities, acceptance liability, and non performing loan made BC needs a very large amount of PPAP. Inability to meet the standard amount of PPAP made its CAR always fewer than 8%. Detail calculation of CAR also shows that the appropriate amount to bail out was USD 5.7 Billions (Rp 5,724.541 million). Regarding the internal condition of BC it was not worthy to bail it out.

The financial report of BC shows that problems of corporate government and fraud in BC were very complex. It was not wise to bail it out as its default was not caused by financial crisis, but by weak governance, imprudent banking, and owner's fraud. Considering corporate governance theory, it was inappropriate to bail BC out. To bail BC out was to bail out any fraud caused by a dominant shareholder and his management, as if the bailout was to cater to certain party's interests. The important finding is that the amount to bail out was excessive and was used inappropriately. There were other interests rather than merely to keep the national banking stabile and to build banking trustworthiness during a global crisis. The decision of bailout shows that political interests have higher priority than other normative criteria.

Macro economically, the decision to bail out was taken to keep national banking stabile and to build banking trustworthiness during the global crisis. This is in accordance with Budiono (2008) who states that government intervention was needed to avoid a domino effect because of BC's bankruptcy. Darmin Nasution (2008) also states that government temporary equity was needed to rescue the bank. The bailout was very important to guarantee more than USD 6.7 Billions depository funds in the Indonesian banking system (Sri Mulyani, 2009). The government of Indonesia decided to settle the liquidity mismatch of this bank. Whether or not BC followed the regulation of the Indonesian Central Bank in accordance with basic rules of the Indonesian Banking Architecture was not being considered in the decision. Frauds that had happened inside the bank were given even broader scope by the big amount of money injected right into the bank. The decision to bailout was viewed in a macro politic context in the multi interests of the decision makers. There was a strong connection between political and economical factors. Failure to understand this big picture will create a narrow-minded financial or banking science. Based on field observations and interviews, the researchers conclude that there was a Grabbing Hand which indicates a relation with political aspects in the process of the bailout. The former owner of BC states that there was a powerful force behind the bailout (Robert Tantular, 2013)."The decisions makers understood that I would not have agreed to bail BC out so that I was not involved in the decision" (JK, 2009).Political interest of BC bailout can be mapped in the figure 1 below.

Was the decision to bail out relevant to national banking stabilization? The case of BC began with liquidity problems when a depositor wanted to draw back his money. BC could not pay its obligation because of its illiquid investment in non-rating, unmarketable securities while BC also did not keep its reserve requirement on the 12% level as it should have. The behavior finance theory was used when the government considered that the world was facing a global financial crisis and believed that if BC was closed, it would cause systemic impact. The government believed that closing any bank would have caused systemic domino effect and would have affected the government credibility. There was also rumor of negative market sentiments, and all the individual investors would have lost their trust in the banking system, and that would have caused chaos. This was dangerous for the national stability. The timing was very close to the presidential and legislative election in early 2009. Considering the timing, to maintain national banking stability and trustworthiness mean maintain political stability. Inevitably the bailout was given to back up massive withdrawals.

Figure 01: Political interest, corporate governance, and fraud in the bail out Of BC

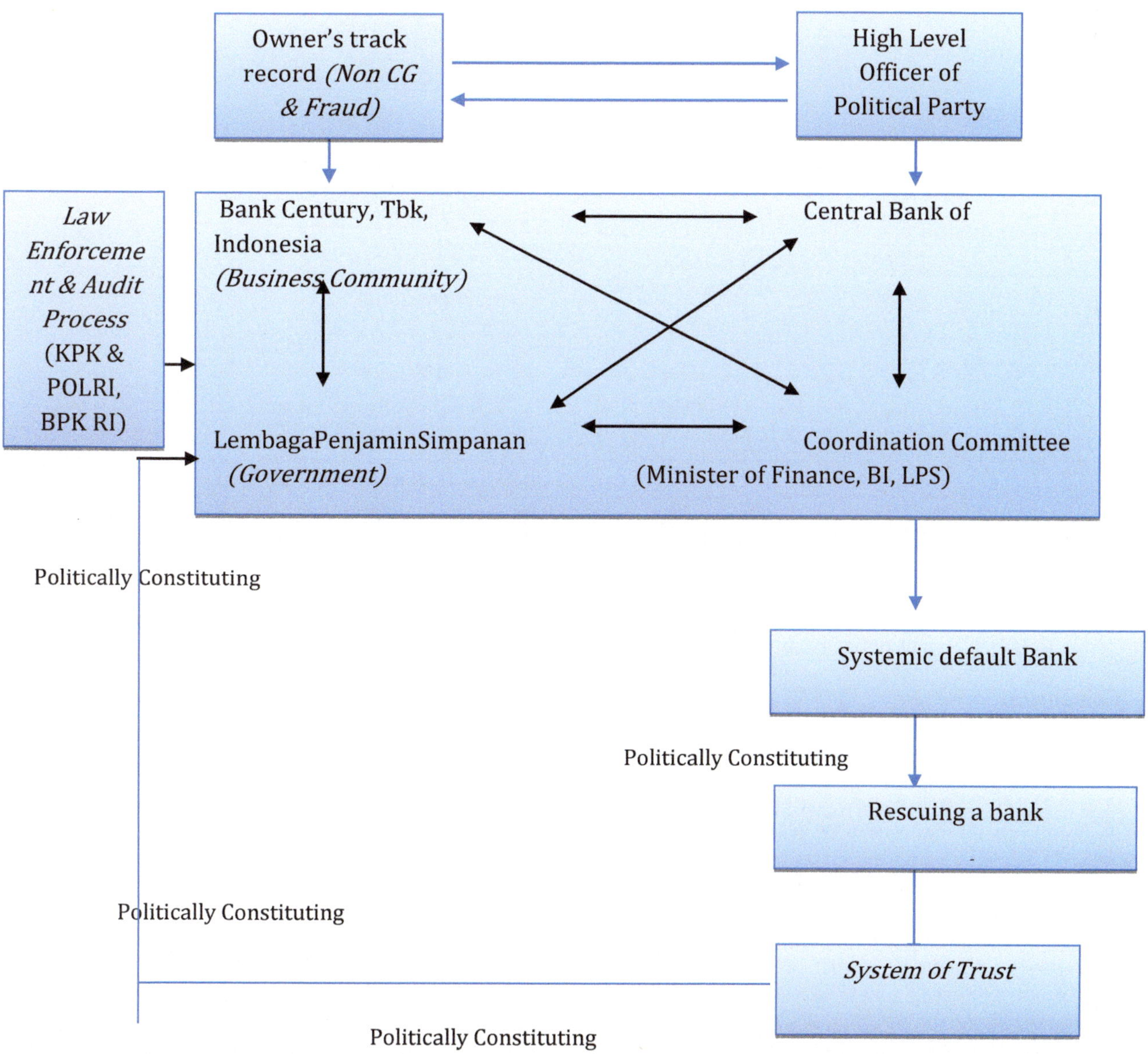

Explanation:
Politically Constituting : Politically causing an act or a decision
←→ : 'influencing each other................'

An election is a door to big change; it is wanted or unwanted by some actors because any major event would cause major shifts in the political arena. Consequently, many decisions will consider various interests of the actors. The decision to bail BC out was one of these decisions. The political, economic reason to bailout is that BC was 'too politically significant to fail'. The diagram can be seen in Picture 2. As a matter of fact, the decision to bail out was able to maintain not only the national banking stability but also the stability of the political situation. The Indonesian economic indicators did improve after the government bailed BC out. Another fact was that the president at that time (Susilo Bambang Yudhoyono/SBY) was then re-elected to his second presidential term.

Picture 02: The economic and non-economic factors that politically constituting the bailout.

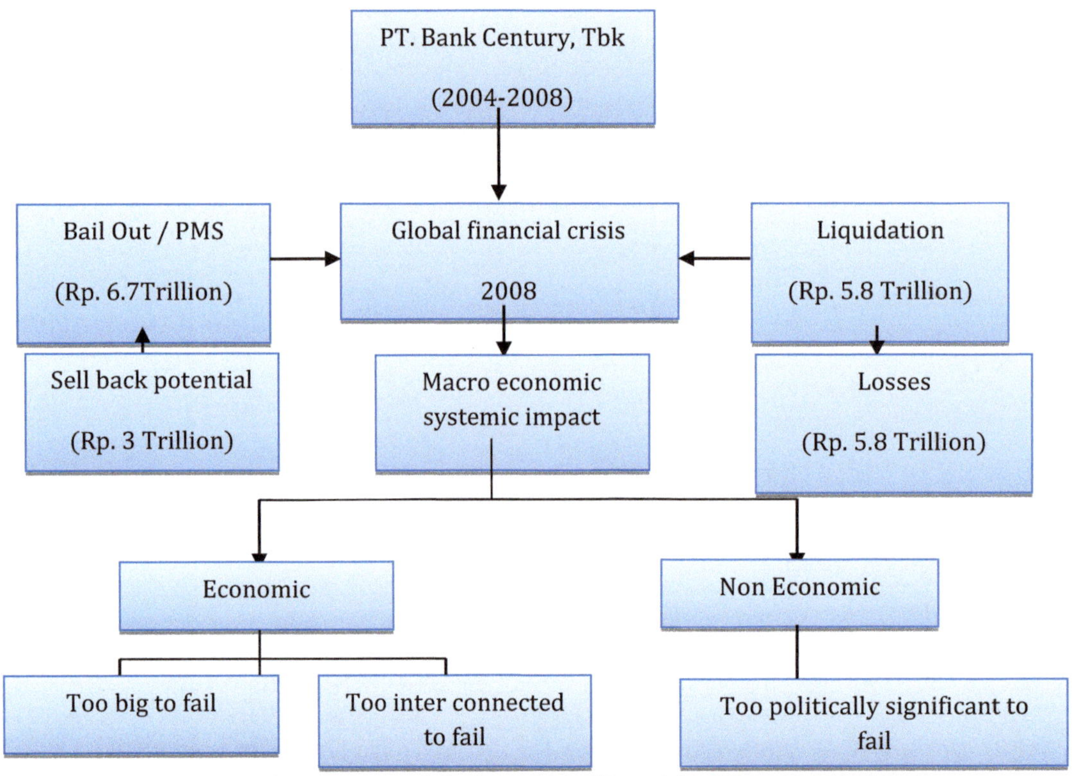

Source: Research findings, 2014 (Note: 1.00 USD = 11,868.75 IDR)

Was the failure of BC in 2008 a symptom of market failure, or a governance failure of BC and a regulation failure of the Indonesian Central Bank? Market failure was only a trigger to BC's default. The complicated frauds in BC made it failed to pay its obligations at the end of 2008. It was a failure to analyze banking system problems. Corporate governance failure was detected as a market failure, in turn, it caused a regulation failure. The Indonesian Central Bank failed to decide the right policy because there was some asymmetry information about BC's internal condition.

5.0 Conclusion

BC was a systematically risk bank, and it was bailed out because of noneconomic reasons. According to the theoretical observation and its implications, the bailout of BC was dominated by non-economical reasons. There was a financial global crisis, and the nation was on the verge of legislative and presidential elections. Regarding the benefit-loss analysis the bail-out of BC was aimed to stabilize the macro-economic and financial sector. In turn, this decision would prevent a domino effect of bank rush. The timing created a political, economic decision to bailout. This research defines it as 'too politically significant to fail'.

To rescue a bank, accountability and transparency in the cash management is needed. So it is better to avoid a cash bailout that tends to cause a conflict of interest. The bail-out technique is not appropriate to rescued BC from bankruptcy. A more effective tool is needed to rescue the bank. The researcher proposes a recapitulation procedure by obligation recapitulation as an additional working capital for the bank to avoid conflict of interest and political effects. This additional working capital could be obtained by overbooking depository premium funds of LPS in other banks, and transferred to the rescued bank either as loan or as time deposit. This alternative would have solved the liquidity problem, which means it would have been able to redeem market volatility. In turn this would have won back the banking system's trustworthiness. This alternative would have been more transparent and accountable because the depository premium funds of LPS would have been recorded in detail in the bank, and the fund would have gained some revenue of interest for the government. This alternative would also have avoided the polemic of a corrupted use of fund. This suggestion can be applied to guide the decision makers if they face a situation 'too politically significant to fail', ceteris paribus.

Finally, Future research needs to analyze the process of a bank takeover. Does the consideration of a negative track record of the shareholders influence the government to take it over? There was much conflict of interest in private banks, and this phenomenon keeps going on. The audit inspectors of BI are still having trouble with some owners of the bank. Future research also needs to investigate why bailouts mostly happen close to legislative/presidential election. Is there any other reason rather than an economic motive to rescue a bank?

Reference

Admati, Anat and Hellwig, Martin. 2013. The banker's new clothes: what's wrong with banking and what to do about it.Princeton University Press.

Akhtaruddin, M, Hossain, MA, Hossain, M & Yao, L 2009.Corporate governance and voluntary disclosure in corporate annual reports of Malaysian listed firms. Journal of Applied Management Accounting Research, vol. 7, no. 1, pp. 1-19.

BadanPengawasKeuanganRepublik Indonesia.2008. Audit forum.http://www.bpk.go.id/webfiles/2009/01/Vol-xi-no.1 may-2008/pdf.

Bank Indonesia, 2008.Metodeanalisis Bank indonesiamenetapkan Bank Century sebagai bank gagalberdampaksistemik.Jakarta, 2008.

Barzelay, Michael. 1993. The single case study as intellectually ambitious inquiry author(s) Journal of Public Administration Research and Theory. J-PART, Vol. 3, No. 3 (Jul., 1993), pp. 305-318.http://www.jstor.org/stable/1181786diaksespada 3 January 2010.

Black, Fischer; Myron Scholes.1973.The pricing of options and corporate liabilities .Journal of Political Economy 81 (3): 637–654.

Boediono, 2009.Rapatpansus Bank Century di Dewan Perwakilan Rakyat Republik Indonesia tanggal 22 Desember 2009.Jakarta, 2009.

Burrel, Gibson and Gareth Morgan, 1979.Sociological paradigms and organizational analysis. Ashgate Publishing Limited, England.

Daniel, Kent and Sheridan Titman, 1997.Evidence on The Characteristics of Cross – Sectional Variance in Common Stock Returns. Journal of Finance, 52 (1): 1 – 33.

Daniel, Kent and Sheridan Titman, 1999.Market efficiency in an irrational world. Financial Analysis's Journal, 55 (6): 28 – 40.

Davis, E.P. 1992. Debt, financial fragility and systemic risk. Oxford: Oxford University Press.

De Long,J. Bradford, Andrei Schleifer, Lawrence H. Summers and Robert J. Waldmann, 1990a. Noise trader risk and financial markets. Journal of Political Economy, 98 (4): 703 – 738.

Darmawati, D. dkk., 2004, Hubungan Corporate Governance dan Kinerja Keuangan, Simposium Nasional Akuntansi VII, Denpasar

Fama, Eugene F., (1970). Efficient capital market: a review of theory and empirical work. Journal of Finance, 25 (2): 383 – 417.

Flannery, M. 1988. Payments system risk and public policy in W.S. Haraf and R.M. Kushmeider (eds) Restructuring Banking and Financial Services in America: 261-87. Washington, D.C.: American Enterprise Institute.

Friedman, Milton. 1953. The case for fllexible exchange rates, in essay in positive economics. Chicago: University of Chicago Press.

Gravitt, J. 2006. Recognizing financial statement fraud red flags. http://www.crowechizek.com/crowe/Publications/pdfs/RecognizingFinancialStateentFraud_PCS6203.pdf (accessed on 9 May 2007) Hamilton, S.,A. Micklethwait.2006.

Greenspan, Alan. 2001. Monetary policy report to the congress. before the committee on banking, Housing and Urban Affair US Senate, February 13,2001. http://www.federalreserve.gov/boarddoslhh/February/testimony/htm.

Grossman, Sanford Jay, Joseph E. Stiglit, 1980. On the impossibility of informational efficient markets.American Economic Reviews, 70 (3): 393 Herwidayatmo. 2000. Implementasgood corporate governance untukperusahaanpublik Indonesia. Artikelpada Majalah Usahawan No. 10 Th XXIX, Oktober 2000.

Hambrick, D. C., and P. A. Mason 1984.Upper echelons: The organization asareflection of its top managers. Academy of Management Review,9: 193-206

Hambrick, D.C. and S. Finkelstein.managerial discretion: a bridge between polar views of organizational fates, in research in organizational behavior, B. Staw and L.L. Cummings (eds.), JAI Press, 1987.
Heilbroner, Robert and Aaron Singer.The Economic Transformation of America. New York: Harcourt Brace Jovanovich, 1977.
Hopkin, Jonathan and Pose, Andres Rodriguez.2007. Grabbing hand or helping hand? Corruption and the economic role of the State.Governance: an International Journal of Policy, Administration and Institutions, Vol. 20, No. 2, April 2007 (pp. 187 - 208).
Ho, Simon S.M. dan Wong, Kar Shun. 2001. A study of relationship between corporate governance structure and extent of voluntary disclosure. Journal of International Accounting Auditing and Taxation, (10): 139-156.
Husnan, Suad., 2001. Corporate governance dankeputusanpendanaan: perbandingankinerjaperusahaandenganpemegangsahampengendaliperusahaanmultinasionaldanbukanmultinasional. Jurnal Riset Akuntansi, Manajemen, EkonomiVol. 1 No.1. Februari 2001:1-12
Iichman, F. Warren and Uphoff, Norman Thomas. 1977. The Political Economy of Change. Oxford University Press.
International Accounting Standard. 2001. IFRS Foundation, Delaware.
Jensen, M.C. and Mecking, W., 1976. Theory of the firm: managerial behavior, agency costs and capital structure, Journal of Financial Economics, Vol. 3, pp: 305-360.
Jones, Charles, P., 2004. Investment, analysist and management. New Jersey: John Wiley and Sons.
Kaufman, George. G. 1996. Bank failures, systemic risk, and bank regulation.Cato Journal, Vol. 16, No. 1 (Spring/Summer 1996).
King, Robert G. and Levine, Ross.Financial intermediation and economic development, in financial intermediation in the construction of europe.Eds.: Colin Mayer and Xavier Vives. London: Centre for Economic Policy Research, 1993a, pp. 156–89.
Krugman, Paul. Maurice Obstfeld, Marc J. Melitz. 2007. International economics, theory and policy. Global Edition, Pearson.
Langevoort, Donald. C, 2002.Taming the animal spirits of the stock markets: a behavioral Approach to Securities Regulation.Berkeley program in law and economics.Working Paper, University of California Berkeley, 64.
Macey, J. R. & O'Hara, M. 2003.The corporate governance of banks. Economic Policy Review 91-107.
Mark J. Flannery &Sorin M. Sorescu, 1995.Pricing bank default risk in subordinated debenture yields,Proceedings 470, Federal Reserve Bank of Chicago.
Markowitz, Harry, 1952. Portfolio selection.Journal of Finance, 7 (1): 77 – 91.
Merton, Robert C. 1973. Theory of rational option pricing".Bell Journal of Economics and Management Science (The RAND Corporation) 4 (1): 141–183. doi:10.2307/3003143. JSTOR 3003143.[2]
Miller, Merton and Franco Modigliani, 1961.Dividen policy, growth and the valuation of shares, Journal of Business, 34 94): 411 - 433.
Nasution, MarihotdanSetiawan, Doddy. 2007. Pengaruhcorporategovernanceterhadapmanajemenlaba di industriperbankan. Simposium Nasional Akuntansi X. Makassar. Ikatan Akuntanindonesia.
Nguyen, Khanh. 2008. Financial statement fraud: motives, methods, cases and detection. Florida. http://www.bookpump.com. Diaksestanggal 25 Oktober 2011.
Olsen, Robert, 1998. Behavioral finance and its implication for stock price volatility.Financial Analysts Journal, 54 (2): 10 -18.
Prasetyantoko, A., 2011.Momentum di tengahkrisis. HarianKompas, 19 September 2011, hal. 6.
Rubinstein, Mark., 2001. Rational market: yes or no? The affirmative case.Financial Analyst Journal, 57 (3): 15 – 29.
Seligman, R.A. Edwin. 1962. The economic interpretation of history. New York, Columbia University Press.
Sharpe William F., 1964.Capital asset pricing – a theory of market equilibrium under condition of Risk. Journal of Finance, 19 (3): 425 – 442.
Shleifer, Andre dan Lawrence Summers, 1990. The noise trader approach to finance, Journal of Economic Perspective, (4): 19 – 33.
Sheifer, Andre dan Robert Vishny, 1998. The grabbing hand, government pathologies and their cures. Cambridge, MA. Harvard University Press.
Shleifer, Andre and Robert Vishny, 1997.The limit of arbitrage. Journal of Finance,52, 35 – 55.
Shefrin, Hersh (2001). Beyond greed and fear; understanding behavioral finance and psychology of investing. Harvard Business School Press.
Skousen, C. And Wright, C. J. 2005.AAA 10th Ethic Research Symposium. Detecting financial statement fraud: an empirical assessment of thesis No. 99 fraud risk factors, American accounting association, ethic section, San Fransisco, California (August 6. 2005 – August 7. 2005).
Slovik, Patrick., 2012. Systematically important banks and capital regulation challenges. OECD Economics Department Working Papers, No. 916, OECD Publishing. http://dx.doi.org/10/1787/5kg0ps8cq8q6-en
Statement on Auditing Standards No. 99.Consideration of fraud in a financial statement audit. American Institute of Certified Public Accountant (AICPA), October 2002.
Statman, Meir., 1999. Behavioral finance; past battles and future engagements.Financial Analysts journal, 55 (6): 18 – 27.

Stiglitz, E. Joseph. Nobel price winner in economics globalization and it's discontents. 2003. WW Norton & Company, New York – London.
SuadHusnan, 2001.Dasar-dasartteoriportfoliodananalisissekuritas, edisiKetiga, Yogyakarta: UPP AMP YKPN.
Supriyatno,2006, Pengaruh Corporate Governance danBentukKepemilikanterhadapKinerjaKeuangan Bank di Indonesia, Disertasi, UGM, Yogyakarta.
The Association of Certified Fraud Examiners.2012.http://www.acfe.com.
Tiscini, Riccardo and Donato, Fracesca di. 2004. The relation between accounting fraud and corporate governance systems: an analysis of recent scandals. http://ssrn.com/abstract=1086624.
Widoatmodjo, Sawidji. 2010. Mencarikebenaranobyektifdampaksistemik bank century. Penerbit PT. Elex Media Komputindo, Jakarta.
World Bank, 2009a. Crisis monitoring and response, using lot quality assurance sampling (LQAS), power point, 11 Mei, Jakarta: World Bank Poverty Team.
Wysocki, Peter. D. 1998. Cheap talk on the web: the determinants of posting on internet stock message boards. Working Paper, University of Michigan Business School.November.
Wysocki, Peter. D. 1999. Short seller and message posting activity on the web.Working Paper, University of Michigan Business School.October.
Wysocki, Peter. D. 2000. Private information, earnings announcements and trading volume.Working Paper, MIT, 29.
Yin, Robert K. 2009.Cases study research: design and methods, fourth edition.Singapore, SAGE Publication.

Appendix: Glossary

BareskrimPolri (Badan Resersedan Kriminal Kepolisian Republik Indonesia) is the Institution under Head of Police Republic Indonesia that doing inspections and investigate the crime in the public.

BI (Bank Indonesia) is the Central Bank of republic Indonesia.

BPK RI (Badan Pemeriksa Keuangan Republik Indonesia) is the auditor that doing on behalf of the Government.

KPK (Komisi Pemberantasan Korupsi) is the Institutions in Indonesia that investigate the corruptions.

KSSK (Komite Stabilitas Sektor Keuangan) is the steering committee of Republic Indonesia had job for stability of macro-economic and finance sector of the nations.

LPS (LembagaPenjaminSimpanan) is the Government Institutions in Indonesia that doing as guarantor of the savings and deposits in the banks up to the amount has appointed by Central Bank regulations.

PMS (Penyertaan Modal Sementara) is the bail-out of the bank by government or is like penetrant equity from the government to the private bank had acquired.

16

An empirical analysis on credit risk model and its application

Joocheol Kim[a*], Eunhwan Kim[b]

[a] School of Economics, Yonsei University, Korea.
[b] School of Economics, Yonsei University, The Korea Development Bank (KDB), Korea.
*Corresponding author's e-mail: joocheol@yonsei.ac.kr

HIGHLIGHTS:

1. Owing to various complexity and validity of model estimation, various credit risk models fail to provide a standard credit risk measurement for the market participants.
2. Most market participants utilize ratings of target firm in measuring credit risk. However, credit ratings have only so many grades that credit ratings do not deliver precise credit risk measure.
3. Inter-bank derivatives transactions in OTC market require credit support to mitigate counterparty's default risk. Threshold level of a bank is determined solely according to its corresponding global credit rating.
4. We suggest standardizing credit risk measurement with distance-to-default value inferred from equity market value and volatility adopted from KMV model, and then applying the outcome to credit support calculation to efficiently allocate resources.

Article History

Keywords:
Collateral management;
Expected default frequency;
KMV.

ABSTRACT

This study intends to focus on introducing credit default risk with widely used credit risk models in an effort to empirically test whether the models hold their validity, apply to financial institutions which usually are highly levered with various types of debts, and finally reinterpret the results in computing adequate collateral level in the over-the-counter derivatives market. By calculating the distance-to-default values using historical market data for South Korean banks and brokerage firms as suggested in Merton model and KMV's EDF model, we find that the performance of the introduced models well reflect the credit quality of the sampled financial institutions. Moreover, we suggest that in addition to the given credit ratings of different financial institutions, their distance-to-default values can be utilized in determining the sufficient level of credit support. Our suggested "smoothened" collateral level allows both contractual parties to minimize their costs caused from provision of collateral without undertaking additional credit risk and achieve efficient collateral management.

1.0 Introduction

Banks measure credit risk of borrowers not only to price their loans but also to diversify portfolio as well as to determine their credit qualities. Among the various risk factors such as market risk or operational risk, credit default risk requires closer attention because the extent of the loss given default is considerably larger despite default is a rare event with lower odds. All Banks regardless of their geographic regions internally allocate majority of their resources to manage credit risk and build models to anticipate future possible event of default. Expansion of use of credit requires forward looking measure to all financial institutions whose products or services mismatch their payment time.

Inter-bank credit risk arises from the counterparties' default possibility in over-the-counter derivatives trades and transactions. All have witnessed in the year of 2008 that default of financial institutions is not an uncommon event. Collapse of financial institutions like Bear Sterns or Lehman Brothers and its contagion can easily cause irrevocable and instantaneous harm to the other side of transaction counterparties and consequently banks emphasize the importance of credit support or collateral requirement to reduce their open exposure to a certain threshold level. Inter-bank traders often reflect credit risk to quoted prices (for example interest rate swap) unless above mentioned credit support is pledged and provided. The provision of collateral then leads to banks' opportunity cost loss and hence determining the adequate level of collateral in legal agreement (e.g. ISDA CSA[1]) would be critical.

Most previous empirical studies on EDF model (Expected Default Frequency) have dealt with various industries ranging from manufacturing to pharmaceutical listed companies in the stock exchange but direct credit risk measure on financial institutions was rarely introduced. This is mostly because financial institutions, especially banks, are the ones who are exposed to credit risk of counterparties and in needs of credit risk protection, not the other way around. Another possible reason is that financial institutions are on a blurring line between private and public sectors[2] for which credit risk could be considered low from the historical point of view. However, exposure accumulated by inter-bank derivatives transactions would be simply larger than any other exposure from loans or investment on firms and consequently, credit measure on financial institutions is no less important. In this study, Merton model and Expected Default Frequency model developed by Moody's KMV will be introduced in order to discover further that the models are acceptable in measuring credit risk of financial institutions. Financial institutions often utilize credit support to mitigate the counterparty risk but the collateral threshold method currently adopted by most financial institutions results in inefficient allocation of bank resource. This study will suggest alternative threshold standard level using the prevailing option pricing model.

The idea of collateral management was developed in the 1980's and became widespread in the 1990's as OTC derivatives trades exploded. Estimated value of total collateral grew from USD 200 billion in 1999 to USD 3,151 billion in 2009[3] and types of assets used as collateral consist of 82 percent of cash and 14.2 percent of government securities. Cash collateral provision typically causes financial institutions a loss of opportunity cost and the increase of collateral provision threatens profitability of financial institutions. Most previous studies on collateral management often focus on the operational risk as margin calls occur daily between the counterparties or on lending and borrowing programs like repo transactions. Another common study field is to quantify credit valuation adjustment and debt valuation adjustment which directly reflect counterparty's credit risk in the quoted prices regarding OTC derivatives transactions. Although it is true that market convention and practice is heavily immersed and pervaded in collateral management, we intend to directly challenge it and offer more efficient fundamental change to collateral management by calculating more precise credit risk level so neither party would provide excess collateral amount.

2.0 Credit risk models

Credit risk is the risk of decline in the credit quality of counterparty in financial transactions and trades, and the core source of credit risk is the default risk that the counterparty may not fulfill its contractual obligations. There are two main streams of modeling credit risk; 1) structural approach and 2) reduced form approach. The following part will introduce few of the renowned models that intuitively measure credit default risk.

2.01 Merton's model[4]

Merton (1974) applied options models to evaluate the credit risk of a firm's debt. This classic model explicitly generates the probability of default at a certain point of time. In order to calculate the default probability, the framework of Merton indicates that the equity of a firm is considered as a call option on the underlying asset value of the firm with a strike at the value of the firm's liabilities. The underlying value of a firm and its volatility are not directly observed from the model and it assumes that the both values are inferred from the market value of equity, volatility of equity and other known variables by solving two non-linear equations which will be discussed further in this study. The inferred values then can be applied to find the probability of default which is the normal cumulative density function of z-value.

2.1.1 Assumptions

Merton's model assumes that (1) a firm only issues a single discount zero coupon bonds with a face value of K and maturity at T for its debt financing. At maturity if the asset value of the firm (firm value) exceeds its book value of

[1] ISDA: International Swaps and Derivatives Association, Inc. CSA: Credit Support Annex

[2] Financial institutions are often "Too big to fail".

[3] ISDA Margin Survey, 2010.

[4] Merton, R., 1974, On the Pricing of Corporate Debt: The Risk Structure of Interest Rates, Journal of Finance, Vol. 29, No. 2, 449-470.

liabilities (K), shareholders would pay off its debt (K) and the firm will continue to exist. On the other hand, if the firm value is less than the redemption amount at maturity then shareholders would file for bankruptcy. The model assumes (2) there is an absence of transaction costs regarding the default event which include bankruptcy costs, taxes or any other relevant cost issues and each of the debt holders has the priority over shareholders. In this case of default, the value of the equity becomes 0. Merton's model assumes (3) constant risk free rate and volatility. The total value of a firm is then assumed to follow geometric Brownian motion,

$$dV_t = \mu V_t dt + \sigma V_t dW_t\,) \qquad \text{..............Eq. (01)}$$

where,
V is the total value of the firm,
μ is the expected continuously compounded return on V (i.e., the asset drift),
σ is the volatility of firm value and dW is a standard Weiner process.

By definition the value of the firm following geometric Brownian motion indicates V_t is normal and lognormally distributed. The value of the firm's asset at time t is given by the following stochastic differential equation,

$$V_t = V_0 \exp\left[\left(\mu - \frac{\sigma^2}{2}\right)t + \sigma W_t\right]\,) \qquad \text{..............Eq. (02)}$$

2.1.2 Modeling[5]

In this model, default occurs when V_t falls beyond the value of the issued discount zero coupon bond (K) at time t. This can be reinterpreted as an option with underlying asset of the value of the firm and strike price at its face value of the bond. In another word, holding the firm's bond equals to taking a long position of risk free asset and a short position of put option with strike price K. The equity of the firm is then a vanilla European call option on the assets of the firm with maturity T and a strike price equal to the face value of the debt.

Table 01: Merton's model and payoffs for equity and bond holders

	Default ($V_t < K$)	Non-Default($V_t > K$)	Payoff
Equity	0	$V_t - K$	$\max[V_t - K, 0]$
Bond	V_t	K	$K - \max[V_t - K, 0]$

Merton adopts option pricing model to derive the value of firm given by
$$v(t,T) = F(t,T) - P(t) \qquad \text{..............Eq. (03)}$$
Where,
$v(t,T)$ is the present value of discount bond with maturity T at time t
$F(t,T)$ is the present value of riskfree discount bond with face value of K at time t
$P(t)$ is the present value of a European put option with strike at K at time t.

Equation (03) shows the value of the corporate bond is given by subtracting the value of a European put option with underlying asset of V_t from the value of risk free discount bond with K. Since the value of risk free discount bond is determined, the value of the firm's bond then depends on the value of the put option. In Merton's model, risk free rate is given as constant and hence the value of put option can be drawn from Black and Scholes option pricing model[6].

$$P(t) = \left[-V(t)\frac{N(-d_1)}{N(-d_2)} + F(t,T)\right]N(-d_2) \qquad \text{........... Eq. (04)}$$

where,

$$d_1 = \frac{\ln\left(\frac{V_t}{K}\right) + \left(r + \frac{1}{2}\sigma^2\right)(T-t)}{\sigma\sqrt{T-t}}$$
$$d_2 = d_1 - \sigma\sqrt{T-t}$$

---

[5] Replication of Merton's model is referred from various text books which includes;
Hull, J., 2002, Options, Futures, and Other Derivatives, Fifth Edition, Prentice Hall.
Caouette, J., Altman, E., Narayanan, P., Nimmo, R., 2008, Managing Credit Risk: The Great Challenge for the Global Financial Markets, Second Edition, John Wiley & Sons, Inc.
Jo, H., 2003, Credit Risk: Measurement and Management, Segyeong.
[6] Put option pricing equation: $P(t) = -S(t)N(-d_1) + Ke^{-r(T-t)}N(-d_2)$

Equation (04) indicates that $[-V(t)\frac{N(-d_1)}{N(-d_2)} + F(t,T)]$ is the expected loss given default and multiplying it with $N(-d_2)$ becomes the expected loss (EL). Therefore, plugging in the value of put option derived from equation (04) into equation (03), we can retrieve the following

$$v(t,T) = F(t,T) + V(t)N(-d_2) \quad \text{........} \quad \text{Eq. (05)}$$

where the $F(t,T)$ is the value of the firm's discount bond without an event of default and $V(t)N(-d_2)$ is the value of the firm's discount bond with an event of default. In the Merton framework, the value of the firm's bond is determined by the difference between the values of its asset and liability, leverage ratio, maturity and asset volatility.

2.1.3 Default probability

The value of asset, V_t, follows a path of geometric Brownian motion and subsequently the default probability can be drawn as

$$Pr(V_T < K) = Pr\left[V_t \exp\left(\mu - \frac{\sigma^2}{2}\right)(T-t) + \sigma W(T-t) < K\right]$$

$$= Pr\left[W(T-t) < \frac{\ln\left(\frac{K}{V_t}\right) - \left(\mu - \frac{\sigma^2}{2}\right)(T-t)}{\sigma}\right] \quad \text{................Eq. (06)}$$

The standard Brownian motion $W(T-t)$ follows a normal distribution with its mean value of zero and variance with$(T-t)$, and can be reiterated as the below cumulative density function,

$$Pr(V_T < K) = N\left[\frac{\ln\left(\frac{K}{V_t}\right) - \left(\mu - \frac{\sigma^2}{2}\right)(T-t)}{\sigma\sqrt{T-t}}\right]$$

where[7] $W(T-t) = Z(T-t)$ and hence the equivalent martingale measure is

$$Pr(V_T < K) = N(-d_2) = 1 - N(d_2) \quad \text{..........} \quad \text{Eq. (07)}$$

2.2 Moody's EDF™ (Expected default frequency)

The EDF Model[8] was developed by the KMV Corporation in the early 1990's then implemented further by Moody's in 2002. The model adopted Black-Scholes option pricing model and previously introduced Merton's Model to generate the default probability of a firm. Measuring default probability requires the following three steps:

1) Estimate asset value and asset volatility
2) Find the value of distance-to-default(DD)
3) Find the default probability

Figure 01: Moody's KMV default process in the model[9]

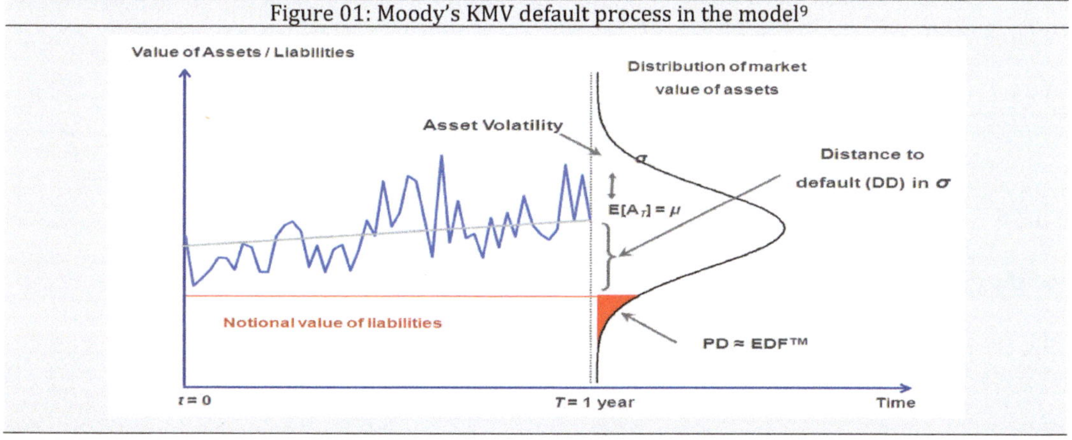

[7] Z is standard normal distribution with $\mu = 0$ and $\sigma^2 = 1$
[8] The model is now provided to subscribers of Moody's.
[9] Default process Figure from Munves, D., Smith, A., Hamilton, D., 2010, Banks and their EDF Measures Now and Through the Credit Crisis: Too High, Too Low, or Just About Right?

2.2.1 Estimate asset value and asset volatility

For a publicly traded company, the asset value and volatility can be estimated from the market price and volatility of equity and the book value of liabilities using options pricing approach which recognizes equity as a call option on the underlying assets of the firm. Suppose a firm with a single class of debt and equity. The equity holder now possesses the right to pay off the debt holder and take over the remaining assets of the firm. In this case, equity is simply a call option on the firm's assets with its strike equal to the book value of liabilities. In practice by solving two equations[10] with two unknowns, the asset value and volatility, we can determine as shown below; (08) and (09).

$$\begin{bmatrix}\text{Equity}\\ \text{Value}\end{bmatrix} = OptionFunction\left(\begin{bmatrix}\text{Asset}\\ \text{Value}\end{bmatrix}, \begin{bmatrix}\text{Asset}\\ \text{Volatility}\end{bmatrix}, \begin{bmatrix}\text{Capital}\\ \text{Structure}\end{bmatrix}, \begin{bmatrix}\text{Interest}\\ \text{Rate}\end{bmatrix}\right) \quad \text{..........Eq. (08)}$$

$$\begin{bmatrix}\text{Equity}\\ \text{Volatility}\end{bmatrix} = OptionFunction\left(\begin{bmatrix}\text{Asset}\\ \text{Value}\end{bmatrix}, \begin{bmatrix}\text{Asset}\\ \text{Volatility}\end{bmatrix}, \begin{bmatrix}\text{Capital}\\ \text{Structure}\end{bmatrix}, \begin{bmatrix}\text{Interest}\\ \text{Rate}\end{bmatrix}\right) \quad \text{............Eq. (09)}$$

The value of underlying assets follows the following stochastic process.

$dV_A = \mu V_A dt + \sigma_A V_A dz$ .... Eq. (10)

where, V_A and dV_A are asset value and change in asset value, respectively. μ and σ_A are asset value drift rate and volatility. dz is simply a standard Wiener process. If K is the book value of the debt due at time t, then the market value of equity and the market value of assets are related as the following expression;

$V_E = V_A N(d_1) - e^{-r(T-t)} K N(d_2)$ .... Eq. (11)

V_E is the market value of the equity and, d_1 and d_2 represent the following equations. r here is the risk free interest rate.

$$d_1 = \frac{\ln\left(\frac{V_A}{K}\right) + \left(r + \frac{1}{2}{\sigma_A}^2\right)(T-t)}{\sigma_A\sqrt{(T-t)}}$$

$$d_2 = d_1 - \sigma_A\sqrt{(T-t)}$$

It follows directly from Ito's lemma that the equity volatility and asset volatility are related as the following expression;

$$\sigma_E = \left(\frac{V_A}{V_E}\right)\left(\frac{\partial V_E}{\partial V_A}\right)\sigma_A \quad \text{................ Eq. (12)}$$

The asset value and volatility implied by the book value of the liabilities, the equity value and volatility are determined by "solving"[11] the call price and volatility equations, (11) and (12) simultaneously.

2.2.2 Find the value of distance-to-default (DD)

Once the asset value and volatility are inferred numerically from the two equations, the distance to default can be calculated simply as

$$DD = \frac{\ln\left(\frac{V_A}{K}\right) + \left(\mu - \frac{1}{2}{\sigma_A}^2\right)(T-t)}{\sigma_A\sqrt{(T-t)}} \quad \text{.......... Eq. (13)}$$

where, μ is an estimate of the expected annual return of the firm's assets. This is nothing but $N(d_2)$[12] in the Black-Scholes model[13].

2.2.3 Find the default probability

In this study, Normal Distribution is assumed to calculate a firm's distance-to-default and its default probability which is expressed as

---

[10] Crosbie, P., Bohn, J., 2003, Modeling Default Risk.

[11] Solver, Mathematical software terminology, provides solution finding for nonlinear equations.

[12] The difference is that DD uses return of assets, μ, whereas d_2 uses risk free interest rate, r.

[13] $N(d_2) = \Pr(V_A > K)$

$$\text{Expected Default Frequency} = N\left(-\frac{\ln\left(\frac{V_A}{K}\right)+\left(\mu-\frac{1}{2}\sigma_A{}^2\right)(T-t)}{\sigma_A\sqrt{(T-t)}}\right) \quad \text{.............. Eq. (14)}$$

But KMV suggests a relationship between distance-to-default and default probability from historical bankruptcy frequencies[14].

2.2.4 Model evaluation

The most significant feature of the KMV's EDF model would be that the model utilizes market value of equity to estimate the firm's asset value. In other words, the model contains future-oriented and forward looking measures functioning as an early warning system because the default probability is derived from option pricing model with equity value which reflects firm's future expected performance at a given time horizon.

3.0 Empirical testing

Financial institutions, especially banks, encounter a performance reliance issue in measuring banks' EDF values because the EDF values are seldom too high or too low in an absolute term according to the subscribers of KMV model as well as Moody's Analytics[15]. This study will tackle such a discrepancy by assessing the level of default risk of each bank using historical financial data and equity market data. The absolute EDF value which does not fully convey the inherent default risk will be replaced with simple d_2 value, distance-to-default value. Then, the acquired values will be observed in line with the movement and momentum of the calculated distance-to-default values in a given time period. The empirical test will be conducted in the following manner: (1) assumptions, (2) distance-to-default movement of defaulted banks, (3) distance-to-default movement of survived banks, and (4) reflection of historical economic impact.

The test results are expected to include (1) valid early signal of EDF values (distance-to-default value in this study as a proxy for EDF value) for South Korean banks and (2) reflection of external economic impact during the test period.

3.01 Test assumption

For this study, 39 data sets of historically delisted banks from South Korean stock exchange and 9 data sets of currently listed banks are retrieved within the period from year 2000 up to year 2013. All sample data were tested to calculate the value of Distance-to-Default. Comparisons are strictly conducted with their Distance-to-Default level movement. All calculations are performed based on the theoretical calculation method introduced EDF model earlier in the study that is to calculate the value of d_2. KTB 1year yield[16] is used as a proxy for risk-free interest rate. Some of the banks only survived short periods within the test years and some of the banks were restructured during the test period. Although we have tested all possible banks that have been listed in the exchange, not all samples showed consistent results due to the above reasons. Also, in this study we eliminate all sudden effect of financial statement (except capital increase or decrease) or any other business impact which could harm the purpose of the study. Nonetheless, the momentum of their movement of Distance-to-Default should suggest significant results. The vertical axis represents distance-to-default and the horizontal axis is the time period in the following figures.

3.02 Distance to default movement of defaulted banks

The values of distance-to-default between year 2006 and year 2012 were calculated for those banks which eventually filed for bankruptcy and delisted. 6 banks, all savings banks, were chosen from the sample data and the banks were divided into two groups, ratings above and below BBB; then one from each sample group was chosen to show the level movement of distance-to-default.

Figure 02: Distance-to-default movement of defaulted banks

[14] Historical data of over 250,000 companies and over 4,700 incidents of default or bankruptcy provides fatter tailed distribution and the default probability, therefore, shows higher value than normal distribution.

[15] Moody's Analytics is a subsidiary of Moody's Corporation

[16] Korea Treasury Bond 1 year yields match well in this model compared to commonly used CD 91 day, KTB 3yr and inter-bank overnight rate.

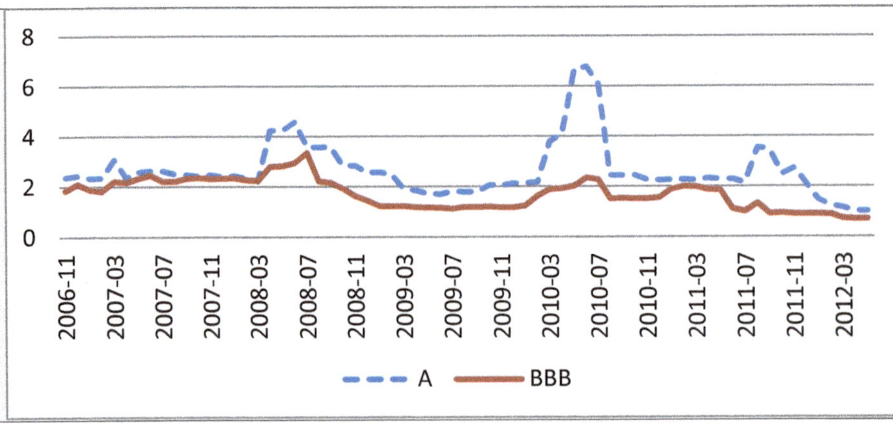

The distance-to-default values were calculated from monthly stock prices and their monthly volatility levels between November 2006 and April 2012. Figure 02 shows that the two values of distance-to-default from both samples move together creating similar paths as they face default. The values of distance-to-default of defaulted banks actually move toward zero which signifies a warning of default. Some of the other samples that went through bankruptcy actually showed negative values of d_2 as they move toward default time.

Another comparison between the distance-to-default values of survived and defaulted banks with ratings[17] of AA and A, respectively, shows clearer path difference for both banks as shown below. The focus is how the value of distance-to-default of default bank moves toward its actual default time.

Figure 03: Comparison of distance-to-default movement of survived and defaulted banks

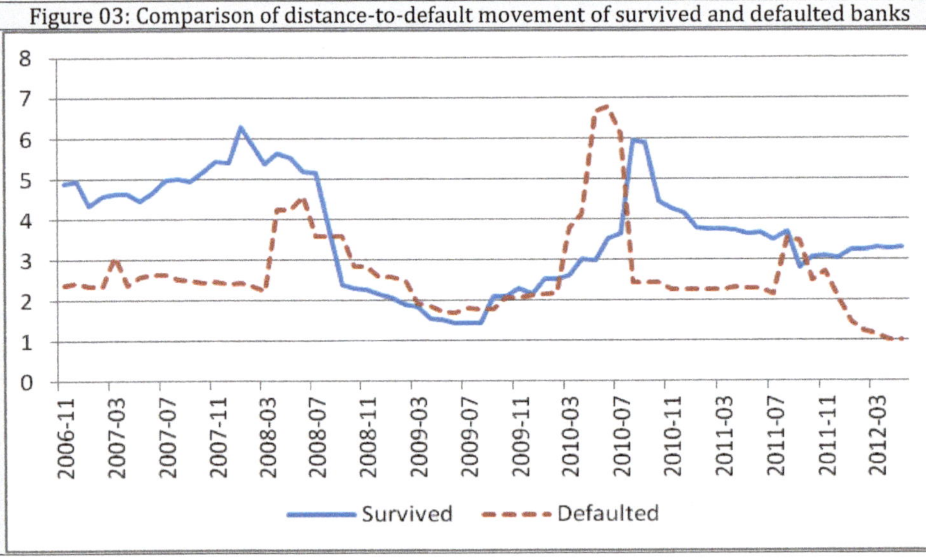

It is possible to see from the figure 03 that the distance-to-default value for the defaulted bank converges toward zero whereas the value of the survived bank maintains its level well above zero. Although the warning signal does not show graphically until the two lines start to diverge after mid-2011, figure 03 still provides the evident interpretation of how momentum of distance-to-default values matches default possibility. The low values between the end of year 2008 and the beginning of 2010 will be discussed later in this study. Also, the high peak around middle of year 2010 will be explained further with another sample.

3.03 Distance to default movement of survived banks

None of the listed banks from year 2000 still are listed as of today. This is because all existing banks either defaulted, were acquired by other banks or were delisted then listed again as a holding group. Survived banks here, then, means mostly delisted banks that are now listed again as holding companies. This study focuses on the values of distance-to-default of those survived banks up until their business events took place. The core target of the empirical test is to show that the obtained values maintain the validity of default probability calculation model. This would mean that the values should stay well above the zero (default point) or should not show any negative numbers.

[17] Ratings by Korea Investors Service as of March 2012

Samples were selected based on the longevity of the survived banks mainly because short time of period may not visually reveal the movement of distance-to-default value. All of the selected banks have the ratings of either AAA or AA as of their last listed month in the South Korea equity market. First, we examine the movement of distance-to-default values of sampled banks years between 2004 and 2008.

The key implication of figure 04 is that despite the distance-to-default values of sample banks do not always move toward the same direction during certain given time periods, they all maintain distant from the default point to a certain extent and if data from JB and BS are excluded from the figure, it would look as figure 05.

Figure 04: Distance-to-default movement of survived banks (before September 2008)

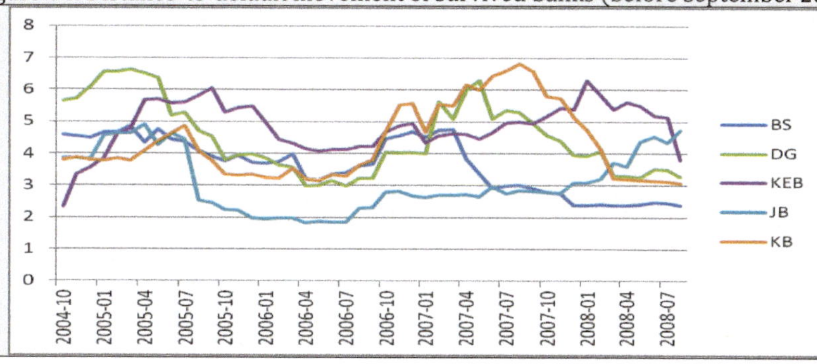

Figure 05: Distance-to-default movement of survived banks (before September 2008)

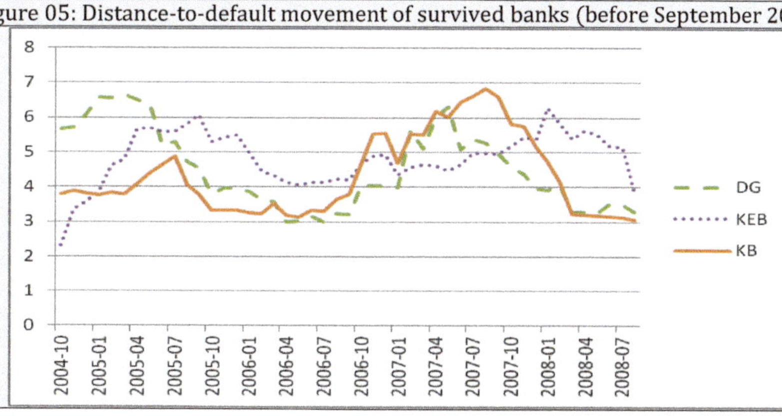

Now, we see clearly that values of all three banks move relatively together along the time period. All move downward in the early years and after hitting the trough around early-2006, all move upward again. Then, all move downward again as they enter global financial distress in 2008. This finding signifies that the distance-to-default values of most survived banks conform in terms of their movement. The direction of d_2 movement matters (whether the values converge or diverge one another) when determining the default signal as shown in the figure 03.

Figure 06: Distance-to-default movement of survived banks: 2008-2011

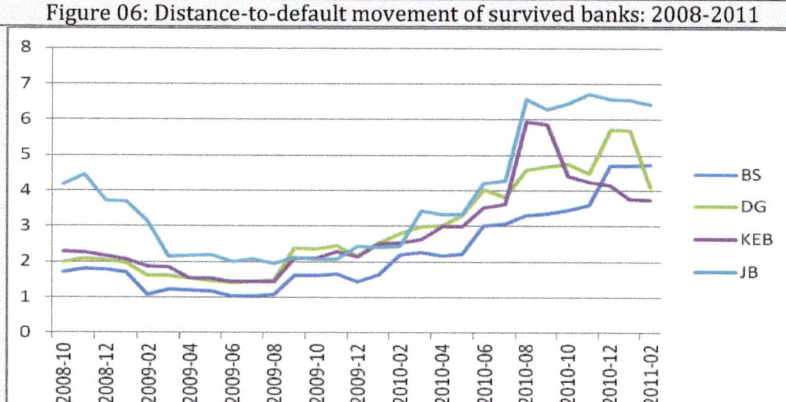

This time we will examine the same sample values observed between 2008 and 2011. Since KB was delisted and listed again as KB Financial Group in the year of 2008, only the rest 4 out of 5 banks will be tested starting 2008 until 2011 for data consistency purpose.

The values of distance-to-default of the sampled 4 survived banks all move toward the same direction within tolerable range and the levels of the obtained values again are consistently placed well above their default point which is at distance-to-default equals zero. Unlike the previously discussed distance-to-default values for the default banks, the survived banks showed their calculated values that have no considerable signs or warnings of default. Much emphasis is on the two critical characteristics in order to visually foresee the upcoming default event: (1) whether the movement of observed distance-to-default value is in line with its peer group; (2) Whether the observed distance-to-default value is actually "distant" from zero[18]. In this case, the observed values of all 4 survived banks hold the above mentioned two conditions and, therefore, presumably we find no particular reason to expect default event.

3. 04 Reflection of historical and economic impact

Now this study will further consider and discuss whether the calculated value of distance-to-default actually reflects the external effect such as economic recession or any internal business event. Default may incur due to a firm's specific capital structure but in most cases, external economic impact indirectly first affects a firm's business environment and then the following poor performance of a firm leads to eventual default. It is also important to check that our calculated values deliver the warning signals of the external impacts.

Figure 06: DG Bank - reflection of events

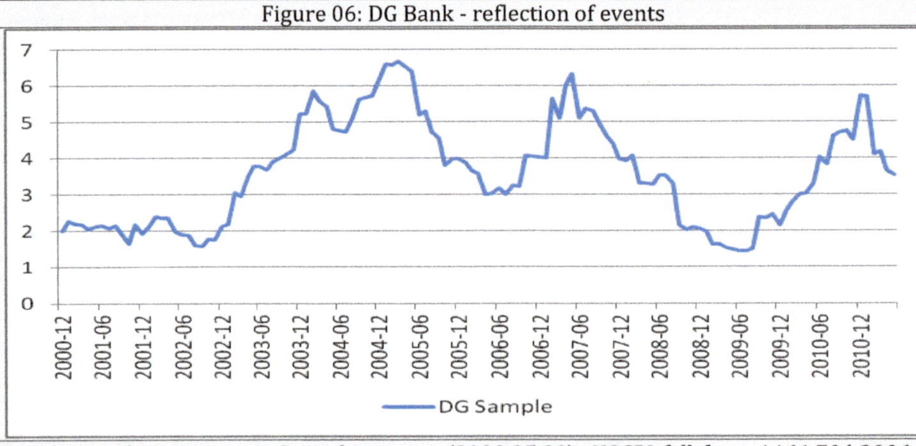

Events that this study targets are: Capital increase (2002.05.23); KOSPI fall from 1464.70(2006.06.11) to 1,192.09(2006.06.14) with high volatility; and global recession (2008-2009)

From the given samples, the longest listed bank is selected to explain whether EDF model holds its validity by cross matching the movement of distance-to-default value with any significant internal and external event occurred at a certain given time. The whole view of the distance-to-default value between year 2000 and 2010 is shown in the figure 07.

In this study, we take one internal effect and two external economic events. The first effect is capital increase. The capital injection of KRW 6.6 billion clearly shows on figure 07 that the distance-to-default value drastically surges in year 2002. Our observed values well reflect the positive effect to the bank's capital structure. Secondly, the drastic fall of KOSPI index level and the increase of relatively high equity volatility[19] of DG bank are well reflected and captured in the figure. Market sentiment often plays a great role that investors seldom sensitively react to future prospect of not only a specific firm but also of overall economy condition. Regardless of a firm's current performance, market expectation on both local and global economy may influence the price of the firm's equity price and the value of distance-to-default. The last impact is the global breakdown and financial recession in 2009 which also could be inferred from the figure where the value of distance-to-default moves deep downward. Although, the inferred value of distance-to-default is determined as a combination of individual performance and economic situation, it is fair to assert that the above findings deliver a fairly accurate glimpse of both internal and external impact.

3.05 EDF model evaluation

The EDF model showed its powerful results in assessing credit default risk of banks that the early warning signs of default could be captured by taking account of the movement and momentum of the distance-to-default values

[18] In fact, zero does not signify the default point. Zero only means high default probability. In standard normal distribution zero distance-to-default will give you 50% chance of default. (e.g. 1% default probability if the distance-to-default value is 2.33.)

[19] Equity volatility of April, May, June and July in 2006 were 10.44%, 10.31%, 9.91% and 10.44%, respectively where equity volatility of the past year with was 4.61%, 4.71%, 5.83% and 5.76%.

compared within the peer group. Although the exact default probability of each bank was not calculated and the absolute default probability level was not deliberately found, the movement trend of distance-to-default itself revealed its significance and contribution to the finding of passage of default risk. Moody's Analytics in their paper[20]published in 2010 stated similar problems incurred from high or low absolute EDF values. Moody's Analytics suggests to focus on the relative EDF values within its peer group and its direction of EDF values in assessing financial institutions, and the high or low EDF values come from different levels of the capital structure[21]. Despite of the concerns of EDF model for financial institutions, the model still holds its validity in applying to banks in South Korea.

4.0 Application

At this point, we have discussed the validity of EDF model in applying to financial institutions and will further investigate how the EDF model can be applied other than its direct application to credit risk management. In the Over-The-Counter (OTC) derivatives market, especially banks, participants are exposed to credit risk from counterparties. Unlike markets with a clearing house, any transaction in the OTC market cannot be protected from credit event and consequently prior to all inter-bank transaction, the participating financial institutions require bilateral legal agreement and they seldom mutually request for credit support of collaterals according to the exposure levels. The legal agreement is called ISDA agreement[22] and the credit support agreement is called Credit Support Annex[23]. Size of posting collateral from negative Mark-to-Market side to the opposite institution grows rapidly due to various OTC derivatives trades and the following large amount of credit support as collateral starts to become a burden to many collateral provider. Minimizing credit risk until all transactions become risk free is not an affordable solution. Collateral management which maintains certain profitability with lowest possible risk is rather preferred and desired.

4.01 Collateral management

Under the agreement of CSA, both sides of transactions require to provide eligible collateral from the negative mark to market side to the opposite side of the transaction in order to mitigate credit risk in unsecured financial transactions. For instance, at a certain time, suppose bank A and bank B have a number of FX swap, CRS or IRS outstanding contracts and both banks would have a mark to market exposure due to the price changes of underlying products. One will have a positive mark to market exposure and the other will have a negative mark to market exposure (also both sides of the exposure could be even but it is highly unlike). The bank with a positive mark to market exposure will claim the counterparty to deliver collateral amount equal to the exposure that exceeds the level of thresholds.

[Required Collateral Amount] = [Total Exposure] − [Corresponding Threshold Amount] ....Eq. (15)

4.02 Problems with threshold

The existence of threshold makes convenient to both parties because repetitive small amount of collateral movement costs more than mitigating counterparty's credit risk. However, setting the threshold levels between the two contractual parties is an often raised problem. The global standard is a bilateral agreement to set the maximum and minimum threshold level that accordingly match each level of ratings provided by global credit ratings agencies such as Moody's, S&P or Fitch. For example, a financial institution with its credit rating of AAA may have a threshold level of USD 40 million. This means that the institution does not have an obligation to provide any collateral to its counterparty as long as its exposure does not exceed negative USD 40 million. If the mark to market exposure becomes negative USD 50 million then the institution must deliver collateral amount of USD 10 million to the counterparty. Also if the credit rating of the financial institution falls to AA, different level of threshold could be applied depending on the agreement. All listed South Korean banks currently show only two ratings that are either AA or AAA from local rating agencies[24] and globally A or Aa[25]. Obviously all South Korean banks with the same ratings do not possess the same or close to the same credit risk level. Among those whose ratings are AAA from the local rating view, some of the banks will have higher intrinsic credit risk than other banks and these banks are confronted to deliver more than a fair collateral level because the threshold is fixed to follow the corresponding

---

[20] Munves, D., Smith, A., Hamilton, D., 2010, Banks and their EDF Measures Now and Through the Credit Crisis: Too High, Too Low, or Just About Right?

[21] Liabilities of financial institution often range from senior obligations to hybrid capital such as preferred shares which rank just above equity.

[22] The ISDA Master Agreement is a development of the Swaps Code, introduced by ISDA in 1985. It is commonly used for OTC derivatives transactions internationally.

[23] CSA is a legal document which regulates collateral for derivatives transactions.

[24] KIS and NICE rating

[25] Moody's rating

ratings. Table 4.1 shows debt ratings of listed banks (or holding group company) as of the first quarter of 2014. In this case, threshold level

Table 02: Credit ratings - South Korea listed banks as of 2014 1Q

Name	Moody's LT	KIS/NICE LT
Cheju Bank LTD	A3	AA+
Woori Finance Holdings Co Ltd	A2	AAA
Woori Bank	A1	AAA
DGB Financial Group Inc		AAA
Daegu Bank	A2	AAA
Industrial Bank of Korea	Aa3	AAA
KB Financial Group		AAA
Kookmin Bank	A1	AAA
Hana Financial Group Inc		AAA
Hana Bank	A1	AAA
Korea Exchange Bank	A1	AAA
JB Financial Group Co Ltd		AA+
Jeonbuk Bank		AA+
BS Financial Group Inc	A2	AAA
Busan Bank	A2	AAA
Shinhan Financial Group Co Ltd		AAA
Shinhan Bank	A1	AAA

* LT: Long term, unsecured and unsubordinated debt

4.03 Suggestions

We further elaborate the current collateral threshold method with "smoother" threshold level from the collateral management stand point by using our distance-to-default values. Universally eligible collateral is always cash, especially hard currencies such as USD or EUR, and financial institutions often utilize cash collateral because cash transfer is quick and convenient to manage. According to ISDA Margin Survey in 2010, 82 percent of collateral used was cash. The main problem with cash collateral we focus is that the return benefit of collateral provider from cash collateral is minimal, meaning the receivable USD cash interest is calculated with effective federal fund rate, and EUR cash interest is calculated with EONIA rate[26]. Both rates would be significantly below the funding rates of all financial institution. Provision of large amount of collateral could then lead to liquidity risk as well. Hence, we suggest a way to minimize loss from posted cash collateral without taking additional credit risk.

4.3.1 Threshold smoothing

The focal idea is that the distance-to-default is calculated from market value of equity and its volatility. Both variables can be directly retrieved from the market data and thus regardless of who calculates the value of distance-to-default, all should agree to a specific value with bearable difference and will hardly encounter large discrepancy. By smoothing threshold level, required collateral amount will be in accordance with a firm's credit quality. The detailed method is as follows.

The adequate collateral amount is determined by deducting upper threshold amount from the total exposure and then adding the difference of upper threshold and lower threshold multiplied with an arbitrary number, K, of scaled between zero and one. Upper threshold implies a step higher threshold level of a firm's credit rating. (for instance, if USD 40 million threshold level at credit rating "A" and USD 50 million threshold level at credit rating "AA" are applied then a firm with its credit rating "A" has an upper threshold is USD 50 million and lower threshold is USD 40 million.) The value, K, is the smoothing factor which is determined by the distance-to-default value.

$$\begin{bmatrix}\text{Collateral}\\\text{Amount}\end{bmatrix} = \begin{bmatrix}\text{Total}\\\text{Exposure}\end{bmatrix} - \begin{bmatrix}\text{Upper}\\\text{Threshold}\end{bmatrix} + K \times [\text{Upper Threshold} - \text{Lower Threshold}] \quad \text{...............Eq. (16)}$$

Where,

$[\text{Upper Threshold}] > [\text{Lower Threshold}]$

Upper threshold means higher credit with higher threshold level such that

$$K = 1 - \frac{(\text{DD} - \text{Min})}{(\text{Max} - \text{Min})} \qquad \text{if Min} < \text{DD} < \text{Max}$$

[26] Federal Fund Rate: 0.06~0.1, EONIA: 0.15~0.25

$$K = 0 \qquad \text{if Max} < DD$$
$$K = 1 \qquad \text{if DD} < \text{Min}$$

Min, minimum value of DD, and Max, maximum value of DD, are decided between the contractual parties.

For example, a bank with A rating(corresponding threshold is USD 1 million) is placed just below AA rating(corresponding threshold is USD 2 million) and the current total exposure is USD 3 million. The distance-to-default value is found to be 8, and the maximum and minimum DD values mutually agreed between the two parties are 5 and 10, respectively. Then the smoothened threshold is calculated as shown below.

$$\begin{bmatrix}\text{Collateral} \\ \text{Amount}\end{bmatrix} = [\text{USD 3M}] - [\text{USD 2M}] + 0.4 \times [\text{USD 2M} - \text{USD 1M}]$$
$$= \text{USD}[3\text{M} - 2\text{M} + 0.4\text{M}] = \text{USD } 1.4\text{M}$$
$$K = 1 - \frac{(8-5)}{(10-5)} = 0.4 \qquad \text{if Min} < DD < \text{Max}$$

Without smooth threshold, the bank from the example requires to deliver USD 2 million worth collateral to the pledgee whereas the bank only requires delivering USD 1.4 million after smoothing its threshold. The benefit of the bank is the opportunity cost of USD 0.6 million.

$$\begin{bmatrix}\text{Opportunity} \\ \text{Cost}\end{bmatrix} = \begin{bmatrix}\text{Funding} \\ \text{Cost}\end{bmatrix} - \begin{bmatrix}\text{Overnight} \\ \text{Cost}\end{bmatrix} \qquad \text{..............Eq. (17)}$$

Overnight Cost: Federal Fund Rate, EONIA Rate, Overnight Call Rate and etc.

4.3.2 Actual practice

Total of 24 brokerage firms are currently listed in the stock market in South Korea as of the first quarter of 2014 and 4 samples of brokerage firms with their long term and unsecured debt capital with "AA" ratings are sampled to apply the "smooth" threshold level.

All 4 firms have similar ratings of which 3 are rated AA+ and one is rated AA-[27]. In 2010, all 4 firms have similar level of distance-to-default values and the values move along together until 2013 then all start to conspicuously diverge. Despite of their ratings in 2014, clear difference between distance-to-default values of the SSS and MRA can be vividly witnessed in the figure 4.1.

The distance-to-default values for the last month of test period, February 2014, and the K value(with max 8 and min 3) from equation 4.2 are shown in table 4.2. The idea is that although the 4 sample firms have the same ratings of AA, levels of their credit risk differ much. However, by calculating previously introduced K-value of each firm, the threshold level can be smoothened individually and credit risk of each firm will be reflected into the threshold level.

Figure 08: AA rated brokerage house in South Korea

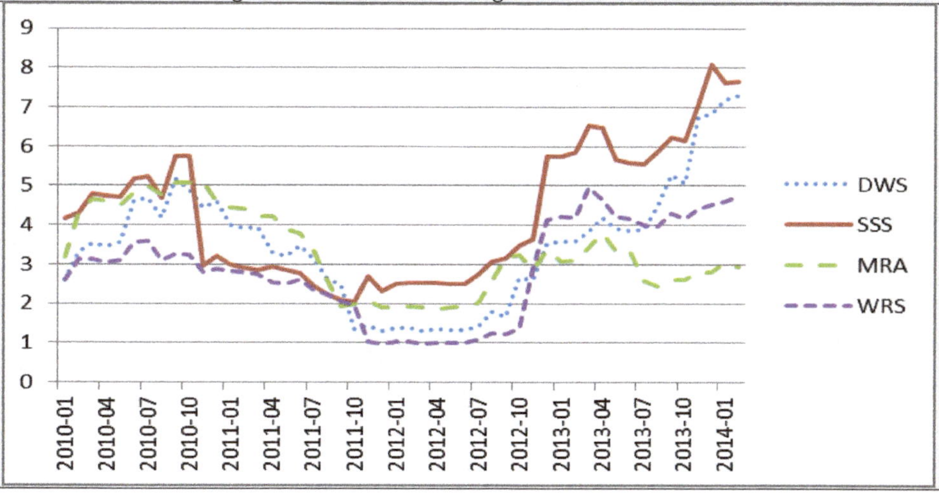

[27] Threshold level does not specify ratings with plus or minus.

Depending on the exposure status, the pledger can become a pledgee within the contractual period as number of transactions increases. This smoothing method will always reflect counterparty default risk as well as help allocate resources efficiently by reducing idle cash provision as a form of collateral.

Table 03: Distance-to-default and K-values for brokerage firms

	DWS	SSS	MRA	WRS
Credit Ratings	AA+	AA+	AA-	AA+
DD(d_2) 2014.2	7.297	7.6417	2.9405	4.7312
K-value[28]	0.1405	0.0717	1	0.6538

5.0 Summary and discussion

5.1 EDF performance

In conclusion, the EDF model performed well enough for financial institutions, especially for banks, acting as an early warning signal of default event and subsequently can be easily applied to collateral management for financial institutions in the OTC market.

Many previous studies showed the validity of EDF model but most of the studies end their findings with testing the model empirically utilizing market observed data. Also, not many papers have dealt with credit risk of financial institutions since in most cases, financial institutions are the ones who need credit risk protection. The application of the EDF model is limited to a certain field of study (e.g. credit risk or default risk related area) but in the actual work environment, many firms and financial institutions, of course, encounter increasing needs to manage counterparty credit risk. Stock market participants, credit risk managers, loan reviewers and more people adopt the model because of the forward looking property of the model and its simplicity.

This study has delivered ideas that the credit risk model, EDF model, is correctly functioning for South Korean banks and it can be applied in collateral management by providing adequate level of collateral according to the level of default risk. We expect our "smooth" threshold level can contribute to enhancement of resource allocation efficiency for participants in the OTC market.

5.2 Discussion on our findings

Global financial policies and reform movements emphasize market stability, and upcoming US and EU regulations may act against OTC market expansion. We expect risk management will become a core issue to all financial institutions. Collateral management for OTC market participants, hence, could become exceedingly important which eventually controls trading activity. In the midst of current atmosphere, we seek for efficiency in use of collateral. We intend to point out that the excess collateral provision between financial institutions may lead to less profitability for all participants. Further, we suggest the bilateral credit support agreement to include a certain level of threshold in accordance with each credit rating to avoid unprofitable daily transactions, and create linear and fine-tuned threshold level to prevent excess or shortage collateral provision.

5.3 Limitations

The critical weakness of EDF model would be that if a firm or, in this study, a bank is not listed in the exchange market the data cannot be retrieved at all. In this case, CDS spread or bond spread implied distance-to-default could be the substitute values but both spreads are not directly observable in the market.

The use of normal distribution throughout the whole study may underestimate credit risk because the actual historical default distribution is known to have fatter tail. The asset value and its volatility are inferred from equity market value and its volatility observed from the exchange market. Equity value not only varies with the firm's intrinsic risk and performance but also with the external impact and moreover non-market impact could also affect the variables due to the inefficiency of secondary equity market. In addition, small trade volumes of a specific firm in the market could also mislead the equity value and volatility.

[28] $K = 1 - \frac{(DD - Min)}{(Max - Min)}$ if $Min < DD < Max$

$K = 1$ if $DD < Min$

Market convention is extremely difficult to ignore. For example, swap dealers still use Yahoo! Messenger to execute trades and each product dealer has market price quote convention as well. Suggesting a new methodology to change the existing standardized contract will be somewhat difficult. The biggest challenge for implementing our findings in OTC market is the latest market trend in which financial institutions prefer cash collateral only with zero threshold level to avoid all possible credit risk regardless of the accompanied cost.

References

Bharath, S., Shumway, T., 2004. Forecasting default with the KMV-Merton model, AFA 2006 Boston Meetings Paper, University of Michigan.

Black, F., Scholes, M., 1973. The pricing of options and corporate liabilities. The Journal of Political Economy, 81: 637-659. http://dx.doi.org/10.1086/260062

Caouette, J., Altman, E., Narayanan, P., Nimmo, R., 2008. Managing credit risk: The great challenge for the global financial markets, John Wiley & Sons. http://dx.doi.org/10.1002/9781118266236

Chan-Lau, J., Jobert, A., Kong, J., 2004. An Option-based approach to bank vulnerabilities in emerging markets, Epub No. 04-33. International Monetary Fund.

Crosbie, P., Bohn, J., 2003. Modeling default risk, Research Paper, Moody's KMV.

Hull, J., 2002. Options, futures, and other derivatives, Prentice Hall.

Hull, J., Predescu, M., White, A., 2004. The relationship between credit default swap spreads, bond yields and credit rating announcements, Journal of Banking and Finance, 28(11), 2789-2811. http://dx.doi.org/10.1016/j.jbankfin.2004.06.010

Jo, H., 2003. Credit Risk: Measurement and management, Segyeong.

Merton, R., 1974. On the pricing of corporate debt: the risk structure of interest rates, Journal of Finance, 29(2), 449-470. http://dx.doi.org/10.1111/j.1540-6261.1974.tb03058.x, http://dx.doi.org/10.2307/2978814

Munves, D., Smith, A., Hamilton, D., 2010. Banks and their EDF measures now and through the credit crisis: too high, too low, or just about right?, Research Paper, Moody's Analytics.

Vassalou, M., Xing, Y., 2004. Default risk in equity returns, Journal of Finance, 59(2), 831-868. http://dx.doi.org/10.1111/j.1540-6261.2004.00650.x

17

Mutual fund flows: Where does the money go?

Harlan Platt [a], Licheng Cai [b], Marjorie Platt [c]

[a] Northeastern University, Boston, MA. h.platt@neu.edu
[b] Currensee Global Inc, Boston, MA. charliecai187@gmail.com
[c] Northeastern University, Boston, MA.

HIGHLIGHTS:

1. Explains the simultaneous relation between mutual fund returns and investment.
2. Demonstrates the interrelationship between equity markets, fixed income and money market.
3. Highlights the impact of lagged returns.
4. Shows how the new investment drives investment returns.
5. Discusses how investment returns influence future fund flows.

Article History

ABSTRACT

We examine three broad mutual fund sectors: equities, fixed income, and money market funds, to ascertain whether fund flows explain investment returns or whether investment returns attract funds. This question has been studied before but for the most part, research results have not been intuitive. Our findings are substantially different from the results of previous studies. We believe that our results are intuitively more obvious. We fail to reject both causal hypotheses. That is, we find that investment returns are affected by funds flows and that funds flows towards high returns.

Keywords:
Lagged returns;
Mutual fund return;
Sectoral allocation.

1.0 Introduction

As of the end of 2012, over $13 trillion had been invested in mutual funds with an additional $265 billion invested in closed-end funds, $1.3 trillion in ETFs, and $72 billion in unit investment trusts (UITs), (see 2003 Investment Company Fact Book). These dollars represent approximately 20.8% of total household wealth.[1] Mutual funds are an important financial intermediary for savings and investment with their holdings comprising more than 24% of all US corporate equities, 14% of US and international corporate bonds, and 12% of US Treasury and government agencies securities.

The industry has more than 776 fund sponsors (or investment companies) some with just a single fund and others with hundreds of funds. The plethora of mutual fund categories, styles, and objectives creates an investment mosaic of surprising depth which includes more than 8,750 mutual funds, 600 closed-end funds, 1,239 ETFs, and 5,787 UITs, (see 2003 Investment Company Fact Book). From amongst these many offerings, investors choose where to place their investable funds. But first they decide whether they want to invest in corporate equities, fixed income securities, or money market funds. These data are summarized below in Table 1.

---

[1] Estimates of total household wealth are taken from the Federal Reserve, see Norris, 2013.

Table 01: Dollars investment in mutual funds, closed-end funds, ETFs, and UITs and the number of funds by category as of December 31, 2012		
	Dollars invested	Number of funds
Mutual Funds	$13 Trillion	8,750
Closed-end Funds	$265 Billion	600
ETFs	$1.3 Trillion	1,239
UITs	$72 Billion	5,787
Source: 2013 investment company fact book		

A plethora of forces influence an individual's decision about which sector to invest in. Amongst these are their age and life expectancy, holdings of other assets, tolerance for risk, liquidity preference and personal expectations of future returns from each investment sector. Our paper is concerned with the choice between equities, bonds,[2] and money market funds - probably the broadest categorization of investment vehicles.

Figure 1: Allocation of Investor's Funds in 2012

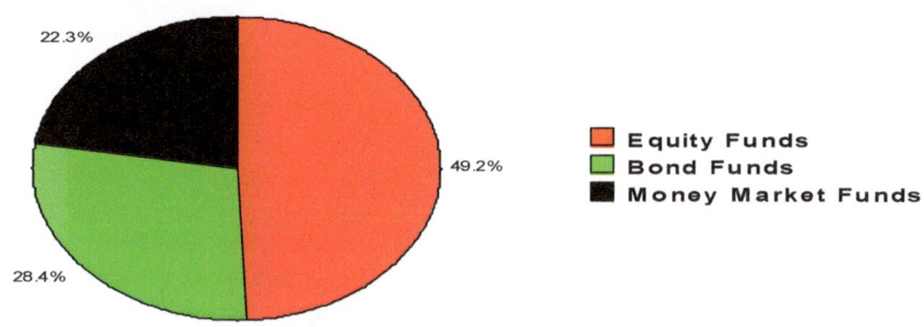

Source: 2013 Investment Company Fact Book, Investment Company Instit

By the end of 2012 as seen in Figure 1, investor's allocation choices placed approximately 50% of their mutual fund investments into the equities category, 28% into fixed income funds, and the remaining 22% in money market accounts. The mix between these three aggregate categories is not fixed. For example, in 2002 fewer than 44% of investment dollars were deployed to equities, slightly more than 37% went to fixed income investments, and about 19% was in money market accounts (2003 Investment Company Fact Book). It is the forces influencing this consumer choice between sectors that are studied in this paper as well as factors affecting investment returns.

For good reason, considerable attention has focused on the substantial and growing mutual fund industry. One topic which has attracted academic researchers is the determination of the causal relationship between fund flows and security returns. There is some evidence that returns are highest in the broad sectors where money has recently flowed into and additional evidence that to some extent money flows where returns are highest. Untangling these simultaneous processes is the key focus of this paper.

Unlike most of the previous work on this topic, this paper views the investor's sectoral financial-allocation decision to be as important as the question of whether higher returns attract new funds or whether the investment of new funds drives returns. We study sectoral allocation decisions, aggregate returns, and fund flows across three aggregate mutual fund sectors: equities, fixed income, and money market funds.[3][4] Our work considers the investor's allocation decision within a simultaneous system of equations thereby recognizing that investment in any one sector is constrained by their total investable funds and that overinvestment of money flows into one sector must be balanced by underinvestment or outflows from another sector. The use of a simultaneous framework enables us to untangle the interrelationship between funds flows and sector returns.

2.0 Previous literature

Relatively few researchers have investigated how investors choose between equity, fixed income, and money market funds. The principal topic studied has been how investment flows influence security returns. These researchers posit the idea that additional money flows into an investment sector leads to incremental demand for

[2] Most U.S. traded investment grade bonds are represented in our sample. Municipal bonds and Treasury Inflation-Protected Securities are excluded, due to tax treatment issues. The AGG index employed in this study includes Treasury securities, government agency bonds, mortgage-backed bonds, corporate bonds, and a small amount of foreign bonds traded in U.S.

[3] Hybrid funds which generally combine elements of fixed income and equity investments are excluded from the analysis for two reasons: their mixed strategic nature and their relative small size.

[4] Mutual fund returns are captured by market returns as an alternative to creating a weighted average value across various mutual funds. Differences between the two series are presumed to be minor.

securities in that sector which results in increased absolute and relative returns. Other researchers have evaluated the opposite relationship: how security returns contribute to the flow of funds. A smaller subset of studies has looked simultaneously at the two relationships, investment flows effect on returns and the impact of returns on flows.

In a key paper, Warther (1995) proposed a multistage-regression process in which to decompose aggregate mutual fund flows into expected and unexpected components. He tested this methodology using monthly data on stock funds, bond funds and gold funds. After decomposing fund flows into two parts, Warther (1995) security returns to be highly correlated with unexpected cash flows but to be unrelated to expected flows. Receipt of unexpected investor deposits result in funds reporting higher returns. Warther (1995) estimated model coefficients to determine an elasticity of market returns with respect to unexpected inflows that equaled 5.7. That is, additional (unexpected) funds given to mutual funds result in substantial boosts in aggregate market returns. He also found fund flows to be correlated with direct (i.e., same sector) security returns but not correlated with the returns of other types of securities. His finding conforms to a reasonable set of expectations about the forces influencing investor decisions. Oddly though, Warther (1995) found a negative relationship between fund flows and lagged security returns which suggests that investors withdraw money from fund categories in the month following their achieving positive returns.

Remolona, Kleiman, and Gruenstein (1997) also considered correlations between mutual fund flows and market returns. Like Warther (1995) they used an early stage regression to generate expected and unexpected mutual fund flows. Three types of stock funds and five types of bond funds were examined with a relatively small database of 118 observations each. Using an instrumental variables regression technique to account for the simultaneity between fund flows and returns, Remolona et.al, (1997) did not generally find a relationship between market returns and fund flows, except for funds with conservative investment objectives where they did find some level of significance for this relationship. For other types of funds, short term market returns had little effect on mutual fund flows. In other words, Remolona et.al, (1997) were unable to confirm Warther's (1995) results. They did not consider the reverse effect, the impact of mutual fund flows on market returns.

In an earlier study, Ippolito's (1992) proposed a different methodology than the two previously discussed studies. His work used annual data on 143 open-ended mutual funds representing 80% of the assets of all mutual funds for the period 1965-1984. He found that investors pay close attention to information about quality (i.e., returns). Ippolito's (1992) shows that investors move their money towards recent good performing mutual funds and away from recent poor performers. Evidence of serial correlation in mutual fund returns led Ippolito's (1992) to argue that better performing mutual funds maintain their return advantage which endorses the idea of investors chasing after good returns.

Cashman, Nardari, Deli, and Villupuram (2012) chose a different methodological approach. They identified how persistence in funds flow is at least as important as fund performance to predict future fund flows. Though not identified as such by the authors, persistence may be functionally equivalent to expected funds flow as identified by both Warther (1995) and Remolona et.al, (1997). In addition, Cashman et.al, identify how some investors evaluate mutual fund performance in a short-term trading like context rather than, as is more traditionally assumed, in a longer run context. Moreover, Bensen, Faff, and Smith (2010) worked with data from 7,000 individual equity mutual funds. They looked for contemporaneous and lagged simultaneously relationships between fund flows and returns. Unlike findings attributed to other recent authors, Bensen et.al, (2010) did not find current and lagged funds flows to affect current returns, across all types of funds. However, they do find that current mutual fund returns significantly affect current investment flows. Ippolito's (1992) argued that higher returns attract investment funds while higher investment flows do not have any effect on returns.

Our research is motivated in part by the Bensen et.al, (2010) paper in that like them we assume endogeneity between fund flows and returns but unlike them we also recognize that investors have a choice between equity, fixed-income, and money market funds. Moreover, while their work analyzes individual mutual funds we propose to study aggregate sectoral mutual funds. Our contribution to the literature then is to evaluate the process of funds flow and security returns with a regression method design for simultaneous models that yields consistent and unbiased coefficient estimates.

3.0 Methodology

3.01 Data

Fund flows

Monthly mutual fund data were obtained for our study from the Investment Company Institute (ICI). The data spans the period 1990-2012. Mutual funds are classified into four categories based on their portfolio components; equity, bond, money market, and hybrid fund. Data for hybrid funds (which combine investment across several fund types) were not included as our research thesis is concerned with investor's discrete choices between specific types of funds.

For the three types of mutual funds the following data series are collected:

1. New Investment Sales - Dollar value of new purchases of mutual fund shares. Does not include shares purchased through the reinvestment of dividends on existing accounts.
2. Reinvested Dividends - Dollar value of distributed income dividends used to purchase more shares of mutual funds.
3. Redemptions - Dollar value of money returned to an investor who has sold shares of a fund (i.e. investor cashes in shares).

Monthly data series measuring investment flows by asset type are generated with the data series as follows:

$$\text{Flow of Investments}_{i,t} = \text{Total Sales}_{i,t} - \text{Redemptions}_{i,t}$$
$$= \text{New Sales}_{i,t} + \text{Reinvested Dividends}_{i,t} - \text{Redemptions}_{i,t}$$

Where, i represent equity funds, fixed income funds, and money market funds and t represents months. Flow of Investments $_{i,t}$ represents the net dollars invested each month in each fund category.

Mutual fund returns

Aggregate equity fund returns are measured by the return on the S&P 500 index. Use of the S&P 500 index is an expedient alternative to the massive task of creating a weighted average of returns for all individual funds. The S&P 500 index is selected because of its substantial correlation with other broad indexes and because it is available for the period of our study.

Aggregate fixed income returns are measured by Barclay's aggregate bond index known as the AGG. The index tracks the broad bond market and is both well-known and highly regarded. The AGG is obtained from Bloomberg.

3.02 Model formulation

Similar to models proposed by Remolona et. al, (1997) and Bensen et. al, (2010), we study two related investment concepts in a simultaneous framework. Our study considers how the flow of dollars into three separate types of mutual fund investments (equities, fixed income, and money market funds) are affected by each sector's investment returns and how sectoral investment returns are affected by investment flows. By using a simultaneous estimation method, the model assumes that investors select between the three investment-vehicles using a conjoint analysis that compares opportunities from each type of investment.

The research paradigm tests whether investors make investment choices after reviewing current and lagged returns reported by equity and fixed income securities. In addition we ask whether investment returns earned in the equity and fixed income markets are affected by current or lagged flows into the three types of funds. The portion of the model representing funds flows is described in equations 1-3 where EQ is the annual net flow of money into equity funds, Bond is the annual net flow of money into fixed income funds, and MM is the annual net flow of money into money market funds. Returns earned by equity funds are measured with the current and lagged returns on the S&P 500, R_SP and R_SPlagged. Current and lagged returns in the fixed income sector are measured by the return on the aggregate bond index, R_AGG and R_AGGlagged. The final factors tested for their effect on investment flows are the flow of investment dollars into the other two markets in both the current and lagged period. That is, for example, we examine how the flow of investment dollars into equities affects the flow of dollars into fixed income and money market funds. For clarity reasons, the subscripts i and t are not included in equations 1 – 3.

$$EQ = a + b_1\,R\_SP + b_2\,R\_SPlagged + b_3\,R\_AGG + b_4\,R\_AGGlagged + b_5\,Bond + b_6\,Bond\ lagged + b_7\,MM + b_8\,MM\ lagged + c_1\,EQ\ lagged + \epsilon 1 \quad \text{Equation (01)}$$

$$Bond = a + b_1\,R\_SP + b_2\,R\_SPlagged + b_3\,R\_AGG + b_4\,R\_AGGlagged + b_5 Eq + b_6 Eq\ lagged + b_7\,MM + b_8\,MM\ lagged + c_1 Bond\ lagged + \epsilon 2 \quad \text{Equation (02)}$$

$$MM = a + b_1\,R\_SP + b_2\,R\_SPlagged + b_3\,R\_AGG + b_4\,R\_AGGlagged + b_5 Eq + b_6 Eq\ lagged + b_7\,Bond + b_8\,Bond\ lagged + c_1 MM\ lagged + \epsilon 3 \quad \text{Equation (03)}$$

The second portion of our work which explains the returns earned by equity and fixed income securities is described in equations 4-5. The basic hypothesis asks whether the flow of funds into a sector drives sectoral returns; our objective is not to explain total return which of course depends on a multitude of factors including economic conditions, interest rates, innovation, and other forces. Rather we focus on the narrower question of how the flow of funds into a sector affects that sectors returns. Returns earned by the S&P 500 is thought to depend upon money flows in both the current and lagged periods into money market accounts, equity funds, and fixed income funds and on the current and lagged returns of fixed income sector. Similarly, the return earned by the aggregate bond fund is thought to depend on the flow of money into the three sectors as well as on the current and lagged return earned by the equity sector. Again, in equations 4-5 the subscripts i and t are not included for clarity reasons.

$$R\_SP = a+C_1*MM+C_2*MM\_LAG+C_3*EQ+C_4*EQ\_LAG+C_5*BOND+C_6*BOND\_LAG+ C_7*R\_AGG+C_8*R\_AGG\_LAG+ \epsilon 4$$
... . Equation (04)

$$R\_AGG = a+C_1*MM+C_2*MM\_LAG+C_3*EQ+C_4*EQ\_LAG+C_5*BOND+C_6*BOND\_LAG+ C_7*R\_SP+C_8*R\_SP\_LAG+ \epsilon 5$$
... . Equation (05)

4.0 Model estimation

The model's five equations are estimated using ordinary least squares (OLS) and then a second time to reflect the simultaneity in the decision process with seemingly unrelated regression techniques (SUR). The need for SUR estimation methods for equations 1-3 arises because the three error terms, $\epsilon 1$, $\epsilon 2$, and $\epsilon 3$, are thought not to be independent of the explanatory variables in each equation. When the error process is related to the covariates in a regression, OLS does not produce consistent or unbiased estimates. The same lack of independence affects regression results for equations 4-5 where the error processes, $\epsilon 4$ and $\epsilon 5$, are related to the independent variables in those equations.

A further complication affecting estimation of the first three equations is the presence of serially correlated error terms. Durbin Watson statistics equaled 0.94 for the equity flow model, 0.42 for the bond flow model, and 1.39 for the money market flow model. The presence of serial correlation is not surprising since there is a strong similarity between successive time periods in many of the factors that influence investor's choice between the three types of investments.[5] To alleviate this problem, lagged dependent variables is added to each equation (1-3). The models depicted above in equations (1-3) include the lagged dependent variables. Estimation results presented below do not include the uncorrected OLS results without the lagged dependent variables. Estimated coefficients on the lagged dependent variables represent the impact on the current dependent variable of past values of independent variables not already included in the equation.

Regression results are presented below in Tables 2a, 2b, and 2c and 3a and 3b. The discussion that follows addresses first the funds flow models (equations 1-3) and then looks at asset returns (equations 4-5).

4.01 Estimation results: funds flow models

The three models explaining the flow of funds into mutual fund sectors are first estimated with OLS. Overall model structures are confirmed with these regressions based on the high significance of the reported F statistics. Each of the three models appears to suffer from serial correlation based on the values of the Durbin Watson statistics. To remedy this situation, lagged dependent variables are added to the three funds flow equations. Re-estimation of the models yielded Durbin Watson statistics in the range that indicates the lack of serial correlation. The remaining discussion of these models is based on the SUR regressions.

The model explaining the flow of money into equity funds estimated with SUR regression has a high adjusted R^2 with a value of 0.52 as seen in Table 2a. The same set of significant independent variables observed in the OLS regression remains significant with SUR regression. A significant positive relationship exists between equity fund flows and the return on the S&P 500, the flow of money into bond funds, and the lagged flow of money into money market funds. Contrasting with these results, there are significant negative relationships found between the flow of money into equity funds and the returns earned on fixed income sector, the lagged flow of money into bond funds, and the flow of money into money market accounts. Two independent variables in the equity funds flow model, lagged returns of both equities and bond sectors are insignificant in the equity flow model.

Unlike equity fund model results, which had the same set of significant independent variables in both OLS and SUR regressions, SUR regression estimation of funds flows into fixed income funds had two additional significant variables beyond those which are significant in the OLS regression as seen in Table 2b. This finding is not unexpected given that OLS estimation is consistent but not as efficient as is SUR regression. A relatively efficient

[5] Ippolito (1992) argues that serial correlation is evidence of better performing funds maintaining their relative return advantage.

estimator has a smaller variance which may reduce the standard errors of coefficient estimates. Like the equity funds flow model above, the return earned in the fixed income sector is a positive determinant of the flow of money into fixed income funds; however, unlike equity fund flows which were unrelated to lagged returns, the lagged return earned in the fixed income sector is significantly related to the current funds flow into fixed income. The comparison between the two sector funds flow models also diverges when examining the impact of the opposite sector's returns on fund flows: equity fund flows are significantly and negatively impacted by bond returns while fixed income fund flows are not affected by equity returns.

Like the equity fund flows model which is significantly related to a) current and lagged fixed income flows and b) current and lagged money market flows, the fixed income flow is significantly related positively (negatively) to current equity (money market) fund flows and negatively (positively) related to lagged equity flows (money market flows).

As occurred in the fixed income flow model, the money market flow model also acquires two significant additional explanatory variables in the SUR regressions when compared with the OLS regression as seen in Table 2c. Fewer significant variables explain money market flows as compared with both equity and fixed income flows. Flows of money into money market funds are negatively related to current flows into equity and fixed income funds and are positively related to lagged bond returns and lagged flows into

Table 2a: Money Flow into Equity Funds

OLS Regressions					SUR Regressions				
Variable	Coefficient	Std. Error	t-Statistic	Probability	Variable	Coefficient	Std. Error	t-Statistic	Prob.
Constant	6481.981	1063.49	6.095*	0.000	Constant	7014.158	1042.017	6.726*	0.000
R_SP	95744.135	12860.00	7.446*	0.000	R_SP	89189.203	12613.080	7.071*	0.000
R_SP_LAG	20357.310	13788.85	1.476	0.141	R_SP_LAG	18306.446	13527.670	1.353	0.176
R_AGG	-145113.95	53641.09	-2.705*	0.007	R_AGG	-167570.441	52600.630	-3.186*	0.015
R_AGG_LAG	22093.032	52652.32	0.420	0.675	R_AGG_LAG	21762.073	51635.28	0.421	0.674
BOND	0.232	0.116	1.997**	0.047	BOND	0.425	0.113	3.762*	0.000
BOND_LAG	-0.426	0.119	-3.569*	0.000	BOND_LAG	-0.640	0.116	-5.495*	0.000
MM	-0.037	0.015	-2.477**	0.014	MM	-0.069	0.015	-4.756*	0.000
MM_LAG	0.065	0.015	4.3996*	0.000	MM_LAG	0.070	0. 015	4.838*	0.000
EQ_Lag	0.514	0.047	10.995*	0.000	EQ_Lag	0.511	0.046	11.154*	0.000
R-squared	0.537	F-statistic	33.085		R-squared	0.522			
Adjusted R-squared	0.521	Prob (F-statistic)	0.000		Adjusted R-squared	0.505			
Durbin-Watson	2.177				Durbin-Watson	2.135			

Note: EQ is the annual net flow of money into equity funds, Bond is the annual net flow of money into fixed income funds, and MM is the annual net flow of money into money market funds. Current and lagged (lag) returns are denoted with R.
* Indicates statistical significance at the 0.01 level; ** indicates statistical significance at the 0.05 level.

Table 2b: Money Flow into Fixed Income Funds

OLS Regressions					SUR Regressions				
Variable	Coefficient	Std. Error	t-Statistic	Probability	Variable	Coefficient	Std. Error	t-Statistic	Prob.
Constant	-595.890	605.349	-0.984	0.326	Constant	-795.696	593.202	-1.341	0.180
R_SP	13591.522	7510.575	1.810	0.072	R_SP	7253.726	7357.780	0.986	0.325
R_SP_LAG	6795.071	7369.141	0.922**	0.357	R_SP_LAG	5430.958	7229.283	0.751	0.453
R_AGG	125517.607	27920.920	4.496*	0.000	R_AGG	132091.431	27890.000	4.823*	0.000
R_AGG_LAG	72206.086	27712.570	2.606*	0.010	R_AGG_LAG	74409.077	27186.570	2.737*	0.006
EQ	0.066	0.033	2.000**	0.050	EQ	0.121	0.032	3.762*	0.000
EQ_LAG	-0.038	0.030	-1.279	0.202	EQ_LAG	-0.068	0.030	-3.762*	0.002
MM	-0.011	0.008	-1.425	0.155	MM	-0.020	0.008	-2.542*	0.002
MM_LAG	0.019	0.008	2.349	0.020	MM_LAG	0.018	0.007	2.285*	0.002
Bond_Lag	0.899	0.033	26.971*	0.000	Bond_Lag	0.898	0.033	27.479*	0.000
R-squared	0.802	F-statistic	115.759		R-squared	0.800			
Adjusted R-squared	0.795	Probability (F-statistic)	0.000		Adj. R-squared	0.792			
Durbin-Watson	2.011				Durbin-Watson stat	2.02			

Note: * Indicates statistical significance at the 0.01 level; ** indicates statistical significance at the 0.05 level.

Table 2c: Money Flow into Money Market Funds

OLS Regressions					SUR Regressions				
Variable	Coefficient	Std. Error	t-Statistic	Prob.	Variable	Coefficient	Std. Error	t-Statistic	Prob.
Constant	17821.582	4554.555	3.913*	0.000	Constant	20811.320	4462.668	4.663*	0.000
R_SP	3396.405	58426.370	0.058	0.954	R_SP	70365.166	57201.090	1.230	0.219
R_SP_LAG	7074.811	57057.160	0.124	0.901	R_SP_LAG	23736.041	55972.570	0.424	0.672
R_AGG	15398.116	221456.901	0.069	0.945	R_AGG	11062.968	219782.700	0.050	0.960
R_AGG_LAG	469422.904	215049.343	2.183**	0.029	R_AGG_LAG	516991.328	210965.201	2.451**	0.014
EQ	-0.629	0.254	-2.477**	0.014	EQ	-1.172	0.246	-4.756*	0.000
EQ_LAG	0.226	0.232	0.972	0.332	EQ_LAG	0.505	0.228	2.217**	0.027
BOND	-0.684	0.480	-1.425	0.140	BOND	-1.193	0.469	-2.254*	0.001
BOND_LAG	-0.728	0.502	-1.450	0.148	BOND_LAG	-0.363	0.491	-0.739	0.460
MM_Lag	0.330	0.060	5.516*	0.000	MM_Lag	0.372	0.059	6.346*	0.000
R-squared	0.283	F-statistic	11.257		R-squared	0.265			
Adj R-squared	0.258	Prob. (F-statistic)	0.000		Adj. R-squared	0.239			
Durbin-Watson	2.104				Durbin-Watson stat	2.09			

Note: * Indicates statistical significance at the 0.01 level; ** indicates statistical significance at the 0.05 level.

Table 3a: Returns of Equity Funds

OLS Regressions					SUR Regressions				
Variable	Coefficient	Std. Error	t-Statistic	Probability	Variable	Coefficient	Std. Error	t-Statistic	Prob.
Constant	-0.010	0.005	-2.075**	0.039	Constant	-0.014	0.005	-2.969*	0.003
MM	3.81E-09	6.65E-08	0.057	0.954	MM	1.18E-09	6.53E-08	0.018	0.986
MM_LAG	-1.95E-07	6.61E-08	-2.949*	0.003	MM_LAG	-1.92E-07	6.50E-08	-2.957*	0.003
EQ	1.85E-06	2.47E-07	7.484*	0.000	EQ	1.92E-06	2.43E-07	7.903*	0.000
EQ_LAG	-8.59E-07	2.35E-07	-3.659*	0.0003	EQ_LAG	-8.48E-07	2.31E-07	-3.673*	0.0002
BOND	9.22E-07	5.10E-07	1.810	0.072	BOND	5.80E-07	5.00E-07	1.159	0.247
BOND_LAG	-4.17E-07	5.36E-07	-0.778	0.438	BOND_LAG	-4.70E-08	5.27E-07	-0.089	0.929
R_AGG	0.547	0.235	2.332**	0.020	R_AGG	1.063	0.228	4.650*	0.000
R_AGG_LAG	-0.043	0.228	-0.186	0.852	R_AGG_LAG	-0.032	0.222	-0.145	0.885
R-squared	0.236	Prob. (F-statistic)	4.43E-12		R-squared	0.222	Durbin-Watson stat		1.978
Adj. R-squared	0.212	Durbin-Watson	2.030		Adj. R-squared	0.197			

Note: * Indicates statistical significance at the 0.01 level; ** indicates statistical significance at the 0.05 level.

Table 3b: Returns of Fixed Income Funds

OLS Regressions					SUR Regressions				
Variable	Coefficient	Std. Error	t-Statistic	Prob.	Variable	Coefficient	Std. Error	t-Statistic	Prob.
Constant	0.008	0.001	6.378*	0.000	Constant	0.008	0.001	6.690*	0.000
MM	4.97E-09	1.72E-08	0.288	0.773	MM	4.78E-09	1.70E-08	0.281	0.778
MM_LAG	-1.81E-10	1.77E-08	-0.010	0.992	MM_LAG	6.99E-09	1.74E-08	0.402	0.687
EQ	-1.90E-07	7.07E-08	-2.680*	0.008	EQ	-2.54E-07	6.94E-08	-3.655*	0.000
EQ_LAG	3.71E-08	6.47E-08	0.574	0.566	EQ_LAG	6.71E-08	6.35E-08	1.057	0.291
BOND	6.21E-07	1.27E-07	4.888*	0.000	BOND	5.76E-07	1.25E-07	4.608*	0.000
BOND_LAG	-6.71E-07	1.34E-07	-5.018*	0.000	BOND_LAG	-6.43E-07	1.31E-07	-4.893*	0.000
R_SP	0.037	0.016143	2.297**	0.022	R_SP	0.073	0.016	4.639*	0.000
R_SP_LAG	-0.026	0.015617	-1.666	0.097	R_SP_LAG	-0.025	0.015	-1.641	0.101
R-squared	0.146	Probability (F-statistic)	1.84E-06		R-squared	0.130	Durbin-Watson stat	1.812	
Adj. R-squared	0.120	Durbin-Watson	1.827		Adj. R-squared	0.103			

Note: * Indicates statistical significance at the 0.01 level; ** indicates statistical significance at the 0.05 level.

equity funds. These results are consistent with the view that money market fund investments are a holding action for many people while they await opportunities in either equity or fixed income funds. That is, when money moves into equity or fixed income funds, balances are drawn down in money market funds to pay for the new equity or bond investments.

As occurred in the fixed income flow model, the money market flow model also acquires two significant additional explanatory variables in the SUR regressions when compared with the OLS regression as seen in Table 2c. Fewer significant variables explain money market flows as compared with both equity and fixed income flows. Flows of money into money market funds are negatively related to current flows into equity and fixed income funds and are positively related to lagged bond returns and lagged flows into equity funds. These results are consistent with the view that money market fund investments are a holding action for many people while they await opportunities in either equity or fixed income funds. That is, when money moves into equity or fixed income funds, balances are drawn down in money market funds to pay for the new equity or bond investments.

Overall our results have some similarity with previous work but it is the differences between the new and older studies that are of most interest. Our findings contrast with Warther (1995) in several ways: a) he did not find, as we did, equity fund flows to be significantly affected by the returns earned by fixed income securities and b) he found a significant negative relationship between flows and lagged returns which we did not replicate. Our findings also differ from Remolona et.al, (1997) who did not find a relationship between current or lagged returns and fund flows. The smallness of their database may influence the differences between our study and theirs. Our findings are consistent with Ippolito's (1992) results that returns influence fund flows though his work was directed only at equity funds and was not estimated simultaneously. Finally, our results support the findings of a positive relationship between current sector returns and fund flows observed by Remolona et.al, (2010) though our finding of an additional significant relationship between lagged returns and current flows extends beyond their results.

4.02 Estimation results: return models

Models explaining returns earned in the equity and fixed income sectors do not evidence the presence of serial correlation in their OLS regressions. Nor is serial correlation a problem in the simultaneous estimation versions of the return's models when using SUR regression. Insignificant independent variables are not dropped from the estimation equation since this paper is exploratory rather than predictive. The two SUR return's models have comparatively high adjusted R^2s given the number of other factors such as economic conditions and corporate earnings that are known to influence investment returns that have purposefully been excluded as explanatory factors.

Returns earned in the equity sector are significantly affected by four independent variables as seen in Table 3a. Equity sector returns are higher the higher are the flow of funds into equities and the contemporaneous returns earned by bond sector; they are also higher the smaller are last period's money flows out of equities and money market funds. These results are not consistent with other researchers such as Remolona et. al, (1997) who did not find that money flows directly affect returns.

Similarly, the returns earned by fixed income funds are also influenced by four significant explanatory factors as seen in Table 3b. Fixed income returns are higher the higher are the flow of funds into fixed income accounts and the contemporaneous returns earned in the equity sector. Higher fixed income fund returns are significantly associated with smaller declines of a) money flows into bond funds last period and b) money flows into equity funds this period. Again, most previous studies do not find this association.

We believe that our findings are more intuitive than those reported by previous researchers; that is, we find that when money flows into either equity or fixed income funds that those sectors earn higher returns. The simple explanation of this phenomenon relies on nothing more than basic supply and demand: a higher demand for funds of either type leads to higher prices and therefore higher returns in corresponding sectors.

Our empirical work spans five separate models, three of which study money flows into equity, fixed-income, and money market funds while the other two models examine the returns earned in the equity and fixed-income sectors. The statistical significance and the direction of the relationship between independent variables and the five dependent variables are discussed above. In this section, we summarize the previous discussion to highlight the critical questions of do funds flow affect returns or do returns affect funds flow. Table 4 below provides an easy reference looking across the five different models with which to answer those questions.

Looking down the column labeled 'Funds Flow' it is clear that in our work current returns earned in the equity and fixed income markets significantly explain the flow of funds into both the equity and fixed income funds while lagged returns earned in the fixed income market also influences fixed income flows. Similarly, looking down the column labeled 'Returns', both current and lagged flows into the equity and fixed income markets are significant influences on the returns earned by both equity and fixed income sectors. Moreover, as our basic hypothesis of simultaneity in the decision process of individuals would suggest, our results show that all three fund types are significantly influenced by both the current and lagged flow of funds into other sectors. Returns earned in the fixed income sector are seen to be affected by the current flow of funds to other sectors while the returns earned in the equity sector is affected by lagged funds flow to other sectors.

Table 04: Identification of Causative Factors Which are Statistically Significant Influences on Models of Money Flows into Various Sectors and on the Returns of Those Sectors

Model/Causative Factor	Funds Flow	Returns
Own current returns	EQ, Bond	
Own lagged returns	Bond	
Own current flow of funds		EQ, Bond
Own lagged flow of funds		EQ, Bond
Other sector current returns	EQ, MM	
Other sector lagged returns		EQ, Bond
Other sector current flow of funds	EQ, Bond, MM	Bond
Other sector lagged flow of funds	EQ, Bond, MM	EQ

Note: EQ, Bond, or MM indicate which sector's funds flow or returns are influenced by a specific causative factor on the left hand side of the table.

These results are substantially different from those found in previous studies. In some respects, our results are more intuitively obvious. For example, we find that investment returns are affected by funds flows. That is what one would expect based on supply and demand analysis. When money flows into sectors those sectors earn higher returns. Similarly, we find that investment decisions are influenced by current investment returns in equity and fixed income funds and lagged returns for fixed-income funds. This too is not surprising given our understanding of how momentum investing and general financial innumeracy are common amongst many investors.

5.0 Conclusions

The results presented in this paper provide a realistic view of forces effecting how investors allocate their investments between equities, fixed income, and money markets. In specific, we find that returns influence the decision to invest in equities and fixed income and lagged returns also influence fixed income investments. Moreover, money flows into the three investment sectors are influenced by the amount of money flowing into other sectors. These results, while unusual in comparison to other researcher, are both logical and intuitive.

Likewise we show that an influx of money from investors both now and in the previous period affects the returns earned in both the equity and fixed income markets. In addition we find that equity and fixed income returns are influenced by the flow of funds into other sectors and by the lagged return in other sectors. These results too are not surprising.

References

2013 Investment company fact book: a review of trends and activities in the U.S. Investment Company industry, Investment Company Institute, 53rd Edition.

Bensen, K., Faff R., and Smith T., 2010. The simultaneous relation between fund flows and returns. Australian Journal of Management, 35(5): 51 – 67. http://dx.doi.org/10.1177/0312896209354217

Cashman G., Nardari F., Deli D., and Villupuram S., 2012. Investor Behavior in the Mutual Fund Industry: Evidence from Gross Flows. Journal of Economics and Finance, April. 1 – 23.

Ippolito, R., 1992. Consumer reaction to measures of poor quality: Evidence from the mutual fund industry. Journal of Law & Economics, XXXV: 45 -70. http://dx.doi.org/10.1086/467244

Norris, F., 2013. Younger households are slower to make gains in net worth. The New York Times, June 14, B3.

Remolona, E., Kleiman P., and Gruenstein, D., 1997. Market returns and mutual fund flows. FRBNY Economic Policy Review, 33 – 52.

Warther, V., 1995. Aggregate mutual fund flows and security returns. Journal of Financial Economics, 39: 209-235. http://dx.doi.org/10.1016/0304-405X(95)00827-2

Bank management in bank decline: Bank mergers as a recovery recipe? ✧

Anders Kjellman [a*], Risto Tainio [b], Taisto Kangas [b]

[a] Novia University of Applied Science, Vaasa, Finland.
[b] Aalto University, Helsinki, Finland.
[*] Corresponding author's email address: anders.kjellman@parnet.fi

HIGHLIGHTS:

1. We find that decline in banking cannot be understood without looking at growth before decline.
2. Based on 309 Finnish bank mergers during 1990 to 2013, we found that many bank managers gradually lost their confidence concerning their capability of successfully running their banks, thus choosing to merge.
3. Mergers have been useful as a mean for continuation of banking activity. However, the Finnish evidence points to the fact that banks that don't merge will perform better than banks that are involved in merger processes.
4. Finally, we have developed a model for explaining bank mergers as a way out from crisis situations.

Article History

Keywords:
Banking crisis;
Bank management;
Decline model;
Merger.

ABSTRACT

The aim of this article is to present a model concerning bank management during the period of decline. Our focus is on bank mergers as a way out in from a crises situation. Generally, the explicit factor behind bank decline usually relates an economic downturn. However, the implicit, triggering factor behind bank decline relates to bank management. The available options for crisis bank management beside mergers are to cut costs, to increase income, to get more own capital, to manipulate bookkeeping data, to sell the bank, to buy banks or to declare failure. Based on 309 bank mergers during 1990 to 2013, we found that bank managers in many cases gradually lost their confidence concerning their capability of successfully running their banks, therefore choosing to merge.

1.0 Introduction

Bank management in a recession is a difficult task and unfortunately there is no obvious strategy recipe available for management dealing with decline. During the ongoing global financial crises Tourish and Harigie (2012) argue that bank managers say that they are pressured, passive observers of events and victims during the decline stages. Based on our evidence we argue that management in decline is much more complex, than previous research has indicated. We therefore saw a clear need to further explore the relationship between bank decline and bank mergers.

The main aim of this paper is to build a model of bank management during a decline period. Thereby we are investigating bank mergers as a recovery recipe. Our findings based on the bank market in Finland during the time period 1990-2013 indicate that the managerial motives behind mergers vary and are crisis dependent. Our data

✧ The authors are most grateful for the discussions with and help received by managers of former or still existing banks. Financial support from the Liikesivistysrahasto is gratefully acknowledged.

indicates that most mergers occur during an economic downturn. Our model is based on Weitzel and Jonssons (1989) and Collins' (2009) decline models. However, adapted to suit the banking industry. We found six stages in the decline process of banks. The first pre-stage of bank decline is in fact a little contradictory, because we found a period of rapid growth before the decline phase starts. Growth seems to breed the seeds of decline in the financial industry. In the first decline stage the bank management is blinded by previous success. In the second decline stage there is inaction and denial of risk. In the third stage the crisis is escalating and becomes visible to the Authorities. If decline escalates further into the fourth stage merges are commonly seen as the natural way out. In the fifth and final decline stage the bank is failing.

We find that during financial crises many bank managers feel that they may have no other option than to merge. However, strategic options behind mergers seem to be different during economic recession and boom times. Based on 309 bank mergers during 1990 to 2013, we found that many bank managers gradually lost their confidence concerning their capability of successfully running their banks, therefore choosing to merge. We found that bank mergers are most often associated with bank decline and failure. The largest banking group, i.e. the savings banks group, in the 1980s went on a growth and merger track and failed. The mergers in the savings banks group did not prove to be a recovery recipe from the crisis. The results instead point towards failure and massive value destruction. On the other hand, the mergers producing Nordea can be seen as a result of a successful recovery strategy. However, let us recall that bank mergers often fail e.g. the four largest Finnish banks – UBF, KOP, Postipankki and Skopbank - that existed in1990 today only exists in the history books. Furthermore, we observed that a loose form of "mergers" like the cooperative bank consolidation in 1997 turned out to be a good recovery recipe.

Bank decline and mergers can be discussed in different contexts (see e.g. Kiefer, 2014; Tri Santoso, 2014). Sinha et al. (2012) as well as Collins (2009) note that having a celebrated CEO may push the institutional culture into the road of decline. It is evident that the role of the management cannot be understated when it comes to running a bank. This is particularly important when the most influential owners might be a diffuse public authority or the depositors of the bank. In the case of the bulk of the bank declines during the 1990s in the Nordic countries, the issue of corporate governance is extremely important. We will use mainly Finnish bank data to create a model for explain bank decline.

One hypothesis that we had was that bank mergers during a decline period would in general follow the same pattern. It does not matter if it is the still ongoing global financial crises, the latest US, UK, Irish or Nordic banking crises. The debt-deflation explanation by Fischer (1933) still seems to be valid. Crises start with growth in the financial sector and indebtedness amongst borrowers, followed by an increase in property prices. Subsequently, the bubble bursts and a financial crisis emerges, hitting the real economy.

In the United States and Europe, rapidly evolving technological changes, deregulation and globalization had in the late 1980s and beginning of the 1990s, as noticed by Amihud and Miller (1998), triggered a wave of bank mergers and consolidation unseen of since the Great Depression. The bank merger wave of the late 1980s and early1990s was followed by a new bank merger wave due to the global financial crises starting with the growth of shadow banking in the USA, followed by the world's largest bankruptcy of Lehman Brothers in 2008. The crisis spread to Europe. In Iceland and Ireland the banking systems collapsed in 2008 and soon all EU countries were hit by the global financial crisis. The banking sector in Finland was no exception from the merger waves of the global financial crisis. Even if the banking sector as a whole remained relatively sound and showing a fairly good profitability 2008-2013.

2.0 Previous descriptions of decline in banking and bank mergers

Greenhalgh (1983 p 232) defines decline as a deterioration in the organization's ability to adapt to its environment: "Decline occurs when the organization fails to maintain the adaptiveness of its responses". McKinley, Latham & Braun (2014 p 90) see decline as a steady downward trend, however they distinguish organizational decline from organizational downsizing: "organizational decline is an involuntary, unintended resource decrease that affects an organization, whereas organizational downsizing is intentional workforce reduction engineered by managers". Collins (2009) again sees decline as partly depending on the management process e.g. in the case of the world's largest bank in the 1980, Bank of America. However, the solution to decline lies not in the simple bromide: "Change or die". Bank of America changed a lot and nearly killed itself. Clearly both internal as well as external factors will affect the decline of a bank. We see bank decline as a process in which a substantial decrease in the banks resource base occurs, over a time period. Often, but not always, the bank decline period is connected to a decline in the economy.

Bank management in a recession period is a difficult task and unfortunately there are no sure 'strategy recipes' available for management dealing with a decline. Weitzel and Jonsson (1989) have, based on earlier research, and introduced a five-stage description of the decline in organizations and the important questions that are associated with each stage. Quite a few studies have been made on the subject of bank performance, and based on international findings we know that there seems to be no evident economies of scale in the banking sector. Contrarily, diseconomies of scale have usually been found instead, i.e. larger banks have been found to be more cost inefficient. It could thereby be argued that the informed bank managers are aware that the economies of scale argument are not really a useful argument in favor of bank mergers.

Bank mergers are here defined as a variety of combinations of banks created by different types of contractual arrangements. While, a bank acquisition can be seen as combination of banks where one bank acquires the other bank(s). Depending on the context and the size combination can be seen as forced or volunteered.

What then are the potential reasons for bank mergers? As noticed by Berger et al (1999) the primary motive for consolidation is maximizing shareholder value. The consolidation activities should be geared towards maximizing the value of the existing shareholders or owners. However, in reality it is not value maximization alone that can explain merger decisions. The motives for mergers can be divided into two subgroups, i.e. value maximizing motives and non-value maximizing motives.

Table 01: Motives behind bank mergers

Value-maximizing motives	Non-value maximizing motives
1. Increasing efficiency	1. Managerial motives
2. Increasing market power (price settings and availability)	2. Authorities motives
3. Other value-maximizing motives	3. Increasing the probability of survival
	4. Other motives

Based on Berger et al (1999). They also provide an excellent overview of the bank merger literature. The motives can naturally be divided into several additional subgroups.

A bank can mainly maximize its' value through consolidation by achieving an increased efficiency or by gaining a greater market power. The increasing efficiency arguments usually involve the arguments of economies of scale (larger units can produce the output at a lower price) and economies of scope (advantages by providing a mix of products and services). These two factors are often combined with other potential efficiency gains and then referred to as X-efficiencies. Case studies of US and EU bank mergers and acquisitions indicate that if a better run bank reforms the practices and operations of a less efficient bank, then the bank merger will appear to have the best potential for successful value creation. According to Vander Vennet (1996), large efficient banks tend to acquire small, less efficient banks. However, Piloff and Santomero (1998), notice that the empirical evidence shows that there is in general no significant value effect emerging from bank mergers. Rhoades (1999), who studied bank mergers between fairly equal sized banks, found that the merging banks would usually cut costs. Most cost cutting was made in personnel, data processing systems and operations. However, it is evident that cost cutting alone will not be enough to increase shareholder value or create a successful merger.

Berger et al (1999) notice that the bank mergers that have occurred during the 1990s have dramatically increased the concentration rate. The largest banks may therefore be able to influence the market price and market development. The increased market power argument may also be used to explain the recent mergers between banks and insurance companies. The legal obligations and other non-value maximizing motives behind mergers were probably more important than the value maximizing motives. In situations where the corporate control elements may be relatively weak, i.e. in banks owned by depositors or the government, managers may be able to pursue their own interests. Empire-building may be one of the managerial objectives, which may be pursued in order to gain more personal power and financial compensation. The risk of overpaying for merger activities is evident when the managerial incentives are not in line with the owner incentives. We can also see that the pursuit of growth blinded a lot of Finnish bankers. Hadlock et al. (1999) found in their study of bank mergers and managerial incentives that banks in which managers hold a substantial share of the stock are less likely to be acquired A merger is not only an intentional economic and technical operation. It also includes elements of a strategic, cultural and mental operation of the CEOs. Kangas (2006) found that the bank Authorities` opinions were important when it came to influence bank managers` decisions to merge.

The Authorities involvement in bank mergers and acquisitions (M&A) mainly emerges from three needs:

1. Prevention of financial failures.
2. Regulation of banks e.g. preventing banks from becoming too big to fail.
3. Government ownership, creating a need for "political correctness". Sometimes public ownership is seen as a good thing and sometimes not.

It is notable, that the Authorities` motives and incentives have seldom been studied in-depth, despite that fact that the European Union is about to create a banking union, and there is an institutional pressure for mergers.

The issue of bank mergers is complex. Firstly, there is no single, unambiguous measure to correctly estimate the merger effects on the banks or society. Secondly, the interpretation of obtained data is a process that involves the human factor. And we know that the capability of all humans is limited. Despite this it is evident, as argued by Tainio et al (1991), that the categories of environment, strategy and organizational structure can be expected to cover the major determinants of performance. Tainio et al (1991), who studied 79 Finnish savings banks during the beginning of the 1980s, found that bank performance could not be described by a single criterion. Instead, they stress the complexity of performance, which is influenced both by the context and the decision-makers. Their result follows in the footsteps of Lenz (1981), who argues that there is no universal cause-effect relationship from the explanatory variable studies to explain the organizational performance. Instead, there seems to be an interaction between time and space, which may explain the puzzle of performance. At one point in time a specific action may lead towards success, while the same action at another point of time may lead towards disaster.

3.0 Bank mergers and acquisitions in Finland 1990-2013

The data in this study consist of the Finnish banking market 1990-2013. During this period the bank mergers and other consolidation activities were analyzed. In all 309 bank mergers and 20 acquisitions occurred. The great Finnish Depression 1991-1995 is affecting the bank market mergers for a long time. During the merger period 1990 to 2000 there are 220 pure bank mergers (138 savings bank mergers and 77 cooperative bank mergers and 5 commercial bank merges), 5 bank acquisitions and 2 banks were taken over by the Authorities and partly sold and thereafter run down. On top of that 252 cooperative banks chose 1.7.1997 to consolidate their balance sheets. This not a merger per se even if the financial institutions chose to start calculating the solvency level as one unit. Only 44 cooperative banks remained outside the consolidation and formed a new bank group, The Local Cooperative Banks (Paikallisosuuspankit). The same had happened in the savings banks group in 1992 when the 44 most profitable and solid banks chose not to merge.

The bank market started to recover during the late 1990s and in 1999 to 2007 the number of banks remained stable at 338, even if the number of financial institutions increased, due to creation of asset management companies. In 2009 the global financial crisis hits Finland with a GDP decline of -8.5% and the number of monetary financial institutions decreases from 360 in 2008 to 298 in 2013. (Source: ECB 2014) In 2008-13 3 banks went bankrupt and one was liquidated and the 72 were merged. Thus we can talk about a new merger wave due to the global financial crisis.

The data used in this study is based on several sources: we have used bookkeeping data, interviews with bank managers and surveys among bank managers. One of the researchers was also a bank manager, who was able to follow the process from within the banking sector. He kept a daily diary of what happened concerning bank management during the years of bank decline. Thus we have used a triangular research method in order to come up with our observations.

Figure 01: Number of bank mergers and acquisitions in Finland 1990-2013.

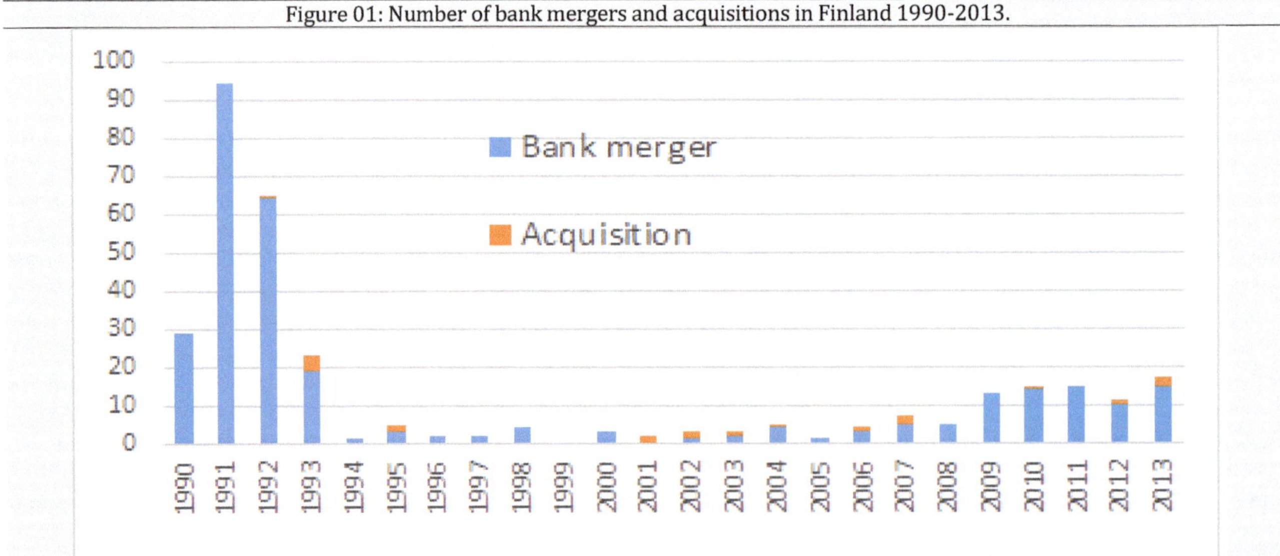

4.0 Remarks concerning mergers as a recovery recipe

The mergers during the period 1990-2013 are particularly due to crises. We can distinguish two merger waves from the data. One emerging from the great Finnish depression 1991-95 and focusing mainly around the savings banks group, and another merger wave relating to the global financial crisis starting from 2008. Thus both merger waves can be related to external economic crisis. In general bank crises can be divided into internally and externally generated crises. We find that particularly in the case of the savings banks mergers 1990-1992 the combination of negative externally and internally produced causes, were devastating. Bad bank management and bad times in combination with bad policies by the authorities created a merger boom never seen before.

The Finnish banking industry is shrinking during the period 1990-2000 and reporting an aggregated net loss of 39.7 Billion marks or about 6% of total assets (Source: Statistics Finland, 1990-2001). Solttila and Vihriälä (1994) find that it is the fast growth of the bank lending in the years before the crisis that can explain this negative impact on the performance of the banking industry. The faster the growth was in the late 1980s, the higher was the rate of non-performing assets.

4.01 The case of the mergers in the savings banks group

At the beginning of the 1990s, the merger process is particularly focused around the savings banks, which in 1990 was the largest banking group in Finland. During 1990-2 138 savings banks will merge merger. A growth and merger process in the Skopbank Group had been revitalized in the 1980s, and usually when a savings bank was facing financial difficulties it was merged into a larger savings bank. However, in the early 1990s the largest savings banks were facing severe financial distress. Thereby the picture had to change. The small profitable savings banks did not have sufficient resources to bail out the often badly run larger savings banks.

On top of this the Skopbank, which was the central bank for the savings banks, started to fail. It was owned and controlled by the savings banks through the Skopbank K share (91.7% of the votes), while Skopbank A shares were listed on the Helsinki Stock Exchange. However, on the 19th of September 1991 the Bank of Finland decided to take control over Skopbank, due to an evident possibility of a failure. This was done through an external equity input by Scopulus (i.e. the Bank of Finland), which implied that the control of Skopbank was in the hands of the authorities.

The "vitalization" of the merger process among the savings banks proved to misfire. During the latter parts of the 1980s, the thought was to create 40 larger regional savings banks. However, the result turned out to be a sense of mistrust in the Skopbank group. During the first part of the 1980s, the Savings bank group was already the largest banking group. However, the savings banks were in some circles regarded as rural and slow-moving, while Skopbank, on the other hand, was seen as fairly small commercial banks, since the corporate banking was concentrated around the two big commercial banks; UBF and KOP. In 1985 a new aggressive strategy was launched, mainly by Skopbank, with the ambition that the Skopbank group should be the leading bank in all fields of the Finnish credit market: the best bank group on the real-estate market, equity market, corporate banking etc. Kjellman (1997) finds that this high ambition is, according to the CEOs of the banks that have survived, more of a contributing factor towards the crisis than what the CEOs of the failed banks argue. This finding may be explained by the fact that the banks that survived in general were more critical towards the growth-merger strategy supported by Skopbank and the Finnish Savings Banks Association.

In the beginning of 1992, the embryo to the Savings Bank of Finland (SBF) had been formed, and in June 1992 the Government Guarantee Fund (GGF) decided to support the merger of the savings banks into a new bank (SBF), which would be controlled by the government. An extensive cost reduction plan was launched and by October 1993 a quarter of the staff had been laid off, and 160 branches had been closed. However, on the 22nd of October, 1993 the Finnish Government, on the recommendation of the Government Guarantee Fund, decided to sell the sound parts of SBF in equal parts to the four major bank groups in Finland, i.e. the Okobank Group, the state owned Postipankki, UBF and KOP. The non-performing assets of the SBF were transferred to the government owned asset holding company, Arsenal Ltd. The four buying banks were also given the option to transfer additional problem credits to Arsenal Ltd. Thereby, the government carried the entire credit risk. Kjellman (1997) noticed that this arrangement was, according to 126 savings banks managers, an important factor behind the problems.

When we discussed with bank managers of savings banks we notice an evident sense that the choice to merge was a mistake. And many CEOs point to the fact that there would have been many more banks and a more stable banking industry in Finland today if they only had not merged. Another interesting fact is that the CEOs in many cases are blaming themselves for the mistakes that were made. To sum up, the mergers in the savings banks group did not prove to be a recovery recipe from the crisis. The results instead point towards a big failure and massive value destruction. Only 40 relatively small and sound savings banks survived.

4.02 The case of Nordea

The case of the merger of the two largest Finnish banks Kansallis-Osake-Pankki (KOP) and Unitas (i.e. Union Bank of Finland, UBF) can be seen as a result of the banking crisis. Both the commercial banks that were of about the same size had been showing highly negative results during the last four years before the merger decision. The financial situation in both banks was therefore strained. The Finnish government had conducted a capital injection into the banking system in 1992 and was thereby the largest single owner in both banks. However, most bankers argued that KOP, in particular, was facing evident financial distress. KOP had shown a loss of 1.8 Billion marks in 1994 and no improvements were expected for 1995. On the 14th of February the merger treaty was signed and on the 2nd of June, 1995 Merita Bank was officially starting its operations.

The arguments: put forward by the CEO of Unitas (and later Merita) Vesa Vainio (1995) in favor of the merger was in brief: 1) that the increased global competition had created a merger pressure, 2) that the cost cuts were potentially very significant, and 3) that the new Merita Bank would be able to create positive synergy effects. Similar arguments were put forward by the CEO of KOP. Occasionally, arguments to create a large and strong Finnish bank were used. However, the real reason behind the merger was most likely the poor results during the years before the merger. Both banks were struggling and additional cost cutting was to be expected.

The outcome of the Merita merger was that the cost cutting process was further accentuated. The plan was to decrease the staff by one-third. The staff, which was about 18,100 before the merger, was planned to be 12,100 by 1997. During the merger year 1995, the staff was reduced by 3,478 work years, and by the end of 1997, there were 10,950 employed. The number of branch offices was planned to be reduced from 775 to 500. However, even this goal was exceeded. By 1997 only 434 branch offices remained. The reduction would be further accentuated during 1998 due to the merger with the Swedish bank, Nordbanken. However, significant cost cutting was made and the cost cutting goals were even exceeded. The Merita merger can thereby be seen as a merger where the bank managers are using the merger to rationalize the banks' activities. In fact, the other megamerger of the early 1990s, i.e. SBF, was also most efficient in cutting staff and activities. However, the paradox is that the mergers will, in the short run, increase costs.

However, the largest merger is still to come. In 1997 it was called the "largest" cross border merger between two equal banks, i.e. the merger between the Finnish Merita Bank and the Swedish Nordbanken. A new era of Nordic banking is starting to accelerate. Both Merita and Nordbanken had identified the Nordic countries and the Baltic Sea area as their home market before the merger. And they were, like many other Nordic banks, looking for opportunities in neighboring countries. In Finland, the Swedish bank Handelsbanken had already opened several branch offices and bought the sound parts of Skopbank, which was put into liquidation.

The argument put forward in favor of the MeritaNordbanken merger was the need to create a large Nordic bank that could compete with the large banks in the world. Furthermore, the CEO of Nordbanken, Hans Dahlborg, stressed the creation of shareholder value, a new financial situation and a long term perspective. He also mentioned the opportunity to use "best practice" when rationalizing the new bank. When cutting costs, the best parts of both banks would be used. CEO Vesa Vainio of Merita also mentioned the fact that the Finnish bank would gain a strong foothold in Sweden. Now several years after the merger we can see that the Finnish part Merita has been the smaller of the two merging partners, e.g. the headquarters that was initially put in Helsinki, Finland has been moved to Stockholm, Sweden. Thereby, one could argue that about half of the Finnish banking industry is highly dependent on the decisions made in Stockholm, Sweden. MeritaNordbanken has, during the year 2000, bought a Norwegian bank Kreditkassen, and decided to merge with a large Danish bank, Unidanmark 1998, which gave the Danish owners 30% ownership in the Bank. Thus, further eroding the Finnish influence in the bank. In 2000 the Norwegian Christiania Bank og Kreditkasse was merged into the bank. And in 2001 the Swedish Postgirot Bank was acquired and the name changed to Nordea (cf Söderberg and Vaara, 2003). We can only speculate on the real reasons behind the MeritaNordbanken merger. However, it seems most likely that some of the managers – who were not real financial stakeholders (only owning a few shares) – were dreaming about building a Nordic bank empire. To sum up the merger process producing Nordea can be seen as a successful recovery strategy.

4.03 The rest of the merging banks in the first merger wave

After five years of negative results in the banking sector (1991-1995) the concentration rate in the Finnish banking industry had increased. Less than one fourth of the savings banks survived, the two largest commercial banks merged and the cooperative banks were drawn closer into the Okobank cooperation. The consolidation activities after the crisis years also appear to have been driven by the economic depression. Good examples of this is the creation of Leonia 1998 from government owned financial institutions, as well as the Sampo-Leonia merger 2000. The effect of the banking crisis is that even 9 years after the banking crisis had started the government is not willing to put more money into the banking system. Instead the state owned Leonia bank was merged with an insurance company Sampo.

One of the most genius banking events in the Finnish history occurs in 1997 when most of cooperative banks decided to consolidate their balance sheets. This activity is not considered a merger because the independent cooperative banks still have their own statutes. In 1997 the Okobank Group consolidation concerned 298 independent cooperative banks. Of these banks 43 solid and profitable banks decided to leave the group and form a new bank group. It is clear the consolidation process was driven by bad results inside the consolidating institutions. In general, the best run cooperative banks opted to leave, while the large cooperative banks that had depleted their financial resources during the hard years, did not have the choice to be able to leave. Old obligations and a lack of funds made it close to impossible to continue with independent banking for most of the cooperative banks. To sum up a loose form of merger like the cooperative consolidation, which allows to banks to remain independent however, calculate their solvency on a group level, seems to be a good recovery recipe.

Kjellman and Nordman (2000) analyzed Finnish bank mergers and acquisitions from 1990 to 1995. During these years 207 bank mergers occurred (138 Savings banks, 67 cooperative banks and 2 commercial banks) creating 60 "new" banks. The results of these mergers were analyzed during the time period two years after and before the mergers. The findings indicate that the Finnish bank mergers 1990-1995 are not reducing but increasing costs; after the merger the operating costs were increasing (excluding the interest rate cost). The potential explanation for the increased cost after the merger is that there are costs associated with merger activities, e.g. laying off personnel is often initially costing (compensation for leaving, early retirement plans etc.), harmonizing the banking cultures, making computer systems compatible, and increased shown credit losses. The findings also indicate that the credit losses are significantly higher the year after the merger, than 2 years before the merger occurs.

4.04 The global financial crises triggered a new bank merger wave 2008-13

The current merger wave during (2008-2013) consists of 72 bank mergers, and more is on the way. The reasons behind these bank mergers relate to the economic downturn and increased global connectivity. The Finnish GDP shrank in 2009, 2012, 2013 and most likely in 2014, while the European Central Bank pushed the market interest levels down to record low levels. Thereby, affecting the Finnish banking market and created a new wave of mergers. While we interviewed CEOs of local banks we noticed that even the bankruptcy of Lehman Brothers carried its wings to the most rural parts of Finland. Many banks had owned commercial papers issued by Lehman Brothers and lost money. However, the "spiritual" effect steaming from the global financial crisis on the bank CEOs was even greater. A spirit of depression and caution about the future could be observed among the bank managers. We found that mergers have been used by the bank managers as a defensive weapon. The merging bank managers seem to have become unsure about their own capabilities and their banks future, and opted to merge. Many small bankers seem to have become afraid of the work load that the new European banking regulation will cause. The increased regulation and control of the banks require more work and it increases the bank costs.

5.0 A model of bank decline and bank merges

We have drawn on the work of Collins (2009) and Weitzel and Jonsson (1989) and adapted their models to decline in banking. We argue that there are six stages in the decline process of banks. The first pre-stage of bank decline is in fact a little contradictory, because we found a period of rapid growth before the decline phase starts. Growth seems to breed the seeds of decline in the financial industry. This growth period may also include bank mergers. However, let us begin by noticing that growth mergers are different from decline mergers. There are different dynamics and motives in growth and in decline. During a growth stage of the banking market many banks are looking for opportunities to expand. Then the banks may be buying market shares through merges and acquisitions, while the bank mergers during a decline period may be more focused around survival of the bank.

In brief the model can by summarized as follows. In the initial pre-decline stage growth seems to breed the seeds of decline. In the first real decline stage the bank management becomes blinded by previous success. In the second decline stage there is inaction and denial of risk. In the third stage the crisis is escalating and becomes visible also to the Authorities. If decline escalates further into the fourth stage merges are commonly seen as the natural way out. In the fifth and final decline stage the banks are failing.

Pre-stage: The Growth stage

Growth seems to breed decline in banking. Before the decline stages all major banking crises have been triggered by a growth phrase in the financial industry. This growth may steam from different sources e.g. deregulation, general indebtedness and creation of a "shadow banking" market. We find that a few years of more than normal growth seems to breed the way towards decline. In particular if the bankers start to talk about a new way of conducting banking to gain more market share. Then the alarm bells should be ringing. The managerial implication in this stage is that bank growth will cause the banks risk exposure to increase. Thus, one should be cautious to expand to fast into potentially unknown territories and customer groups. Based on our evidence, success breeds failure. As one of our sources said about the spirit in Skopbank: "We're so great, so just let us just agree on one thing and that is to never be poor again". The undisciplined pursuit of more scale, more growth, more of whatever those in power see as "success" leads right to the following stage.

Figure 02: Decline in a bank. The real performance of the bank is usually first improving and after that gradually deterring. The figure is based on Weitzel and Jonsson (1989) and Collins (2009), however adapted to suit the financial sector.

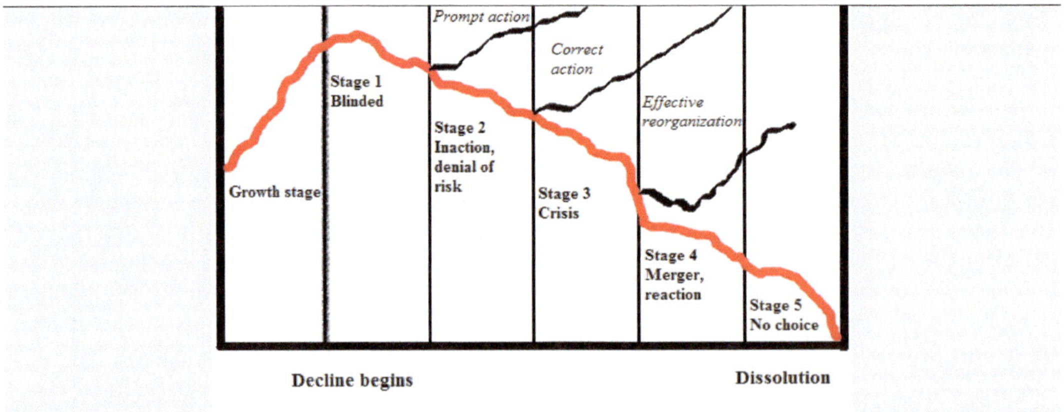

Stage 1: The blinded stage
Great banks can become insulated by success; accumulated momentum can carry an enterprise forward for a while, even if its bankers make poor decisions. Military discipline with arrogant leaders is a blinding cocktail. This was typical in the case of Skopbank, which had experienced a strong growth case during the 1980s. Success made the management of both Skokbank and KOP arrogant and too brave. Good examples of the arrogance and complancement can be found in Tainio et al (2002). The first mistake was that the Board of Skopbank had delegated the power to young managers. The initial success of the young management breaded the failure of Skopbank. They were talking about a new type of banking. And one lesson to be learned is that when that is happening, things may start to go wrong. Stage 1 usually kicks in when people become arrogant, regarding success virtually as an entitlement, and they lose sight of the true underlying factors that created success in the first place. The casino economy of the late 1980s blinded most of the larger banks in Finland. Luck and chance play a role in many successful outcomes. Many bank managers failed to acknowledge the role luck may had played in their success and thereby overestimated their own merit and capabilities.

Many CEOs just does not seem to see the evident. If the times are good and the customers are borrowing too much, it will lead to indebtedness and problems. It is not so hard to see that too rapid bank growth may cause future problems. Nor is it hard to see that derivative contracts and sophisticated financial products may cause banks to go under. It is not only the oldest and respected British bank, Barings banks that have dissolved due to derivative contracts. In Finland the failure of Helsingin Osakepankki (currency option speculation 1985) and the state owned Postipankki (a swap loss 1995 in the USA) are due to miscalculated speculations. You just might find yourself surprised and unprepared when you wake up to discover your vulnerabilities too late.

The managerial implication in this blinded stage is that bank growth has caused the banks risk exposure to increase. At this stage the previous growth strategy of the bank should be questioned and reevaluated. Very few organizations can grow forever.

Stage 2: Denial of risk and inaction to maintain or get needed own capital
Banks in Stage 2 stray from the disciplined creativity that led them to greatness in the first place, making undisciplined leaps into areas where they cannot be great, often do to the simple fact that they have very little experience from the new areas. A good example of this is the internationalization of the Finnish commercial bank in the late 1980s. The banks expanded to UK, Luxemburg and the USA and tried to create new business opportunities. The problem was in these countries the good customers were already taken, and expansion into unknown areas was very risky. Virtually no actions were made to maintain a sufficient level of own capital, nor to get rid of bad customers nor reducing the risk exposure. When we look at the savings banks and Skopbank, we find many examples of denial of risks. When a bank grows beyond its core business it has set itself up for potential problems. Those in power start to blame external factors for setbacks rather than accept responsibility. Examples of bank manager behavior in this stage could be meltdown of the bank's team spirit and internal fighting, which keeps the managers busy. The vigorous, fact-based dialogue that characterizes high-performance teams dwindles or disappears altogether. Taking action inconsistent with your core values is common and increasing the risks.

The managerial implication of this stage is that the bank is now in decline and prompt actions are needed to turn the development around. A natural strategy is to first identify and examine the risk exposures and then deal with them. Inaction and denial of risk exposures will lead to a severe crisis situation for the bank. The inaction to not see this and react will gradually lead the bank towards stage 3.

Stage 3: Crisis
As banks move into the crisis stage, internal warning signs begin to mount. As Collins (2009) noted external results may remain strong enough to "explain away" disturbing data or to suggest that the difficulties are "temporary" or

"cyclic" or "not that bad," and "nothing is fundamentally wrong." At this stage intentional downsizing is a hard but typical option for the potential turnaround banks. "In reality assets can be sold off at a bargain price or the bank's real estate holdings can be "written upwards" in order to increase the shown own funds." Kangas (2006) noted that not even at this stage some managers gasp the danger. In fact it is sometimes hard to see hidden problems like real value losses in assets, derivative exposures and potential counterpart problems. Real performance results may either be hidden in off balance transactions or not reported properly in the balance sheets. The bank managers start to blame external factors for setbacks rather than dealing with the problems at hand. The vigorous, fact-based dialogue that characterizes high-performance teams dwindles or disappears altogether.

At this stage also the Authorities and politicians starts to realize that they may be facing a banking crisis and potential costs for the public sector. Banks may need to be rescued by the government. The stability of the entire economy may be at stake and the politicians feel a need to act. In Finland the typical solution presented by the Authorities was to urge the crisis banks to merge both in the 1990s and after 2008.

The managerial implication in the crisis stage is to find turnaround solutions for the bank. Potential solutions are cost cuts, increase capital inflow, reorganization, increase solvency, customer driven innovations & services, mergers and in special cases even acquisitions. As noticed by Tourish and Harigie (2012) many bank managers became influenced by the behavior of "significant" others, and these bankers found themselves to become passive observers of events. A real danger is inaction in combination with starting to imitate and believe in big and loud bank players. When the bank is in the crisis stage, it is important not to rely on others to solve your problems, but instead try to solve them yourself. Good bank management at least includes the element of being able to solve your own problems, while an imitating, passive and on others relying strategy can be linked to bad bank management.

Stage 4: Bank mergers as a recovery recipe

The potential of a disaster is visible to all informed in the bank. The critical question is: what can the CEO and the boards do? A quick salvation in the form of e.g. a merger may seem appealing? In Finland bank merges were the most common crisis response to a severe crisis situation. When the pressure from the Authorities, bank owners and depositors are increasing our findings indicate that a bank merger was considered an appealing solution. If the bank merged with another bank the unpleasant reconstruction work could be moved over to another part. Thereby the responsibility of the bank managers and board could be shifted away.

We found that bank managers at this point in reality may have lost a lot of their room to maneuver. In fact further cost cutting may not be enough, and during a decline phase it usually is harder to receive additional funding in order to increase the solvency level. This in most cases leaves the bank manager with no other real option than to merge or declare bankruptcy. Kangas (2006) argues that when the bank managers' room to maneuver decreases and decreases, then finally the mental process will lead to a situation that the bank manager feels like he has no room to maneuver. We argue that if the bank managers found themselves cornered with the options to leave the bank, declare bankruptcy or try to find a buyer, or merge with another financial institution, then the option would be to merge. Faced with two real options, i.e. to merge or to declare bankruptcy, the bankers chose to merge. Thereby, we argue that this no-way out argument may be used to explain most of the Finnish bank mergers from 1990 to 1997 and 2008-13. The "satisfactory" solution for the latent financial problems was by many CEOs seen to be, to merge. Thereby the profitability problem could be dealt with in an acceptable way. The required shake-up of the bank did not call for a declaration of mistakes made by the CEO. The layoffs could be blamed on the merger, and the CEO could continue as a bank manager. An interesting observation that we make is that in Finland "all" banks involved in a merger process seem to have potential solvency problems.

The managerial implication for this stage is that a merger can be a potential crisis response, however, it most likely also means the end of the bank. However, let us recall that a bank manager cannot decide about a bank merger alone, also the owners and the authorities must agree to the deal.

Stage 5: No choice, belly up,..., or merge?

In the fifth stage the bank managers have realized that the bank cannot be saved by the bank itself, but the preferred and often only way out is to rely on the authorities. To start playing the game for receiving help from the central bank or the tax payers is on. The accumulated setbacks and expensive false starts erode financial strength and individual spirit to such an extent that a banker abandons all hope of building a future. In some cases the bank's leader just sells out like in the case of the mergers of the state owned financial intuitions creating the state owned Leonia bank; and in the most extreme cases the bank simply goes belly up, like in the case of Skopbank or the two Icelandic banks' Finnish branches 2008. All in all however, only 3 small banks goes bank bankrupt 1990-2013. All the other declining banks were either merged or taken over by the authorities. In stage banks may be forced by the Authorities to merge like in the case of the Savings Bank in Finland. Thus, the bank merges in this dissolving crisis stage can be seen as no other way out solutions.

When we interviewed bank CEOs we became convinced that the basic decline model as given in figure 2 gave a good description of what had happened. However, there was one problem. The different roles of the bank manager in pursuit of turnaround and the personal qualities of the CEO are not stressed sufficiently. We became convinced that a model which would explain bank consolidation should stress the activities of the bank CEOs. Some CEOs were able to create opportunities for turnaround, while other CEOs were not capable of corrective actions during the decline process.

We also have to recall that the bank managers are socially influenced individuals. They live in their current life space, and have experienced the past as well as have aspirations for the future of themselves and the bank. These aspirations will be one factor among many other potential factors that will explain how the bank manager will lead his bank in decline. If the bank has got to a truly critical stage then in reality the bank manager only has got two real potential choices: To merge or declare failure. Most bank managers will opt for a merger process instead of admitting that, they believe, that the banks operations cannot continue.

Finally, it can be noticed that the consolidation activities inside the EU and the USA show no sign of stopping. Since the large seem to get larger, we can most likely expect more mergers and acquisitions in the future. However, let us recall that bank mergers often fail e.g. the four largest Finnish banks – UBF, KOP, Postipankki and Skopbank - that existed in1990 today only exists in the history books.

6.0 Conclusion and policy implications

We have created a model concerning bank decline. In banking we argue that decline cannot be understood without looking at growth before decline. Based on 309 bank mergers during 1990 to 2013, we found that bank managers in many cases gradually lost their confidence concerning their capability of successfully running their banks, therefor opting for a bank merger. The reasons behind merges seem to be time and context dependent. In our model of bank decline we see the role of the bank manager as crucial. The major reasons behind the Finnish bank merger waves seem to be bad bank management and real economic crisis, which was caused by the Finnish depression of the 1990s as well as the global financial crisis starting in 2008.

After a bank growth phase, some banker became blinded and led their banks into a crisis phase. Faced with two perceived options, i.e. to merge or to declare "bankruptcy", the bankers often chose to merge. Thereby, we argue that this no-way out argument may be used to explain most of the Finnish bank mergers from 1990 to 2000 and 2008-13. The "satisfactory" solution for the latent financial problems was by many CEOs seen to be, to merge. Thereby the profitability problem could be dealt with in an acceptable way. The required shake-up of the bank did not call for a declaration of mistakes made by the CEO. The layoffs could be blamed on the merger, and the CEO could continue as a bank manager. The board members were given an excuse for retirement, or handed the argument that they were doing something about the profitability problem. The personnel that were not laid-off were promised a future in the new banking organization and thereby some of their lost trust could be regained. The customers were promised a larger (however leaner) bank that certainly offered increased security and improved service capability. In fact the choice to enter into a merger seems to be appealing at least partly to all of the involved stakeholders.

Why do so many bank mergers fail to generate recovery? During the period 1990-2000 the mergers were particularly due to the banking crisis. In fact, the banking industry is, during this period, is reporting a net loss. We are still today feeling the effects of the banking crisis of the 1990s. However, we also find that managerial incentives and empire building seem to have been a triggering factor behind some mergers. We cannot see that shareholder value creation would have been the main motivating force behind the mergers of the 1990s, even if the argument has been used by e.g. Nordea. Today it seems like many bankers seem to have become afraid of the work load that the new European banking regulation will cause. The increased regulation and control of the banks requires more work and increases the bank costs, thus this fair is creating more mergers and bigger banks.

We found that in almost all of the cases of merging banks, the bank managers had started to lose their confidence in being able to maintain the CEO position or the bank as independent unit. Even if the absolute bulk of the bank mergers in the 1990s and from 2008 and forwards in Finland cannot be characterized as successful mergers, it is still not wise to condemn a merger strategy. Mergers have been useful as a mean for continuation of banking activity. However, the Finnish evidence points to the fact that banks that don't merge will perform better than banks that are involved in merger processes.

One policy conclusion is that we need to be alert when the banks become strongly growth-driven. The lesson for bankers, owners, depositors and Authorities is that rapid growth in banking seems to breed failure. And this we should remember. Another policy implication is that bank mergers are not a universal panacea for solving decline problems. When the mergers occur it is often too late.

References

Amihud Y., Miller G., 1998. Bank mergers & acquisitions. Kluwer Academic Publisher, Dordrecht. http://dx.doi.org/10.1007/978-1-4757-2799-9

Berger A.L., Demsetz R.S., Strahan, P.E., 1999. The consolidation of the financial service industry: Causes, consequences, and implications for the future. Journal of Banking and Finance, 23(2):135-194. http://dx.doi.org/10.1016/S0378-4266(98)00125-3

Collins, J., 2009. How the mighty fall and why some companies never give in. New York, USA. Harper Collins Publishers Inc.

European Central Bank (2014) Statistical data warehouse http://sdw.ecb.int/browseChart.do?REF_AREA=152&type=&MFI_LIST=102&node=4586742&q=&sfl2=4&SERIES_KEY=187.MFI.M.FI.102.T.1&DATASET=0&sfl3=4&trans=AF Accessed 16.3.2014

Fisher, I.,1933. The debt-deflation theory of great depressions, Econometrica, October, 337-357. http://dx.doi.org/10.2307/1907327

Greenhalgh L., 1983. Organizational decline, In Samule B. Bachanach (ed.) Research in the sociology of organizations, Greenwich, CT: JAI Press, 2:231-278.

Hadlock C.J., Houston J.F., Ryngaert M., 1999. The role of managerial incentives in bank acquisitions. Journal of Banking and Finance, 23(2-4), 221-249. http://dx.doi.org/10.1016/S0378-4266(98)00092-2Hiilamo H., 1995. SKOP lyhyt historia, WSOY, Juva.

Kangas T., 2006. Suomen pankkikriisin alueellinen ulottuvuus: Esseitä paikallisista toimijoista ja toteuttajista. PhD Thesis. Helsinki School of Economics, Acta Universitatis Oeconomicae Helsingiensis, Helsinki.

Kiefer M. V., 2014. Bank failures and mergers in Turkey: 1992-2014. International Journal of Finance and Banking, 1(3): 45-64.

Kjellman A., 1996. What can we learn from the Finnish banking crisis? The case of the failures in the savings bank sector, Meddelanden från Ekonomisk-Statsvetenskapliga Fakulteten vid Åbo Akademi A:420, Turku.

Kjellman A., 1997. Essays on performance and financing decisions during the 1990s recession in Finland. PhD Thesis. Åbo Akademi University Press, Turku.

Kjellman A., Nordman M., 2000. Strategies behind and effects of bank mergers in Finland, Meddelanden från Ekonomisk-statsvetenskapliga Fakulteten vid Åbo Akademi, A:517.

Lenz R., 1981. Determinants of organizational performance: An interdisciplinary review, Strategic Management Journal, 2(2): 131-154. http://dx.doi.org/10.1002/smj.4250020204

McKinley W., Latham S., Braun M., 2014. Organizational decline and innovation: Turnarounds and downward spirals, Academy of Management Review, 39(1): 86-110. http://dx.doi.org/10.5465/amr.2011.0356Pietilä, A-P., 1995. Pankkikirja, Helsinki, Art House.

Piloff S.J., Satomero A.M., 1997. The value effect of bank mergers and acquisitions. Published in Amihud, Y. and Miller G., eds. 1997. Bank Mergers & Acquisitions. Dordrecht, Kluwer Academic Publisher.

Rhoades S.A., 1999. The efficiency effects of bank mergers: An overview of case studies of nine mergers. Journal of Banking and Finance, 22(2-4):273-291.

Saari M., 1992. Minä Christopher Wegelius. Jyväskylä, Gummerus.

Santoso T. R., Hartono M., Agung Prabowo M., Riyanto G., Eferin S., Tjiamudjaja Y., 2014. The arena of multiinterest, governance and fraud – a critical review of BC bailout. International Journal of Finance and Banking, 1(2):25-35.

Solttila, H., Vihriälä, V., 1994. Finnish banks' problem assets: Result of unfortunate asset structure or too rapid growth, Bank of Finland Discussion Papers 23/94.

Söderberg, A-M.,Vaara, E., 2003 (Eds.). Merging across borders. People, cultures and politics. Copenhagen Business School Press. Copenhagen.

Tainio, R., Korhonen P.J., Santalainen, T.J., 1991. In search of explanation for bank performance - Some Finnish data, Organization Studies, 12(3): 425-450. http://dx.doi.org/10.1177/017084069101200305

Tainio R., Santalainen T., Sarvikivi K., 1991. Organizational changes in a bank group: The merger process and its generative mechanisms, Scandinavian Journal of Management, 7(3): 191-203. http://dx.doi.org/10.1016/0956-5221(91)90033-W

Tourish D., Hargie O., 2012. Metaphors of failure and the failures of metaphor: A critical study of root metaphors used by bankers in explaining the banking crisis. Organization Studies 33 (8): 1045-1069. http://dx.doi.org/10.1177/0170840612453528

Weitzel W., Jonsson, E., 1989. Decline in organizations: A literature integration and extension. Administrative Science Quarterly, 34:91-109. http://dx.doi.org/10.2307/2392987

Vainio V., 1995. Konkurrensen omvälver bankmarknaden, Unitas 1:3.

Vander Vennet R., 1996. The effects of mergers and acquisitions on the efficiency and profitability of EC credit institutions. Journal of Banking and Finance, 20(9):1531-1558. http://dx.doi.org/10.1016/S0378-4266(96)00014-3

Vihriälä V., 1993. Suomen pankkikriisi - Mitä opimme? The Finnish Economic Journal, 4:581-589.

19

Destined to be defaulted: Local government insolvency and bailout in post-transition Hungary✧

Izabella Barati-Stec [a*]

[a] Central European University, Hungary & Budapest Business School, Hungary
*corresponding author's email address: izabella.barati@gmail.com

HIGHLIGHTS:

1. The paper shows how Hungarian decentralization has unfolded since the early 1990s.
2. Summarizes and gives a critical overview of the current legislative changes.
3. Unveils the systemic risks associated with municipal borrowing in post transition economies.
4. Highlights how inadequate planning can lead to municipal financial distress.

Article History

Keywords:
Local public finance;
Local insolvency;
Municipal bail-out;
Sub-national debt.

ABSTRACT

This paper reviews the waves of democratization and the development of the public administration and public finances in Hungary, with special attention municipalities caused by the changes in sub-national finance regulation since 2010. During the transition yeas, Hungary was very forward looking and the first among CEE countries to end central planning and to introduce market rules into the economy. Everybody expected the decentralization to be a success story. 25 years later, Hungary not only failed to meet the expectations, but also undergone though a situation in 2008 to start a massive recentralization process. This paper puts fiscal decentralization in Hungary in a historical context while critically investigating the findings of recent literatures on decentralization process in Hungary. The critical investigation of past experiences and reform steps of the current government suggest possible reform measures to solve the financial problems of Hungarian municipalities.

1.0 Introduction

In Hungary, as in many other Central and Eastern European (CEE) countries, 1990 was a time of euphoria. With the end of centralized planning, local communities obtained the right to form local self-governments and to make decisions about the community on their own. Although expenditures have been decentralized, revenues have remained fairly centralized, even two decades after the transition to democracy.

In Hungary, the result of this failure to provide adequate fiscal autonomy has been tension and asymmetries among Hungarian municipalities. In order to address these concerns, Hungary has introduced a series of structural and financial reforms to its administrative system since 1990. After 2005, further government reform plans focused on the need for some recentralization instead of broadening fiscal freedom at the local level. Current reforms include creating a new administrative level between the level of the counties and municipalities, moving from a passive form of control over borrowing to an authorization process, and centralizing the provision of services such as education and health care.

✧ This paper was supported by the Hungarian Academic Research Fund.

The second section of this paper describes the Hungarian public administration system and gives an overview of the main laws passed since 1990 concerning municipalities and their effects on municipal finance, describes local borrowing and its regulation in Hungary while in the third section, I evaluate the current changes taking place, and, in the conclusions I make a few suggestions for possible reforms.

2.0 Designing a new system: the Hungarian public administration

In Hungary, three main waves of legislation were passed after 1990. The first created the framework for a decentralized public administration system. The second preceded accession to the European Union and ensured enhanced public accountability. In 2010, Hungary's public administration entered a third phase with the recentralization of certain tasks and finances.[1]

2.01 The levels of administration

In 1990, the Hungarian Parliament guaranteed the independence of municipalities through several laws, among which the most important were the Constitution and Act LXV (1990) on Local Governments. The old Constitution in force before January 2012 listed the rights of local governments and also regulated the organizations and mechanism for the protection of these rights. Act LXV (1990) created a new form of public administration, laid down its operational rules, and regulated the scope and duties of public administration at each level of government.

Hungarian municipalities – which have an average population of 2,600[2] – are smaller than municipalities in most OECD countries. More than half of Hungary's municipalities have a population below 1,000. Although we can find other fragmented systems in countries such as France or Switzerland with its average municipal size of 1800 and 2800 respectively, Hungarian municipalities have greater responsibilities than municipalities of the same size in other OECD countries. This situation raises the question of economies of scale. Many small settlements, although obliged by Act XCV (1990) to provide services such as collecting and treating waste water and garbage, are not able to fulfill such responsibilities or carry out the necessary investments on their own. In older democracies,[3] forced amalgamations have sometimes been used[4] to solve this problem.

In Hungary, the strongest impediment to forced amalgamation is the negative memory of the council system before 1990,[5] when forced cooperation among municipalities deprived small villages of basic services. As a result of this history, voluntary municipal associations were favored by the state subsidy system in the early 1990s. The creation of notary districts[6] and municipal associations[7] was another way to counter high administration and service delivery costs.

There are two main differences between notary districts and municipal associations. First, notary districts are parts of the state administration system and serve administrative tasks, while associations are specifically created to deliver public services. Second, creating notary districts is obligatory under the aforementioned conditions, whereas creating associations is voluntary.[8]

The national administration also created "micro-regions" and although the geographical boundaries of these in many cases corresponded with those of the associations, they were not the same. The associations had real service functions, while micro-regions were created only for statistical reasons, that is, after accession to the EU, Hungary needed a territorial system that corresponded to the EU's regional policies – a level of organization that could be the recipient of EU regional grants.[9]

---

1. For more on this question, see Krugman (2011) and Scheppele (2011).

2. Without Budapest, the capital city, the average population is 2560. If Budapest is included, this number is 3,100 (based on KSH (Central Statistical Office) data, 2013)

3. Such as Denmark, Sweden, the Netherlands, Germany, or Canada.

4. As pointed out by Swianiewicz, (2010), amalgamations, of course, also have negative effects, such as distancing citizens from decision-making bodies, the overuse of some services, and decreases in service quality.

5. Hungary's public administration system before 1990 could be characterized by a vertical integrity and hierarchy of settlements, in which bigger municipalities had greater rights and more political power, and upper tiers of the hierarchy were responsible for lower tiers.

6 A "notary district" in Hungary is a group of municipalities that employs only one person as notary for fulfilling administrative tasks in all of them, thus saving on administrative expenses. These municipalities also offer their public services together. Neighboring municipalities with fewer than 1,000 inhabitants (the number in 2012 rose to 2,000) are required to create notary districts for the purpose of fulfilling their administrative responsibilities. The higher the number of inhabitants within a notary district, the higher the level of central government subsidies. The number of notary districts has risen slowly; there were about 500 of them in 2000 and there are about 700 today.

7 Municipal associations have also been created between the local and the county level. The central government's tool for encouraging municipal associations was not to give them direct subsidies, but rather to threaten them with lower subsidies if they did not form an association. If the number of recipients of a particular service did not reach a level set by the government,[7] the municipality – or association - was not eligible for a subsidy. Municipalities could be members of more than one association for different purposes. According to Hungarian legislation, municipal associations were financed through their members and entitled to state subsidies. They cannot levy taxes, making it difficult for them to issue bonds or borrow from a bank for investments. If a development is financed by an association and a bank loan is needed – which is typically the case – the bank would need to make contracts with each municipality. Given that some associations have more than 30 members, transaction costs were very high.

8 Creating municipal associations also meant that Hungary could have moved from type I multi level governance to type II, according to the MLG classification by Hooghe and Marks (2001).

9 Interestingly, this level used to be a formal government tier under the communist era, but its tasks were taken away in 1990.

The next level of government is the county. Counties are responsible for tasks that must be carried out at a higher level than that of municipalities, although a municipality can take such tasks over if it has the necessary fiscal and management capacity. An example for this could be the maintenance of high schools or art schools. The potential hazard of this practice is that the county is often left with the most expensive tasks to carry out. The revenue-raising capacity of the county is limited, as under Act XCV (1990); a county government cannot levy taxes or collect fees. Having the most expensive tasks to carry out and not being able to raise their own revenues has meant that counties needed to borrow to maintain the level of their services.

Figure 1(a): The council system - before 1990

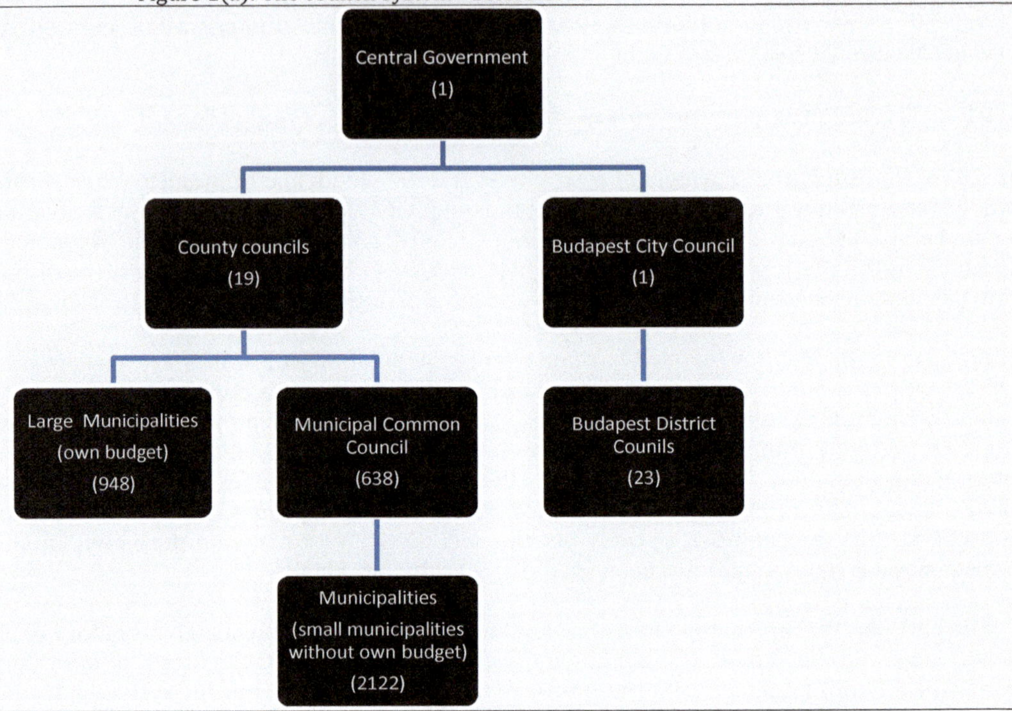

Hungary's territory is divided into seven regions. The circumstances of their creation were similar to those of the micro-regions; that is, the creation of regions was a requirement of the European Union for statistical reasons. The regional territorial development offices were delegated to this level and these offices were also responsible for the approval of EU grants. Figure 1 gives an overview of the Hungarian Territorial System (a) before the transition, (b) between 1990 and 2013 and (c) the most recent situation.

Figure 1(b): The Hungarian territorial system between 1990 and 2013

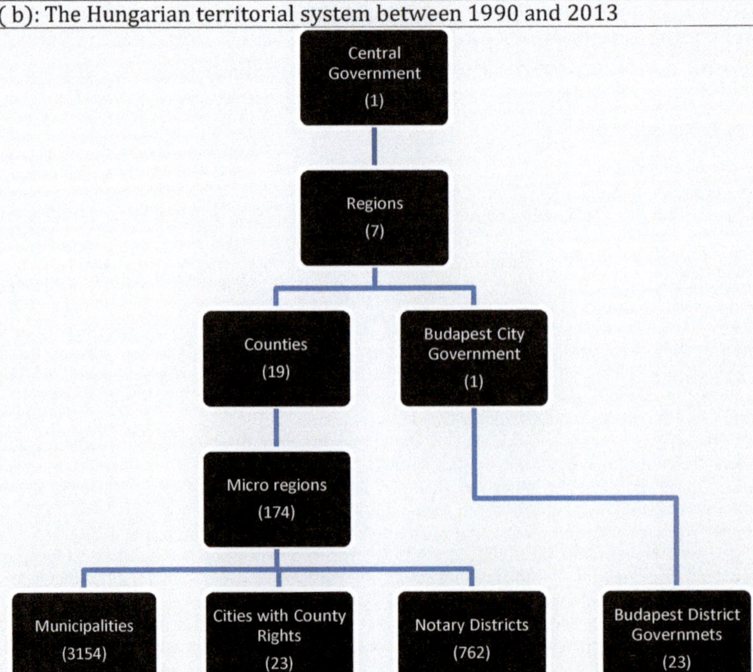

Figure 1(c): The current Hungarian territorial system as a result of the 2013 reform

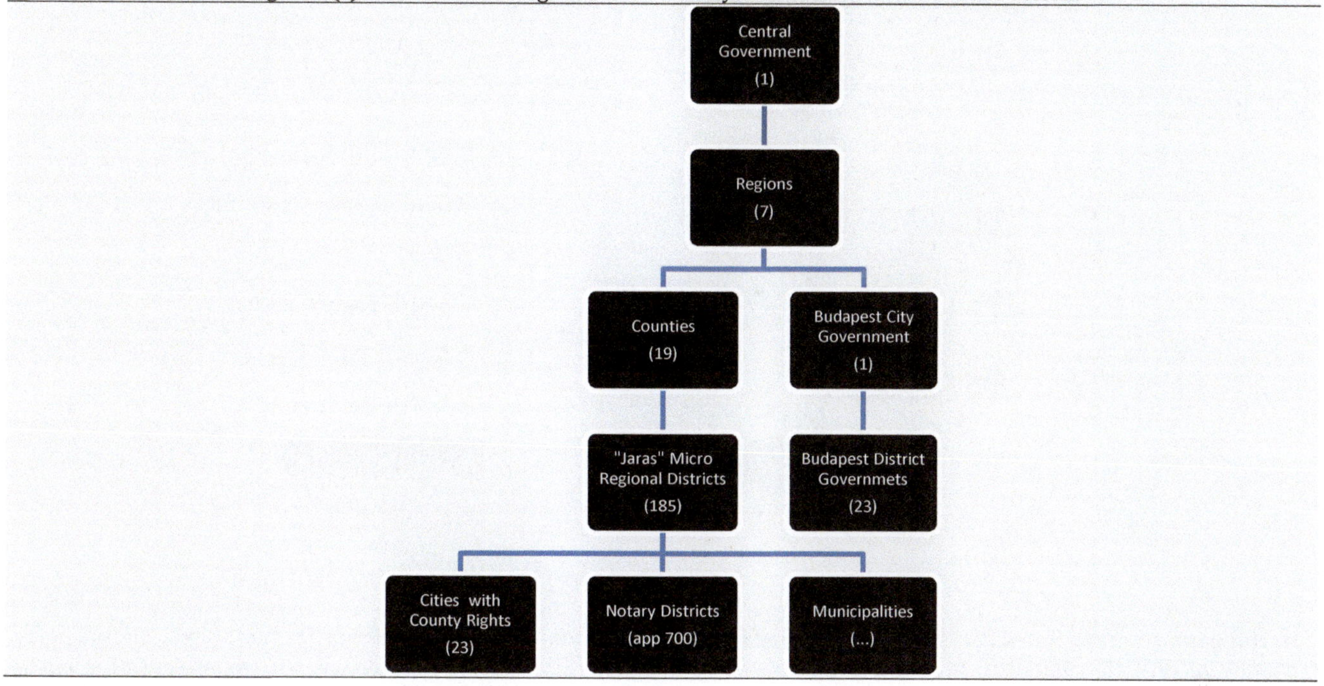

Transfer of property rights in 1990 - A source of asymmetry:
After 1990, municipalities acquired the assets necessary to fulfill services at their level, such as water treatment plants or garbage dumps, as well as buildings for administrative offices and schools. Many of these assets were sold in the early 1990s, as municipalities found it difficult to maintain them. The revenue from privatization was spent partly on other capital investments and partly on operating expenses. Of course, the value of these buildings and land depended on the economic development of the area, so more fortunate municipalities received assets that were much more valuable than those of other municipalities. The result was a gap among their fiscal capacities.

The value of buildings and land a municipality possesses is important for creating public-private partnerships (PPPs). Because those who engage in PPPs and provide foreign direct investments prefer bigger cities and richer areas for their investments (where the level of the available infrastructure is higher), and because the business turnover tax is the most important local tax, richer municipalities tend to fare better than smaller, less wealthy ones. According to the study by Barati-Stec and Hogye (2012) [10] some municipalities have been able to finance large investments such as water and sewage infrastructure out of their operating budgets, because they had large business turnover tax revenues; other municipalities that cannot collect this tax and use it as collateral for loans or spend tax revenues directly on investments must rely on state funds. This situation has further exacerbated the differences in fiscal capacity among municipalities.

[10] The Department of Public Policy at Corvinus University has conducted several surveys among Hungarian municipalities. In this paper, the author refers to two surveys, one done in 2010, the other in 2011. The research in 2010 examined the 100 largest Hungarian municipalities' investment techniques and economic and political expectations. The method used was in-depth interviews with mayors, other political leaders, and managers of the municipalities. In 2011, public policy students at Corvinus University interviewed representatives of 19 municipalities (they approached 24 municipalities, but only 19 responded) in the Budapest region. The purpose of the research was to identify municipal budgeting techniques and economic expectations and to assess municipal views about the current economic situation and legislative process in Central Hungary. These settlements are typically better off than the rest of the country, are most likely to have larger tax base and had substantial investments even during the economic downturn.

Figure 02: The distribution of FDI in Hungary after the transition, 1993

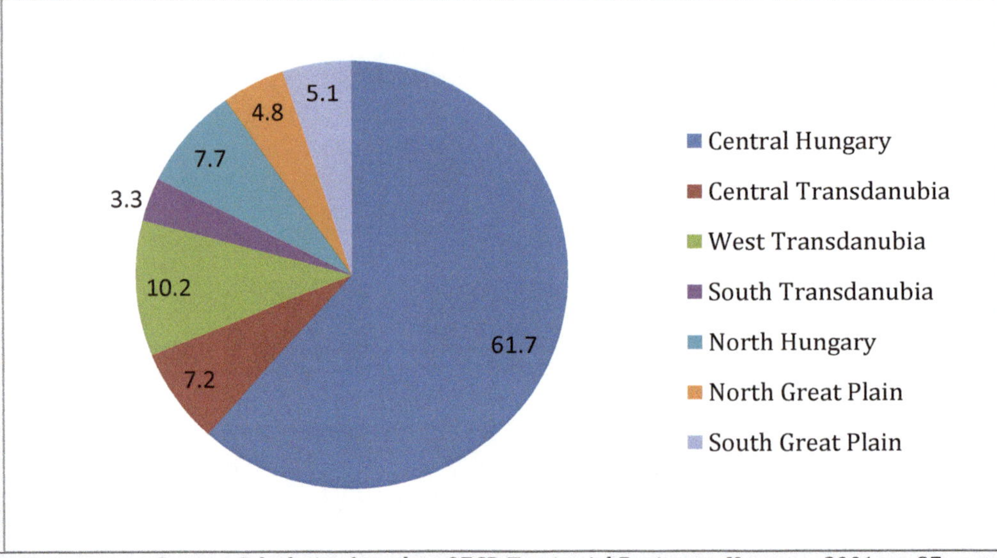

Source: Calculation based on OECD Territorial Reviews – Hungary. 2001. pp 87.

In Hungary, municipalities can sell property (land or buildings) only under two circumstances. First, the property cannot be directly related to fulfilling obligatory local services. Second, the income cannot cover operating costs. Regulations also prohibit municipalities from using strategically important land and buildings as collateral for loans.[11]

Municipalities, however, have found loopholes in these regulations, since it is possible to reclassify municipal property.[12] Consequently, municipalities with operating deficits often reclassify their properties. Another way to get around the regulation is to sell assets through off-budget institutions. This can happen only with the approval of the municipality. Practices like this also raise the question of corruption.[13]

2.02 The composition of Hungarian municipal revenues

Although Hungarian municipalities have financial resources – such as local taxes and fees on services – that are independent from centralized decision making, own-source revenues represent less than one-third of the local budget. According to the local tax law – Act C on local taxes that came into force in 1991 and has been amended by the Parliament almost every year since - , local governments have discretion over levying local taxes and over the tax rate. Act C describes the tax types (the objects and payers of the tax) and the maximum level of tax a municipality can levy. Local decrees on taxation must stipulate (i) who pays the tax, (ii) the basis of the tax, (iii) any exemptions, (iv) the rate of the tax, and (v) the conditions of beginning and ending tax obligations.

As is most EU countries, Hungarian municipalities are obliged to separate their current and capital budgets. A general rule is that current expenses should not be financed from investment income, but in practice this does sometimes happen as municipalities may sell assets through off -budget institutions[14] or, as described later, issue general-purpose bonds and use the income for financing operation[15]. State subsidies and shared taxes may not be used for repaying loans. With creative accounting, however, municipalities can evade these rules. In the same year, they may prove to creditors that they are in a sufficiently good financial situation to borrow for new investments while proving to the central government that they need emergency or "vis major" grants.[16],[17]

---

[11]. Using buildings as collateral was a highly criticized practice of the Hungarian municipal credit market. On the one hand, the value of the asset often surpassed the amount of the loan; on the other hand, using an asset to finance a project to which it is not otherwise related is not economically efficient. The market for buildings and land can also be very volatile.

[12]. For example, buildings belonging to a local school cannot be sold, but if the school is moved into another building, the property becomes saleable.

[13]. In October 2011, Sandor Pinter, Hungary's Minister of Interior Affairs, denied the existence of corruption in Hungary. One month later, the Ministry of Public Affairs and Justice announced that the level of corruption threatens the operation of public administration.

[14]. Off-budget institutions are institutions of the municipality that have a separate budget from that of the municipality. In fact, the budget of these institutions does not appear in the municipal budget, therefore it is very difficult to trace and publicly control their revenue flows and transactions.

[15]. . The assets sold through off- budget institutions are school and office buildings, land, etc. that were originally qualified as non-sellable assets – directly related to the obligatory tasks of the government - , but after reclassification - e.g. moving the institution into another, usually less valuable building - became sellable assets – not directly related to the core functions of the government. At this point the municipality authorizes the off-budget institution with its management, which very often means it will be sold. This can happen if the municipality decides to "rationalize" the service of education and moves two schools into one building. Than one of the original school buildings will go under the management of the off-budget institution -- to be sold over a matter of some time. Municipalities could also become indebted through their off-budget institutions as guarantors of their debts. The amount borrowed by the off budget institutions were only considered as part of the total of municipal loans if they defaulted.

[16]. In Hungary, the Latin term "vis major" is the equivalent of "Force Majeur" in English Common Law. A vis major grant in Hungary is given to a municipality that has become indebted because of reasons outside its control (such as a flood).

2.03 Local taxes in the context of municipal borrowing

Under current legislation in Hungary, the main local taxes are the business turnover tax, the communal tax, the property tax, and the tax on tourism. The shared taxes are the personal income tax (PIT) and the vehicle tax.

The business turnover tax:
The main local tax is the business turnover tax and it constitutes about 10 % of total municipal income. The business turnover tax is levied on the net income of the company, after the costs of services and materials (that is, non-labour inputs) are deducted. The business turnover tax has been widely criticized in Hungary for increasing differences among the different sub-national units and because it is very sensitive to economic cycles: in 2008 local governments relying largely on this kind of tax almost went bankrupt when their biggest taxpayers had to close down.[18] Its volatility - as shown in figure 3 - makes the business turnover tax an unreliable source for example backing investment loans or financing services at the local level. Another criticized feature of the tax relates to its calculation, that is, if this tax covers services (benefit principle, see Ebel and Taliercio (2010)) than not profitable companies should also have pay it[19].

Figure 03: Local taxes as % of own source revenues between 2001- 2013

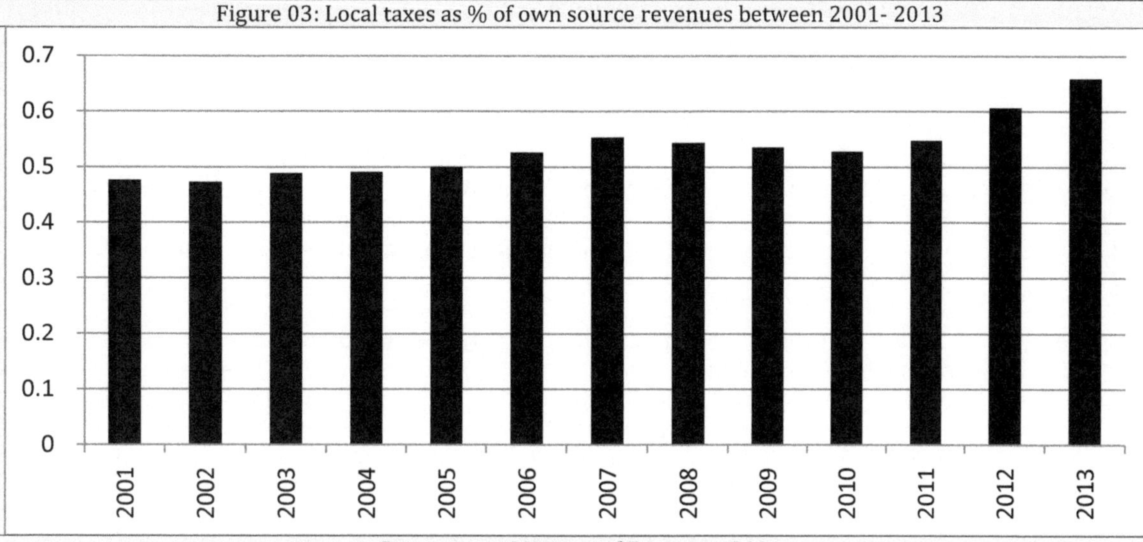

Data source: Ministry of Economy, 2014

Figure 04: Business tax as % total local tax between 2001- 2013

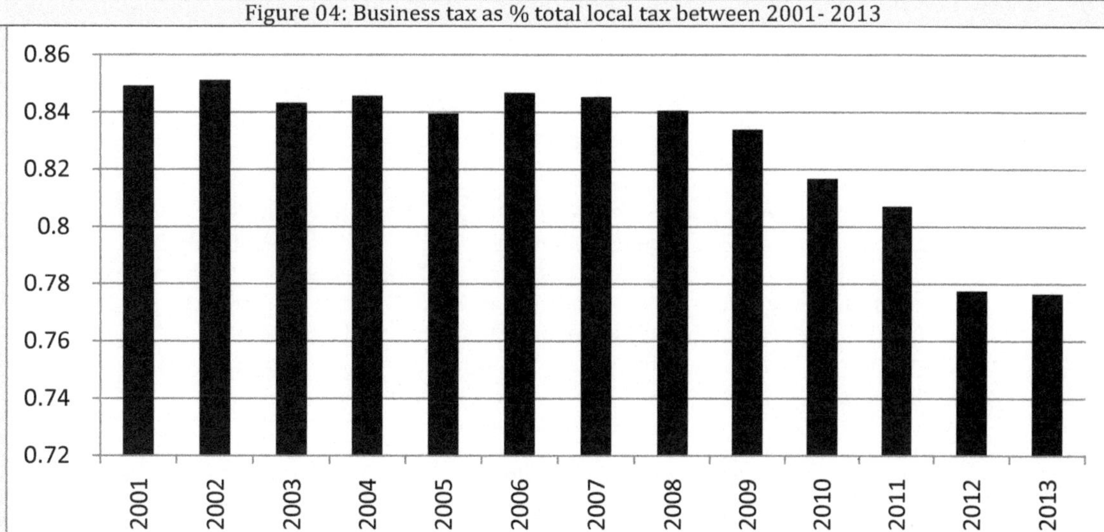

Data source: Ministry of Economy, 2014

[17] Large cities, like Pecs, with very high debt was also eligible for a 'vis major' grant 1.5 billion HUF in 2012. Hódmezővásárhely, a city with a debt of 20 billion Huf also got more than 1,5 billion state grant under different purposes the month before the 2012 interim local elections. Among the smaller municipalities one example is Harkany, a small settlement famous for its thermal bath. When the baths was to be sold by its private owner, the municipality offered more for the it than private bidders did. This transaction – the village had to operate the baths – caused insolvency. Harkany was the biggest winner of vis major grants in 2012 in its county.

[18]. When the Russian market collapsed, some Hungarian municipalities with taxpayer companies producing mainly for the Russian market almost went bankrupt.

[19]. For more about the benefit principle and evaluating local taxes see Ebel and Taliercio (2005). For other possible classification of taxes see Boadway and Kitchen (1999), Slack (2009) and Szalai and Tassonyi (2004).

The maximum rate is 2 percent, but the municipality can set a lower rate or can choose not to levy this tax at all. Since 2010 it has been collected through the central tax authority (Nemzeti Adó- és Vámhivatal, or NAV), but the recipients are local governments. Even with this low rate many settlements are reluctant to levying at the maximum[20], but as the example of Budapest - where the number of tax payers did not decrease compared to its neighbors with a lower tax rate - shows, being afraid of tax competition should not influence decision making, companies value the available infrastructure more than the low rate of tax in the given settlement[21] (benefits principle).

The communal tax:
The Hungarian Communal Tax is a head tax, levied on a per-capita base. It is a typical form of lump-sum tax. Although 60 percent of municipalities have introduced it, its revenue generating capacity and economic impact are not significant. Communal tax income represents only 2 percent of municipal budgets.

Property tax:
The rate of the tax is set by the municipality. Property tax in Hungary in most cases is levied based on the size of, and the geographic area where the property is. The law on local taxes says that municipalities can levy property tax based on market value, at a maximum 3% rate, in reality, many municipalities choose not to levy it value based[22, 23].

Tax on tourism:
This tax is typical in tourist areas[24]. The interesting feature of this tax is that the central government, when calculating normative transfers,[25] takes into account the tax capacity of the municipality, including the tax on tourism in the touristic areas. If this tax is levied and collected, then the amount of the grant is raised with its amount. This provision encourages municipalities to levy this tax to the maximum level. The amount of tax can be calculated based on the number of guest nights (300 huf per night) or based on the rate paid, in which case it is 4%.

Personal income tax:
Personal income tax (PIT) is a centrally collected tax that is partly redistributed to the local level. In 1990, 100 percent of the PIT was redistributed to the municipality from which the revenues originated, but in 2006, only 8 percent went to the originating municipality, and another 20 to 25 percent to other municipalities, while the remaining app. 65-70 percent was kept by the state. In 2011 the remaining 8 percent share of PIT that had stayed at its origin also got turned over to the central government. Employees have a choice of filing their returns themselves or authorizing their employers to file for them.

Vehicle tax:
The vehicle tax was originally levied based on the weight of the vehicle, but in 2007 its calculation was changed. Now it is levied based on the horsepower (or kilowatts) of the vehicle and calculated on a sliding scale, meaning that the first deductions are possible after the car reaches four years of age. The starting amount is 340 Hungarian Forints per kilowatt (at the time of writing the paper about $1.70). The income from the vehicle tax constitutes about 2% of local budgets. Hungarian municipalities cannot use the income from the PIT and the vehicle tax for repaying loans, because they are shared taxes.

Transfers from the central government:
Central grants represent another revenue source at the local level. The aim of transfers is to create a balance between the revenues and expenditures of different regions, because municipal responsibilities must be fulfilled everywhere. The main question is whether it is possible to design a grants system that balances expenditure needs and the allocation of revenues. Hungary gives grants to municipalities for capital investments and also for operating purposes; the latter are known as normative grants. Normative grants could be conditional or unconditional. In 2014 they represent approximately 20% of local income. Unconditional grants[26] are rare in Hungary, although this

---

[20] This fear was the reason why Budapest postponed introducing the highest rate until 1996.

[21] Here I would like to refer to the benefits principle, as this tax is paid by non residents indirectly for benefitting from local infrastruture services.

[22] If a property is sold, the new owner has to pay a duty that is based on the sale price. The sale price and the duty are then recorded in the land registrar of the municipality. Municipalities sometimes use this data for assessing the value of property. In general we can say that property value assessment in Hungary is

[23] The property tax is best administered by the local level, since it means identifying each parcel of land, as well as tracking land improvements and changes in ownership – records that are kept at the local level. This tax produces the most stable income for the municipality, and has a positive impact on improving creditworthiness. Nevertheless, if property values fall as they did in the United States and some European Union countries such as Spain and Ireland after 2008, the property tax could also prove to be an unstable basis. As we can read in Paulais (2009), in the USA, where property tax provides the largest source of local revenues some municipalities them reported a more than 45% decline compared to previous year.

[24] The owner of the business is a "tax collector agency" and the tax is for covering the indirect services the municipality offers to tourists. See again the benefits principle Ebel and Taliercio (2005).

[25]. Normative grants are the contributions of the state to maintain public services. For calculating the sum of the normative grant, an indicator and a per-unit cost element are used. Indicators usually reflect the "load" measurement, e.g., the number of children in school. The cost elements are the same for every municipality, even though the real costs can vary.

[26]. The main forms of grants are unconditional (general) grants, conditional non-matching grants, and matching grants. With unconditional (general) grants, the central government supports the municipality without any conditions on the use of the grant. Conditional non-matching grants are earmarked grants; the municipality can use it only for specific purposes. This type of transfer is the most appropriate method for local governments to meet national

type of transfer would give the most autonomy to municipalities and is most consistent with Article 9 of the European Charter on Local Self-Government.[27],[28]

Figure 05: Normative grants as % of total municipal revenues

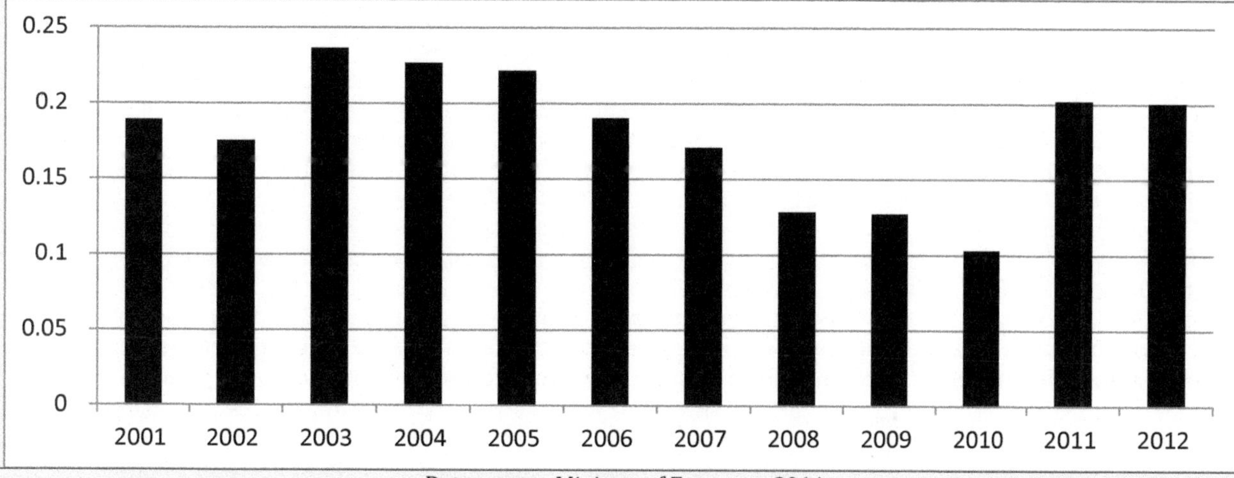

Data source: Ministry of Economy, 2014

Although centrally allocated resources in Hungary cannot be used for loan repayment, the assessment of the creditworthiness of a municipality is affected by the perception of transfer dependence. The available amount of central transfers in Hungary has never been predictable, since the central level can cut transfers without agreement from the local level. Moreover, the factors affecting the changes in grant amounts are not set out in law. Thus municipalities are largely defenseless against central decisions over transfers. Cuts in subsidies can cause difficulties in debt repayment and municipalities that cannot raise local income must decide between fulfilling a service and repaying the debt. For many municipalities, the solution – which represents a serious threat to the state budget – is to keep repaying the debt from the local budget and to apply for emergency grants for providing local services. The availability of emergency grants creates the illusion that the municipality is able to maintain its services and finance its debt at the same time.

Table 01 summarizes the number of municipalities that asked for emergency grants in various years between 1993 and 2011. In 2011, more than one-third of Hungarian municipalities needed this type of aid and almost two third in 2013.

Table 01: The number of Hungarian municipalities receiving emergency grants[29]

Year	Emergency grants	% of all municipalities
1993	165	5
1998	888	27
2002	1,279	40
2007	1,050	33
2011	1,182	37
2012	1,743	54
2013	1,894	61

Sources: www.kormany.hu, www.allamkincstar.hu, Ministry of Economy

2.04 Municipal borrowing in Hungary

Loan practices and moral hazard:

In Hungary, municipalities borrow directly from domestic banks and also issue bonds. In the case of bond issues, however, the buyer will also be the bank itself and since there is no secondary market for these bonds either, these "issues" are really bank loans. Loan-financed investments are subject to central approval as part of the subsidy system and lenders often presume that the government has also approved the loan. By implication, the central

standards, regardless of their revenue capacity. Matching grants require subnational governments to contribute to a subsidized program. A typical form of matching grants is a partial cost reimbursement, which can be a very effective tool for the central government as it can direct municipal spending by lowering the local "price" of services.

27. Notwithstanding the provisions of the Charter, even EU grants come earmarked.

28. The purpose of unconditional grants could be to develop rural areas, create jobs, and reduce differences in regional development. Unfortunately, these grants rarely meet their goals. Their effect is usually smaller than the central government expects due to substitution – that is, the revenues that the municipality previously used for that purpose may be spent on another program and the municipality may reduce its own expenditures in the area of the grant. This is called the "fungibility problem" of grants. For a discussion on the fungibility of transfers, see Boadway and Shah (2009), 309–312.

29 In 2012 the name of the grant changed, but its purpose remained the same.

government's approval was perceived as taking responsibility and offering guarantees for the loan. The guarantee made loan financing cheaper through reduced interest rates, enabling municipalities to access more borrowing than they could otherwise undertake.[30]

If a municipality pursues an unsafe fiscal policy resulting in the need for a bailout – and the central government is ready to take this action, the burden it imposes on every other municipality in the country is small but the overgrazing municipality's gain is measurable. For this reason, more and more municipalities will try to raise more loans than what they are able to repay as observed by Gillette (2011)). If over-borrowing occurs on a large scale, the provision of public services can be jeopardized. If more than one municipality raises larger loans than they are able to repay, the financial system is burdened as a whole and the creditworthiness of the country can be adversely affected as described by Liu and Webb (2011).

The 1995 Budget Act in Hungary introduced the first limits on municipal borrowing. The relevant paragraph was abolished by the Constitutional Court, however, for violation of procedures, but the main ideas on setting constraints on local borrowing were incorporated into the Act on Local Governments in 1996. According to these new rules, municipal borrowing could not exceed 70 percent of the municipality's own adjusted current income, which meant that a municipality could not incur loans that exceeded 70 percent of the difference between its short-term income and short-term obligations in a given year.[31] Act XXV (1996) on Municipal Bankruptcy was unique among the countries of the region. It aimed to introduce hard budget constraints on local governments by asserting that the state is not responsible for local debt. This legislation was passed at a time when many municipalities, facing hard budget constraints, had introduced new local taxes to finance their obligations.

Figure 06 shows the sudden increase in the number of municipalities imposing some form of local tax in 1996 in response to the new regulation. Almost all Hungarian municipalities introduced local taxes by 2000.

Figure 06: Number of municipalities introducing some form of local tax

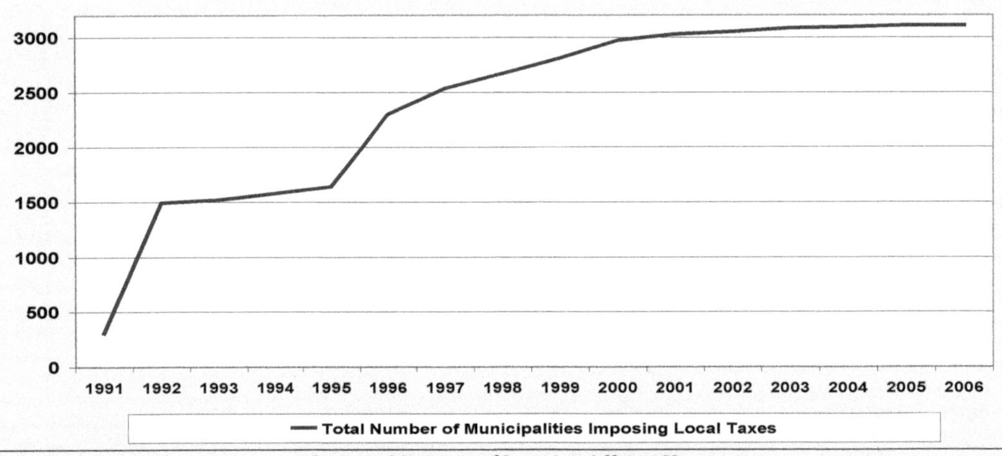

Source: Ministry of Interior Affairs, Hungary

At the same time that many municipalities were introducing new local taxes, some sought out private partners for infrastructure investments. Figure 07 indicates the increasing number of contracts between the two sectors (contracting out) and the amounts transferred by the municipalities to the private sector.

---

30. If a municipality pursues an unsafe fiscal policy resulting in the need for a bailout, the burden it imposes on every other municipality in the country is small, but the overgrazing municipality's gain is measurable. For this reason, more and more municipalities will try to raise more loans than what they are able to repay as described by Gillette (2011).

31. The enforcement of this law was questionable. According to Gal (2012), some municipalities went beyond their borrowing limits and the Ministry of Internal Affairs only found out about these cases much later.

Figure 07: Amounts transferred by the municipalities to the private sector
(in million Hungarian Forints, nominal values)

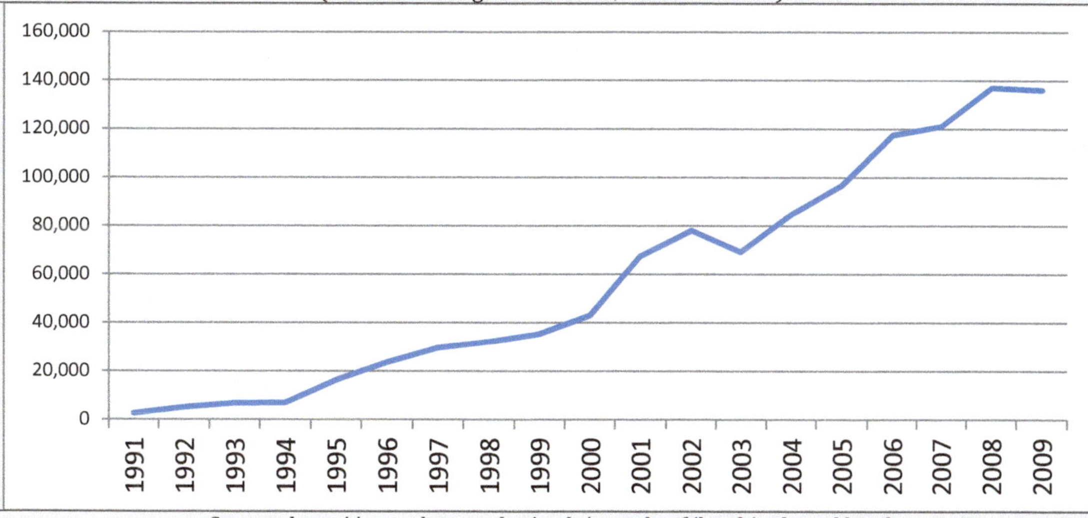

Source: http://www.bm.gov.hu/web/portal.nsf/html/onkgazd.html

The Municipal Bankruptcy Act also laid down the procedures to be followed if a municipality falls 60 days behind its obligations. A key element of the process is the appointment by the court of a trustee who prepares an emergency budget, makes decisions on what services will be carried out in the future (usually only the obligatory services), and prepares a plan about how to restructure the debt and reorganize municipal services. In reality, lenders assumed that the state would sooner or later give additional "emergency" grants to cover municipal deficits and as the result of a legal case, they likely would have had to write off a portion of their debt. Therefore, a safer strategy for lenders was to wait and almost all cases of municipal bankruptcy have been initiated by the municipality itself.[32]

Foreign currency loans:
Municipalities can also borrow in foreign currencies. As the chart below shows in 2009-2012 almost 70% of local debt - bonds and loans - was denominated in Swiss Franc and Euros (Figure 8), making debt service payments very expensive due to the very high value of the Franc (see Figure 9).

Figure 08: The proportions of foreign currency and forint denominated local debt

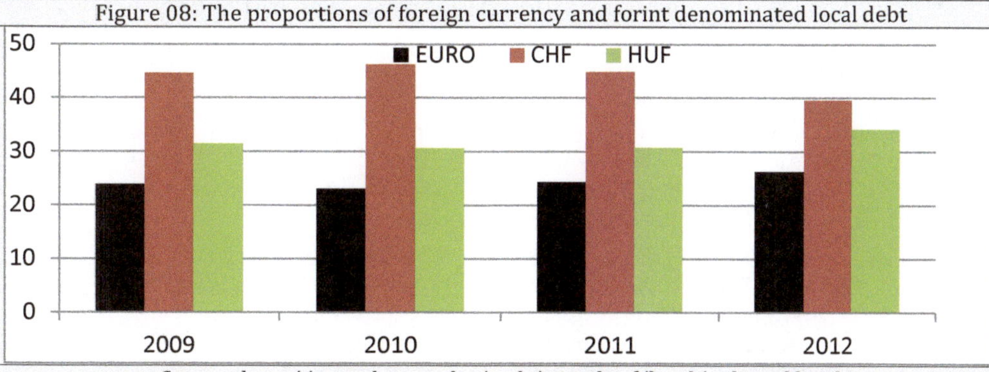

Source: http://www.bm.gov.hu/web/portal.nsf/html/onkgazd.html

In 2010, municipal indebtedness amounted to US$6 billion, 5 percent of the country's GDP, partly due to changes in the exchange rate. By itself 5 percent does not seem to be very high in comparison with other European countries. The average local public debt in the 27 EU countries was 5.6 percent in 2008. Higher numbers applied to Italy and France (both about 8 percent) or Spain (10 percent). What makes the Hungarian data alarming is the rate of change. The amount of Hungarian public debt rose more than 20 percent from 2007 to 2008, while the EU average for the same period is only 4 percent (Chatrie 2009). From 2009 to 2010, $4 billion local public debt grew to $6 billion – another 50 percent change.

[32] As a result, only a few municipalities have undergone this process, since most come to an agreement with their creditors before the court makes a decision, although many more have threatened strategic bankruptcies. About half the cases that have made it to the court have ended in rescheduled repayments; in other cases, the lender banks have had to write off the loans so the municipality could start with a "clean slate."

Figure 09: The change of foreign currency denominated loans and bonds of the Hungarian municipal sector (Amount in billion HUF)

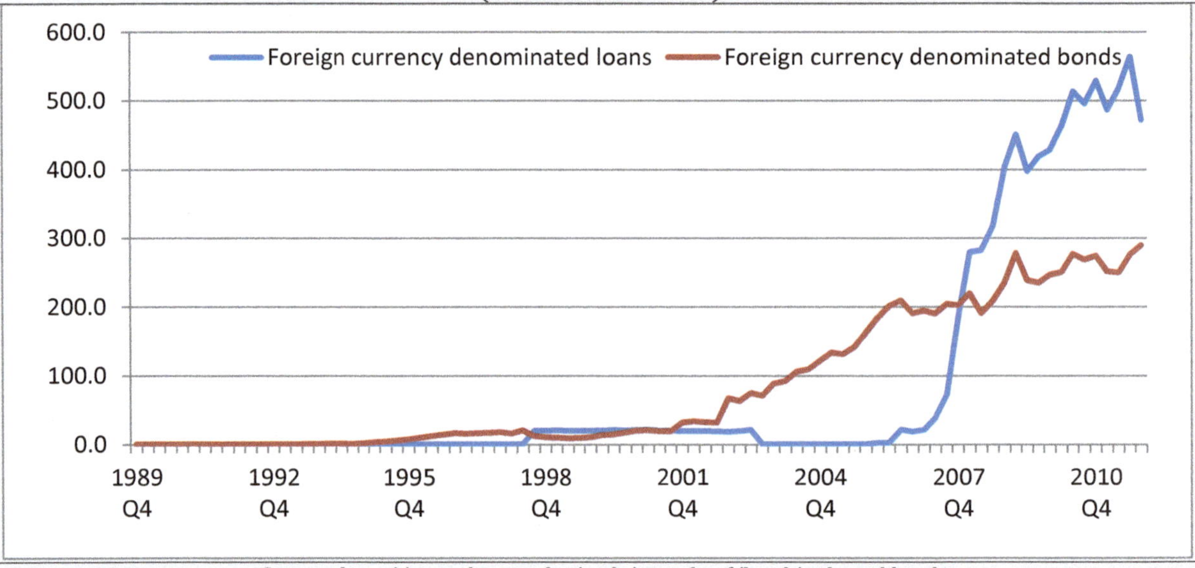

Source: http://www.bm.gov.hu/web/portal.nsf/html/onkgazd.html

2.05 Systemic risks of borrowing of Hungarian municipalities

The economic downturn in 2008 had a strong impact on municipal finance all over the world. In countries in which municipalities depend on property tax revenues, municipalities watched their property tax revenues sink as property prices fell, leading to difficulties in maintaining the level of services. Local governments that depended on more volatile revenue sources that directly depended on the economy, such as sales taxes or income taxes, were even worse off after 2008. In post transition countries, where granting debt-raising power to local levels was an important part of the decentralization process and was often done without regulations that would ensure avoiding over-indebtedness, the problems were even bigger.

Some of the risks associated with local borrowing were born at the time when the rules about Hungarian public administration were laid down. This section summarizes and examines these risks one by one,

2.06 The risk of unbalanced budgets

Diminishing state subsidies, as a consequence of the hard budget constraint of the central budget, would not be a problem if municipalities were able to raise revenues on their own. The absorption capacity of Hungarian municipalities, however - especially after the economic downturn in 2008 – is very low. The debt payments of municipalities were also considerably higher than they had been before 2008, which can be explained in part by the change in the value of Hungarian Forint relative to the Euro and the Swiss Franc. Since the expenditures of municipalities are increasing and other revenue sources are shrinking, the risk of budget deficits is significant.

2.07 Lack of public accountability and access to information

Hegedüs and Tönkö (2006) have documented that since 2000, many municipalities in Hungary have used public-private partnerships to create infrastructure, so that the costs of the investment were deferred. It is thus difficult to assess the real indebtedness of a municipality at any given date. Furthermore, due to the lack of regulation, future debt service does not have to be calculated ahead of time, so municipal decision makers have avoided appearing responsible for future indebtedness.

The main purpose of the public-private partnerships was to avoid direct municipal borrowing and to lengthen the financing period of the investment. In these cases, private borrowing is backed by municipal guarantees. After a certain period, the municipality assumes ownership of the assets. If the municipality has to repay the loan instead of a private company, the responsibility is further deferred.

2.08 Moral hazard and the risk of over-indebtedness of the sector

Moral hazard in the practice of Hungarian municipal borrowing is very high and deserves special attention. The indebtedness of the municipal sector increased 1260% from 2001 to 2007. In 2007, according to Homolya and

Szigel (2008), about 83 percent of municipal borrowing was not backed by any revenue stream or immobile assets. When a bank officer was asked why the bank had offered a Swiss franc–based loan to an obviously not creditworthy small municipality, the officer replied: "If we do not do it, another bank will." This behavior increases the risk of over-indebtedness of the sector and makes one doubt whether municipalities were aware at all of the risks associated with foreign currency borrowing.

In 2007, municipalities borrowed substantially more than in previous years. This boom had several reasons. Some municipalities borrowed while they still could, since tightening the borrowing regulation had been on the government's agenda for years. Others raised loans in foreign currencies with a speculative purpose, because the interest rates made the loans appear to be a good investment. Homolya and Szigel (2008) also observed that the borrowed money then ended up in Forint-based deposit accounts. The foreign currency debts were not hedged.

According to the results of the research of Barati-Stec and Hogye (2012) municipal decision makers often assumed that the central government would bail out insolvent municipalities. Furthermore, local officials often lacked basic financial knowledge about borrowing. For example, they were unfamiliar with the risks associated with foreign currency loans and could rarely afford to hire budgeting, planning, infrastructure, or finance advisors to guide them.

2.09 Carrying out unnecessary and costly investments

The targeted grants set priorities for municipalities from the higher levels and distort local preferences. Under-financed local governments seek all possible revenues that they can raise and are likely to apply for grants for investments they do not need if that is the only way to get access to government funding and at the same time, the long-term maintenance cost of the investment is not taken into consideration. As a result of centralized financing, local decision makers are not publicly accountable for their actions and in some cases informing the public before making an investment means only a short announcement in the local paper. Although they are obliged to do so by law, they do not organize public hearings to discuss major investments as Barati-Stec and Hogye (2012) found during their research.

2.10 Unhealthy financing mechanisms

Since municipalities can issue bonds for a "general purpose," it is also possible that some of these bond issues are needed to cover operating expenses. According to Homolya and Szigel (2008) only 50 percent of bond issues had a direct investment purpose, 10 percent were explicitly for financing operating expenses, and 40 percent were "general-purpose" bonds. Although "general purpose" means that the use of the bonds was not clarified at the time of the issue, so they could have been spent on investments or operating costs, it is likely that 50 percent of total bond issues were used to cover current expenses.

As loans and bond issues are made in subsequent years, each one with a different grace period set in a negotiation process between the lender and the municipality, the municipality may have to start repaying all the loans at once. This, besides indicating incompetence on the municipality's side also raises questions about the incentives of the banks in these situations. There are between 10 and 15 financial institutions in the Hungarian local credit market, making it very competitive. Even though municipalities' creditworthiness is low, the financial sector is willing to take the risks associated with local borrowing. Moreover, the market is not particularly transparent, so the banks find it difficult to estimate the creditworthiness of a municipal borrower.

Municipalities sell land and buildings through off-budget institutions, which makes it hard to trace how the revenue from these transactions is used. This practice further decreases transparency and suggests that capital income is being used to cover operating expenditures.

3.0 Changes in regulation & finance of Hungarian municipalities after the economic downturn

Since the spending of the municipal sector represents almost 14 percent of Hungarian GDP, municipal finance imbalances will have a significant effect at the macroeconomic level. Having high subnational spending in relation to the GDP is a characteristic of the northern countries (the proportions for Norway and Denmark are 32.9 and 13.1 percent of GDP, respectively). Decentralized spending is also a characteristic of some of the former Communist countries; in the Czech Republic the proportion is 11.9 percent and in Ukraine it is 12.6 percent of GDP (Slack 2009: Table 5). However, Escolano et al. (2012) concluded that the positive effect of decentralized expenditures is reduced if local governments depend largely on central transfers at the same time – another characteristic of former communist countries.

After 2008, Hungarian municipalities, as well as the central government, found themselves in a difficult economic situation. Markets were shrinking and the state sovereign rating in November 7, 2008, was changed to A3 from A2 by Moody's. On March 1, 2009, it was downgraded to Baa1. S&P changed the rating on the November 17, 2008, from BBB+ to BBB and, in March 2009, to BBB-. Some companies that had provided the largest tax base for local governments closed down and the number of unemployed increased rapidly, placing an extra burden on municipal budgets. The state cut back subsidies to the local sector for stabilization purposes by 6 percent in 2009 (from 66.6 billion to 62.4 billion Hungarian Forints). Another 70 billion Forints for raising public servants' wages were also taken away from the public sector. The Hungarian government that was elected in 2010 and re-elected in 2014 introduced a series of reforms concerning all levels of public administration and their finances.

3.01 Constitutional changes

The new Constitution took effect on January 1, 2012. When the old Constitution was no longer in force, many regulations that were included in it that affected municipalities also became nullified while new laws to regulate municipalities had not yet been created. The old Constitution included a paragraph about municipal associations, stating that forming associations is a free decision of the member municipalities and higher levels of government cannot force municipalities to carry out tasks together. The new Constitution, however, vaguely states that other sectoral laws can oblige municipalities to cooperate while carrying out tasks. Also, the new Constitution does not comply with the requirement of the European Charter of Local Self-Governments, which states that municipal rights should be protected by the country's Constitution. This provision was also criticized by the Venice Commission.[33]

3.02 Structural changes and reallocation of tasks

The creation of a new formal level of micro-regions that would replace free associations of municipalities has been among the government's plans for more than 10 years. This step shifts some of the more expensive tasks to this level from the local level. In-depth interviews with municipal representatives in 2010 by researchers at Corvinus University suggest that municipalities generally did not oppose a new formal level between them and the counties. The services that municipalities would have preferred to "upload" to the micro-regional level were education, health care, solid waste, and sewage collection and treatment. As a final decision of the government the education became centralized - so instead of stepping one level up, it skipped and went directly to the center - and now it is under one single national authority, even though municipalities strongly opposed to the state taking over this service[34]. While other infrastructural services remained local services the new level still mainly only fulfils administrative tasks (issuing ID cards, passports). Numerous services – like mid and higher level education, health care - that had been provided by counties also got uploaded to the central level, making the role of the counties in public administration even lighter if possible.

3.03 Local finance

Instead of the normative grants – discussed before – a new form of operational subsidy was introduced that took into consideration the total tax capacity of the municipality. The subsidy is calculated based on the difference between the sum of the maximum possible per capita PIT and business turnover tax (tax potential) of the municipality and an amount assigned by the government based on the size of the municipality (the bigger the municipality the higher this amount is). If the tax potential is lower than the amount assigned by the government, the normative grant will make up for the difference, if the potential is more than the normative amount, than the grant will be reduced by the amount of the difference.

The number of municipalities declaring insolvency between 1996 and 2007 was 22. Since 2009, however, there have been 23 new cases. Although the insolvent municipalities during the first 10 years were mainly small settlements, the recent cases involved larger municipalities as well. The government set new regulation on local borrowing (Act CXCIV (2011) on Economic Stability) as well. Under the new act, municipalities can only borrow short term without direct permission but decisions about loans for investments – with some exemptions[35] - will be made on a case-by-case basis at the central level. Debt can only be taken on if the debt service in any year will be under 50% of the own source municipal revenues, forcing decision makers to take into consideration the different grace periods of borrowing in subsequent years.

3.04 Sector-wide bailout

---

33. The European Commission for Democracy through Law (the Venice Commission) was established in 1990 for dealing with emergency issues in constitutional matters.

34. Municipalities are so desperate to maintain this control that some have even re-classified school buildings as residential rental units, so that the state cannot take them over.

35 According to the Act CXCIV of 2011 on the economic stability of Hungary (article 10/2), there is no need for approval for (i) liquidity loans, (ii) for providing the own part of already approved EU or other international financed project, (iii) reorganization loans and (iv) in case of investmnet loans up to 100.000.000 HUF for Budapest and other cities with county rights, 20.000.000 HUF for national minority self governments and in all other cases 20% of own revenues, but maximum 10.000.000 HUF.

The central government and county-level representatives signed an agreement in October 2011 about the bailout of the counties' debt and taking over county tasks and assets. Before the details of this transaction were discussed, municipal associations were noting that the county assets are worth more than the amount of debts, so bailouts would not be needed. After a lengthy negotiation period, the counties signed the agreement according to which the state took over all of the assets of and the tasks performed by these institutions leaving the counties even more weightless. In 2012 a new announcement came about the partial bailout of the municipal sector and was followed by decisions resulting in the total bailout by March 2014, just 4 weeks before the new elections.

In case of smaller settlements the main reason for the very high level of indebtedness was the asymmetrical financing system and lack of fiscal capacities - as described before in this paper - , matched with the undifferentiated obligatory service provision (vertical fiscal imbalance). Bigger municipalities were better off financially, but started investments that were beyond their limits. In 2012, the government announced taking over the entire debt burden of municipalities with less than 5000 inhabitants (more than half of Hungarian municipalities fall in this category). Later, 14 municipalities were taken out from the first round of consolidation, as the per capita debt was higher than 200.000 HUF (1000 USD) and the government started a special investigation to reveal the reasons behind this relatively high per capita debt.[36] In case of municipalities with more than 5000 inhabitants, 40-70% of the total debt was going to be taken over by the state with the exact amounts to be determined in case by case negotiations. Even though the government elaborated a formula for calculating these amounts in each settlement, the practice suggested that decisions were made on an ad hoc basis again, giving ground to rumors about political influence. In March 2014, despite the negative critics, the central government took all municipal debt regardless their causes, size and financial situation of the indebted municipality[37].

4.0 Conclusions: reforms based on Hungarian tradition and international examples

We can conclude that the municipal level wished for reforms leading to greater fiscal decentralization, more local autonomy, and increased transparency. The government elected in 2010 had the chance of completing the decentralization process that started 20 years ago, but instead, has used the situation in 2008 to start a massive recentralization process.

Given that the main problem of Hungarian local finances was the inability of small settlements, a vast majority of the sector, to finance their operations, and as a consequence, their over indebtedness due to the constant rollover of liquid loans, it is questionable whether the new regulations discussed in the previous section are going to meet their expectations.

The negotiations about the debt between the state and the banking sector are still going on. There is little doubt about the need for re-regulating small settlements' service obligation and financing practices, however, the new rules just shift some of the tasks and revenues away while making long term borrowing stricter, without easing normal, everyday service provision and operation in these settlements. The new laws do not address the difficulties of small local governments since they will have to continue to borrow short term, taking out liquidity loans, reproducing the old problems. The author's suggestions based on the findings of recent literature on decentralization, after evaluating the reform steps of the current government are as follows:

1. The current bailout sends the message that the central government is ready to 'save' the insolvent municipalities and sets a bad example for the fiscally prudent ones. This practice favours the fiscally imprudent and should be given up.
2. Differentiation among different-sized governments is needed when regulating subnational borrowing practices to ease normal, everyday service provision and operation of small settlements.
3. The right of larger municipalities[38] to introduce special taxes should also be examined. Special rights could be given to cities that are or could be the centre of economic development in their region. This reform could be introduced gradually. First, the city of Budapest could be given this special right (about one-fifth of Hungary's population lives in the capital), then, based on the lessons learnt, the group of special-tax cities could be broadened to the five to seven largest Hungarian cities. [39]

The decentralization process follows a different path in each country and change does not occur all at once. Hungary has a historical heritage that made it difficult to introduce the amalgamation of municipalities to provide services or

[36] A revealing fact about the whole process and indication of that the effects of the bailouts were not examined thoroughly, is that the government learnt about these 14 cases only after the total bailout of the sector was already announced.

[37] When the value of the Hungarian Forint relative to the EURO and the Swiss Franc, the currencies in which most households' debt was denominated, fell, the government accepted a law on the of these debts at a centrally given rate, which in case of the EURO was 250, and for the Swiss Frank 180. The market rates at that time were 295 and 236 respectively. The first idea of doing the same thing in case of public debt came from one of the Ministers of State for the Prime Minister's Office and mayor of Hódmezővásárhely, a town seriously indebted in Swiss Frank.

[38] About 50 percent of Hungarian local debt is raised by 30 municipalities, out of a total of 3200 municipalities.

[39] The largest Hungarian cities are Budapest (pop. 2.000.000) Debrecen (206.225), Miskolc (170,234), Szeged (169,678), Pecs (156,974), Gyor (130476), Nyiregyhaza (117,597).

delegating revenue-raising power to the micro-regional level. However, over time, Hungary could learn from the practices and examples of mature democracies to broaden municipal rights rather than curtailing them, provided that the necessary financial safeguards are in place.

References

Barati-Stec, Izabella and Mihaly Hogye, 2012. Önkormányzatok költségvetéskészítési gyakorlata (Budgeting Technics of Municipalities. Pro Publico Bono Online. ISSN 2062-9966 (online)

Boadway, Robin and Anwar Shah, 2009. Fiscal federalism: Principles and practice of multi-level governance. New York: Cambridge University Press.

Boadway, Robin, and Harry Kitchen, 1999. Canadian tax policy. Third Edition. Toronto: Canadian Tax Foundation.

Chatrie, Isabelle, 2009. Economic outlook: Sub-national public finance in the European Union. Dexia Crédit Local, presentation made in Brighton, December 11.

Ebel, Robert and Robert Taliercio, 2005. Subnational tax policy design and administration. Tax Notes International: 919-936

Escolano, Julio, Luc Eyraud, Marialuz Moreno Badia, Juliane Sarnes, and Anita Tuladhar, 2012. Fiscal performance, institutional design and decentralization in European Union countries. IMF Working Paper. WP/12/45. Washington, D.C.: International Monetary Fund: 1-32.

Gál, Erzsébet, 2012. Az önkormányzati adó- és követelésminősítésének elmélet és gyakorlati problémái. (Theoretical and Practical Challenges of Municipal Credit Rating). Ph.D. Dissertation. Miskolc University.

Gillette, Clayton P., Political Will and Fiscal Federalism in Municipal Bankruptcy (March 23, 2011). NYU School of Law, Public Law Research Paper No. 11-22; NYU Law and Economics Research Paper No. 11-13: 1-54. Available at SSRN: http://ssrn.com/abstract=1793173 or http://dx.doi.org/10.2139/ssrn.1793173

Hegedüs, J. and Tönkö, A., 2006. Az önkormányzati gazdasági társaságok szerepe a helyi önkormányzatok vagyongazdálkodásában: feltételes kötelezettségvállalás problémája. (The "contingent liability" problem.) Budapest: Városkutatás Kft.: 1-17

Homolya, Dániel and Gábor Szigel, 2008. Lending to local governments: Risks and behaviour of Hungarian banks. Hungarian National Bank Bulletin 3(2): 20–29.

Hooghe Liesbet and Marks, Gary, 2001. Types of multi level governance, Department of Political Science, University of North Carolina:1-32.

Krugman, Paul, 2011. Depression and democracy. New York Times, New York Edition, December 12, page A23.

Liu, Lili, and Steven B. Webb, 2011. Laws for fiscal responsibility for sub-national discipline: International Experience. WPS5587. Washington, D.C.: World Bank, 1-56.

Paulais, Thierry. 2009. Local governments and the financial crisis: An analysis. Washington, D.C.: The Cities Alliance, 1-26.

Scheppele, Kim Lane, 2011. Hungary's constitutional revolution. The New York Times, Opinion Pages. 19th December.

Slack, Enid, 2009. Guide to municipal finance. Nairobi: UN-HABITAT, 1-90.

Swianiewicz, Pawel, 2010. If territorial fragmentation is a problem, is amalgamation a solution? An East European Perspective. Local Government Studies. 36(02):183-203.

Szalai, Akos, and Almos Tassonyi, 2004. Value-based property taxation: options for Hungary. Environment and Planning C: Government and Policy 22(4): 475–632.

20

Does oil price uncertainty transmit to the Thai stock market?

Komain Jiranyakul [a*]

[a] School of Development Economics, National Institute of Development Administration, Thailand
[*] Corresponding author's email address: komain_j@hotmail.com

HIGHLIGHTS:

1. Thailand is an emerging market economy in Southeast Asia that heavily depends on oil imports.
2. The Stock Exchange of Thailand has been the source of equity financing of listed firms from various equity sectors.
3. Fluctuations in world crude oil prices cause volatility transmission from oil to the Stock Exchange of Thailand.
4. The country needs to rely more on renewable energy and natural gas to maintain or improve the production processes of listed firms.

Article History

Keywords:
Bivariate GARCH;
Emerging markets;
Real stock price;
Real oil price;
Volatility transmission.

ABSTRACT

This study investigates the impact of oil price uncertainty on the Stock Exchange of Thailand. Monthly data from May 1987 to December 2013 are applied to the two-stage procedure. In the first step, a bivariate generalized autoregressive conditional heteroskedastic (GARCH) model is estimated to obtain the volatility series of stock market index and oil price. In the second step, the pairwise Granger causality tests are performed to determine the direction of volatility transmission between oil to stock markets. It is found that movement in real oil price does not adversely affect real stock market return, but stock price volatility does affect real stock return. In the sense of causality, there exists a positive one-directional volatility transmission running from oil to stock market. Oil price change and its uncertainty also adversely affect two main sub-index returns. These important findings give some implications for risk management and policy measures.

1.0 Introduction

The Stock Exchange of Thailand is an emerging stock market in Southeast Asia. It has been the source of equity financing of listed firms from various equity sectors. Capital inflows (portfolio and foreign direct investment) have been in a rising trend since the financial liberalization in the early1990s. The data from the Bank of Thailand show that net capital flow of the country was 1.1 billion US dollars in 1985 and increased to 11.3 in 1991 and 21.5 in 1995. In 2000, three years after the 1997 financial crisis, the net capital flow was -9.8 billion US dollar, but recovered in 2005 and reached the highest point of 24.8 in 2011. Even though the net capital flow is fluctuating, a surge of capital inflow was observed in recent years. Capital inflow to the Thai stock market in terms of portfolio investment has caused foreign investors to play an important role in recent years. Foreign investors can freely invest in government bonds, debentures and stocks. A surge in capital flows to domestic capital market can impose important economic impacts on the Thai economy such as an appreciation in exchange rates, a rising trend in the price level and stock prices.

Thailand is an oil-importing country that has been relying on imported machinery and equipment. In 1996, one year before the financial crisis, this category of imports accounted for 47.2 percent of total imports, but decreased to 44.3 in 1998 and steadily decreased to 32.6 percent in 2011 and a little recovered thereafter. This can be due to exchange rate fluctuations during the floating regime. As a matter of fact, this category of imports is essential to the production of exported manufacturing goods and is also dependent on imports of crude oil. In Asia, crude oil consumption increased from 11.3 million barrels per day in 1987 to 32.9 million barrels in 2011 (US Energy Information Administration). China and India are the leading demanders in the region. In Southeast Asia, Thailand is the second largest net oil importer behind Singapore. Oil price hike episodes in the world oil markets can exert the impacts on the Thai stock market.

There were several episodes of oil price surges. The data from IEA World Energy Outlook show that the first and second oil price hikes occurred in 1974 and 1978. The world oil price reached its peak in 1981, and declined thereafter. The third oil price surge occurred again in the early1990s due to the Gulf war and gradually declined. After 2002, the rising trend of oil price was observed. Oil price fluctuations caused mainly by these episodes can create real oil price uncertainty that transmits to the stock markets, especially those of oil-importing countries. Fluctuations in stock market index can be caused by various factors. One main factor that cause stock market index to fluctuate can be fluctuations in crude oil price. In the context of volatility transmission, oil price fluctuations caused mainly by the episodes oil price surge can create real oil price uncertainty that transmits to the stock markets, especially those of oil-importing countries. Most studies that focus on volatility transmission from oil to stock markets have been conducted for advanced countries, such as the United States, Japan and Euro area countries. Only few studies have been conducted for developing countries. Therefore, it is worth investigating more on volatility transmission in a developing country.

This paper collects the dataset covering the period from May 1987 to December 2013 to answer the following research questions. Does real oil price Granger cause the stock market index? Can oil price change adversely affect real stock market return and real sub-index returns? Does oil price uncertainty transmit to overall market return and sub-index returns? Newly econometric techniques are used to answer the above questions. If the results show that oil price uncertainty affects stock returns, there should be implications for investors and portfolio managers as well as the government. The implications for Thailand might not be different from other developing economies that are dependent on imports of crude oil.

The paper is organized as the following. The next section presents literature review. The third section describes the data and econometric methodology. The fourth section presents empirical results and implications from the empirical results. The last section concludes.

2.0 Literature review

Theoretically, real oil price shocks rather than nominal oil price shocks should affect decisions by economic agents in an economy. However, movements in real oil price are caused by both nominal oil price and the price level. If nominal oil price and the price level move together in the same direction, the effect of real and nominal oil prices on macroeconomic variables should be the same. Otherwise, real stock price should be the determinant of economic decision. The effect of oil price shocks on macroeconomic variables has been widely examined.

Recently, the focus is on the response of real stock prices to crude oil price. Jones and Gautam (1996) investigate the relationship between oil and stock markets. They find that the reaction of stock prices in the United States and Canada to oil price shocks depends on the impact of the shocks on real cash flows. However, oil price shocks cause larger changes in stock prices than subsequent changes in real cash flows in the United Kingdom and Japan. Their results are based on the standard cash flows/dividend valuation model. Using monthly data, Sadorsky (1999) finds the evidence showing that oil price volatility affects real stock returns in the United States. Ciner (2001) investigates the relationship between oil prices and the stock market in the United States using daily data and finds the evidence that oil shocks affect stock index returns. In addition, the linkage between oil and stock markets is stronger in the 1990s. Papapetrou (2001) uses a multivariate vector-autoregression to examine the dynamic relationship among oil prices, interest rates, real economic activity and employment in Greece. One of the main findings is that oil price significantly explains stock price movements. Basher and Sadorsky (2006) employ a multi-factor model to examine the impact of oil price changes on a large set of emerging stock market returns. The find strong evidence that oil price risk affects stock returns in those economies. Using monthly data, Park and Ratti (2008) examine the impact of oil price shocks on stock markets in the United States and 13 European countries. They find that an increase in real oil price shocks has a significant impact on real stock returns within the following month. The increased volatility of oil prices depresses real stock returns in many European countries, but not in the United States. For Norway, an oil-exporting country, there exists a positive response of real stock return to real oil price shocks. Furthermore, the asymmetric effect of oil price shocks on real stock returns is found in the United States and Norway. Cong et al. (2008) find that oil price shocks do not affect real stock returns of most Chinese stock market indexes, except for the indexes of manufacturing and oil companies.

Apergis and Miller (2009) investigate the impact of oil price changes on stock market returns in the United States, Japan, Canada, and other five European countries under the vector autoregressive framework. They find that stock market returns do not respond in a large way to oil market shocks.

Narayan and Narayan (2010) use daily data for the period 2000-2008 to investigate the impact of oil prices on Vietnam's stock prices. They find a positive and significant impact of oil prices on stock prices. One of the main findings by Kim and Yang (2011) is that the surge in capital inflows in South Korea, Indonesia, Malaysia, Philippines and Thailand cause a rise in stock prices.

Few studies emphasize the mechanism of return and volatility transmission between oil and stock markets and their sector indices. Malik and Hammoudeh (2007) find that oil price volatility affects the volatility of equity indexes in the Gulf countries. Malik and Ewing (2009) use weekly data during 1992 to 2008 to examine volatility transmission between oil prices and equity sector returns. They employ bivariate GARCH models to estimate the mean and conditional variance simultaneously and find the existence of significant transmission of the United States sector index returns and volatility of oil prices.

Arouri et al. (2011) employ a generalized vector autoregressive-generalized autoregressive conditional heteroskedastic (VAR-GARCH) approach to examine volatility transmission between oil and stock markets in Europe and the United States at sector level using weekly data. Their results show that there is a widespread direct spillover of volatility between oil and stock sector returns. Furthermore, the volatility cross effects run only from oil to stock sectors in Europe while bilateral spillover effects are observed in the United States. Masih et al. (2011) find a negative impact of oil price volatility on real stock return in South Korea.

Jouini (2013) employs the VAR-GARCH procedure to investigate the link between world oil price and stock sectors in Saudi Arabia using weekly data during 2007 to 2011. The results show the existence of return and volatility transmission between oil price and stock sectors.

Awartani and Maghyereh (2013) investigate dynamic spillovers of returns and volatilities between world oil prices and stock market indexes in the Gulf Cooperation Council countries, which comprises Bahrain, Kuwait, Oman, Qatar, Saudi Arabia and the United Arab Emirates. One of their main findings is that there exist net spillovers from oil to stock markets.

3.0 Materials and methods

Monthly data of stock market index, consumer price index, the dollar exchange rate, and crude oil price are used in this study. The stock market index series is obtained from the Stock Exchange of Thailand website while consumer price index and the dollar exchange rate series are obtained from the Bank of Thailand. The Brent crude oil price series expressed in dollar per barrel is obtained from Energy Information Administration. The data set covers the period from May 1987 to December 2013[1] with 320 observations.[2] Real stock price index is calculated by deflating nominal index by consumer price index. Real oil price is calculated by multiplying crude oil price by the dollar exchange rate and deflating by consumer price index. Real stock market return (r^{SP}) and real oil price change (r^{OP}) are the percentage rates of change of real stock market index and real crude oil price. The plots of two time series data are shown in Figure 1 (a and b). Both of them fluctuate regularly with the spike in the early 1990s for real oil price series resulting from 1991 Gulf War. These figures (1a and 1b) could exhibit multiple structural breaks. However, the series are stationary as reported in Table 1.

Table 01: Unit root test results, 1987M5-2013M12

	ADF test with constant	ADF test with trend and constant	PP test with constant	PP test with trend and constant
r^{SP}	-16.822 [0] (0.000)***	-16.795 [0] (0.000)***	-16.825 [11] (0.000)***	-10.643 [11] (0.000)***
r^{OP}	-6.266 [12] (0.000)***	-6.270 [12] (0.000)***	-13.434 [16] (0.000)***	-13.430 [16] (0.000)***

Note: r^{SP} stands for the percentage change in real stock market index (real stock market return), and r^{OP} stands for the percentage in real oil price. The number is bracket is the optimal lags chosen by Akaike information criterion (AIC) for ADF tests and is the optimal bandwidths chosen by Newey-West using Bartlett kernel for PP test. The number in parenthesis is the probability of accepting the null of unit root. *** indicates significance at the 1 percent level.

The results of unit root tests using Augmented Dickey-Fuller (ADF) and Phillips-Perron (PP) tests for real stock market return (r^{SP}) and change in real oil price (r^{OP}) are stationary.

[1] The period is limited by the availability of crude oil price.

[2] In fact, the size and significance of parameters in the conditional variance depend on the data frequency being used. Monthly data set allows for a longer time span and can capture the long-run impact of volatility on other variables.

Figure 01: Real stock market return and change in real oil price, 1987M5-2013M12

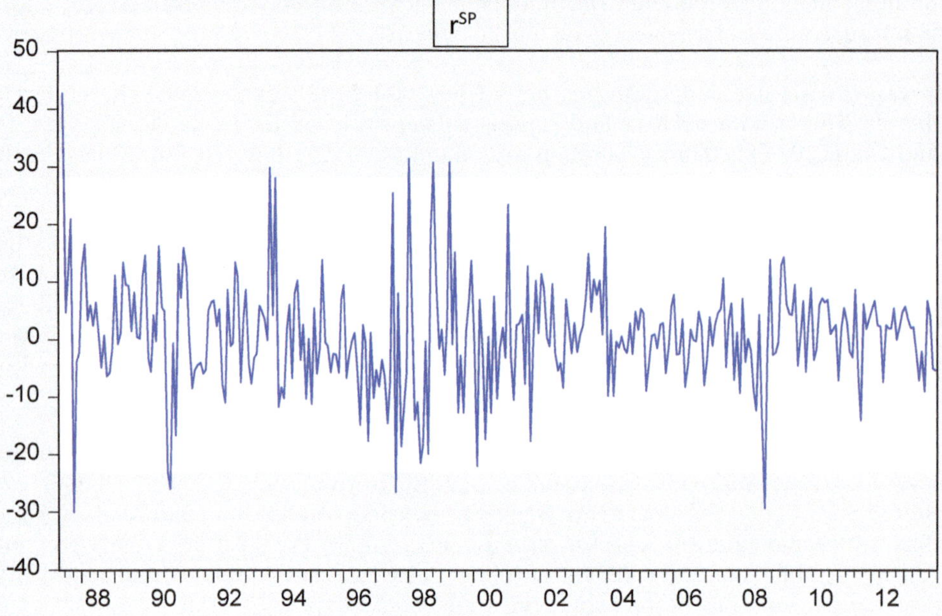

a. Real stock market return

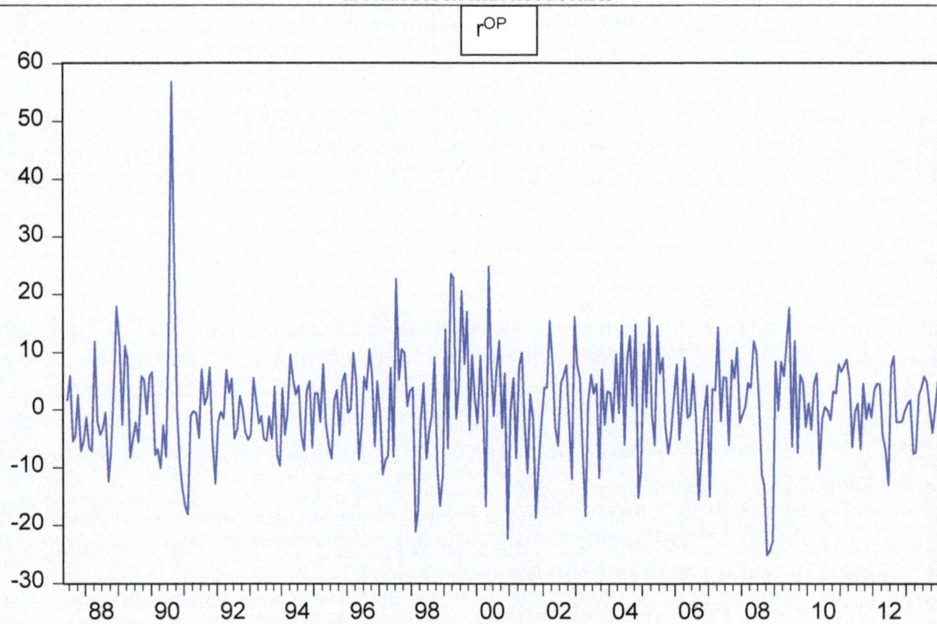

b. Change in real oil price

The stationarity property of the two series enables one to perform the estimation of a bivariate GARCH model.

Summary statistics of real oil movement and real stock return series are reported in Table 2. The average monthly stock return is 0727 whereas the average monthly oil price rate of change is 0.728. The Jarque-Bera normality test rejects the null of a normal distribution of both series, indicating that least squares estimation is not suitable.

Table 02: Summary statistics, 1987M5-2013M12

	r^{SP}	r^{OP}
Mean	0.727	0.728
Standard deviation	9.524	8.963
Skewness	0.273	0.654
Kurtosis	5.351	7.745
Jaque-Bera Statistic	77.152	321.973
	(0.000)	(0.000)

Note: r^{SP} stands for the percentage change in real stock market index (real stock market return), and r^{OP} stands for the percentage in real oil price. The number in parenthesis is the probability of accepting the null of normality.

In an empirical model, some researchers include oil price variable as one of various determinants of stock market index. However, cointegration tests in a bivariate framework often fail to find a long-run equilibrium relationship between crude oil prices and stock prices in emerging stock markets. This might be because of omitted variables in the regression. Testing for causal relationship in a bivariate framework can also capture the relationship between real stock market index and real oil price.

The first attempt is to conduct the test for causal relationship between real oil price and real stock market index in a bivariate framework using the non-causality test proposed by Toda and Yamamoto (1995). This method has significant advantage since prior knowledge whether the variables are cointegrated is unnecessary as long as the order of integration does not exceed the lag length. The variables in the model are tested in their levels. This bivariate vector autoregressive (VAR) model is specified in equations (1) and (2) below. Equation (1) is used to test whether real oil price causes real stock market index while equation (2) is used to test whether real stock market index causes real oil price. The error terms are white noise.

$$LRSP_t = \alpha_0 + \sum_{i=1}^{k} \alpha_i LRSP_{t-i} + \sum_{j=k+1}^{k+d_{max}} \alpha_j LRSP_{t-j} + \sum_{i=1}^{k} \beta_i LROP_{t-i} + \sum_{j=k+1}^{k+d_{max}} \beta_j LROP_{t+j} + \varepsilon_t \quad (1)$$

$$LROP_t = \gamma_0 + \sum_{i=1}^{k} \gamma_i LROP_{t-i} + \sum_{j=k+1}^{k+d_{max}} \gamma_j LROP_{t-j} + \sum_{i=1}^{k} \phi_i LRSP_{t-i} + \sum_{j=k+1}^{k+d_{max}} \phi_j LRSP_{t+j} + u_t \quad (2)$$

Where LRSP is the log of real stock market index, LROP is the log of real oil price.

The testing procedure consists of the following steps: the first step begins with testing for zero restrictions of the coefficients of all lag variables since the extra lagged variables are included in the model. Testing whether the variables in the model cause each other is a test of the joint restriction where all coefficients are zero, the second step determines the optimal lag length (k) using Schwertz information criterion (SIC), the third step estimates a VAR of order $k^*=k+d_{max}$, where d_{max} is the maximum anticipated order of integration, and the final step uses the Wald tests for linear or non-linear restrictions whether the series is I(0), I(1) or I(2) according to Rambaldi and Doran (1996). This procedure can prevent biases that may occur when using the standard unit root and cointegration tests.

Another estimation method that can capture the link between crude oil and stock markets is the model of volatility spillovers. The two-step approach is employed in the second attempt to explain the relationship between oil price volatility and the Thai stock market. In the first step, a bivariate generalized autoregressive heteroskedastic model with constant conditional correlation (ccc-GARCH model proposed by Bollerslev (1990) is employed to generate stock and oil price volatilities. In the second step, these generated series along with real stock market return and the rate of change in oil price series employed in the standard Granger (1969) causality test. Pagan (1984) criticizes this procedure because it produces the generated series of volatility or uncertainty. When these generated series are used as regressors in Granger causality test, the model might be misspecified. However, the full information maximum likelihood method that simultaneously tests the impact of volatility in the mean equation can give the same results (see Oteng-Abayie and Doe, 2013).[3] Furthermore, the main advantage of the two-step procedure is that it provides room for the ability to establish causality between variables. The system equations in a ccc-GARCH(1,1) model comprises the following five equations.

$$r_t^{SP} = a_{1,0} + \sum_{i=1}^{p} a_{1,i} r_{t-i}^{SP} + \sum_{i=1}^{p} b_{1,i} r_{t-i}^{OP} + e_{1,t} \quad (3)$$

$$h_t^{SP} = \mu_1 + \alpha_{1,1} \varepsilon_{t-1}^{2,SP} + \beta_{1,1} h_{t-1}^{SP} \quad (4)$$

$$r_t^{OP} = a_{2,0} + \sum_{i=1}^{p} a_{1,i} r_{t-i}^{OP} + e_{2,t} \quad (5)$$

$$h_t^{OP} = \mu_2 + \alpha_{2,1} \varepsilon_{t-1}^{2,OP} + \beta_{2,1} h_{t-1}^{OP} \quad (6)$$

$$h_t^{SP,OP} = \rho_{12} (h_t^{SP})^{1/2} (h_t^{OP})^{1/2} \quad (7)$$

[3] The possible case indicating the difference of the two procedures is that when the GARCH-in-mean model fails to detect the impact of current period of one variable on current period of another variable does not imply that some of its lags will have no impact at all.

Where r^{SP} is the real stock market return, and r^{OP} is the movement in real oil price (the rate of change), h^{SP} is the conditional variance of real stock market return, h^{OP} is the conditional variance of real oil price change, and $h^{SP,OP}$ is the conditional covariance of the two variables. The constant conditional correlation is ρ_{12}. The system equations can be estimated simultaneously. The coefficients of ARCH term (ε^2_t) and GARCH term (h_t) as well as the intercept must be non-negative. The sum of these coefficients should be less than one if the conditional variance series will be stationary.

The pairwise Granger causality test is performed in the following equation.

$$y_t = a + \sum_{i=1}^{k} \alpha_i y_{t-i} + \sum_{i=1}^{k} \beta_i x_{1,t-i} + \sum_{i=1}^{k} \gamma_i x_{2,t-i} + \sum_{i=1}^{k} \phi_i x_{3,t-i} + u_t \qquad (8)$$

Where y is a dependent variable, and x_1, x_2, and x_3 are independent variables. If any independent variable causes the dependent variable, there should be at least one significant coefficient of that lagged independent variable. This also indicates that the F-statistic in the standard causality test must show significance for each pair of variables. In the present study, the sequence of variables that will enter into a vector autoregression is $\{r^{SP}, r^{OP}, h^{SP}, h^{OP}\}$, $\{r^{OP}, r^{SP}, h^{SP}, h^{OP}\}$, $\{h^{SP}, r^{SP}, r^{OP}, h^{OP}\}$, and $\{h^{OP}, r^{SP}, r^{OP}, h^{SP}\}$. The optimal lag length is determined by AIC. It should be noted that all variables in the test must be stationary. An unrestricted vector autoregressive (VAR) model is used to detect the sign of lagged variables.

4.0 Results and implications

The results of Granger non-causality tests are shown in Table 3. In the VAR model, the optimal lag length determined by SIC is two. The anticipated maximum order of integration of all variables is one resulting from the unit root test in Table 1. Thus, the whole lag length is three specified as VAR(3) model. The misspecification tests for serial correlation, normality, and heteroscedasticity in the VAR(3) model are also reported.

Table 03: Results of non-causality test, 1987M5-2013M12

Hypothesis	$\chi^2_{(3)}$	p-value
LROP does not cause LRSP	2.828 (-)	0.419
LRSP does not cause LROP	0.425 (-)	0.935
Misspecification tests	Test statistic	p-value
LM	5.856	0.210
WH	96.111	0.000
JB	14.173	0.001

Note: LRSP stands for the log of real stock market index, and LROP stands for the log of real oil price. LM is the Lagrange multiplier test for serial correlation up to third order in the residuals, WH is the White heteroskedasticity test of the residuals, and JB is the Jarque-Bera statistic for testing the null hypothesis that the residuals are multivariate normal. The minus sign in parenthesis indicates negative causation.

The results in Table 3 show that the null hypotheses that real oil price does not cause real stock market index and that real stock market index does not cause real oil price are accepted. Further tests are conducted to investigate the misspecification of the augmented VAR(3) models used in the analysis. The Lagrange multiplier (LM) test statistic indicates the acceptance of the null hypothesis that there is no serial correlation in the residuals up to the third order of lags. Furthermore the White heteroscedasticity (WH) test shows that the null hypothesis of the presence of autoregressive conditional heteroskedastic (ARCH) effect can be rejected at the 1 percent level of significance. In addition, the Jarque-Bera (JB) statistic indicates that the residuals are not multivariate normal. Therefore, it cannot be concluded that the augmented VAR model is suitable for testing non-causality between the two series.

The bivariate GARCH estimation for the system equations (3) to (7) to obtain the volatility series are reported in Table 4.

The assumption of constant conditional correlation facilitates the simplicity of the system estimation. The model performs quite well in the data set. The mean equation for real stock market return is assumed to be dependent on the lag of real oil price change while the mean equation for real oil price change is assumed to be independent of the lag of real stock market return.[4] The lags are chosen so that the system equations are free of serial correlation. Panels A and B contain the results of the conditional means and variances for stock market return and oil price change, respectively.

[4] The country is an oil-importing country. Therefore, its stock market cannot affect world oil price.

Table 04: Results from the estimates of a bivariate AR(p)-cccGARCH(1,1) model, 1987M5-2013M12

Panel A: Real stock return equation	
Conditional mean equation:	$r^{SP}_t = 0.893 + 0.085\, r^{SP}_{t-1} - 0.065\, r^{OP}_{t-1}$
	(1.747)* (1.403) (-1.273)
Conditional variance equation:	$h^{SP}_t = 4.433 + 0.128\, \varepsilon^{2,SP}_{t-1} + 0.186\, h^{SP}_{t-1}$
	(2.125)**(3.702)*** (17.279)***
	(t-statistic in parenthesis)
Panel B: Equation of oil price change	
Conditional mean equation:	$r^{OP}_t = 0.265 + 0.208\, r^{OP}_{t-1}$
	(0.621) (3.105)***
Conditional variance equation:	$h^{OP}_t = 7.583 + 0.128\, \varepsilon^{2,OP}_{t-1} + 0.186\, h^{OP}_{t-1}$
	(0.099) (4.799)*** (9.282)***
	(t-statistic in parenthesis)
Panel C: Conditional covariance equation	
	$h^{SP,OP}_t = -0.062 (h^{SP}_t)^{1/2} (h^{OP}_t)^{1/2}$
	(-1.033)
	(t-statistic in parenthesis)
Panel D: System diagnostic test using residual Portmanteau tests for autocorrelation	
	$Q(8) = 34.242$
	(0.361)
	(p-value in parenthesis)

Note: r^{SP} stands for the percentage change in real stock market index (real stock market return), r^{OP} stands for the percentage in real oil price, h^{SP} stands for stock return volatility, and h^{OP} stands for oil price volatility. ***, **, and * denote significance at the 1, 5, and 10 percent, respectively.

Referring to Panel A, stock market return is not affected by oil price change. In Panel B, Oil price change is affected by its one-period lag. The coefficients in the two conditional variance equations are non-negative. Both conditional variance equations give significant ARCH and GARCH terms (α and β). The sum of the coefficients of the ARCH and GARCH terms for real stock return is 0.998 whereas the sum of coefficients for real oil price change is 0.939. These results show that the GARCH variance series as measures of volatility or uncertainty is stationary. The constant conditional correlation in Panel C is -0.062, which is low and not statistically significant. The system diagnostic test using residual portmanteau test for autocorrelation accepts the null of no autocorrelation as indicated by Q(8) statistic. Therefore, the system equations are free of serial correlation. The volatility series are generated so as to examine their impacts on stock market return and volatility in the standard Granger causality test. The threshold GARCH model proposed by Zakoian (1994) is also estimated, but the asymmetric is not found. Therefore the standard Granger causality test are conducted by relying on the generated variance series from the AR-ccc-GARCH(1,1) model.

The results of the pairwise Granger causality test are reported in Table 5. The results show some important findings. First, an increase in real oil price seems to cause real stock market return to fall, but this result is not statistically significant. Therefore, there is no evidence that real oil price change can cause a decline in real stock market return. This finding does not support the findings by Ciner (2001) and Papapetrou (2001). Second, stock price volatility negatively affects real stock market return, i.e., an increase in oil price volatility causes stock market return to increase, and vice versa. This confirms the finding by Sadorsky (1999). Third, stock market return does not affect stock price volatility. Fourth, real oil price volatility does not affect real stock market return, which is contradictory to the results of Masih et al. (2011). However, real oil price does affect real stock price volatility. An increase in oil price volatility causes an increase in stock price volatility and vice versa. This is an evidence of volatility spillover in one direction. Finally, a movement in real oil price causes stock price volatility to increase. The results do confirm the finding by Awartani and Maghyereh (2013).

Table 05: Pairwise Granger causality test results, 1987M5-2013M12

Hypothesis	F-statistic	p-value
r^{OP} does not cause r^{SP}	0.913 (-)	0.435
h^{SP} does not cause r^{SP}	2.392*(-)	0.069
r^{SP} does not cause h^{SP}	0.988 (+)	0.399
h^{OP} does not cause r^{SP}	1.991 (+)	0.115
r^{OP} does not cause h^{SP}	4.126***(+)	0.007
h^{OP} does not cause h^{SP}	4.792***(+)	0.003

Note: r^{SP} stands for the percentage change in real stock market index (real stock market return), r^{OP} stands for the percentage in real oil price, h^{SP} stands for stock return volatility, and h^{OP} stands for oil price volatility. The optimal lags of 3 are determined by AIC. ***, **, and * denote significance at the 1, 5, and 10 percent, respectively. The signs + and – in parenthesis indicate positive and negative causality.

The estimate from VAR with the optimal lags of 3 gives the impulse responses of variables as shown in Figure 2. The information contained in the VAR (3) can be represented by graphs of the impulse response functions. The impulse responses illustrate the dynamic response path of a variable due to a one-period standard deviation shock to another variable. The graphs give some further evidence on the pattern of linkages between oil and stock markets. All variables of interest are shown in the figure, i. e., oil price movement and its volatility that affect stock return and its volatility. Referring to Figures 1a and 1b, the response of real stock return to oil price shock is negative but lasts for 3 months only while the response of real stock return to oil price volatility is also negative but lasts for only 4 months. The response of stock price volatility to oil price shock in Figure 1c is negative and lasts only 2 months whereas the response of real stock return to oil price volatility shock (Figure 1d) is negative but becomes positive within 4 months and dissipates within 9 months. In Figure 1e, the response of oil price volatility to oil price shock is positive and lasts for 10 months. The positive response of stock price volatility to oil price volatility shock is positive and decreases within 3 months, but never dissipates as shown in Figure 1f. The results seem to confirm those from Granger causality tests.

Monthly data for three sub-indices are also available from the Stock Exchange of Thailand website, but at different time periods. The two-step procedure is used to test the impact of real oil price movements on returns and the impact of real oil price volatility on returns and stock price volatility for each sub-index.

For SET50 index comprising 50 stocks of listed companies from various equity sectors, the data are available from September 1995 to December 2013 with 220 observations. The SET100 index comprising 100 stocks of listed companies are available from May 2005 to December 2013 with 104 observations. The market for alternative investment (MAI) index comprising small and medium sized companies are available from September 2002 to December 2013 with 136 observations.

Figure 02: Impulse responses from VAR estimate

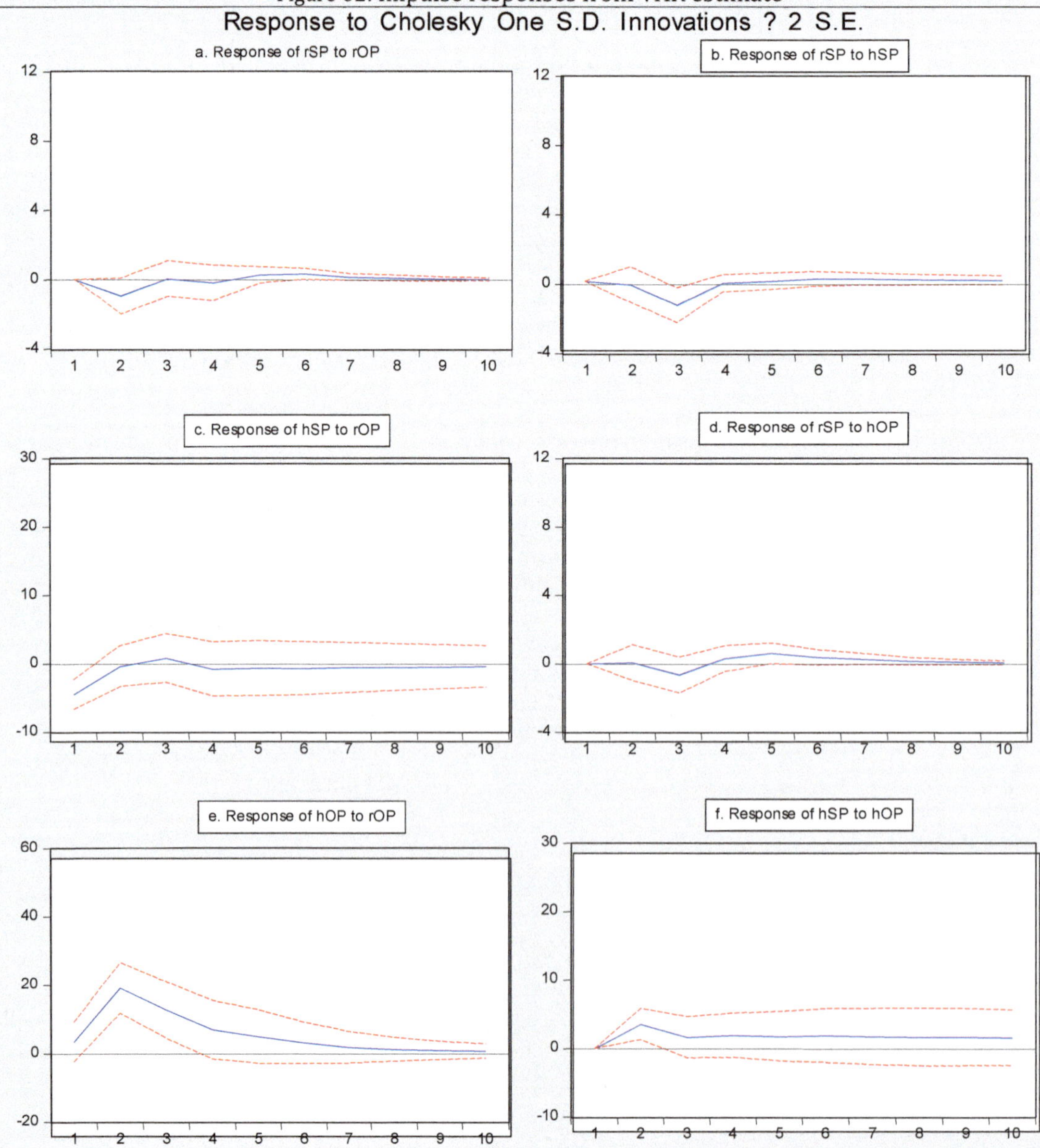

The results from pairwise Granger causality test for the rate of change of these indices that are linked to the rate of change in real oil price and its volatility generated from a specified bivariate GARCH model similar to the estimated model in Section 3.1 are reported in Table 6.

The results in Panel A of Table 6 show that oil price shock does not affect the index return for SET50, but oil price uncertainty does adversely affect this index return. In Panel B, oil price shock significantly causes the index return of SET100 to decrease, but oil price uncertainty does not negatively affect the index return. In Panel C, the impact is different. Oil price shock and oil price volatility does not affect in the index return. For oil price uncertainty transmission, there seems to be no transmission to sub-index volatility at all. As a matter of fact, the MAI index comprises stocks of small and medium sized companies. These companies use less oil for production and thus are not affected by oil price shock and its volatility. On the contrary SET 50 index is the market capitalization weighted index and is the subset of the SET index. This index is calculated from stock prices of enterprises with large market capitalization in main equity sectors, such as energy and utilities, telecommunication, banking and finance, agro and food industry, and properties. The SET 100 index is calculated from stock prices of 50 more enterprises.

Table 06: Pairwise Granger causality test results for sub-indices

A. SET 50 index, 1995M8-2013M12		
Hypothesis	F-statistic	p-value
r^{OP} does not cause r^{SP}	0.117 (-)	0.977
h^{OP} does not cause r^{SP}	2.112*(-)	0.081
h^{OP} does not cause h^{SP}	0.872 (+)	0.481
B. SET 100 index, 2005M5-2013M12		
Hypothesis	F-statistic	p-value
r^{OP} does not cause r^{SP}	6.164*** (-)	0.001
h^{OP} does not cause r^{SP}	0.839 (-)	0.476
h^{OP} does not cause h^{SP}	0.258 (+)	0.784
C. MAI index, 2002M9-2013M12		
Hypothesis	F-statistic	p-value
r^{OP} does not cause r^{SP}	0.766 (-)	0.467
h^{OP} does not cause r^{SP}	0.034 (-)	0.967
h^{OP} does not cause h^{SP}	0.126 (+)	0.806

Note: r^{SP} stands for the percentage change in real index, r^{OP} stands for the percentage in real oil price, h^{SP} stands for index return volatility, and h^{OP} stands for oil price volatility. The optimal lags are determined by AIC. ***, **, and * denote significance at the 1, 5, and 10 percent, respectively. The signs + and – in parenthesis indicate positive and negative causality.

Therefore, the two index returns are more prone to oil price movements and uncertainty. In addition, the SET 50 and SET 100 indices are constructed to accommodate the issuing futures and options. Therefore, portfolio managers should be aware of the impact of oil price shock and its uncertainty on these sub-indices when they rely on passive portfolio management. For active portfolio managers, it should be necessary to use options as a hedge against risk so as to reduce a portfolio risk when that portfolio return tends to fall due to oil price uncertainty. The government can also impose some measures such as encouraging firms to improve energy efficiency and finding alternative fuels (renewable energy and natural gas). These measures can prevent large fluctuations in listed firms' profitability resulting from oil price uncertainty, which in turn can adversely affect the stock market.

5.0 Conclusion

In this study, the impact of oil price volatility on the Thai stock market is investigated. The monthly data used in this study are real stock market return and oil price. The period covers May 1987 to December 2013. The estimation method used is the two stage approach, which comprises the estimation of the ccc-bivariate GARCH(1,1) model to generate volatility series and the use of standard Granger causality test to determine the directions of causation. One of the main findings in this study is that there exists volatility transmission from oil to domestic stock market. For sub-indices, there is no impact of oil price uncertainty on stock price volatility, but oil price movement and its volatility adversely affect two main sub-index returns. Since the SET50 index comprises 50 blue-chip stocks from main equity sectors, index fund managers should realize that a fall in this sub-index return can be caused by the impact of real oil price uncertainty.

The evidence that oil price shocks and oil price volatility that cause an increase in volatility of the stock market and causes a decrease in sub-index returns gives some implications. For risk management, portfolio managers should be aware of the impact of increasing portfolio risk caused by oil price shocks and volatility. They should diversify well enough to reduce their portfolio risk. For policy implications, the government can also impose some measures such as encouraging firms to improve energy efficiency and finding more renewable energy and natural gas to maintain or improve the production processes of listed enterprises in the stock market.

References

Arouri, M. E. H., Jouini, J., Ngugen, D. K., 2011. Volatility spillovers between oil prices and stock sector returns: implications for portfolio management. Journal of International money and finance, 30(7): 1387-1405.

Awartani, B., Maghyereh, A. I., 2013. Dynamic spillovers between oil and stock markets in the Gulf Cooperation Council countries. Energy Economics, 36(C): 28-42.

Apergis, N., Miller, S. M., 2009. Do structural oil-market shocks affect stock prices? Energy Economics, 31(4): 569-575.

Basher, S. A., Sadorsky, P., 2006. Oil price risk and emerging stock markets. Global Finance Journal, 17(2): 224-251.

Bollerslev, T., 1990. Modelling the coherence in short-run nominal exchange rates: a multivariate generalized ARCH model. Review of Economics and Statistics, 73(3): 498-505.

Ciner, C., 2001. Energy shocks and financial markets: nonlinear linkages. Studies in Nonlinear Dynamics and Econometrics, 5(3): 203-212.

Cong, R-G., Wei, Y-M., Jiao, J-L., Fan, Y., 2008. Relationship between oil price shocks and stock market: an empirical analysis from China. Energy Policy, 36(9): 3544-3553.

Granger, C. W. J., 1969. Investigating causal relations by econometric models and cross spectral methods. Econometrica, 37(3): 424-438.

Jones, C. M., Gautam, K., 1996. Oil and the stock markets. Journal of Finance, 51(2): 463-491.

Jouini, J., 2013. Return and volatility interaction between oil prices and stock markets in Saudi Arabia. Journal of Policy Modeling, 35(6): 1124-1144.

Kim, S., Yang, D.Y. 2011. The impact of capital inflows on asset prices in emerging Asian economies: is too much money chasing too little goods? Open Economies Review, 22(2): 293-315.

Malik, F., Ewing, B. T., 2009. Volatility transmission between oil prices and equity sector returns. International Review of Financial Analysis, 18(1): 95-100.

Malik, F., Hammoudeh, S., 2007. Shock and volatility transmission in the oil, US and Gulf equity markets. International Review of Economics and Finance, 16(3): 357-368.

Masih, R., Peters, S., De Mello, L., 2011. Oil price volatility and stock price fluctuations in an emerging market: evidence from South Korea. Energy Economics, 33(5): 975-986.

Narayan, P. K., Narayan, S., 2010. Modelling the impact of oil prices on Vietnam's stock prices. Applied Energy, 87(1): 356-361.

Oten-Abayie, E. F., Doe, S. K., 2013. Inflation and inflation uncertainty in Ghana. E3 Journal of Business Management and Economics, 4(12): 259-266.

Pagan, A., 1984. Econometric Issues in the analysis of regressions with generated regressors. International Economic Review, 25(2): 221-247.

Papapetrou, E., 2001. Oil price shocks, stock market, economic activity and employment in Greece. Energy Economics, 23 (5): 511-532.

Park, J., Ratti, R. A., 2008. Oil price shocks and stock markets in the US and 13 European countries, Energy Economics, 30(5): 2587-2608.

Rambaldi, A. N., Doran, H. E., 1996. Testing for Granger non-causality in cointegrated system made easy. Working papers in Econometrics and Applied Statistc, 88, University of New England.

Sadorsky, P., 1999. Oil price shocks and stock market activity. Energy Economics, 21(5): 449-469.

Toda, H. Y., Yamamoto, T., 1995. Statistical inferences in vector autoregressions with possibly integrated process. Journal of Econometrics, 66(1/2): 225-250.

Zakoian, J. M., 1994. Threshold heteroskedastic models. Journal of Economic Dynamic and control, 18(5): 931-955.

Permissions

All chapters in this book were first published in JEFS, by LAR Center Press; hereby published with permission under the Creative Commons Attribution License or equivalent. Every chapter published in this book has been scrutinized by our experts. Their significance has been extensively debated. The topics covered herein carry significant findings which will fuel the growth of the discipline. They may even be implemented as practical applications or may be referred to as a beginning point for another development.

The contributors of this book come from diverse backgrounds, making this book a truly international effort. This book will bring forth new frontiers with its revolutionizing research information and detailed analysis of the nascent developments around the world.

We would like to thank all the contributing authors for lending their expertise to make the book truly unique. They have played a crucial role in the development of this book. Without their invaluable contributions this book wouldn't have been possible. They have made vital efforts to compile up to date information on the varied aspects of this subject to make this book a valuable addition to the collection of many professionals and students.

This book was conceptualized with the vision of imparting up-to-date information and advanced data in this field. To ensure the same, a matchless editorial board was set up. Every individual on the board went through rigorous rounds of assessment to prove their worth. After which they invested a large part of their time researching and compiling the most relevant data for our readers.

The editorial board has been involved in producing this book since its inception. They have spent rigorous hours researching and exploring the diverse topics which have resulted in the successful publishing of this book. They have passed on their knowledge of decades through this book. To expedite this challenging task, the publisher supported the team at every step. A small team of assistant editors was also appointed to further simplify the editing procedure and attain best results for the readers.

Apart from the editorial board, the designing team has also invested a significant amount of their time in understanding the subject and creating the most relevant covers. They scrutinized every image to scout for the most suitable representation of the subject and create an appropriate cover for the book.

The publishing team has been an ardent support to the editorial, designing and production team. Their endless efforts to recruit the best for this project, has resulted in the accomplishment of this book. They are a veteran in the field of academics and their pool of knowledge is as vast as their experience in printing. Their expertise and guidance has proved useful at every step. Their uncompromising quality standards have made this book an exceptional effort. Their encouragement from time to time has been an inspiration for everyone.

The publisher and the editorial board hope that this book will prove to be a valuable piece of knowledge for researchers, students, practitioners and scholars across the globe.

List of Contributors

Nor Azam Abdul-Razak
Senior Lecturer, School of Economics, Finance & Banking, Universiti Utara Malaysia, Malaysia

Russayani Ismail
Associate Professor, School of Economics, Finance & Banking, Universiti Utara Malaysia, Malaysia

Roslan Abdul-Hakim
Professor, Othman Yeop Abdullah Graduate School of Business, Universiti Utara Malaysia, Malaysia

Ugur Ergun and Zehra Mahmutović
Management Department, Faculty of Economics, International Burch University, BIH

Yueh-Chiang Lee
Department of Business Administration, Vanung University, Taiwan

Yao-Hung Yang
Department of Business Administration, Chung Yuan Christian University, Taiwan

Gabriel Caldas Montes
Department of Economics, Fluminense Federal University Rio de Janeiro, Brazil

Biru Paksha Paul
Department of Economics, State University of New York at Cortland, NY 13045, USA

Raymond Osi Alenoghena
Department of Economics, Faculty of Social Sciences, University of Lagos, Nigeria

Yong-Ching Chiou
Department of Insurance and Finance , National Taichung University of Science and Technology, Taiwan

Yao-Chih Hsieh
Department of Public Finance, Feng Chia University, Taiwan

Wenyi Lin
Graduate Institute of Financial and Economic Law, Feng Chia University, Taiwan

Chris I. Enyinda
Department of Marketing and International Business, Canadian University of Dubai, UAE

Meral Varish Kiefer
Department of Economics, Cornell University, Ithaca, NY 14850, US
Faculty of Management, Sabanci University, Istanbul, Turkey

Mehdi Hojjat
Professor, Neumann University, Aston, PA, USA

Srinivasa Konduru
Assistant Professor, Dept. of Agricultural Business, California State University, USA

Tae Hun Kim
Department of Agricultural Development Research, Korea Rural Economic Institute (KREI), South Korea

Mechel Paggi
Director, Center for Agribusiness, California State University Fresno, Fresno, CA

Tobias Olweny
Department of Finance and Accounting, Jomo Kenyatta University of Agriculture and Technology, Kenya

Ikhlaas Gurrib
Coordinator, MBA (Finance) program, Canadian University of Dubai, Dubai, United Arab Emirates

Amir Behnam Izadyar
Darulmaali Financial Consulting Group, LLC, Maryland, USA

Feroza Ragnath
Darulmaali Financial Consulting Group, LLC, Maryland, USA

Ruddy Tri Santoso, Hartono, M. Agung Prabowo and Guntur Riyanto
Faculty of Economic and Business, University of Sebelas Maret (UNS). Surakarta

Sujoko Efferin
Faculty of Business and Economic, University of Surabaya (UBAYA) Surabaya

Yenny Tjiamudjaja
Editor, translator

Joocheol Kim
School of Economics, Yonsei University, Korea

Eunhwan Kim
School of Economics, Yonsei University, The Korea Development Bank (KDB), Korea

Harlan Platt
Northeastern University, Boston, MA

Licheng Cai
Currensee Global Inc, Boston, MA

Marjorie Platt
Northeastern University, Boston, MA

Anders Kjellman
Novia University of Applied Science, Vaasa, Finland

Risto Tainio and Taisto Kangas
Aalto University, Helsinki, Finland

Izabella Barati-Stec
Central European University, Hungary & Budapest Business School, Hungary

Komain Jiranyakul
School of Development Economics, National Institute of Development Administration, Thailand

Index